Chinese Mythology:
An Introduction

Chinese Mythology

An Introduction

Anne Birrell

with a foreword by
Yuan K'o

THE JOHNS HOPKINS
UNIVERSITY PRESS
Baltimore and London

Johns Hopkins Paperbacks edition, 1999
4 6 8 9 7 5 3

The Johns Hopkins University Press
2715 North Charles Street
Baltimore, Maryland 21218-4363
www.press.jhu.edu

The Library of Congress has cataloged the hardcover
edition of this book as follows:
Birrell, Anne.
Chinese mythology : an introduction /
Anne Birrell ; with a foreword by Yuan K'o.
p.   cm.
Includes bibliographical references and index.
ISBN 0-8018-4595-5 (acid-free paper)
1. Mythology, Chinese.   2. Tales—China.
I. Title
BL1825.B57   1993
299'.51—dc20   93-14738

ISBN 0-8018-6183-7 (pbk.)

A catalog record for this book is available
from the British Library.

To
Yuan K'o, Derk Bodde,
Jaan Puhvel, Victor Mair,
and Norman J. Girardot
and to the Memory of
Bernhard Karlgren and
Wolfram Eberhard

Contents

4. Destroyers · 89

5. Miraculous Birth · 113

6. Myths of the Yellow Emperor · 130

7. Myths of Yi the Archer · 138

8. Myths of Yü the Great · 146

9. Goddesses · 160

10. Immortality · 181

11. Metamorphoses · 189

Foreword

For a long time people have admired the mythologies of ancient Greece and Rome and Northern Europe for their rich variety and beauty of form and content. At the same time, they have thought that China had a dearth of myth, or they even considered that China was a nation that had no myths at all. This is a profound mistake. There is, in fact, a treasure trove of ancient Chinese myths, and they are so extraordinary, so magnificent, and so full of imaginative power that they stir the human soul to its very depths.

There are three major reasons why people are under the false impression that China lacks a recognizable mythology. In the first place, China did not enjoy the phenomenon of gifted poets like Homer and Hesiod of the ninth and eighth centuries B.C., who retold ancient myths in an eloquent literary mode. In the Chinese case, myths at first appeared in a piecemeal fashion, in a variety of versions, fragmented and truncated, and were collated as mythological material only fairly late, if at all.

The second reason for this general misconception about Chinese myths is that in the archaic and ancient period, Chinese writing, because of its unwieldy and ideographic forms, was not yet sufficiently developed or a sophisticated enough medium to express the complexities of a systematic classical mythology. Myths were preserved and kept alive through oral traditions.

Finally, and most important, Chinese myths were prevented from becoming fully developed by the negative attitude of scholars of the early Chinese empire and throughout the centuries, especially scholars of the Confucian persuasion. They viewed the fantastic elements and antisocial aspects in tales of marvels and wonders with a very deep prejudice, ignoring their imaginative flair, color, emotive power, and deeper levels of meaning. As a consequence, they did not consider it important to preserve myths in written records, and so in time Chinese myths were neglected, and many were lost forever.

These factors contributed to a situation in which Chinese mythology stagnated in the earliest stage of written records. Myths did not undergo the enhancing process of being transformed into literature or being systematized by creative authors. Mythological material was absorbed, and thereby preserved in literary amber, in a disorganized way in a number of miscellaneous books. Writers made very different use of myths: historians incorporated them into their histories, literary writers wove them into their prose and poetry according to the dictates of literary fashion and generic requirements, and philosophers of contending schools used them, sometimes exactly the same one, to argue quite opposite points of view. Even that treasury of classical Chinese mythology, *The Classic of Mountains and Seas,* selected mythological material in a fragmentary manner, fitting it into a new structure, half-fact, half-fiction, to create a geographic survey and folkloric compendium of the ancient world.

The diffuse and fragmentary nature of the Chinese repertoire of myth is the legacy of these historical factors during the process of oral or textual transmission. Yet is this to be viewed as a total misfortune? In their very diversity, in their sprawling, disorganized confusion, the myths have been used by a great many different authors. Significantly, they have been used piecemeal, and so they have not suffered a complete reworking at the hands of literary authors or others. One might argue that in their present fragmentary state, preserved in a large number of classical books, they must appear as Greek and Roman myths once did before Homer, Hesiod, or even Ovid transformed, reshaped, and rewrote them. It is possible to argue that by an accident of history, Chinese myths remain in a more or less pristine condition compared with mythological texts of the Greco-Roman and Judaic traditions. One may further conclude that for this reason Chinese myths, despite their protean and contradictory forms, are more reliable documentary evidence of a primitive and archaic oral tradition in the world of myth.

In the late 1940s, I commenced my life's work of compiling, sorting, and researching Chinese myths. Over the past decade this has resulted in the publication of a dozen or so books and about fifty articles. Now it is the younger generation of Chinese scholars who are examining Chinese mythology from a multidisciplinary approach—history, folklore, religion, anthropology, minority nationality studies, philosophy, psychology, and comparative mythology. Their research has been published in a total of eight hundred articles. My own research has been conducted from the standpoint of literature and literary scholarship. But my work in this field is to be considered only a first stage.

My early research work *The Mythology of Ancient China* has been translated into Japanese, Russian, and Korean. Now readers in the English-speaking world have a new book on Chinese mythology, this one. It is not a translation of my work into English but an independent research work by Professor Birrell which builds on my four main research works. Taking *The Mythology of Ancient China, One Hundred Myths: An Anthology with an Annotated Translation, A Source Book of Chinese Myth Texts,* and *A Dictionary of Chinese Myths and Legends,* with some recent revisions, as a foundation, Professor Birrell has translated the classical texts anew into English, reorganized and selected from the data, and added much that is new. Most important is her systematic discussion of content and context, in which she views the myths from a comparative perspective and draws on a fund of new research material in that field. She has also added a full bibliography of Chinese, Japanese, and Western research; a glossary of mythical figures, motifs, and place names; an index of concepts; and an introductory essay, in which she discusses numerous aspects of and problems in the study of myth.

Professor Birrell recently consulted me at the Szechwan Academy of Social Sciences in Ch'eng-tu about the selection of classical texts. I believe that the book she has written combines originality with convincing methodology and is a more advanced book on Chinese mythology than has yet appeared in any language. Through her meticulous attention to detail she has achieved a high standard of scholarship. That she "did not think ten thousand leagues too far to come" and discuss with me personally the many problems of research is in the true spirit of learning and cannot be too highly praised.

I am therefore delighted to write a foreword for this book. I trust that Western readers will come to understand Chinese culture more closely and will enjoy the marvels of Chinese mythology. I also hope that they will appreciate more fully the enduring power of myth in the birth and development of this country and its people.

Yuan K'o

Szechwan Academy of Social Sciences

Ch'eng-tu

Acknowledgments

I wish to thank the British Academy and the Chinese Academy of Social Sciences for sponsoring my research visits to China in 1988 and 1990. I particularly wish to thank the Szechwan Academy of Social Sciences for arranging lengthy research sessions with China's foremost authority on mythology, Professor Yuan K'o, and his research assistant, Dr. Chou Ming, with the help of Mr. Chang Hsiang-jung. I am also most grateful to the Carnegie Foundation for their writing grant. I acknowledge a debt to the late Professor Angus C. Graham of the School of Oriental and African Studies, University of London. I am also indebted to Professor Chih-tsing Hsia, of Columbia University, and his wife, Della, for their encouragement in this project since they visited me in Cambridge in 1991. Colleagues around the world have been a fine support these last few years: Professor Noel Barnard of the Australian National University, Professor Norman Girardot of Lehigh University, Professor Rémi Mathieu of the Collège de France, and Professor Victor Mair of the University of Pennsylvania. Charles Aylmer and Koyama Noboru, Chinese and Japanese Sections, Cambridge University Library, have also been very helpful. I am grateful to Eric Halpern, editor in chief of the Johns Hopkins University Press, for his courtesy and expertise in guiding my manuscript to publication. To Barbara B. Lamb, managing editor, and Irma F. Garlick I offer my sincere thanks for their excellent editorial assistance. Thanks go, too, to E. G. M. Mann & Son and Miss Shirley Blythe, of Fordham, Cambridge, for their technical printers' assistance. Final thanks go to Fra Ewen G. Cameron, Enid and Stan Adelson, Elizabeth Scott Blair and her brother David, and Bob Tignor, Princeton University, and his wife, Marian, for their friendship and interest.

Abbreviations

Chronological
Table

Shang/Yin	?1766–?1123 B.C.
Chou Dynasty	?1123–221 B.C.
Western Chou	?1123–771 B.C.
Eastern Chou	
Spring and Autumn Era	722–481 B.C.
Warring States Era	403–221 B.C.
Ch'in Dynasty	221–207 B.C.
Han Dynasty	202 B.C.–A.D. 220
Former Han	202 B.C.–A.D. 8
Latter Han	A.D. 25–220
Three Kingdoms	221–280
(Han, Wei, and Shu Kingdoms)	
Chin Dynasty	265–419
Six Dynasties Era	386–589
(Wu, Eastern Chin, Sung, Ch'i,	
Liang, and Ch'en Dynasties)	
Sui Dynasty	589–618
T'ang Dynasty	618–907
Five Dynasties	907–959
Sung Dynasty	960–1279
Yuan or Mongol Dynasty	1280–1368
Ming Dynasty	1368–1644
Ch'ing or Manchu Dynasty	1644–1911
Republic of China	1912
People's Republic of China	1949

Chinese Mythology:
An Introduction

Introduction

This book offers for the first time a comprehensive range of texts of myths of the classical Chinese tradition translated from the Chinese into English with an analysis of their context and significance. A representative corpus of over three hundred narratives has been selected from more than one hundred classical texts. These constitute the most authentic texts in the Chinese mythic tradition. The organizational principles are based on thematic categories and classes of motif familiar to mythologies worldwide. A perusal of the chapter headings in this book reveals the wide range of Chinese mythic themes: cosmogonic myths, creation myths, etiological myths, myths of divine birth, mythic metamorphoses, myths of strange places, peoples, plants, birds, and animals, myths of the primeval and the lesser gods, mythical figures, and myths of the semidivine heroes who founded their tribe, city, or dynasty at the dawn of history.

The narratives are mostly fragmentary texts, often written in a lapidary style in obscure language and meaning. The texts are therefore accompanied by discussions that explain and clarify the obscurities and difficult textual background. While these analyses are firmly based on the cultural traditions of classical China, the motifs and themes of the myths are also elucidated from the aspects of interdisciplinary studies and of comparative mythology. Thus significant research on a variety of subjects is cited in order to highlight relevant aspects of archeology, anthropology, religion, sociology, and psychology, together with the application of works on mythologies worldwide.

Unlike late nineteenth- and early twentieth-century studies of Chinese myth, which incorporated late ethnographic or folkloristic material with ancient myth texts without due regard for chronological consistency, this book focuses primarily on mythology as a subject in its own right and with its own raison d'être apart from other disciplines. Thus ethnographic aspects are referred to but do not form a major part of the discussion. Similarly, non-Sinitic aspects of classical Chinese myth are not pursued at length, because of the special linguistic and historical problems that have yet to be adequately researched. Also excluded are the mythic systems of Confucianism, Taoism, and Buddhism, besides the network of local and regional cults. This, again, is partly for reasons of disciplinary integrity, mythology being separate from philosophy and religion, and partly because these systems of belief, of which Buddhism is comparatively late, spawned immensely complex mythologies and pantheons of their own, which would require a brave new generation of mythologists to assimilate, codify, and elucidate. Despite these large exclusions and minor emphases, however, the repertoire of classical Chinese myth which remains to be studied is still so extensive and complex that only a representative proportion of it can be offered here. Nevertheless, this basic repertoire constitutes a corpus of over three hundred texts of varying length, which are sufficient to introduce readers to the field. The material is presented in a form that makes it accessible to specialists in Chinese and nonspecialists alike, in the disciplines of Sinology, religion, history, anthropology, archeology, art history, and literature.

Definitions of Myth

The Chinese term for *myth, shen-hua,* almost exactly coincides with one of the many contemporary Western definitions of myth as sacred narrative. *Shen* means 'god', 'divine', 'holy'; *hua* means 'speech', 'oral account', 'tale', 'oral narrative'. In this respect, the second part of the Chinese term, *hua,* is equivalent to the original meaning of the word *mythology:* the root of the word *myth* begins with the Proto-Indo-European root *mu 'to mutter or murmur', from which the Greek stem *my* and the noun *mythos,* meaning 'word' or 'story', are derived, while the Greek noun *logos* denotes 'word', 'ordered discourse,' or 'doctrine.'

Mythologists today are generally in agreement that the basic definition of *myth* is 'account', 'tale', 'story', or 'narrative'. There is considerable disagreement, however, whether myths are necessarily always sacred or limited to the gods and the divine. For it is clear from reading texts of mythologies from throughout the world that other elements, such as the supernatural, the folkloric, the strange and marvelous, natural phenomena, the inexplicable, and also basic concerns such as eating belong to the corpus of myth. As a definition, therefore, the terms *shen-hua* and *sacred narrative* are of limited use, since they exclude too much valuable material from the Chinese and other mythological traditions.

In a recent study of myth, William G. Doty recorded that he had collected over fifty different definitions and that a more rigorous search would have yielded many more (1986, 9). This embarrassment of riches can be explained in part by the fact that scholars from such diverse disciplines as religion, psychology, and anthropology, who have discovered in myth a rich vein of human knowledge and experience, have formulated different working definitions of the term based on the prerequisites of their own disciplines. In the nineteenth century universalistic theories of the nature myth school predominated, exemplified by the meteorological interpretations of myth by Friedrich Max Müller. For the evolutionist school of Edward B. Tylor, myth was an expression of primitive philosophy. There was also the etiological interpretation of myth as an explanation of origins characterized by the works of Andrew Lang. In the early twentieth century the myth-as-ritual school in Cambridge, led by Jane Ellen Harrison, defined myth thus: "The primary meaning of myth . . . is the spoken correlative of the acted rite, the thing done" (1963, 328). For Franz Boas myth was a kind of autobiographical ethnography by which the culture of a primitive tribe could be deduced from an analysis of its myths. For Bronislaw Malinowski the function of myth was explained within its cultural context as a "sociological charter." Claude Lévi-Strauss has accepted Malinowski's definition that "myth is a charter for social action," but he develops the functionalism of Malinowski with a new theory that myth embodies the structure of mind and society in a given community. Central to the structural-analytical approach of Lévi-Strauss is his object of revealing the paradigms of binary oppositions in a mythic narrative to arrive at a deep stratum of meaning. From the standpoint of psychology, Freud held that myths were the reflections of an individual's unconscious fears and desires, whereas Jung defined myth as the expression of the "collective unconscious," developing the thesis of archetypal patterns of thought and symbol. In recent times the late Joseph Campbell elaborated Jungian concepts of the archetype in myth. Mircea Eliade, who was influenced by the myth-as-ritual school of Cambridge and by the Jungian concept of archetypes, defined myth as the vital link between the ancient past and contemporary realities, while emphasizing its etiological characteristics.

These definitions by scholars from a wide spectrum of disciplines have greatly enlarged the scope and content of myth. Yet in appropriating myth for its own purpose, each discipline or school remains jealous of its own concerns, aims, and methodology. In the end, myth is not anthropology, nor is it religion, or sociology, psychology, or literature. As Friedrich Schelling insisted as early as 1857, myth has its own autonomy; it is a human experience that must be understood on its own terms and in its own right. Any attempt to graft it onto another discipline will result in its diminution and loss (cited by Puhvel 1987, 12).

This brief review of the definitions of myth which have evolved over the past century and a half may now be usefully followed by Doty's eight ways of categorizing it in most interdisciplinary works on myth: (1) myth as aesthetic device, narrative, literary form; (2) myth containing subject matter having to do with the gods, the "other" world; (3) myth explaining origins (etiology); (4) myth as mistaken or primitive science; (5) myth as the text of a rite, or depending on ritual that it explains; (6) myth making universal truths or ideas concrete or intelligible; (7) myth explicating beliefs, collective experiences, or values; (8) myth constituting "spiritual" or "psychic" expression (Doty 1986, 9). Doty also provides a definitive statement of the significance, context, and function of myth:

> A mythological corpus consists of a usually complex network of myths that are culturally important imaginal stories, conveying by means of metaphoric and symbolic diction, graphic imagery, and emotional conviction and participation, the primal, foundational accounts of aspects of the real, experienced world and humankind's roles and relative statuses within it.
>
> Mythologies may convey the political and moral values of a culture and provide systems of interpreting individual experience within a universal perspective, which may include the intervention of suprahuman entities, as well as aspects of the natural and cultural orders. Myths may be enacted or reflected in rituals, ceremonies, and dramas, and they may provide materials for secondary elaboration,

the constituent mythemes having become merely images or reference points for a subsequent story, such as a folktale, historical legend, novella, or prophecy. (Ibid., 11)

While this working definition lacks the brevity of more traditional definitions, it has the virtue of constituting a comprehensive statement of the major components of myth. As such, it serves as a useful reference point for collating and evaluating cross-cultural mythic narratives.

It is pertinent here to note the distinction among myth, legend, and folk tale. The most convincing differentiation among these three forms of narrative has been proposed by William Bascom (Table 1). In order to draw distinctions among the three generic forms of myth, legend, and folk tale in the classical Chinese tradition, some classical myths are presented side by side with their legendary or folk tale versions.

Approaches to Chinese Myth

Of the remarkable variety of approaches to myth, the meteorological (naturist), the ethnographic, the myth-as-ritual, the sociological, and the etiological have most influenced Sinologists working on Chinese myth. Henri Maspero, in "Mythological Legends in the *Classic of*

Table 1. Formal Features of Prose Narratives

	Prose Narratives		
Form	*Myth*	*Legend*	*Folk Tale*
Conventional opening	None	None	Usually
Told after dark	No restrictions	No restrictions	Usually
Belief	Fact	Fact	Fiction
Setting	Some time and some place	Some time and some place	Timeless, placeless
Time	Remote past	Recent past	Any time
Place	Earlier or other world	World as it is today	Any place
Attitude	Sacred	Sacred or secular	Secular
Principal character	Nonhuman	Human	Human or nonhuman

Source: Based on Bascom 1984, 11, Table 2.

History" (1924), and Eduard Erkes, in "Parallels in Chinese and American Indian Myths" (1926), followed the nature myth school, itself influenced by nineteenth-century romanticism, in their research on Chinese solar myths. The monomythic definition and approach of the naturist school has long since been rejected, as is epitomized by the title of Richard M. Dorson's article "The Eclipse of Solar Mythology" (1955), and has been modified to take into account the polyfunctionality of myths within a culture. The ethnographic approach to the study of Chinese myth dominates the work of Marcel Granet (1959) and Wolfram Eberhard (1968). Granet, who was influenced by the sociological-anthropological school of Emile Durkheim, characterized his work *Dance and Legend in Ancient China* as "a sociological analysis" of myths derived from ritual drama and religious dance (Granet 1959, 1). The main value of his work today resides in his useful collation of mythic texts and his perceptive discussions of individual narratives. Eberhard's ethnographic study of the role of myth in the cultures of south and east China, *The Local Culture of South and East China,* attempts to identify specific Chinese subcultures with individual classical and traditional myths. Again, his research has yielded a valuable source of mythic narratives and the ways in which minority cultures in China have utilized them. The myth-as-ritual school, whose influence has now declined, is also represented in Sinology by Carl Hentze's study *Lunar Myths and Symbols* (1932). Hentze's aim was to reconstruct the meaning of lunar and stellar myths by the comparative method, interpreting narratives in terms of their ritual and symbolic meaning. Since Bernhard Karlgren's harsh attack on these early studies with their various approaches, few Sinologists have attempted to participate in the general academic discussion of approaches and methodology in mythic studies. Karlgren's own contribution to the study of Chinese myth, which ended with his critique of the work in this field by his European colleagues, is his monumental "Legends and Cults in Ancient China" (1946). This article is sociological in orientation, focusing on the relationship between both primal and evolved myth and the founding myths of clans in ancient Chinese society. This work remains a valuable source for its collation and analyses of mythic references and their later reworkings as fable and legend. His translations of texts are reliable, and his work is still a useful study.

The etiological approach is exemplified by Derk Bodde's "Myths of Ancient China" (1961). Within its brief confines, this essay covers, in an intelligent, well-organized way, the major creation myths, solar myths, and flood myths of early China. Despite its brevity, it offers a study that is rigorous and scholarly in its methodology, questioning traditional concepts of prehistory, and applying, where relevant, the findings of comparative mythology. Bodde has made an important contribution to Chinese ethnographic and ritual studies in his more recent work *Festivals in Classical China* (1975). In this pioneering study his subsidiary aim of tracing certain Han rituals to their mythic counterparts by means of textual and iconographic documentation is of major importance for the study of the evolution of Chinese myth. Combining the data of iconographic records with the disciplinary approaches of history and archeology, Michael Loewe has examined mythic motifs attached to the mythologem of immortality as it is manifested in the mythical figure of the Queen Mother of the West in *Ways to Paradise: The Chinese Quest for Immortality* (1979).

The younger generation of Sinologists has also begun to develop studies in this emerging field. Sarah Allan has applied the methodology of Lévi-Strauss, especially his concept of transformations, in her examination of the succession myths and foundation myths of the protohistorical and historical dynasties of archaic China, and she has successfully utilized the Lévi-Straussian theory of binary opposition in her counterpointing of the sage-king and negative or subordinate mythical figures (Allan 1981). William G. Boltz has conducted research on the figure of Kung Kung with illuminating insights and has explained in the clearest terms the long-term misunderstanding of many Sinologists in applying the term *euhemerization* to Chinese mythical figures (1981). Mark E. Lewis has focused on the theme of violence in classical China, proposing the thesis that some forms of aggression in this period found their archetypal pattern in sacred narrative and so came to be sanctioned by the authority of myth (1990). Wolfgang Münke has adopted a more general approach in a work that constitutes a dictionary of Chinese myth (in German). For the most part, he refers to, but does not translate, the classical sources. His introductory essay deals with some important issues, such as the Chinese terms for God. In the text of his dictionary he also discusses a variety of problematic questions, such as the gender of the earth deity Hou-t'u. Occasionally, his discussions are marred by value-laden epithets, such as "Satan," in respect of the God of War, Ch'ih Yu, and of the god, Kung Kung (Münke 1976, 5–28, 142–43, 71, 219). The French Sinologist Rémi Mathieu has produced two significant works on classical Chinese mythology. The first is his two-volume annotated translation of *The Classic of Mountains and Seas,* a major repository of mythic narratives (1983). In his introductory essay, Mathieu states that he follows the comparative method in mythology and that he particularly acknowledges his debt to Georges Dumézil in reconstituting the historical and ethnological elements of the origin of the primitive peoples of Central Asia and East Siberia and minority nationalities of China (1983, 1:xxvii). His copious annotations of this classical text, translated *in toto,* reveal his special interest in the ethnographic and socioreligious approaches to myth. More recently, Mathieu has published a source book of Chinese myth (in French) with briefer annotation but very little discussion of the myths themselves. His selection follows the textual research work of Yuan K'o, which he has supplemented with his own collation of texts. The texts are organized into thematic categories (Mathieu 1989). Sarah Allan has utilized a recognized approach in comparative studies of myth, although this is limited to the methodology of Lévi-Strauss. Her more recent work does not reveal a comparativist approach (1991). It is generally true to say that most Sinological work on myth has been conducted without serious reference to comparative mythology.

A number of general books have been published on Chinese mythology which have achieved some sort of status in the field by reason of the dearth of scholarly publications for the general reader, or even the specialist. These books are not useful for the purposes of this study, for several reasons. They indiscriminately assemble and confuse the myths of quite separate mythological traditions of Taoism, Confucianism, Buddhism, local hero cults, and regional cults, so that the lay reader is unable to distinguish their lines of demarcation or chronology. Moreover, instead of translating the texts, they paraphrase the myth, without indicating their sources. Worse still, they tend to use strands from several, often contradictory narratives, so that they end up by creating virtually new mythic narratives. In many cases these writers are not Sinologists, or even specialists in myth, and they rely on the older myth material that happens to have been translated into English rather than researching the subject using classical and modern Chinese sources.

Insofar as this study is concerned, I have utilized a number of different disciplinary approaches rather than adhering to one individual theory or definition. The etiological approach is evident in the first chapters on the origin of the universe, the creation of humankind, and the origin of cultural benefits having to do with food, tools and weapons, hunting, the domestication of animals, and medicinal plants (chaps.

1 and 2). Etiological myths are also evident in narratives of the foundation of a tribe, people, city, or dynasty (chaps. 5 and 16). Another important influence has been Raglan's approach to myth, that is, the delineation of the characteristics of the mythical figure as hero, based on Raglan's formulation of twenty-two stereotypical features of the hero to be found in the biographies of major Indo-European and Semitic heroes (1937). Raglan's work followed on from the studies of Otto Rank in *The Myth of the Birth of the Hero* (1959) and was developed by Joseph Campbell, with the influence of Jungian archetypes, in *The Hero with a Thousand Faces* (1968). The use of Raglan's hero pattern is evident in my study in the patterns of miraculous birth, the pattern of the savior figure, and the mythology of divine heroes such as the Yellow Emperor, Yi the Archer, and the semidivine figure Yü the Great (chaps. 3, 5, 6–8, and 13).

At a more complex level, certain approaches to Chinese myth have been used to interpret opaque, fragmentary, or corrupt mythic narratives that express a surface meaning but also convey a deeper underlying reality. Often in such cases the most fruitful approach has been that pioneered by Malinowski, who suggested that some myths contain the vestige of a social or communal practice that may or may not still be followed. Two of his statements on this concept are particularly relevant:

> Myth serves principally to establish a sociological charter, or a retrospective moral pattern of behavior. . . .
> Myth fulfills in primitive culture an indispensable function: it expresses, enhances, and codifies belief; it safeguards and enforces morality; it vouches for the efficiency of ritual and contains practical rules for the guidance of man. Myth is thus a vital ingredient of human civilizations; it is not an idle tale, but a hard-worked active force; it is not an intellectual explanation or an artistic imagery, but a pragmatic charter of primitive faith and moral wisdom. (Malinowski 1954, 144, 101)

Several Chinese myths lend themselves to Malinowski's interpretation of myth as a sociological, or pragmatic, charter. I have applied it to the myth of the virgin brides and the river god and the myth of Yao's son, Tan Chu, to show that beneath their surface meaning lies a more powerful layer of mythic significance (chaps. 3 and 11).

Another valuable approach to the interpretation of obscure or ambiguous Chinese mythic narratives has been Eliade's concept of archetypes, derived from the Jungian mode. In *The Myth of the Eternal Return*

(1971), Eliade discussed the concepts of "the symbolism of the Center," "celestial archetypes of cities and temples," and "the Sacred Mountain" as an *axis mundi*. These concepts have provided illuminating insights into the Chinese motifs of the world-tree, such as the Chien-mu and Leaning Mulberry, the sacred K'un-lun mountains, and so forth. Moreover, pivotal to an understanding of the juxtaposition in mythic narratives of clashing opposites has been the fruitful concept of binary opposition proposed by the structural anthropologist Lévi-Strauss. This concept has been particularly rewarding in discussing symbolic opposites, such as Ch'ih Yu and the Yellow Emperor, or the failed hero, Kun, and his successful son, the hero Yü the Great. One of the seminal theories of Georges Dumézil on dual sovereignty or joint rule (1940) has been helpful in recognizing and elucidating the complex myth of the divine (half-)brothers, the Yellow Emperor and the Flame Emperor, who each ruled half the world but who later fought for total supremacy.

The Comparative Method
in the Study of Chinese Myth

The fertile theories of the productive scholar Georges Dumézil are synonymous with modern methods of comparative methodology. In introducing the work of Dumézil in *The New Comparative Mythology: An Anthropological Assessment of the Theories of Georges Dumézil* (Littleton 1973), C. Scott Littleton proposed the following useful definition of the term *comparative mythology*: "Comparative mythology refers to the systematic comparison of myths and mythic themes drawn from a wide variety of cultures and involves attempts to abstract common underlying themes, to relate these themes to a common symbolic representation (e.g., the forces of nature, fertility, or . . . social organization) and/ or to reconstruct one or more protomythologies" (ibid., 32).

The comparativist approach has resulted in a major contribution to the study of mythologies. This new science was generated two hundred years ago during the Enlightenment, when the idea of universal human progress was prevalent. Those eighteenth-century scholars who studied myth, religion, and ritual included in their research the oriental myths and rituals of ancient India and Persia. In the nineteenth century, the rise of romanticism and philosophical idealism, together with a pantheistic view of nature, further inspired studies of myth, especially in Germany, as is exemplified by theories on naturism put forward by Friedrich Max Müller. Initially, comparative mythology was dominated by the discipline of philology, but it gradually moved toward the analysis of mythic type and motif. In the early twentieth century, the theories and theses of the anthropologist Sir James Frazer had a profound influence on scholarship in many fields, especially his concept of the "dying god," epitomized by his reconstruction of the myth of the sacred grove at Nemi. Frazer's comparative method was exhaustive: he collated every known manifestation of a motif in mythologies throughout the world and recorded them in voluminous publications. Nowadays his magnum opus, the thirteen-volume *Golden Bough*, with *Das Kapital* by Karl Marx and Charles Darwin's *Origin of Species*, rank as the three outstanding *unread* works of the nineteenth century.

There are several reasons why Frazer's work is not so influential, or fashionable, today. His method of documenting examples of mythic motifs resulted in their being presented without a textual or historical context, thus robbing them of their ethnographic relevance and their chronological significance. Frazer also based his research on the late nineteenth-century concept of unilineal evolutionism, derived from the Darwinian model, that all societies evolve along the same linear path from "savagery" and "barbarism" to civilization; that myths belong to the initial period of "savagery"; and that as society develops from the primitive to the civilized, so myths gradually decline until only their vestiges remain. Finally, Frazer's work is often dismissed today as "armchair anthropology" by those who favor ethnographic fieldwork with firsthand documentation by the scholar, or scientist, living among the community under study.

Nevertheless, it would be absurd to reject Frazer's work in its entirety, and many of his findings have provided me with valuable insights into the workings of early Chinese myth. For example, the moon goddess, Ch'ang O, has hitherto been viewed in a limited way in the contexts of immortality and lunar iconography. But Frazer's study of the Coyote Indian trickster figure prompts the realization that Ch'ang O possesses the typical features of the trickster figure in myth and folklore. Similarly, other rewarding parallels have been suggested by the work of mythologists on other myth systems, such as Doty and Bruce Lincoln. For example, the P'an Ku myth has up till now been read as an etiological myth on the origin of the cosmos. But from Doty has been borrowed the useful term *the cosmological human body* to advance our understanding of this important myth, while from Lincoln the terms *homologic sets* and *alloforms* have been applied to demonstrate that it is much more than a cosmogonic myth. The value of Lincoln's method lies in his systematic tracing, through narratives preserved in the ancient literatures of Indo-European language groups, of the mythic motif of the dying god whose body creates the universe (1986, 1–40). Moreover, Lincoln's discussion of myths relating to food and eating, for which he coins the term *sitiogonic* to mean 'explaining the origin of food', has also been applied to interpret the underlying significance of some Chinese myths, such as the conflict between the Lord of the Granary and the Goddess of Salt River (ibid., 65–86).

A major Chinese mythic motif, the separation of sky and earth, has also been explicated in the light of comparative mythology. The Chinese narratives of this motif are extremely resistant to comprehension today because early on in the classical tradition, the root mythic motif became inextricably entangled with sociopolitical and ethical theories, with the result that the motif became almost unrecognizable in its extant form. In fact, Derk Bodde was the first to read the obscure Chinese mythic narratives relevant to this motif as the myth of the separation of the sky and earth (1961, 389–92). I have developed his interpretation in the light of the cross-cultural study of this motif by the mythologist K. Numazawa, "The Cultural-Historical Background of Myths on the Separation of Sky and Earth" and by means of the study of Sándor Erdész, "The World Conception of Lajos Ámi, Storyteller" (1984, 183–92; 316–35). To clarify this motif, reference has been made to the pertinent reminder of the classicist G. S. Kirk that it is linked to the idea of a Golden Age and that it has as much to do with the relationship between gods and humans as with the physical aspects of sky and earth in a purely cosmogonic myth (1970, 209, 226–38).

One of the most valuable works I have used to interpret Chinese myth has been the recent study by Jaan Puhvel, *Comparative Mythology* (1987). With its judicious use of descriptive terminology, its concepts informed by extensive reading, and its organizing principle of thematic categories, this seminal work examines in an instructive manner the myths of India, Iran, Greece and Rome, the Celts, Germans, Scandinavians, and Slavs. Puhvel's descriptive term *ornithomorphous hierogamy* in his illuminating discussion of bird motifs in myth provided a key to understanding the significance of recurring Chinese myths of divine conception through eating a bird's egg, which in turn forms the basis of a major Chinese myth of dynastic foundation. My indebtedness to Puhvel's work is testified to by my application of several of his analyses of motifs, especially mythic geography, world measuring, animal features of the gods, polycephality in gods, bestiovestism, the berserk warrior-god, and antithetical archetypes, such as fire and water. Because of his comparativist study, several Chinese mythic motifs that might otherwise have passed unnoticed have been discovered, identified, and clarified.

In any discussion of comparative mythology, Greco-Roman parallels predominate, of course, and since the myths of Greece and Rome are so familiar, it has seemed natural and helpful to draw some parallels in this book. But this has not been done to the exclusion of parallels with other cultures, particularly Indian, Iranian, and Scandinavian. Moreover, the temptation to label Chinese mythical figures as "the Chinese Orpheus," "the Chinese Odin," or "the Chinese Prometheus" has been resisted in order to keep the cross-cultural parallels from converging on the line of inquiry and so endangering the authenticity and integrity of Chinese myth.

Modern Chinese and Japanese Studies of Chinese Myth

In a study of Chinese myth, William G. Boltz has reiterated a basic problem confronting Western Sinologists specializing in Chinese myth, namely, that for over two thousand years "the Chinese historized their mythology" (1981, 142). In fact, it was only as late as the 1920s that Chinese historians grasped the nettle of their traditional mode of historiography and historical method. The eventual process of disentangling the mythical era from the historical period was primarily due to the open-minded approach and clarity of vision of the young historian Ku Chieh-kang and other scholars, including Yang K'uan, in the decade and a half after 1926. (For a study of Ku's life and thought, see Schneider 1971.) Ku Chieh-kang has rightly been termed the "founder of modern mythological studies in China" (Mitarai 1984, 5). Ku, however, aroused considerable controversy between 1926 and 1941 when he published his views on the demarcation between history and mythology in a seven-volume collection of essays by himself and others, *Critiques of Ancient [Chinese] History*. Some of his ideas and methodology, such as the rigid dating of myth according to the known date of its textual *locus classicus,* have long since been rejected. But Ku's scholarly method of separating mythical figures from historical personages and of detaching the mythical age from the historical era constitutes a major contribution to the modern study of Chinese history, and especially to the study of Chinese myth, since he was the first to establish this as an independent discipline. Yang K'uan developed these ideas into recognizably mythological formulations. For example, he reordered traditional "emperors" of antiquity into various categories of god, such as supreme being, earth deity, and so forth (K. C. Chang 1976, 169, citing Yang K'uan's preface to "A Discussion of Ancient Chinese History" [1941], in *Critiques of Ancient [Chinese] History*, vol. 7).

At the same time as Ku's monumental historical research appeared, other Chinese writers and scholars began to publish work on Chinese mythology which clearly acknowledged their debt to Western studies of myth. The most notable Western influences were Edward Burnett Tylor's *Primitive Culture* in 1871, Andrew Lang's *Myth, Ritual and Religion* in 1887, N. B. Dennys's *Folk-Lore of China . . .* in 1876, and Edward T. C. Werner's *Myths and Legends of China* in 1922. Dennys and Werner properly demarcated the line between history and other specialist disciplines, though they did not always make a sharp distinction between mythology and religion. It is significant that the work of Tylor and Lang, besides many other Western research works on myth, had a major impact on Chinese authors and writers of fiction in the 1920s and 1930s. The earliest of these was the novelist and short story writer Shen Yen-ping, or Shen Ping, otherwise known by his nom de plume of Mao Tun. In two essays on myth published in 1925 and 1929, he classified Chinese myth on thematic lines, such as cosmogony, nature myths, the origin of nature, the wars of the gods, myths of darkness, and metamorphoses. In his 1929 work, in particular, he drew on resources of comparative mythology, citing mythic narratives of the Australian aborigines and North American Indians, and of ancient Greece and India and Northern Europe. In 1928 another writer, Hsuan Chu, classified Chinese myth on a regional basis—those of North, Central, and South China—noting that most extant mythic texts derived from Central China. Hsuan Chu also organized myths into thematic categories under the general rubric of "Worldview," under which he listed motifs such as cosmogony, creation of humankind, giants, nature gods, heroic deities, monsters, and culture gods. His contribution is distinguished by the comparative method, and he was one of the first to introduce the myths of other cultures to Chinese readers.

In the 1930s a valuable research work on myth was published by Lin Hui-hsiang. In his *Mythology*, Lin presented the significant Western approaches to myth and offered a critical overview of the major specialists, notably F. Max Müller and Andrew Lang (Allen, 1982, 145–46). In 1932, Cheng Te-k'un made an important methodological advance by focusing attention on the myths of one classical text, *The Classic of Moun-*

tains and Seas. His system of classification was based not on thematic principles but on disciplinary or subject categories, namely, philosophy, science, religion, history, and sociology (1932, 127). For example, he subsumed myths on primal matter, cosmogony, and the creation of humans under the category of philosophy, and celestial and meteorological myths under science. But when he subsumed myths of divine beings and divine culture bearers under the category of history, he appeared to have disregarded Ku Chieh-kang's reconstruction of mythology and ancient history. Another important methodological advance was the publication of an article by K. C. Chang in which he showed the value of applying comparative approaches to the analysis of Chinese creation myths, citing the major authors in the discipline: Durkheim, Boas, Eliade, Bascom, Leach, Lévi-Strauss, Malinowski, Raglan, and Thompson (K. C. Chang 1959, 47–79). In a later study, in English, a chapter entitled "A Classification of Shang and Chou Myths," he usefully discussed the sources of Chinese myths and organized the classical narratives into a five-part typology including the separation of gods and heroes, natural calamities and human saviors, and heroes and their descents (K. C. Chang 1976, 149–73).

The novelist Chou Tso-jen was also influenced by Western mythology, especially the writings of Andrew Lang and Jane Ellen Harrison, and by anthropological and psychological studies. He argued (1950) for the authenticity and autonomy of myth as a subject in its own right and was instrumental in introducing Chinese readers to the mythical figures of ancient Greece (C. H. Wang 1977, 5–28).

One of the major writers and scholars who specialized in the study of Chinese myth in the 1930s and 1940s was Wen Yi-to. Basing his research on the classics, especially the *Songs of Ch'u, The Classic of Change,* and *The Classic of Poetry,* he attempted to combine the philological method of Müller with the anthropological approach of Lang. Wen's main contribution resides in two methodological approaches. First, he singled out an individual classic as a special focus for studies of myth, as Cheng Te-k'un had already done, instead of ranging across the broad spectrum of classical texts. Second, he devoted individual monographs to specific motifs, such as the fish motif (Wen Yi-to 1948, 1:117–38). Nevertheless, Chinese and Western scholars have criticized Wen's philological method as idiosyncratic and unscientific. His overeager tendency to identify totems such as the dragon or the snake with mythical figures has also been questioned on the grounds of a lack of evidence. Despite these drawbacks, Wen Yi-to ranks as the foremost exponent of Chinese myth in the first half of this century (Allen 1982, 146–58).

Japanese researchers into Chinese myth, such as Izushi Yoshihiko in 1943, have generally followed the thematic principle of classification. In 1944, Mori Mikisaburō developed a more sophisticated classification system with a four-part division into the gods, ancestral myths, nature myths, and minor deities. More recently, Mitarai Masaru has devoted a monograph, *The Deities of Early China* (1984), to a variety of problems relating to Chinese myth. Like many Japanese research works, Mitarai's monograph is a valuable source of new research data, and it contains a thorough survey of traditional and modern problems in this field. His methodological approach, however, makes his otherwise useful work difficult to assimilate. He proposes the thesis that the foundation of China's protohistoric and historical dynasties may be identified with primeval gods and suprahuman figures who came to be associated with the emergence of the most important clans in antiquity. Interspersed uneasily among the discussions of this central thesis are fundamental cosmological myths and numerous important others, which, because of their artificial linkage to dynasties and clans of remote antiquity, are diminished in terms of their authenticity, narrative content, and mythic significance. Also published in 1984, Kominami Ichirō's *Chinese Myths and Tales* usefully discusses sources of myth in the post-Han era, besides the meaning of specific mythic themes.

A number of recent Chinese scholars have published impressive work in the field of comparative mythology, for example, Hsiao Ping, Ho Hsin, Tu Erh-wei, and Wang Hsiao-lien. They have produced a wealth of new data, but their work is not without its problems. Ho Hsin, for example, bases his work on myth on the outdated theory of solar myth propounded by Müller (1891) and deploys a dubious phonological argument for the primacy of a sun god in China and the worship of solar deities (1986). Similarly, Tu Erh-wei places undue emphasis on the lunar theory of myth, now equally outmoded as a monomythic approach. With little substantive evidence, he postulates the existence of numerous moon deities in the Chinese mythic tradition and argues for a lunar significance in narratives where none is to be found (Tu Erh-wei 1977). Hsiao Ping has written a monumental study of the myths relating to the classic *Songs of Ch'u* using a multidisciplinary approach with an emphasis on ethnology. The value of his work lies in his skill, convincingly backed by textual and ethnographic evidence, in tracing the living elements of myth motifs that have their origin in classical myths. These vestiges are to be found in the minority peoples of China, and Hsiao Ping has produced impressive charts showing the recurring elements of vestigial myth in the present-day cultures of twenty-five different Chinese nationality groups (1986, 108–11). Today in China, research on mythology maintains an ideological stance based on the outmoded writings of Hegel, Marx, and Engels. At the same time, there is a marked difference between the readiness of pre-1950 Chinese writers to incorporate the findings of Western mythologists in their work on Chinese myth and the reluctance of post-1950 Chinese specialists to assimilate the developments in mythic studies throughout the world over the past few decades. The career and publications of Wang Hsiao-lien are an exception here. He has relied heavily on Japanese research on myth to develop his ideas and methodology. He has translated numerous Japanese articles and books into Chinese. In 1983 he translated Shirakawa Shizuka's (1975) *Chinese Mythology* into Chinese, and he has published a valuable survey of twenty-three Japanese specialists on Chinese myth (1977, 273–97).

For the past forty years the doyen of Chinese mythology has been Yuan K'o, a scholar at the Szechwan Academy of Social Sciences in Ch'eng-tu. Of his numerous contributions to the field, his two source books (1980.2; 1985) and his annotated critical edition of *The Classic of Mountains and Seas* (1980.1) constitute a foundation for the development of the subject. I am indebted to the pioneering research of this dedicated scholar whose work is acknowledged by the international community of Sinologists as an outstanding contribution to the emerging discipline of Chinese myth studies.

The Nature of Chinese Mythic Narratives

The piecemeal way in which mythic narratives were recorded in classical texts is compensated for by the inclusion of these texts, for the most part, in the body of canonical literature which scholars and aristocratic families in the period between the fourth century B.C. and third century A.D. sought assiduously to preserve and maintain. The mythic narratives have remained preserved in amber, in their original contexts of works on history, philosophy, literature, political theory, and various treatises and miscellaneous works, for over two millennia. Thus readers today can evaluate them in their earliest recorded form, in their original written context, and in all the variety of versions from one text to another. Because China lacked a Homer or a Hesiod, a Herodotus or an Ovid, who recounted myth and shaped its content and style, early Chinese myth existed as an amorphous, untidy congeries of archaic expression. So, to the extent that it was not reworked and extrapolated from early texts into an *Iliad,* an *Odyssey,* or a *Metamorphoses,* it retained a measure of authenticity.

On the other hand, as Rémi Mathieu and others have pointed out, early Chinese writers of different intellectual persuasions who used myth may have distorted it in order to make better use of it in their works (1989, 12). Another major disadvantage of the manner of their preservation in various classical texts is that mythic narratives were deployed by writers of different persuasions to illustrate this or that point of view, and as a consequence the narratives often remained tied to and, to some extent, colored by that viewpoint. This is particularly noticeable in the philosophical work *Chuang Tzu,* dating from the fourth century B.C. For example, it is the sole source that preserved the myth of the P'eng bird, which metamorphosed from a monster fish, yet the reason for the recounting of that myth was to explain complex ideas of relativity and objectivity which were central to early Taoist thought. Similarly, the mythical figure of Shun in *Mencius* is identified with the ethical principle of filial piety, central to the humanistic doctrines of Confucianism, yet other mythic narratives in several classical texts relate contradictory aspects of this figure. The very existence of these variant versions is rewarding for the modern mythographer, since it permits a comparison of different modes of narrative and, in some cases, allows of a piecing together of a composite myth from overlapping fragments of the same textual period. It is because the corpus of Chinese myth is so rich in variant forms, perhaps uniquely so in respect of other mythological traditions, that in this book multiforms of a myth are presented together wherever possible, in order to give the reader an idea of the range, variety, and vitality of mythic expression.

The texts of the mythic narratives presented in this book may be classified into three main periods. The first is the pre-Han or early classical era from the middle to late Chou dynasty, that is, circa 600 B.C. to 221 B.C. Although the earliest written records date from circa 1300 B.C., discovered at the site of the Shang dynasty capital, Yin, near Anyang in Honan province, these texts, in the form of oracle bones, are mainly divinatory and are to do with religion, ritual, and mundane affairs. No myths are recorded among these oracle bones. Although no mythological texts from the archaic or historical Shang period exist, there is the possibility that fragments of Shang mythic narratives have been preserved in the texts of the Chou period.

The main period for early classical mythic narratives is the Eastern Chou era, circa 450 to 221 B.C., and this late dynastic era is rich in texts. It is important to note that while it is true to say that myths preserved in the late Chou period constitute the earliest extant recorded version, this is not the same as their earlier pristine, or pure version, which cannot be known.

The second period of mythic texts is the late classical and postclassical eras of the Ch'in, Han, and post-Han periods, from circa 221 B.C. to the fifth century A.D. A textual problem immediately confronts us here because several important texts containing mythic material are of uncertain date in terms of the original compilation, and many such texts contain mythic material that belongs to a much earlier period than the conventional date of the text as a whole. It is safe to conclude that such texts represent a transitional phase between the late Chou and the Ch'in and early Han eras, in terms of much of their material if not of the biographical date of their author or compiler.

Texts dating from the Han proper and post-Han periods, between the first century B.C. and fifth century A.D., mark a sharp break from the earlier classical era because writers were beginning to modify, codify, distort, embroider, and erroneously explain early mythic narratives to such an extent that their mythopoeia created an alternative body of myth. Moreover, as Mathieu observes, one direct result of the unification of feudal states into one empire during the Ch'in and early Han eras was that a process of homogenization of local mythological traditions occurred (1989, 10). This mythopoeic and homogenizing trend is noticeable in several important texts of the period. In "Genealogy of the Gods," chapter 63 of *The Elder Tai's Record of Ritual* by Tai Te (first century B.C.) and in "Basic Annals of the Gods," the first chapter of Ssu-ma Ch'ien's monumental *Historical Records* (late second century B.C.) are to be found pseudobiographical data for the shadowy figures of the primeval gods of the early classical era.

Mythopoeia was not confined to the fabrication of biographies of the gods. Ssu-ma Ch'ien's history, the first history of the Chinese empire, records a pentad of gods, which in fact constitutes a new pantheon that differs fundamentally from the older pantheons. The Yellow Emperor, who was a latecomer to the primeval pantheons of the Chou mythologies, stands preeminent as the first and foremost god, the fountainhead of Chinese civilization and cultural history. His new preeminence is due to the adoption of this deity by the Taoist philosophers whose doctrines were finding favor among the rulers of the empire. Although the mythic texts of this second period have to be approached with caution because of this mythopoeic tendency, they are invaluable for the way they demonstrate how mythologies evolve to meet the exigencies of social, intellectual, and political life. They are also important documents insofar as they contain surviving mythic narratives that do not appear in the Chou classical texts, or offer variant versions. For example, the eclectic writer Wang Ch'ung, of the first century A.D., alluded to a great number of fragments of myth for which his work *Disquisitions* is the *locus classicus,* and in some cases these fragments may be presumed to long predate their author (Huang Hui 1938).

The third period may be termed the traditional era of Chinese mythic narratives, that is, from the Sui-T'ang to the Ming dynasty, from the sixth to the early seventeenth century. The most valuable repository for this material is the Sung encyclopedias, which usually cite early texts verbatim. Another source is the commentaries of scholars from the seventh century and later, which cite authors several centuries earlier whose work has not survived. Whereas the texts of the first period are to be found in works of moral philosophy, political theory, and literature, the texts of the two later periods are much more general, ranging from commentaries on the classics, to alchemical handbooks, botanical treatises, local gazettes, geographical tracts, and ethnographic studies. Mythology, however, does not allow of classification into overly neat periods and all manner of "awkward" materials will be found obtruding from this tripartite time scale.

The Polyfunctionality of Myth as an Organizing Principle

One of the major characteristics of myths worldwide is their polyfunctionality. That is, a mythic narrative may be read in many different ways and at several levels. For example, the myth of the Chinese deity Hou Chi may be viewed as a myth of the grain god, of the miraculous birth of a god, of the child hero overcoming attempts on his life, or of the inauguration of temple sacrifice to the grain god, and again as the foundation myth of the Chou people. Similarly, myths of the Yellow Emperor may be interpreted as facets of his contradictory roles of warrior-god, bringer of cultural benefits, peacemaker, avenging god, or, later in the mythological tradition, the supreme deity of the Taoist pantheon, and yet again as the amalgam of homogenized local mythic traditions.

It is partly because of the polyfunctionality of myth that this book has been organized into chapters marked by thematic categories that underscore major worldwide motifs, such as cosmogony, the creation of humankind, etiological myths of culture and civilization, foundation myths, and so forth. In order to highlight the way in which myths may serve several functions, some narratives have been repeated within different thematic chapters to reveal their rich aspectual multiplicity. This scheme will be found to be not too different from the arrangements of motifs devised by Stith Thompson in *Motif-Index* (1955, 1:61–345).

Future Research on Chinese Myth: A New Dimension

This book offers a foundation in basic readings in mythic narratives, together with explications of the texts in the light of traditional Chinese scholarship and from the perspective of major developments in mythic studies worldwide and comparative mythology. Though I hope that this book will pave the way to a deeper understanding of and a wider acquaintance with the content and nature of Chinese myth, much research remains to be done. In fact, a supplementary volume of readings and analyses now waits to be compiled on additional versions of myths, minor mythical figures, and fugitive fragments, still within the confines of classical mythic texts.

Another rewarding line of inquiry, following on from the research of Wen Yi-to and others, would be to study the myths within individual classical texts and to compare them with other textual versions. Some major repositories, such as the *Huai-nan Tzu*, still await a full, annotated translation in the style of recent classical translations by Rémi Mathieu (1983) and Roger Greatrex (1987). Monographs could also be written on primary motifs, such as the flood, with all its ramifications of mythical figures, themes, and comparative elements. Mythic motifs or mythical figures might be examined from a diachronic and synchronic perspective to demonstrate the potency of a myth within a society over a historical period. The mythic traditions of the major belief systems of Confucianism, Taoism, and Buddhism should be studied separately in orderly sequences of historical period, not lumped together in a confusing hodgepodge. Thereafter the interplay among the three mythological systems could be explored.

At a more complex level, researchers equipped with linguistic expertise in the languages of non-Sinitic peoples along China's historical frontiers will be able to analyze myths preserved in Chinese texts from the aspect of non-Sinitic influences, or even origins. Technical monographs on the phonological elements of mythic narratives will no doubt throw light on the interrelationships among mythical place-names, plant names, and the singular or multiple names of deities. The important areas of Sinological ethnography, already under way in China with a new generation of scholars, will be vitalized by further interaction in the international sphere, especially with the translation of the best Chinese and Western monographs in this field. Studies on local and regional cults, peripheral to but dependent upon the main belief systems in traditional China, will add to our understanding of how religious belief functions in a specific community in a given historical period. Japanese monographs, too, which are continuing to make important contributions to the fields of anthropology, ethnography, archeology, and mythic studies, should be translated and discussed in an international academic forum. In taking up these essential areas of research, the next generation of scholars will be exploring new frontiers in this developing field of humanistic scholarship.

I

Origins

Chinese etiological myths of cosmogony, which explain the origin of the universe, describe how the world came to be ordered out of chaos. These myths are ways of conceptualizing the universe at the moment when it was created, *in illo tempore,* or "in the beginning" of mythological time. Chinese cosmogonic myths fit the general pattern of myths worldwide in the sense that they do not describe creation *ex nihilo:* the cosmos is created from "some already existing matter" (Dundes 1984, 5). Many mythologies containing accounts of the origin of the world and of human life reveal a deep interest in ultimate origins, in tracing the world back to a single primeval element that existed from the time before "the beginning" and from which all things emerged. In the ancient cosmologies of Greece, Egypt, Mesopotamia, and elsewhere, the mythic narratives describe this primeval element as water. In Vedic Indian myth, it is fire in water. By contrast, the basic principle of Chinese cosmology is a primeval vapor, which was believed to embody cosmic energy governing matter, time, and space. This energy, according to Chinese mythic narratives, undergoes a transformation at the moment of creation, so that the nebulous element of vapor becomes differentiated into dual elements of male and female, Yin and Yang, hard and soft matter, and other binary elements.

Besides the concept of a primeval element, most ancient cosmologies contain narratives that present a picture of the cosmos that emerged from it. The ancient Chinese conceived the world as a square area of land or earth, above which was the round sky, held up like a dome by four supports from the earth. In some accounts these supports are said to be four giant pillars, or eight pillars fastened by cords to the sky's canopy, or four immense mountains reaching from earth to the sky, which they prop up. This world picture bears a strong resemblance to the ancient Egyptian view, an account of which is given by J. M. Plumley (1975, 17–41). Since Egyptian mythic narratives predate the Chinese by about two and a half millennia, the resemblance may well reflect a cross-cultural influence from Egypt to China through Central Asia.

Another important point is that the ancient Chinese conceived of the cosmos in this world picture as the only world, not as part of a vast, limitless universe. One of the Chinese accounts from the fourth century B.C., "Questions of Heaven," makes it clear that the edges and boundaries, seams and corners are all observable in this world picture. And like the Babylonian, the Chinese cosmogonic myths describe how the stars, sun, and moon became fixed and ordered in their trajectories soon after the moment of creation.

The cosmogonic myths differ fundamentally from those of other traditions, such as the Judeo-Christian, in the absence of a creator and lack of any necessity for a divine will or benevolent intelligence to ordain the act of creation. Consequently, Chinese cosmogonic myths are not marked by the seal of authority within a monolithic religiocultural system, such as is the function of the account in *Genesis,* which serves as the authorized version of the origin of the world in the Judeo-Christian tradition. Rather than one authorized version in the Chinese tradition, there are several accounts of the creation of the world and of human beings. G. E. R. Lloyd has observed of ancient Greek cosmology, "There is no such thing as *the* cosmological model, *the* cosmological theory, of the Greeks" (1975, 205). Thus Lloyd speaks of "Greek cosmologies" in the plural. Similarly, it is more accurate to discuss the pluralism of Chinese cosmological conceptions. This point is important for the Sinological debate on ancient Chinese cosmology, for many scholars have asserted that the cosmological tradition in ancient China is negligible, or even nonexistent, as N. J. Girardot amply demonstrates in his seminal article on this subject, "The Problem of Creation Mythology in the Study of Chinese Religion" (1976, 289–318). Exceptions to this "benign neglect" in Sinology are the scholars Wolfram Eberhard, Derk Bodde, Eduard Erkes, Max Kaltenmark, and K. C. Chang.

Using the pluralistic approach to ancient Chinese cosmologies, therefore, it will be seen that five main traditions emerge based on mythic narratives drawn from six classical texts, which are early or relatively late. The five main traditions are: (1) the cosmogonic myth that describes the world picture in "Questions of Heaven," dating from about the fourth century B.C.; (2) the cosmogonic myth that describes the creation of the universe and humans out of formless misty vapor in *Huai-nan Tzu*, dating from the second century B.C., and also in the *Tao yuan*, a recently excavated mortuary text believed to date from the fourth century B.C.; (3) the cosmogonic myth that describes the separation of earth from sky and the origin of the firstborn semidivine human in *Historical Records of the Three Sovereign Divinities and the Five Gods*, dating from the third century A.D.; (4) the myth of the cosmological human body in *A Chronicle of the Five Cycles of Time*, dating from the third century A.D.; and (5) the myth of the making of human beings by a creatrix in *Explanations of Social Customs*, dating from the late second century A.D.

Within these cosmogonic mythic narratives there are four separate accounts of the creation of human beings, which range from nature-oriented myths to anthropogonic ones and from a male-dominated creation myth (in which the firstborn semidivine human is male) to a female one. In terms of dating, the earliest cosmogonic Chinese myths are from the fourth to the second century B.C., and the latest appears in the third century A.D. It is significant that as the early myths began to be codified and rationalized in the late and postclassical era, it was the latest, male-dominated creation myth of P'an Ku which became the generally accepted account and acquired a sort of orthodoxy in the ensuing centuries. Compared with other cosmogonic myths in the ancient world, Chinese accounts appear relatively late in the mythographic tradition.

In his essay "The Cosmology of Early China," Joseph Needham usefully summarizes the three schools of cosmological thought which had become current by the late Han period. His discussion does not, however, take into account the earliest texts cited in this chapter, which date from the fourth century B.C. These three schools, which so dominated and informed astronomical science in the late classical period, were described by Ts'ai Yung (A.D. 133–192) as the K'ai t'ien, or domed universe school; the Hun t'ien, or celestial circles of the astronomical sphere school; and the Hsuan yeh, or infinite empty space school (Needham 1975, 87–93).

Finally, it will be seen that whereas in Chinese cosmogony an upper world and an earthly world are described, little mention is made of an underworld. None of the accounts gives a detailed description of the geography of the world of the dead, or the underworld, such as that ruled by Hades, brother of the sky god, Zeus, in Greek myth, or in Mesopotamian myth.

The Origin of the World

The source of the first reading in this section is "Questions of Heaven," chapter 3 of *Songs of Ch'u*. "Questions of Heaven" is the most valuable document in Chinese mythography. Written in about the fourth century B.C., it presents a systematic account of the main myths of ancient Ch'u in its 186 verses. The account opens with a narrative of the creation of the world and proceeds to the acts of the gods and suprahumans, and of mythical figures of the prehistorical era, ending with the deeds of historical personages up to the kings of Ch'u in the late sixth century B.C. An earlier date than the fourth century B.C. may be surmised for the myths related in the text, since it clearly draws on a preexisting fund of myths. The reasons the text is so valuable are that it is a rich store of ancient myth; that it constitutes the earliest repertoire of most primary and some minor myths; and that it serves as a control text by which to compare and contrast other mythic texts, whether earlier fragments, contemporary accounts, or later narratives. It is a unique document in the Chinese tradition because it contains in its brief confines the totality of deeply held beliefs at a single point in the mythological tradition.

The format of "Questions of Heaven" is a series of questions, about 160 in all (David Hawkes arrived at 172 [1985, 122], and Chiang Liang-fu found over 100 [1984, 337]). The questions contain fairly substantial information, so that if they do not hold the answer to the question posed, they point toward it. They are often expressed in such an arcane, convoluted manner that they form what might be termed sacred riddles. Another difficulty in interpretation is that the context or background of the myth referred to in some riddling questions has not been preserved in another version or contemporaneous document.

The purpose of these questions remains enigmatic, although their general substance has to do with cosmology, mythology, and history. Yet the unwritten answers to them were indubitably fixed in the mind of the person who framed them and in the minds of the audience for whom they were formulated. It is possible to infer that the puzzling questions were meant to prompt a long-remembered knowledge and were designed to stir the mind, to entertain, and to serve as a sort of catechism concerning the most basic beliefs and sacred truths of the community of Ch'u which engendered them.

The anonymous author of "Questions of Heaven" was clearly an authoritative member of the sophisticated society of Ch'u state in Central China during the Warring States period of the late Chou dynasty. Well educated, deeply versed in his rich cultural traditions, he was probably an official of aristocratic standing in the Ch'u court. The unknown author served as custodian of the cultural heritage of Ch'u in its religious, historical, and political aspects. Traditionally, authorship of the text has been ascribed to Ch'ü Yuan, a shadowy figure in the aristocratic court circle of Ch'u, but modern scholarship views him more as an adapter of a priestly textual tradition than the author (Hawkes 1985, 126). The mythopoeia created by the mystique of this and other texts in *Songs of Ch'u* ascribed by tradition to Ch'ü Yuan has been brilliantly — and one would have thought conclusively — exposed by James Robert Hightower in "Ch'ü Yüan Studies" (1954, 192–223).

The first reading in this section marks the opening of the anonymous account, which declaims the sacral words *It says*, similar to the Western scriptural refrain *It is written*, for both appeal to a dim and distant tradition. The phrase distinguishes the mythic narrative of "Questions of Heaven" as sacred history, since the account of the more recent kings of Ch'u at the close of the text traces their ancestry back to the beginning of time, linking the Ch'u kings of history to the primeval era of gods and heroes.

The mythic narrative of the origin of the world in "Questions of Heaven" presents a vivid world picture. It mentions no prime cause, no first creator. From the "formless expanse" the primeval element of misty vapor emerges spontaneously as a creative force, which is organically constructed as a set of binary forces in opposition to each other — upper and lower spheres, darkness and light, Yin and Yang — whose mysterious transformations bring about the ordering of the universe. First the heavens and the celestial bodies appear. The vaulted sky, nine layers deep with nine celestial gates, is propped up by eight pillars rooted in the earth below. The cosmological question "Why do the eight pillars lean to the southeast and why is there a fault?" is answered in other mythic narratives that tell of the cosmic disorder caused by the marplot, Kung Kung (chap. 4). The play of mythic numbers is significant. There is the duality of binary forces, the trinity of the threefold changes of Yin and Yang which wrought the cosmos, and the nonary system in the nine layers of sky and gates, besides the numerological significance of the number eight. The number nine is endowed with special meaning in the early culture of Ch'u, as is evidenced by several titles in *Songs of Ch'u*, such as "Nine Songs," "Nine Declarations," "Nine Arguments," and others (Hawkes 1985, 8). The number nine generally has a divine connotation, being especially linked to the sacred sphere of the sky. The number eight has distinctively Chinese connotations of cosmic harmony and felicity. The number three is of worldwide significance as a mystical or magical figure, and the number two, especially in its dualistic aspect, is distinctively Chinese.

The cosmological account ends with a description of the ordered movement of the sun, moon, and stars, "Dipper's Ladle," "the Cord," and "the twelve divisions." It is clear that although there is an interest in astronomy, the concept of heliocentricity does not play a significant role. Moreover, the world presented in this picture is conceived of as the only world, one that is not part of a limitless universe. Thus the narrative tells of the "ends" of the sky and their "corners and edges," which are observable and comprehensible to the human mind.

The second reading is from a newly discovered text, believed to date from the fourth century B.C. and from the same region of Ch'u as the first text. It was excavated from a Han tomb in Ch'angsha, Hunan, the area of ancient Ch'u culture (Jan Yün-hua 1978, 75). The narrative describes the chaos prior to creation, when everything was a wet, dark, empty space. Its concept of unity before creation, "all was one," strikingly resembles the modern cosmogonic concept of "singularity" at the moment of creation.

The third and fourth readings are from the *Huai-nan Tzu,* an eclectic work compiled in the early Han period, circa 139 B.C., by Liu An, king of Huai-nan (ca. 170–122 B.C.) and by members of his coterie of scholars and thinkers, mainly of the Taoist persuasion. The first of the two citations is from chapter 7, "Divine Gods." The second is from chapter 3, "The System of the Heavens." To some extent, the narratives provide some kind of answer to questions posed in "Questions of Heaven," but, together with the second reading, they present a cosmogonic picture that is quite different. Their mode of expression is discursive rather than interrogative. They also reveal an impetus toward natural philosophy in their conceptualization of the world at the moment of creation. Although in method and style the *Huai-nan Tzu* does not approach the Latin classic *De rerum natura* of Lucretius (ca. 94–55 B.C.), a near contemporary of Liu An, there is an affinity between the two cosmogonic accounts in *Huai-nan Tzu* and the works of Roman nature philosophers in their reference to the theory of the elements, lightness, density, vapor, and so forth.

Both passages from *Huai-nan Tzu* develop the dualistic concept of Yin and Yang in "Questions of Heaven." The first citation narrates that there were "two gods born out of chaos," who divided into Yin and Yang and became "the hard and the soft"; the second citation elaborates this dualism. This dualism lends itself to Lévi-Straussian analysis, but if one looks beyond his theory of binary opposites and mediation, the use of abstract concepts in this dualism suggests that they may be the vestige of a much older mythological paradigm that was then rationalized and diminished. It is useful to hypothesize that the Chinese dualism of Yin and Yang and of the two primeval gods may be the rationalized remnant of the sort of motif to be found in Akkadian cosmogony, the mythic narrative of which was preserved in seventh-century B.C. texts but probably is much older. The Akkadian myth relates that in the beginning there were Apsu and Tiamat, male sweet water and female salt water; from them another male-female pair (possibly signifying silt), Lahmu and Lahamu, were born, and from them Anshar and Kishar (aspects of the horizon), who produced the sky god, who in turn produced Ea, the earth god (Kirk 1970, 121).

The second of the *Huai-nan Tzu* readings (the fourth reading) differs from the other cosmogonic accounts in its introduction of the mechanistic concept of a primal generator, the Tao, or Way. Though both extracts narrate the birth of all living things, the first specifies that "the pure vapor became humans," but the second integrates human beings into a generalized idea of all creatures, "the ten thousand things in nature."

The fifth reading is a late mythological account from *Historical Records of the Three Sovereign Divinities and the Five Gods* by Hsu Cheng, of the third century. The work now exists only in fragments preserved in later works. The text is important, even though it is late in the mythological tradition, because it has acquired the status of orthodoxy as the most generally accepted account of the cosmogonic myth in China. Rémi Mathieu suggests that the myth may derive from Tibetan peoples of the southwestern region, where the author, Hsu Cheng, lived in the era of the Three Kingdoms (1989, 29 n. 1). The text differs radically from the other accounts in its use of the cosmic egg as an image of primordial chaos. But the presentation of the egg motif through a simile rather than a statement of truth or fact, in the mythic mode, betrays the lateness and literariness of its composition. The text also differs from those preceding in its presentation of an anthropogonic account of cosmogony, in which P'an Ku, Coiled Antiquity, is the firstborn semidivine human who takes his place in the universe as an equal in the cosmic trinity of Heaven, earth, and human. This tripartition was not new with Hsu Cheng but was derived from early Han philosophers such as Tung Chung-shu (?179–?104 B.C.), a Confucian scholar and putative author of the sociopolitical philosophical work *Heavy Dew of the Spring and Autumn Annals.* His school of thought sought to prove a line of reciprocal interaction among Heaven, earth, and human, the reigning Han emperor mediating among the three spheres as the archetypal human (Fung Yu-lan 1953, 2:16–87).

A further difference between the organismic cosmogony of "Questions of Heaven" and the *Huai-nan Tzu* and the anthropogonic account of the P'an Ku myth is the clear, but as yet unelaborated, narrative of the myth of the separation of sky and earth. It relates that at creation the sky rose higher with the light elements and the earth sank deeper with the heavy matter, and in the mesocosm between sky and earth P'an Ku was born. This myth of the separation between sky and earth receives a more elaborate treatment in narratives presented in chapter 4, from much earlier sources of the late Chou era.

The last reading tells of the transformation of P'an Ku's body into the various parts of the universe. It is from *A Chronicle of the Five Cycles of Time,* a work also attributed to Hsu Cheng, of the third century A.D., which again is extant only in fragments. The narrative presents the motif of the cosmological human body, in which the microcosm of the human body of P'an Ku becomes the macrocosm of the physical world. It is important to note that this is also a myth of the dying god: P'an Ku is the firstborn, not quite a god nor yet fully human; he is a giant who shares the cosmic powers of Heaven and earth. He is also the first dead, and the creation of the world results from the metamorphosis of his dying body. In a recent study, Bruce Lincoln compiled a list of the characteristics of the Indo-European myths of the cosmological human body, epitomized by the Norse creation story of Ymir. The features of the P'an Ku myth fit Lincoln's general pattern for the most part. The most striking similarities occur in what Lincoln terms homologic alloforms, or homologic set. That is, the physical world was made from various parts of the body, natural forms corresponding in a logical way to bodily parts (Lincoln 1986, 2–3, 5–20). In the P'an Ku myth there are sixteen such alloforms, as against nine typical Indo-European alloforms, and they conform in such aspects as flesh becoming earth, hair becoming plants, and so forth. The P'an Ku narrative is expressed with lyricism and elegance. Just as the simile of the chicken's egg for primordial chaos denoted a literary rather than an authentically mythological genesis, so too does the P'an Ku transformation narrative. It is possible to conclude that this myth did not originate from the native Chinese tradition, for two reasons. First, it does not appear in the early mythic texts of classical China but emerges only in late sources of the third century A.D. Second, the myth shares so many features with the Indo-European mythologem of the cosmological human body that it seems likely that it was borrowed at a late date, perhaps through Hsu Cheng himself, from Central Asian sources reaching China. The specialist Jaan Puhvel suggests that it is traceable to the traditions of the ancient Near East (1987, 285).

> It says: At the beginning of remote antiquity, who was there to pass down the tale of what happened? And before the upper and lower worlds were formed, how could they be explored? Since darkness and light were hidden and closed, who could fathom them? In the formless expanse when there were only images, how could anyone know what they were? When were brightness and gloom created? Yin and Yang commingled three times; what was their original form and how were they transformed? The round sphere and its ninefold gates, who planned and measured them? Whose achievement was this? Who first created them? How are Dipper's Ladle and the Cord fastened, and how were the poles of the sky linked? Why do the eight pillars lean to the southeast and why is there a fault? Where are the ends of the Nine Skies situated and where do they join up? Their corners and edges are so many that who knows what they number? How do the heavens coordinate their twelve divisions? How are the sun and moon connected? How are the serried stars arranged? (*Ch'u Tz'u, T'ien wen*, SPTK 3.1b–4a)

> In the beginning of the eternal past
> When all was the ultimate sameness in vast empty space,
> Empty and the same, all was one,
> One eternally at rest,
> Moist-wet and murky-dim,
> Before there were darkness and light.
> > (*Tao yuan*, from Jan Yün-hua, TP 63, 1978: 75,
> > Chinese text, English trans. emended)

Long ago, before Heaven and earth existed, there were only images but no forms, and all was dark and obscure, a vast desolation, a misty expanse, and nothing knew where its own portals were. There were two gods born out of chaos who wove the skies and designed the earth. So profound were they that no one knew their lowest deeps, and so exalted were they that no one knew where they came to rest. Then they divided into Yin and Yang and separated into the Eight Poles. The hard and the soft formed, and the myriad living things took shape. The dense cloudy vapor became insects, and the pure vapor became humans. (*Huai-nan Tzu, Ching shen,* SPPY 7.1a)

Before Heaven and earth had formed, there was a shapeless, dark expanse, a gaping mass; thus it was called the Great Glory. The Way [Tao] first came from vacant space, vacant space gave birth to the cosmos, the cosmos gave birth to the Breath, and the Breath had its limits. The limpid light [Yang] rose mistily and became the sky, the heavy turbidness congealed and became earth. Because rare limpidity easily condensed but heavy turbidity congealed with difficulty, the sky was the first to form, and earth settled into shape later. The double essence of sky and earth became Yin and Yang, the complex essence of Yin and Yang became the four seasons, the diffuse essence of the four seasons became the ten thousand things in nature. The hot Breath of concentrated Yang gave birth to fire, the essence of the fiery Breath became the sun, and the cold Breath of concentrated Yin became water, the essence of watery Breath became the moon. The excess from sun and moon became the stars. The sky received the sun, moon, and stars, and the earth received rivers and rain water, and dust and silt. . . .

Heaven is round; earth is square. (*Huai-nan Tzu, T'ien wen,* SPPY 3.1a, 3.9b)

Heaven and earth were in chaos like a chicken's egg, and P'an Ku was born in the middle of it. In eighteen thousand years Heaven and earth opened and unfolded. The limpid that was Yang became the heavens, the turbid that was Yin became the earth. P'an Ku lived within them, and in one day he went through nine transformations, becoming more divine than Heaven and wiser than earth. Each day the heavens rose ten feet higher, each day the earth grew ten feet thicker, and each day P'an Ku grew ten feet taller. And so it was that in eighteen thousand years the heavens reached their fullest height, earth reached its lowest depth, and P'an Ku became fully grown.

Afterward, there were the Three Sovereign Divinities. Numbers began with one, were established with three, perfected by five, multiplied with seven, and fixed with nine. That is why Heaven is ninety thousand leagues from earth. (*San Wu li chi*, cited in *Yi-wen lei-chü*, CH 1.2a)

When the firstborn, P'an Ku, was approaching death, his body was transformed. His breath became the wind and clouds; his voice became peals of thunder. His left eye became the sun; his right eye became the moon. His four limbs and five extremities became the four cardinal points and the five peaks. His blood and semen became water and rivers. His muscles and veins became the earth's arteries; his flesh became fields and land. His hair and beard became the stars; his bodily hair became plants and trees. His teeth and bones became metal and rock; his vital marrow became pearls and jade. His sweat and bodily fluids became streaming rain. All the mites on his body were touched by the wind and were turned into the black-haired people. (*Wu yun li-nien chi*, cited in *Yi shih*, PCTP 1.2a)

The Goddess Nü Kua Creates Human Beings

The mythical figure of Nü Kua appears early in the tradition, as the brief reference to her in "Questions of Heaven," the first reading below, dating from circa the fourth century B.C., attests. Another short passage in *Huai-nan Tzu* describes Nü Kua's creative role: "Nü Kua made seventy transformations," which the commentator, Hsu Shen (ca. A.D. 100) interpreted to mean Nü Kua's creative power. Clearly, Nü Kua predates P'an Ku in classical mythology by six centuries. The second reading is from a compendium of explanations of the origins of social customs compiled by the Latter Han author, Ying Shao (ca. A.D. 140–ca. 206). The reading opens with the words "People say that," referring to beliefs held to be true in the late Han era about the primeval goddess. This text recounts an etiological myth about the origins of the human race, and it constitutes the fourth different account among our readings. It predates both P'an Ku myths of the firstborn human and of the body mites that became humans when P'an Ku died. But it postdates the *Huai-nan Tzu* myth that humans were created from "pure vapor." Thus Ying Shao's narrative of Nü Kua the creatrix is about a century earlier than that of the male creator of humans (from P'an Ku's body) in the Chinese tradition.

Several motifs in Ying Shao's brief account feature in similar myths worldwide. The first is the substance from which the goddess made humans. Various Greek myths, for example, narrate that humans were made from dragons' teeth, as in the story of Cadmus, or from a "mother's bones," or from stones, as in the story of Pyrrha and Deucalion, or from the ashes of Titans destroyed by Zeus. The Norse myth of Ymir tells how humans were made from the murdered corpse of Ymir. Most etiological myths of the creation of humankind narrate that the substance from which humans were made was dust, as in *Genesis*, or else earth, or dirt, or clay. The motif of clay, dirt, soil, or bone to create the first humans is examined in a cross-cultural survey by Frazer (1935, 5–14). In this myth of Nü Kua, humans are made from the materials of yellow earth and mud. A second worldwide motif is that of social stratification. In the Nü Kua myth humans are polarized into "rich aristocrats" made from yellow earth and "poor commoners" made from mud. A distinctive motif is the tool that Nü Kua uses for creation, a builder's cord. It is with this emblem that she is represented in later iconography. The early pottery of the pre-Shang and Shang periods shows the motif of twisted cord, perhaps registering a vestige of this or a similar myth. In Han iconography, Nü Kua is also shown holding a builder's compass.

From the period of the Former Han, the female gender of Nü Kua was underscored (some primeval gods being of indeterminate gender), and at that time she began to be paired with the mythic figure of Fu Hsi, the two being presented as a married couple and patrons of the institutions of marriage.

The third reading on the Nü Kua myth is from *A Treatise on Extraordinary and Strange Things* by the T'ang dynasty writer Li Jung (fl. ca. A.D. 846–874). This much later tradition presents Nü Kua as the first mortal, with her brother; the two institute marriage and become the progenitors of humankind. In this narrative, the goddess has been demoted from primal creatrix to a mortal subservient to God in Heaven (T'ien), and also a lowly female subservient to the male, in the traditional manner of marital relations. This late version of the Nü Kua myth shares with the Garden of Eden mythologem the motif of shame and guilt in sexual intercourse, the fan covering brother and sister as the figleaf covered Adam and Eve. Implicit in the Adam and Eve narrative is the theme of incest; it is also present in the Chinese myth, and it recurs in the repertoire of Chinese mythology. In this narrative the incest is condoned. In sum, the three readings demonstrate the ways in which an arcane primal myth develops into a specific theme, from creative power to the act of creation, and then further evolves, or degenerates, into a myth that contradicts the original intent and meaning of the early mythic expression.

How was Nü Kua's body made? How did she ascend when she rose on high and became empress? (*Ch'u Tz'u, T'ien wen*, SPTK 3.20b)

People say that when Heaven and earth opened and unfolded, humankind did not yet exist. Nü Kua kneaded yellow earth and fashioned human beings. Though she worked feverishly, she did not have enough strength to finish her task, so she drew her cord in a furrow through the mud and lifted it out to make human beings. That is why rich aristocrats are the human beings made from yellow earth, while ordinary poor commoners are the human beings made from the cord's furrow. (*Feng su t'ung-yi*, CFCE 1.83)

Long ago, when the world first began, there were two people, Nü Kua and her older brother. They lived on Mount K'un-lun. And there were not yet any ordinary people in the world. They talked about becoming husband and wife, but they felt ashamed. So the brother at once went with his sister up Mount K'un-lun and made this prayer:

Oh Heaven, if Thou wouldst send us two forth as man and
wife,
then make all the misty vapor gather.
If not, then make all the misty vapor disperse.

At this, the misty vapor immediately gathered. When the sister became intimate with her brother, they plaited some grass to make a fan to screen their faces. Even today, when a man takes a wife, they hold a fan, which is a symbol of what happened long ago. (*Tu yi chih*, TSCC 3.51)

Sunrise, Sunset

Chinese solar mythology is a very large topic and has been the subject of a specialist study by Henri Maspero (1924), no doubt inspired by the nineteenth-century nature mythologists, who were mainly concerned with origins in myth and proposed different single natural phenomena as the most important for the study of primitive man (de Vries 1984, 31–40). Since Maspero's monograph, no Sinologist or specialist in

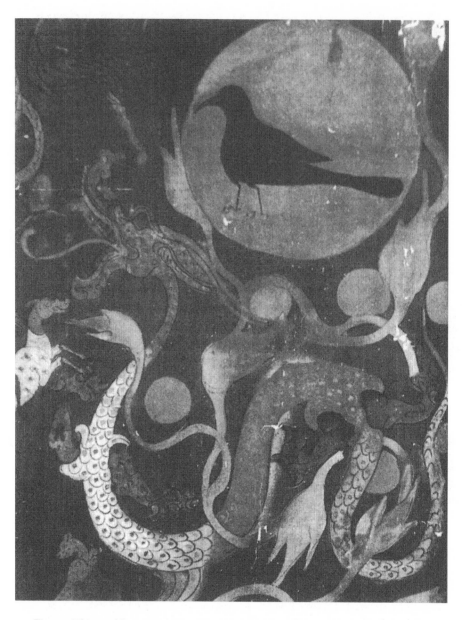

Figure 1. The world-tree, Leaning Mulberry, with the crow in the rising sun and other suns. Funerary Ch'u silk painting, tomb of the wife of the Marquis of Tai, Ma-wang-tui, Ch'ang-sha, Hunan province, circa 190 B.C. Wen-wu, *The Western Han Silk Painting,* 1972, detail from Fig. 1.

myth has dealt fully with Chinese solar myths using recent findings in Sinology and comparative mythology. Ho Hsin's monograph is based on the outdated theory of Max Müller and employs unscientific phonology to argue for the primacy of a sun god and the worship of solar deities in archaic China (1986).

The three readings on solar myth which follow contain several primary myths. Though they do not belong to cosmogonic myths per se, they are of major importance in terms of cosmological narratives, and so they are included here. Various solar motifs are examined in later chapters.

The first two readings here are from *The Classic of Mountains and Seas*. This is an anonymous work of mixed authorship and dating, compiled in the late Chou and the Han periods from earlier source material. After the Ch'u "Questions of Heaven," this text is the second most valuable source of classical myths. Rémi Mathieu, who has made a special study of this classic, dates its first five chapters to the third century B.C., chapters 6–13 to the second century B.C., and the last five chapters to the Latter Han period, circa the first century A.D. (1983, 1: c–ciii). The text of the classic itself contains two valuable indicators of its dating. At the end of chapters 9 and 13 appear the official signatories, Wang, Kung, and Hsiu, with the statement that they checked the material, that is, chapters 1–13, in the year 6 B.C. That the signatories read this part in the late first century B.C. means that the material clearly dates from an earlier period (Yuan K'o 1980.1, 266, 334). The presence of these official editors may also indicate that the material was censored.

The classic differs from "Questions of Heaven" in that it is not so culture bound and does not reflect a single belief system or cultural tradition but seeks to explore the known and imagined world of the classical era in terms of its mythology, geography, ethnography, medicine, and natural history. In form, style, and content it may be characterized as an uneasy mélange of several styles — a snatch of Ovid's *Metamorphoses*, a whiff of Lucretius's *De rerum natura*, and an echo of Ctesias's fabled descriptions of India. Compiled in an age of travel and exploration and appearing at the dawn of Chinese geographical science, this repository of myth and fable clearly does not seek to convey scientifically verifiable information about Chinese regions and foreign lands and peoples; rather, it aims to amuse, delight, shock, horrify, and at times inform its readers. Its first five chapters, especially, advise on remedies for numerous and varied ailments (Mathieu's list of 69 ailments, 1983, 2:1046–48). Although the text was finally compiled in the Han period, the classic contains a great deal of mythographic material which is corroborated by earlier sources. But there is a fundamental difference between this classic and those earlier: whereas they utilized myth for the purposes of philosophy, history, ritual, law, or political theory, the primary intent of *The Classic of Mountains and Seas* was to gather together, and so preserve, a vast repertoire of mythic narratives about various parts of China in all their contradictory, enigmatic, and seemingly useless variety.

The two readings from this classic narrate separate solar myths. The first tells how the ten suns (one for each day of the ancient ten-day week) are each washed clean after their passage through the world and are hung to dry in the world-tree, Leaning Mulberry (Fu-sang), in the east. The classic recounts six myths of the rising of the sun and moon, and six of their setting. The second reading gives another version: a crow carries the sun to the crest of a leaning tree before it departs for its daily journey. The gigantic tree described is probably Leaning Mulberry. The crow motif in this account is unique among versions of this solar myth, for usually the crow (sometimes said to be three-legged) is described as being in the center of the sun.

The third reading comes from the chapter entitled "The System of the Heavens" of *Huai-nan Tzu*. It relates the sun's journey from dawn to dusk as it passes through the Seven Halts in the sky and over the Nine Provinces on earth. There are fifteen stages of the sun's journey, and each is named: five refer to variations of the sun's light, three signify human mealtimes, four relate to the sun's position, and two refer to a pestle and one to a carriage. The last name, "tethered carriage," refers to the place where the charioteer of the sun rests the dragon-steeds. In this edition of *Huai-nan Tzu*, the charioteer of the sun is called "the Woman" (*ch'i nü*). In a citation of this passage in a much later text, *Sources for Beginning Scholarly* Studies, complied by Hsu Chien (A.D. 659-729), the words *the Woman* are replaced by the name Hsi-Ho. The identity of Hsi-Ho is problematic. One tradition has it that Hsi and Ho were two male ministers of the semidivine ruler, Yao. Another makes Hsi-Ho a single person, a man who was Master of the Calendar. A quite separate tradition makes Hsi-Ho a female who was the charioteer of the sun, and this is followed by Hsu Chien in his citation of the *Huai-nan Tzu* passage. Yet another tradition makes Hsi-Ho the mother of ten suns, who cares for them after their journey through the sky. This motif and its attendant problems are addressed in chapter 5.

Beside T'ang Valley there is the Leaning Mulberry, where the ten suns are bathed — it is north of the Land of Black-Teeth — and where they stay in the river. There is a large tree, and nine suns stay on its lower branches while one sun stays on its top branch. (*Shan hai ching, Hai wai tung ching,* SPPY 9.3a–b)

In the middle of the great wasteland, there is a mountain called Nieh-yao Chün-ti. On its summit there is a leaning tree. Its trunk is three hundred leagues tall; its leaves are like the mustard plant. There is a valley called Warm Springs Valley. Beside Yang Valley there is Leaning Mulberry. As soon as one sun arrives, another sun rises. They are all borne by a crow. (*Shan hai ching, Ta huang tung ching,* SPPY 14.5a–b)

The sun rises from Yang [Sunny] Valley and is bathed in Hsien Pool, and when it brushes past Leaning Mulberry it is called bright dawn. When it climbs Leaning Mulberry and is about to begin its journey, it is called daybreak. When it reaches Winding Riverbank, it is called daylight. When it reaches Ts'eng-ch'üan, it is called breakfast. When it reaches Mulberry Wilds, it is called supper. When it reaches Pivot Sunshine, it is called angle center. When it reaches K'un-wu, it is called perfect center. When it reaches Mount Niao-tz'u, it is called small return. When it reaches Sad Valley, it is called evening meal. When it reaches Nü-chi it is called great return. When it reaches Yuan Yü, it is called high pestle. When it reaches Lan-shih it is called low pestle. When it reaches Sad Springs and stops the Woman and rests its six dragons with stunted horns, it is called tethered carriage. When it reaches Yü Yuan, it is called yellow gloaming. When it reaches Meng Valley, it is called fixed dusk. When the sun rises from Yü Yuan's riverbank and brightens the slopes of Meng Valley, and then passes over the Nine Provinces and the Seven Halts, it has covered 517,309 leagues. (*Huai-nan Tzu, T'ien wen,* SPPY 3.9b–10b)

2

Culture
Bearers

Mircea Eliade has shown that in most mythologies there is a central myth that describes the beginnings of the world and that this cosmogonic myth is accompanied by a sequence of myths that recount the origin of plants, fire, medicine, animals, and human institutions (1984, 140–41). This was the primordial era of divine beings, mythical ancestors, and culture heroes. Eliade also notes that "all the important acts of life were revealed *ab origine* by gods or heroes" (1971, 32). He points out that their value lay not in their cultural benefit per se but in the fact that the cultural benefit was first discovered by a god and revealed to humans by a god (ibid., 30, 31). The rich variety of Greek first-finders is matched by their Chinese parallels: Prometheus and the Fire Driller brought fire, Cadmus and Fu Hsi brought writing, Triptolemus and Hou Chi brought grain, Demeter (or Ceres) and the Farmer God brought agriculture, Athena brought horsemanship while Po Yi brought domestication of animals and fowl, and Athena and Ch'ih Yu brought war and arms. But the surface equations of the divine functions of the Greek and Chinese traditions are immediately diminished when their myths are compared, for beyond simplistic similarities lies a great wealth of particular differentiation.

In most mythological accounts of culture bearers or first-finders, importance is attached to the concern the gods feel for the physical well-being and nourishment of humans and to the great care they take to teach and show humans how to perform the cultural act, such as sowing, weaving, hunting, or producing fire. Thus the myths deal not so much with the first plant or the first animal as with the first teachings of the techniques and arts of culture and civilization. This is not to say that the gods are not jealous of their gifts, as Prometheus discovered when he stole the sacred fire, or Tantalus when he stole the food of the gods, the food of immortality, and as Kun in the Chinese tradition knew when he stole the divine soil from God in order to save humans from the flood. Similarly, the beneficent role of the gods does not exclude their visiting upon humans disaster, plague, and war. This jealous, punitive aspect of divinity is examined in chapter 3.

In his recent study of mythological motifs, Bruce Lincoln focuses on the nature and origin of food, for which he has devised the neologism *sitiogony,* from the Greek *sitos* 'food, bread, grain' (1986, 65). Certainly, in Chinese mythology the origin and production of food and the cultivation, reclamation, and nurture of the land are major mythological themes. Another theme having to do with the physical well-being of humans is the search for the drug of immortality and the art of healing. But the dominant motif is water, its management and control, its resources, its gods, its abundance and scarcity, and its power for good or evil. It is with this motif that the readings begin.

The River God Chü Ling

The myth of the river god, Chü Ling, contains several important themes. It recounts the beneficial act of the river god in easing the flow of water for the good of humans. It describes the colossal strength and awesome energy of the elemental deity. The text does not specify which river Chü Ling presides over, but the word *Ho* in this and other texts usually denotes the Yellow River in North China. The name Chü Ling means Giant Deity, or Divine Colossus. The god is also known as Chü Ling Hu.

The first reading below contains two terms from philosophical Taoism: the Tao, or Way, and Yuan, or Prime Cause. This terminology reflects the Taoist nature of the source that preserved the myth, *A Chart of The Magic Art of Being Invisible,* an anonymous work probably dating from the Latter Han period, which is extant only in fragments. It is a compendium of the techniques of Taoist adepts. The second reading is from *A Record of Researches into Spirits,* a collection of myth, fable, legend, and folklore compiled by Kan Pao in the fourth century A.D. Its narratives incorporate supernatural phenomena, such as portents, the links among gods, humans, and spirits, strange creatures, metamorphoses, magic, miracles, and divine retribution (K. S. Y. Kao 1985, 4–11). Although the text is of late provenance, it contains a great deal of pre-Han mythological material. This reading illustrates how a pristine myth, such as that of Chü Ling, is reworked to suit the postclassical idiom, with its appeal to tourism and its antiquarian interest in ancient monuments. Both texts exemplify the mythological tenet that although mythologists rely on the earliest texts for source material, they must also explore the vast range of later eclectic writings in order to discover vestiges of myth which might otherwise be overlooked. In the case of the Chü Ling myth, although it has been overlaid with philosophical or antiquarian elements, it can be stripped down to its original base of the river god utilizing his primeval force for the benefit of humankind.

> There was one Chü Ling. He chanced to obtain the Way of Divine Prime Cause, and he could create mountains and rivers and send forth rivers and water courses. (*Tun chia k'ai shan t'u, Shuo-fu* 5/43.1a)

> The hills of the two Hua mountains were originally one mountain that looked down on the river. As the river passed it, it took a winding course. The river god, Chü Ling, split the mountaintop open with his hand and rent it below with his foot, dividing it in two down the middle in order to ease the river's flow. Today one may view the print of his hand on Hua Peak — the outline of his fingers and palm is still there. His footprint is on Shou-yang Mountain and still survives to this day. (*Sou shen chi*, TSCC 13.87)

The Fire Driller

The first-finder myth of the Fire Driller, Sui-jen, deals with the discovery of fire and cooking. The Fire Driller may be classified as a mesocosmic mythological figure in the sense that he is not a god, nor yet quite a human being, but a being somewhere in between. The account in the reading relates that he predates Pao Hsi, another name for Fu Hsi, who is one of the major culture bearers in the primeval pantheon. It also relates that the Fire Driller was a sage who was able to traverse the cosmos. The moral function of gods and culture heroes is a repeated motif, and it is clearly stated here: "He provided food to save all living creatures."

The name Sui-jen, Fire Driller, is based on a pun. The myth is linked to a strange dark land of beings who never die called Sui-ming Country, and in this land grows a Sui-wood tree. Both Sui-ming Country and Sui-wood have the same written form for *Sui*, but the *Sui* of *Sui-jen* is a homophone of the *Sui* of *Sui-ming* and *Sui-wood* and is written differently, not surprisingly with the fire indicator. *Sui-jen* may be translated as 'Fire Producer' or 'Fire Driller' and is phonetically linked to the igneous Sui-wood and thereby to Sui-ming Country.

An interesting feature of the Fire Driller myth is that the first-finder learns from a bird how to produce fire from an igneous tree and then teaches humankind the art of fire making and cooking. Mimesis recurs in mythology worldwide, as does the motif of the bird's creative role. The best known is the myth of the earth-diver bird, which is wide-spread in the North American continent (Rooth 1984, 168–70).

Other myths in the Chinese tradition relate the discovery of fire. One tells how the Yellow Emperor used the friction method (as opposed to drilling) and then taught humans how to cook to avoid food poisoning. Another relates that it was the god Fu Hsi who gained knowledge of the origin of fire by observing the natural phenomenon of fire arising from lightning strikes (Yuan K'o 1957, 54 n. 37, n. 51).

None of the three myths expresses the themes of theft, guilt, and punishment which are central to the myth of the theft of fire by the Titan, Prometheus. Where the two traditions of Greece and China converge is in the theme of the demigod or culture hero bringing humans the gift of fire, which benefits their lives. The distinctively Chinese characteristic of the fire myth lies in the keen observation of nature, which may be viewed as a prototype of natural science, and the application of acquired knowledge to create technology. The Fire Driller reading is from *Researches into Lost Records*, compiled by Wang Chia, circa the fourth century A.D. This extract does not appear in the extant edition of *Researches*, but it is preserved in chapter 869 of a major Sung dynasty encyclopedia. In general, *Researches* is a valuable source of early myth, especially for mythological geography.

Ten thousand miles from the capital of the Shen-mi Kingdom there is Sui-ming Country. It knows nothing of the four seasons, or day or night. Its people never die. When they get tired of life, they live in Heaven. There is a fire tree called Sui-wood. Twisted and gnarled, it spreads over ten thousand hectares. Clouds and fog drift out of it. If twigs broke from it and rubbed together, they produced fire. After many generations there was a sage who traveled beyond the sun and moon. He provided food to save all living creatures. He came to Nan-ch'ui. He looked at the tree and saw a bird like an owl, and when it pecked the tree with its beak, fire shot out in a blaze. The sage realized what had happened, so he took a small twig to drill for fire, and he was called Sui-jen, the Fire Driller. This was before Pao-hsi, and roasted food cooked by a fire came from that. (*T'ai-p'ing yü-lan,* citing *Shih yi chi,* SPTK 869.2a)

Fu Hsi's Inventions and Discoveries

Of seven important classical sources from the Chou period which in various textual contexts place the primeval gods in a sequence, indicating a rudimentary chronology and pantheon, four sources list Fu Hsi as the earliest god in the archaic pantheon. Yet these same texts also frequently mention the names of faded gods who are only shadowy figures in the mythological tradition but may in their pristine form have been mighty gods who predated even Fu Hsi. Fu Hsi is also mentioned in these texts as the earliest of a series of three major cosmogonic gods, Fu Hsi, the Farmer God (Shen Nung), and the Yellow Emperor (Huang Ti). Although these texts imply that Fu Hsi is a major mythical figure, he in fact plays only a minor role in ancient mythology and was made famous in the Han era through such arcane texts as "Appended Texts" to the *Chou Change,* or *The Classic of Change,* the earliest sections of which date from the middle Chou period, circa 800 B.C. Curiously, Fu Hsi does not feature in that storehouse of early myths, *The Classic of Mountains and Seas.*

In the mythic narratives, Fu Hsi is a multifaceted god who brought many benefits to humankind. Among his many functions are the invention of nets for hunting and fishing, the discovery of melody and music, the invention of musical instruments, the invention of divination through the Eight Trigrams (*Pa kua*), the invention of knotted cord for calculating time and measuring distance, and, according to one version of the fire myth, the discovery of fire.

In the Latter Han era, Fu Hsi was given the courtesy name T'ai Hao, as is evidenced by the "Chart of Personages Ancient and Modern" in the *History of the Han* by Pan Ku (A.D. 32–92). But in pre-Han sources, T'ai Hao appears as an independent divinity, and although he is a shadowy figure in these early texts, he is never identified there with Fu Hsi (Karlgren 1946, 230). *The Classic of Mountains and Seas* identifies T'ai Hao as the founder of the Pa people (modern Szechwan). *T'ai* means 'Great' or 'Supreme', *Hao* means 'Brilliant Light'.

Unlike the names of most other gods, Fu Hsi's name is not fixed but occurs in at least six variations. The most common is Fu Hsi, which may mean Prostrate Breath. There are also Fu Hsi, or Silent Sacrificial Victim; P'ao Hsi, or Kitchen Sacrificial Victim; Pao Hsi, or Embracing Breath; Pao Hsi, or Embracing the Victim; P'ao Hsi, or Roasted Sacrificial Victim; and Fu Hsi, or Hidden Play; in which Fu, Hsi, Pao, and so forth are written with different characters. The common denominator in most of these names is sitiogonic and sacrificial, and the variants may have to do with regional phonetic variations of the god's name.

In the Han dynasty the multifunctional figure of Fu Hsi frequently became associated with the goddess Nü Kua. The two deities are represented in Han iconography as two human figures linked by serpentine lower bodies, Fu Hsi holding a carpenter's square, Nü Kua a pair of compasses, and both deities holding a length of knotted cord. Thus the primordial and independent goddess of cosmogonic myth is domesticated by Han mythographers and made to serve as the exemplar of the human institution of marriage. The same systematizing impulse in the late Chou and Han periods resulted in the designation of Fu Hsi as the god who reigns over the east and controls the season of spring, having the tree god, Kou Mang, as his lesser god.

The first of the following readings is from the "Appended Texts," written in the Han dynasty, attached to *The Classic of Change,* which dates from circa 800–100 B.C. According to tradition, Fu Hsi is believed to have written the "Eight Trigrams" section of this *Classic,* King Wen of the Chou the "Appended Texts," and Confucius the "Ten Wings" to the *Classic.* The last two date from the Han era, according to modern textual scholarship. In the reading from "Appended Texts," Fu Hsi's name appears as Pao Hsi, Embracing the Victim. The text is a mimetic paradigm: the god observes and imitates the natural order of things and teaches his knowledge to humans.

The second reading also dates from the Han period. It is by the author Wang Yi (A.D. 89–158), who came from the region of ancient Ch'u and was the compiler and editor of the earliest extant edition of *Songs of Ch'u,* which includes a piece in nine parts by him. Wang Yi was the first commentator of *Songs of Ch'u.* In this extract he seeks to explain the divine origin of Ch'u music.

The third reading is from *Researches into Lost Records* by Wang Chia (4th century A.D.). Here Fu Hsi's role as culture bearer is recorded, but, more importantly, he is shown as a god who is a divine king come down to earth and enthroned on an earthly altar. In ancient mythic geography the cosmos was believed to be a square earth vaulted by a round sky and surrounded by four seas. The text is interesting since it reiterates Wang Yi's designation of Fu Hsi as an ancient king. Clearly, by the late Han and post-Han eras, the process of demythologization was beginning to take effect, and Fu Hsi the god was being rationalized as a partly human king of the remote archaic past. The fourth reading is by Ko Hung (A.D. 254–334). Again the narrative accentuates the mimetic function of the culture bearer. It also illustrates how in the post-Han era the identification of T'ai Hao with Fu Hsi had become a convention. Ko Hung, whose text goes by his sobriquet, the Master Embracing-Simplicity, was a Taoist philosopher, alchemist, and pharmacist.

Although the term *euhemerization* has often been used in Chinese studies to define the process of rationalizing gods into humans, in fact it means the exact opposite. The original term signifies the rationalization of human hero kings into gods. The Greek writer Euhemerus, of the late fourth century B.C., wrote a travel novel entitled *Sacred Scripture*, which survives only in quoted fragments. In this he explained that Uranus, Cronus, and Zeus had originally been great kings but were later the objects of worship by a grateful people (Rose 1970, 414–15). This misunderstanding and misuse of the term by Sinologists has recently been discussed critically by William G. Boltz: "euhemerism . . . *more sinico* is technically the precise opposite of euhemerism in its proper Greek usage" (1981, 141).

> Long ago, when Pao Hsi ruled the world, he looked upward and meditated on the images in the skies, and he looked downward and meditated on the patterns on the ground. He meditated on the markings of birds and beasts and the favorable lie of the land. He drew directly from his own person, and indirectly he drew upon external objects. And so it was that he created the Eight Trigrams in order to communicate with the virtue of divine intelligence and to classify the phenomena of all living things. He made knotted cord for nets and fishing pots in hunting and fishing. He probably took these ideas from the hexagram "Clinging." (*Chou yi, Hsi tz'u*, 2, *Chuan*, SPPY 8.3a)

> Fu Hsi was an ancient king. He ordered the creation of the zither instrument. The "Chia pien" and "Lao shang" are the names of tunes. It is said that Fu Hsi made the zither and composed the "Chia pien"

tune. Someone from Ch'u state composed the "Lao shang," based on the "Lao shang" tune. They are divine pieces of music, a delight to listen to. Some people say that the "Fu Hsi" and the "Chia pien" are divine song tunes. (Wang Yi's commentary on *Ch'u Tz'u, Ta chao,* SPTK 10.6a)

Fu Hsi was enthroned on a square altar. He listened to the breath of the eight winds and then designed the Eight Trigrams. (*T'ai-p'ing yü-lan,* citing *Shih yi chi,* SPTK 9.5b)

T'ai Hao imitated the spider and wove nets. (*Pao-p'u Tzu, Nei p'ien, Tui su,* SPTK 3.5a)

The Farmer God Thrashes Herbs

The Farmer God (Shen Nung) is the culture bearer who taught humans the methods of agriculture and pharmacopoeia. The etiological myth of the Farmer God underscores several motifs: divine intervention to aid human beings, a god who teaches humans how to manage complex techniques, and the soteriological aspect of a god who suffers for the sake of humans.

Of seven major pre-Han sources, four rank the Farmer God after Fu Hsi in the cosmogonic chronology, and one ranks him as the first of the primeval gods (Karlgren 1946, 207). Like Fu Hsi, the Farmer God was a mythical figure who played a minor role in the early texts but became famous through the mythographers of the Han period, especially in the "Appended Texts" of the Han, added to the Chou *Classic of Change.* Also like Fu Hsi, the Farmer God shares some functions with other deities, for example, agriculture, by which the god Hou Chi is identified. And in the same way as the god Fu Hsi was mistakenly identified with T'ai Hao, so the Farmer God came to be identified with Yen Ti, the Flame Emperor. But the separate identities of the Farmer God and Yen Ti are consistently attested in the pre-Han sources, which recount their individual roles, functions, and attributes.

The first reading below, from the *Huai-nan Tzu,* underscores the themes of godly self-sacrifice, medical help for suffering humans, and agricultural knowledge. The second, from *The Classic of Change,* focuses on the invention of the plow and how to utilize it and survive in a hostile world. The third reading, from Kan Pao, recounts how the Farmer God whipped the kernel and seed box of every known plant and its foliage to release its essence, which he himself tasted for its toxic or non-

Figure 2. a, the Farmer God, Shen Nung, with his plow; inscription reads, "The Farmer God taught agriculture based on land use; he opened up the land and planted millet to encourage the myriad people"; *b,* the Yellow Emperor, Huang Ti; inscription reads, "The Yellow Emperor created and changed a great many things; he invented weapons and the wells and fields system; he devised upper and lower garments, and established palaces and houses"; *c,* the God Chuan Hsu; inscription reads, "The God Chuan Hsu, Kao Yang, was the grandson of the Yellow Emperor and the son of Ch'ang Yi"; *d,* the God K'u, Ti K'u; inscription reads, "The God K'u, Kao Hsin, was the great grandson of the Yellow Emperor." Funerary stone bas-relief, Wu Liang Shrine, Chia-hsiang county, Shantung province, A.D. 151. From Feng and Feng, *Research on Stone Carving* (1821) 1934, chap. 3.

toxic qualities. The method of discovery is one of trial and error, or a rudimentary experimentation, leading to a protoscientific system of botanical classification. Rémi Mathieu suggests that the motif of the whip signifies regeneration, as with the ancient Roman Lupercalian fertility rites (1989, 68 n. 1). The color motif of the god's whip is significant: the word for the rust color, *che*, derives from the root word *ch'ih* 'scarlet red,' which is a recurring emblematic color in Chinese mythology. The color *che* 'rust' came to be used for prisoners' uniforms and as an emblematic color of banishment; thus the motif appears to denote punishment. It is also worth nothing that the color resembles dried blood.

The fourth reading is from *A Record of Accounts of Marvels*, attributed to Jen Fang (A.D. 460–508). It is a late text that cites early myths, and several of its passages are written in the antiquarian and touristic mode. Arising from the myth of the Farmer God's experiments with plant substances is his later association with medicine. Several pharmacological works, such as *The Classical Pharmacopoeia of the Farmer God*, written by Wu P'u in the third century A.D., bear his name.

In ancient times the people ate plants and drank from rivers, and they picked fruit from trees and ate the flesh of shellfish or crickets. At that time there was much suffering due to illness and injury from poisoning. So the Farmer God taught the people for the first time how to sow the five grains and about the quality of the soil—which soils were prone to be arid or wetland, which were fertile or barren, which were highland and lowland. He tasted the flavor of every single plant and determined which rivers and springs were sweet or brackish, and he let the people know how to avoid certain things. At that time he himself suffered from poisoning seventy times in one day. (*Huainan Tzu, Hsiu wu*, SPPY 19.1a)

After the Pao Hsi clan had died out, the clan of the Farmer God emerged. He split wood to make a plowshare and molded wood to make a plowhandle. With the plow he dug the soil and taught the benefit of this to the world. He probably took this from the hexagram "Advantage." (*Chou yi, Hsi tz'u*, 2, *Chuan*, SPPY 8.3a)

The Farmer God thrashed every single plant with a rust-colored whip. In the end he learned their characteristics—the bland, the toxic, the cool, and the hot, taking their smell and taste as a guide. He sowed the hundred grains. And so all under Heaven called him the Farmer God. (*Sou shen chi*, TSCC 1.1)

On Holy Metal Ridge in the Central Plain there still exists the tripod the Farmer God used for thrashing herbs. On Ch'eng-yang Mountain is the spot where the Farmer God thrashed the herbs. One name for it is Farmer God Plain, or Thrashed Herbs Mountain. On its summit is Purple Yang Lookout. Tradition has it that the Farmer God distinguished every single herb, and for over a thousand years one of these herbs, Dragon Brain, still grows there. (*Shu yi chi,* HWTS 2.5a)

Ch'ih Yu Invents Metallurgy and Weapons

The god Ch'ih Yu was a culture bearer who invented metallurgy and metal weapons. He is also known as the god of war, and as such he shares many attributes and functions with Indra, Thōrr, and Mars. The martial function of Ch'ih Yu is attested by three major late Chou accounts, including the *Kuan Tzu,* attributed to Kuan Chung (d. 645 B.C.), from which the first reading below is taken. This text relates that the Yellow Emperor opened up the mountain and that Ch'ih Yu was the first to work metal from there. Several early texts also recount that Ch'ih Yu fought the Yellow Emperor for supremacy but lost. A tradition deriving from *The Classic of History* casts Ch'ih Yu in the role of the first rebel. This might suggest that the god Ch'ih Yu resembles Lucifer in the biblical tradition, except that in later myth he is treated sympathetically as a hero and became the object of local worship in the Shantung region. In addition to his being a violent warrior and an inventor of weapons, Ch'ih Yu's other attribute is a bull-like appearance with horns and hooves.

The second reading, from Jen Fang's *Record of Accounts of Marvels,* recounts these attributes of the god from an antiquarian perspective, accentuating the metallurgical substance of iron ore in the description of Ch'ih Yu and his brothers as having "bronze heads and iron brows, and they ate stone pebbles." A further attribute of the god, as befits the god of war, is the color motif of brilliant red. Several texts relate that at his execution, Ch'ih Yu's fetters turned into maple trees, significant for their red foliage. (These and other motifs are discussed in chap. 11, "Metamorphoses.")

This second reading is an important document since it summarizes the antiquarian, legendary, ethnographic, and religious aspects of the god which had accumulated by the fifth century. Jen Fang's presentation of Ch'ih Yu bears some resemblance to the Norse Odinic warriors

Figure 3. The God of War, Ch'ih Yu, inventor of metal weapons. Funerary stone bas-relief, Wu Liang Shrine, Chia-hsiang county, Shantung province, A.D. 151. From Feng and Feng, *Research on Stone Carving* (1821) 1934, chap. 3.

described by the Old Icelandic writer Snorri Sturluson (A.D. 1178–1241). Snorri recounts that Odin's warriors "bit their shields, and were as strong as bears or bulls. They slew men, and neither fire nor iron bit on them. This is called going berserk" (paraphrased by Puhvel 1987, 196). The motifs of biting metal and bull-like features are close parallels.

Jen Fang also mentions the local musical game of head butting (*chiao-ti*) with horns, called "Ch'ih Yu's Game," which he traces back to the Han era. In his monograph on early Chinese poetry, Jean-Pierre Diény contests the connection between the "Ch'ih Yu Game" and the head-butting game of the Han (1968, 58). Derk Bodde notes that the first mention of the horn butting game occurs in 208 B.C. but that not much is known about it. He suggests that human head-butting contests in the Han were a vestige of or a humanization of actual bullfights

(1975, 206). The name Hsien-yuan in Jen Fang's account is a pseudo-name of the Yellow Emperor and belongs to that category of names borrowed from faded mythical figures which has been noted in the case of Fu Hsi/T'ai Hao and the Farmer God/Yen Ti.

In his discussion of the Ch'ih Yu myth, Mark E. Lewis examines attributes of the god from the standpoint of his thesis of "sanctioned violence" (1990, 156–211). The head-butting aspect of later legend is discussed by Michael Loewe (1990, 140–57).

> Then Ko-lu Mountain burst open and there came out water, and metal followed it. Ch'ih Yu gathered it up and fashioned it into swords, armor, spears, and lances. That year he brought under his power nine lords. Then Yung-hu Mountain burst open and there came out water, and metal followed it. Ch'ih Yu gathered it up and fashioned it into the lances of Yung-hu and the dagger-axes of Jui. That year he brought under his power twelve lords. (*Kuan Tzu, Ti shu*, SPTK 23.1b)

> When Hsien-yuan first came to the throne, there were Ch'ih Yu and his brothers, seventy-two in all. They had bronze heads and iron brows, and they ate stone pebbles. Hsien-yuan executed them in the wilderness of Cho-lu. Ch'ih Yu was able to stir up a dense fog. Cho-lu is now in Chi Province. The spirit of Ch'ih Yu is there. People say that it has a human body, the hooves of an ox, four eyes, and six hands. Recently the people of Chi Province unearthed a skull that looked like bronze and iron, and it turned out to be the bones of Ch'ih Yu. And now there is Ch'ih Yu's tooth, which is two inches long and so hard that it is unbreakable. During the Ch'in and Han eras it was said that Ch'ih Yu's ears and temples were like swords and spears and that his head had horns. It was also said that when he fought against Hsien-yuan, he butted people with his horns and no one could stand up to him. Nowadays there is a piece of music from Chi Province called "Ch'ih Yu's Game." The local people form into twos and threes and wear horns on their heads and butt each other. The horn-butting game that was devised in the Han period was probably based on this tradition. In the villages and in the country-side of T'ai-yuan, horned heads do not feature in the sacrifice to Ch'ih Yu's spirit. In modern Chi Province there is the Ch'ih Yu River, which is in the wilderness of Cho-lu. In the reign of Emperor Wu of the Han, Ch'ih Yu's spirit was visible in daylight. He had tortoise feet and a serpent's head. When [textual lacuna] a plague broke

out, the local people had the custom of setting up a spontaneous shrine to him. (*Shu yi chi,* HWTS 1.2a –b)

Ti K'u Makes Musical Instruments

Ti K'u, also known as Kao Hsin, figures in the late Chou cosmogonic chronology as a deity coming after the Yellow Emperor and before the three demigod heroes Yao, Shun, and Yü. The first reading in this section traces Ti K'u's magnificent but spurious descent from the Yellow Emperor. The text comes from the first history of China by the Han historian Ssu-ma Ch'ien (ca. 145–ca. 86 B.C.). The history charts the development of Chinese civilization from the beginning of time to the historian's own day, ending circa 100 B.C. The first chapter opens with accounts of the gods whom the historian considered to be the primary deities of the old pantheon, but his list is a distortion of early myth mingled with legendary and fictional Han material.

The second reading also reflects the rationalizing trend of the Han. It is from a text dating three centuries later by Huang-fu Mi (A.D. 215–282). His divine genealogies are essentially a reworking of early mythical accounts to make arcane passages, lacunae, inconsistencies, and old-fashioned ideas more comprehensible and more amenable to third-century A.D. readers.

Like other early gods, such as Fu Hsi and Ch'i, the son of the demigod Yü, Ti K'u is the god of music. Like them, too, he is particularly associated with specific music titles, such as "Nine Summons," "Six Ranks," and "Six Blooms." Ti K'u is also identified with the invention of six percussion instruments (drums, chimes, and bells), and four wind instruments. In this function the god is linked to the mythical Yu Ch'ui, also known as Ch'iao Ch'ui, the divinely gifted inventor and craftsman.

Chinese mythology has a great number of sacred beasts and birds, some of which have recognizable shapes, such as felines, eagles, owls, and so forth, while others are multimorphic or fantastic hybrids. Few of these, however, are connected with individual gods, as the eagle is with Zeus, the cow and peacock with Hera, the owl with Athena, the wolf and woodpecker with Mars, the swan with Apollo, and the sparrow with Aphrodite. These creatures of the Greco-Roman mythological tradition, moreover, have a symbolic meaning, such as the owl's wisdom and the sparrow's lust (Rose 1970, 65, 169). The birds in the Ti K'u myth narrated in the third reading, from the late Chou text *Annals of Master Lü,* feature the birds of paradise, the phoenix and the sky-pheasant. Yet these are not emblematic of Ti K'u himself but are part of the divine sphere. Here they function as divine messengers visiting a lesser god as a mark of divine favor. This reading underscores Ti Ku's function as a divine king endowed with the harmonious gift of power. Thus the birds of paradise serve as a motif of harmony in the idealized image of Ti K'u's divine rule.

Ti K'u, Kao Hsin, was the Yellow Emperor's great-grandson. (*Shih chi, Wu ti pen chi,* SPPY 1.7b)

When Ti K'u was born, there was a divine miracle: he uttered his own name, "Ch'ün." (*Ti wang shih chi,* TSCC 3701.8)

Ti K'u commanded Hsien Hei to compose the music and songs "Nine Summons," "Six Ranks," and "Six Blooms." He ordered Yu Ch'ui to create the small war drum, drum, bell, chime, panpipe, pipe, clay ocarina, flute, hand drum, and hammer bell. Ti K'u then ordered people to play them. Some drummed on the drum and war drum, some blew the panpipe, some performed on the pipe and flute so that they made the phoenix and sky-pheasant dance to it. Ti K'u was very pleased, and serene in his regal power. (*Lü-shih ch'un-ch'iu, Ku yueh,* SPTK 5.9b)

Hou Chi Teaches How to Sow Grain

The functions of the Farmer God and the god Hou Chi overlap. But whereas the Farmer God has several functions, Hou Chi has two: he is the god of agriculture and the founder of the Chou people. Nothing is known of the birth and career of the Farmer God, but for Hou Chi a considerable amount of biographical material appears in one of the earliest sources of the mythological tradition, *The Classic of Poetry,* compiled circa 600 B.C. Among its 305 poems are long dynastic hymns that praise the founding gods of the Chou and their predecessors the Shang. Poem 245, the first of the readings below, is a hymn that honors the founding god of the Chou. It is written from the point of view of a Chou noble house and recounts the myth of Hou Chi from his miraculous conception to his inauguration of the sacrifice to his name, which sacrifice is performed and described in the closing stanzas of the hymn. The poem combines the themes of commemoration of the founder god Hou Chi, praise to the ancestors of the living members of the household, propitiation for a good harvest, and the continuity of the family line descended from the god. The narrative fits the pattern of the first-finder and links this motif to two foundation myths, the founding of the Chou and the founding of the first Chou sacrifice to the god of agriculture.

The second reading is a prose account of the Hou Chi myth from the "Basic Annals of the Chou" by Ssu-ma Ch'ien. Although it was written some five centuries after the poem's compilation date, it follows the early version with remarkable fidelity. But halfway through his narrative the Han historian grafts on another, late mythologem of Yao and Shun derived from *The Classic of History*. According to the author of *The Classic of History*, time began with Yao. Thus the primeval gods of the traditional pantheon are subsumed under the figures of Yao and his successor Shun and made to serve subordinate roles. (The mythical figure Ch'ih Yu is the only exception to this rule.) By the Han era, *The Classic of History* had acquired the status of orthodoxy, constituting the true version of historical events and also the ideal model for the writing of ancient history. Many writers, including Ssu-ma Ch'ien, therefore, sought to give the subjects of their biographies the seal of approval by linking them to the sage-rulers of the Golden Age of Antiquity, Yao, Shun, and Yü. Consequently in Ssu-ma Ch'ien's biography of Hou Chi, the primeval god is subordinated to Yao and Shun and is demoted from god of agriculture to a mere minister of agriculture in their administration. It is possible to hypothesize that in using the paradigm of Yao and Shun in *The Classic of History*, Ssu-ma Ch'ien intended to demonstrate that the gods of the Chou were desacralized when the sociopolitical structure of the Chou dynasty had been dismantled by the Ch'in and Han conquerors.

The designation Hou in the name Hou Chi is the subject of considerable debate. Many Sinologists translate it as the title of a male deity, rendering it as Lord Millet. Yet the title is of ambiguous gender. The deity Hou t'u, for example, is rendered as Lord Earth or as Empress Earth or Earth Goddess. The rendition of Hou-t'u as a female sovereign divinity is followed by Edouard Chavannes (1910, 521–25) and more recently by Rémi Mathieu (1989, 195). If the title of Hou Chi were rendered in the feminine, as Empress Millet or Goddess Millet, this mythical figure would find a parallel with the general pattern of female cereal deities, of whom Demeter (Ceres) is the foremost example. In the readings below the name Hou Chi is rendered as Lord Millet.

She who first gave birth to our people
Was Chiang Yuan.
And how did she give birth to our people?
She performed the Yin and Ssu sacrifices well
So that she might not be without child.
She trod in the big toe of God's footprint
And was filled with joy and was enriched;
She felt a movement and it soon came to pass
That she gave birth and suckled
The one who was Hou Chi.

She fulfilled her due months
And her firstborn came forth,
With no rending or tearing,
Without injury or harm.
And this revealed the miraculous,
For did not God give her an easy birth,
Was he not well pleased with her sacrifice?
And so she bore her child with comfort.

She laid it in a narrow alley
But ox and sheep suckled it.
She laid it in a wood on the plain
But it was found by woodcutters on the plain.
She laid it on chill ice
But birds covered it with their wings.
Then the birds went away
And Hou Chi wailed,
Really loud and strong;
The sound was truly great.

Then he crawled in truth;
He straddled and strode upright
To look for food for his mouth.
He planted large beans,
And the large beans grew thick on the vine;
His ears of grain were heavy, heavy;
His hemp and wheat grew thick;
The gourd stems were laden with fruit.

Hou Chi's gardening
Was the way of the natural plant.
He cleared the rank grass

And planted a yellow crop there,
Growing even and rich,
Well planted and well eared;
It was firm and it was good,
The ears well ripened, the grain well thickened.
Then he made his home in T'ai.

He sent down cereals truly blessed,
Both black millet and double-kernel millet,
Pink-sprouting millet and white;
Black and double-kernel millet spread all over,
And he reaped many an acre.
Pink-sprouting and white millet spread all over,
Carried on his back, carried over his shoulder.
He brought them home and inaugurated the sacrifice.

Our sacrifice, what is it like?
Some pound, some bale,
Some sift, some tread.
We wash it soaking, soaking wet;
We steam it piping, piping hot.
Then we plan with thoughtful care:
Gathering southern-wood, offering rich fat,
We take a ram to make the Wayside Sacrifice,
Roasting and broiling,
To usher in the New Year.

The bronze pots filled to the brim,
The bronze pots and cauldrons.
As soon as their aroma rises up,
God on high enjoys it with pleasure.
The rich fragrance is right and proper,
For Hou Chi inaugurated the sacrifice;
With no fault or blemish his people
Have continued it to the present day.

  (*Shih ching*, 245, *Sheng min*, SPPY 17.1.1a–12a)

Hou Chi of the Chou was named Ch'i, the Abandoned. His mother, the daughter of the Yu-t'ai clan, was called Chiang Yuan. Chiang Yuan was Ti K'u's first consort. . . . When Ch'i was a child, he looked imposing, as if he had the bold spirit of a giant. When he went out to play, he liked planting hemp and beans, and his hemp and beans were very fine. When he became an adult, he also grew very skilled at plowing and farming. He would study the proper use of the land, and where valleys were suitable he planted and he reaped. Everyone went out and imitated him. Emperor Yao heard about him and promoted Ch'i to master of agriculture, so that the whole world would benefit from him and have the same success. Emperor Shun said, "Ch'i, the black-haired people are beginning to starve. You are the Lord Millet [Hou Chi]. Plant the seedlings in equal measure throughout the hundred valleys." He gave Ch'i the fiefdom of T'ai with the title of Lord Millet, and he took another surname from the Chi clan. (*Shih chi, Chou pen chi,* SPPY 4.1a–b)

Po Yi Tames Birds and Beasts

One of the confusing aspects in the study of myth is the phenomenon of names. Either one mythical figure has a multiplicity of names, or a variety of figures have the same name. Both aspects come into play with the name of the mythical figure Po Yi. In the first reading below one Po Yi, originally named Ta Fei, is said to be the ancestor of the Ch'in people, an assistant of Yü in the task of controlling the flood, besides being a minister of Shun and domesticator of birds and beasts. The passage is by Ssu-ma Ch'ien, who relates the myth of the ancestor of the Ch'in people, who gained supremacy in the ancient world and conquered the mighty Chou. The same technique the historian used in the myth of Hou Chi of linking the mythical figure to the sage-rulers Yao and Shun is evident here, in addition to the historian's convention of adducing a divine genealogy for his biographical subject.

The second reading refers to another mythical Po Yi, the name Yi written with a different character. In the early tradition this Po Yi is a separate figure, although both share the function of the domestication of beasts. By the Han period, however, the Po Yi who was ancestor of the Ch'in and the Po Yi who was the legendary domesticator of animals had coalesced into one and the same figure. A third Po Yi, written with yet another graph for Yi, is the ancestor of the Chiang clan. A fourth, with his brother Shu Ch'i, was a hero of the Shang Dynasty (chap. 13).

Another characteristic of mythology is the impulse toward creating lines of descent from a god to the ancestor of a clan or individual. In chapter 5 of his history "Basic Annals of the Ch'in Dynasty" Ssu-ma Ch'ien provides the line of Po Yi with divine descent from the god Chuan Hsu and with a miraculous birth. Such genealogies do not, on the whole, occur in mythic narratives in the late Chou tradition, and they are to be judged as fallacious concoctions to flatter a royal line. Their very tidiness when compared with the often inchoate matter of early mythic narratives makes them particularly suspect.

The mythic narrative of Po Yi in *The Classic of History* contains designations of animal names which have been taken to imply the practice of animal totemism in archaic China. Although such passages as this may have as their underlying pattern a correlation with the bear cult of the Ainu tribe of Japan and other animal cults, it is salutary to be mindful of the dangers of superficial parallels and hasty judgments. In his discussion of the pitfalls of what he termed the "totemic illusion," the anthropologist Michael A. A. Goldenweiser noted that there is not necessarily a totemic link among the three factors of clan organization; clan appropriation of animal, bird, or plant emblems; and a belief in a kinship or genealogical relationship between clan or clan member and such an emblem (cited in Mendelson 1968, 127). Since the second reading, from *The Classic of History*, clearly indicates the appropriation of animal emblems but fails to show either totemic descent of humans from those emblems or the cult of the animal totem by those humans, the passage must be ruled out as textual evidence for totemism in archaic China.

> The ancestor of the Ch'in people was a descendant of the god Chuan Hsu. His granddaughter was called Nü-hsiu. When Nü-hsiu was weaving, a black bird dropped an egg. Nü-hsiu swallowed it and gave birth to Ta Yeh. Ta Yeh took the daughter of the Shao-tien as his wife, and her name was Nü-hua. Nü-hua gave birth to Ta Fei, who controlled the inundated earth with Yü. Once he had completed this work . . . he aided Shun in taming birds and beasts. A great number of birds and beasts were tamed, and that is why he became known as Po Yi. (*Shih chi, Ch'in pen chi*, SPPY 5.1a–b)

> Emperor [Shun] said, "Who will control the plants and trees, the birds in the highlands and lowlands?" Everyone said, "Yi is the one." The Emperor said, "Excellent! Now, Yi, you will do the work that has been giving me cause for concern." Yi bowed and kowtowed, and he assigned tasks to Scarlet, Tiger, Bear, and P'i-bear. The emperor said, "Excellent! Set out, then. They will go with you." (*Shang shu, Shun tien*, SPPY 3.14b–15a)

K'ung Chia Rears Dragons

By traditional accounts, K'ung Chia was the thirteenth king of the legendary dynasty of the Hsia, and the fourth last dynastic king of the Hsia. It is worth noting at this juncture that although writers of the Chou dynasty believed in the existence of a Hsia dynasty, preceding the Shang dynasty, which the Chou had overthrown, and although many Sinologists accept that the Hsia dynasty existed, it is prudent to adopt the cautious approach, exemplified by Morton H. Fried, to the lack of historical evidence for the Hsia: "Of course, the existence of the Hsia is not yet verified; much less is anything known of its political structure" (1983, 488).

Perhaps because the reign of K'ung Chia came so close to the end of a dynasty made glorious by its supposed founder, the demigod Yü the Great, and because K'ung Chia was the great-grandfather of the infamous Chieh, the tyrannical last ruler of the Hsia, he is given a bad press in mythological accounts. Both of the readings that follow exemplify this unfavorable portrayal. Ssu-ma Ch'ien and the later author of *Biographies of Immortals* list the king's crimes of sacrilege, depravity, misrule, and murder, and other authors even embroidered their accounts of his villainy. Both readings have as the main theme the rearing of divine dragons by human kings and their ennobled keepers. The first reading is from Ssu-ma Ch'ien's "Basic Annals of the Hsia Dynasty," and it is concerned with the tradition of the noble office of dragon tamer from the time of Yao (known as the T'ao T'ang era) to the era of the Hsia king K'ung Chia. Some of the names of dragon tamers appear to be professional titles, such as the Master Who Rears Dragons. The second reading is from a fanciful compendium of biographies of seventy-one immortals compiled between the third and fifth centuries A.D.

A few dragons in mythology themselves have distinctive names, such as Chu Lung or Torch Dragon and Ying Lung or Responding Dragon. The former controls the powers of darkness and light, the latter the powers of water and drought. The *lung* dragon possesses an elemental energy, and although it is often fallacious to seek to give myths a symbolic interpretation, some dragon myths may be said to deal with the problem of how to harness and utilize colossal physical force and elemental energy.

> When Emperor K'ung Chia acceded to the throne, he enjoyed imitating the behavior of spirits and gods, and he became befuddled with depravity. When the power of the Hsia lord declined, his nobles

rebelled against him. Heaven sent a pair of dragons down to earth, one male and one female. K'ung Chia could not make them eat because he had not yet received the expertise of Huan-lung. When the T'ao T'ang era declined, there was Liu Lei, who descended from that time, and he had learned how to tame dragons from Huan-lung. He came to serve K'ung Chia. K'ung Chia granted him the name Yü-lung and permitted him to receive the lordship of the descendants of Shih-wei. When one of the dragons died, Liu Lei presented it to K'ung Chia, the Hsia lord, to eat. The Hsia lord sent an official to find out what had happened. Liu Lei panicked, and fled to another part of the world. (*Shih chi, Hsia pen chi,* SPPY 2.20a)

Shih-men was the disciple of Hsiao-fu. He, too, had the ability to create fire. He ate from peach and plum trees and flowers. He became the dragon trainer of K'ung Chia of the Hsia. But K'ung Chia could not make Shih-men abide by his wishes, so he murdered him and buried him in outlying fields. One morning a storm blew up there and when it was over the mountain forest was completely on fire. K'ung Chia offered sacrifice to Shih-men and prayed to him, but on the way home he fell down dead. (*Lieh hsien chuan,* TSCC 1.12)

Ts'an Ts'ung Encourages Sericulture

Ts'an Ts'ung is the first-finder who taught the techniques of sericulture to humans. Ts'an means 'a silkworm', and Ts'ung means 'a cluster', indicating that the divine silkworm was a prolific producer. The first historically verifiable sacrificial ceremony to the god of sericulture, made to the name of Hsien Ts'an, Ancestral Ts'an, or First Sericulturalist, occurred in the Latter Han era (Bodde 1975, 263–72). It seems that Hsien Ts'an and Ts'an Ts'ung are identical, and the different names may indicate local variants of the same etiological myth. Sericulture itself was probably first practiced in Neolithic times in China. The earliest record of the discovery of a cocoon is at an archeological site in Shansi, dating 2600–2300 B.C. (Li 1983, 36–37). Remnants of woven patterned silk from the Shang era (trad. 1766–1123 B.C.) have been discovered, and by the Chou era (1123–256 B.C.) silk was relatively plentiful.

The first of the passages that follow is from *Basic Annals of the Kings of Shu,* which may date from the middle Han era, and is attributed, probably erroneously, to the famous author Yang Hsiung (53 B.C.–A.D. 18), who came from Ch'eng-tu city in ancient Shu (modern Szechwan).

The text states that the Shu kings were descended from the god Ts'an Ts'ung, the bringer of sericulture. Yuan K'o proposes the theory that the ancient graph for Shu is similar to the graph for silkworm (1980.2, 283). Such a cultural origin has yet to be proved by archeological and historical evidence. The second reading, from the same work, affirms this descent with some added ethnographic data. The third reading is cited in the compendium *A Continuation of "The Origin of Things"* by the T'ang author Feng Chien, which has survived only in fragments cited in various works. The citation is from *Supplementary Material to "Biographies of Immortals" and to "Biographies of Holy Immortals"* by the Former Shu author Tu Kuang-t'ing of the tenth century A.D. *Biographies of Immortals* is attributed to Liu Hsiang (79–8 B.C.) of the Former Han period, and *Biographies of Holy Immortals* is attributed to Ko Hung (A.D. 254–334). It is clear that Tu Kuang-t'ing has added fictional color to the earlier myth.

The fourth reading is from an anonymous popular work of the Yuan dynasty, edited circa A.D. 1592, *A Compendium of Information on the Gods of the Three Religions* (that is, Confucianism, Taoism, and Buddhism). This late account of the god Ts'an Ts'ung adds several motifs: color symbolism (green being the color of spring silkworms), the god teaching humans the technique of sericulture, miraculous cure, local worship, and touristic data.

> The first ancestor of the Shu kings was called Ts'an Ts'ung. In the next era his descendant was called Po Huo, and in the era after that his descendant was called Yü Fu. Each of these three eras lasted several hundred years. In each era they became gods and did not die. Their people followed their kings, taking another shape and vanishing like them. (*T'ai-p'ing yü-lan,* citing *Shu wang pen chi,* SPTK 888.2b)

> The king of Shu's ancestor was called Ts'an Ts'ung. The first ancestors of Shu with the title of king were Ts'an Ts'ung, Po Huo, and Yü Fu. In the K'ai-ming reign people used to pile their hair up, and they wore their collar on the left. They did not understand writing and they did not yet have ritual or music. From the K'ai-ming reign back to Ts'an Ts'ung was an aeon of 34,000 years. (*Ch'üan Shang ku, Ch'üan Han wen,* citing *Shu wang pen chi,* 53.5a)

> Ts'an Ts'ung set himself up as king of Shu. According to tradition, he taught the people about silkworms and mulberry. He made several thousand golden silkworms. At the start of each year, he took the

golden silkworms and gave the people one silkworm each. The silk-worms the people raised always multiplied prolifically, so that in the end they could return the gift to the king. When he went on a royal tour of his realm, wherever he stopped on his journey, the people created a market town. Because of his legacy people in Shu hold a silkworm market every spring. (*Hsu shih shih*, citing *Hsien chuan shih yi, Shuo-fu* 10.45a)

The god in the green clothes is Ts'an Ts'ung. According to tradition, Ts'an Ts'ung began as the lord of Shu and later took the title of king of Shu. He always wore green clothes. When he conducted a royal tour of the city limits and countryside, he taught his people the man-agement of silkworms. The countryfolk appreciated his kindness, and so they set up a temple to sacrifice to him. Shrines to his name spread all over the western region, and they proved without excep-tion to have miraculous powers. He was generally called the god in the green clothes, and that is how Green-God County got its name. (*San chiao sou-shen ta ch'üan, Lien-ching* 316)

Master Yen Presents His Invention

The narrative of Master Yen's invention recalls the myth of Dae-dalus and Icarus in the sense that both inventions went disastrously wrong. But whereas the Daedalus myth is recounted in the tragic mode, the story of Master Yen is told in the comic mode. The narrative of Mas-ter Yen, though it is set in archaic times, is from the late source of the *Lieh Tzu*. This problematic text was traditionally believed to date from the fourth century B.C., after the shadowy figure of an early Taoist phi-losopher named Lieh Yü-k'ou, or Lieh Tzu, who was made famous by Chuang Tzu. The text is now thought to be a fourth-century forgery by Chang Chan (fl. A.D. 370).

According to the *Lieh Tzu*, the legendary inventor Master Yen lived in the reign of King Mu of Chou of the tenth century B.C. But King Mu is himself a figure who attracted a great deal of lore and legend, and so any associated narrative would be likely to be a late fiction. If indeed the dating of Master Yen to the reign of King Mu were correct, then Master Yen would come midway between the mythical figure of Ch'iao Ch'ui, or Yu Ch'ui, who is credited with the invention of miscellaneous instru-ments such as the compass, plow, hunting bow, measuring rope, boats, and bells, and inventors such as Master Shu Pan of Lu state of the sixth century B.C. and Mo Tzu of the fourth century B.C., one of whose inventions was the kite. But the *Lieh Tzu,* itself of dubious authenticity, especially cannot be relied on for its dating in this case, for the reason that none of the late Chou texts mentions a Master Yen, but they frequently refer to Ch'iao Ch'ui, Master Shu Pan, Mo Tzu, and other ingenious inventors, both mythical and historical.

This long narrative from the *Lieh Tzu* contrasts strongly with the typical mythological narrative of the late Chou era, which is usually brief, elliptical, disjointed, and lacking in informative links. The prose style of the *Lieh Tzu* narrative is sophisticated in its portrayal of the inventor, its dramatic denouement, and its humorous asides. Its punch line, moreover, contravenes the norm of mythic accounts since the author speaks in the voice of a modern man of the post-Han era seeking to demythologize the divine nature of creation: "Such human ingenuity can be judged to be just as worthy as the Creator!" Master Yen's invention itself, a realistic automaton, was a product of the post-Han era and may have originated in Central Asia. As such, the *Lieh Tzu* text belongs to legendary rather than mythological literature.

King Mu of Chou went on a royal tour to his western dominions. He crossed the K'un-lun mountains, descended Mount Yen, and then made his return journey. Before he had reached China, he met someone on the way who presented an artisan to him called Master Yen. King Mu received him and asked him, "What special talent have you?" Master Yen said, "Your humble servant will try whatever you command, sir, but I have already made something that I would like Your Majesty to be the first to see." King Mu said, "Bring it with you another day and we will view it together." The next day, Master Yen requested an audience with the king. The king received him and said, "Whatever sort of a person is that you've brought with you?" He replied, "The object your humble servant has made can entertain you." King Mu looked at it in amazement. Then he hurried forward and looked it up and down, and it was a real human being. What a marvel it was! Master Yen lowered its jaw and it began to sing in tune to the music. He lifted its hands and it danced in time to the rhythm. A thousand and one different things it did, as fast as you thought of it. The king was sure it was a real person, and he examined it with the First Palace Lady and the court attendants. When the entertainment was almost over, the singer winked and beckoned to the court ladies on each side of the king. The king was furious. He stood up and was about to have Master Yen executed. Master Yen was terrified. He stood up and tore the singer apart to show the king—it consisted entirely of leather, wood, gum, lacquer, and the colors white, black, red, and blue. The king examined the materials. Its insides, that is, its liver, gall bladder, heart, lungs, spleen, abdomen, and stomach, and its exterior, that is, its muscle and bone, limbs and joints, skin and bodily hair, and its teeth and head hair—everything was what you would expect to find, except that it was all artificial. When it was put together again, it was just as it had first appeared. The king tried removing its heart, but then its mouth could not speak. He tried moving its liver, but then its eyes could not see. He tried moving its testicles, but then its feet could not walk. Only then did the king show his delight. He sighed, "Such human ingenuity can be judged to be just as worthy as the Creator!" Then he ordered a fine carriage to be made ready to take them back with the royal entourage to the capital. (*Lieh Tzu, T'ang wen*, SPPY 5.16b–17b)

Minor Culture Bearer Traditions

The last chapter of *The Classic of Mountains and Seas* contains numerous references to culture bearers descended from the gods. Since their creations and inventions coincide in this chapter of the *Classic,* they are presented sequentially here. It should be noted that this last chapter is much later than the earlier chapters and probably dates from the first century A.D., although the material is no doubt prior to that. The intrinsic interest of these mythic narratives is augmented by the fact that in some cases they constitute different traditions from the main mythic tradition presented earlier in this chapter on culture bearers. Some musical instruments, in particular, have several divine claimants for their creation. In the following readings the god Ti Chün predominates, and he is a major deity in this *Classic.* The recurring motif of divine genealogy indicates the lateness of this version compared with mythic narratives of the Chou period.

Po Ling, the grandson of the Flame emperor [Yen Ti], shared Wu Ch'üan's wife, A-nü Yuan-fu. Yuan-fu was pregnant for three years, and then she gave birth to Ku, Yen, and Shu, the first to create the rank of marquis [Hou]. Ku and Yen were the first to create bell instruments and musical airs. (*Shan hai ching, Hai nei ching,* SPPY 18.7a)

Ti Chün gave birth to Yü Hao, Yü Hao gave birth to Yin Liang, Yin Liang gave birth to Fan Yü, who was the first to create boats. Fan Yü gave birth to Hsi Chung, Hsi Chung gave birth to Chi Kuang, and Chi Kuang was the first to use wood to make carriages. (*Shan hai ching, Hai nei ching*, SPPY 18.7a)

Shao Hao gave birth to Pan, and Pan was the first to create bows and arrows. (*Shan hai ching, Hai nei ching*, SPPY 18.7a)

Ti Chün gave birth to Yen Lung. It was Yen Lung who created the lute and the zither. (*Shan hai ching, Hai nei ching*, SPPY 18.7b)

Ti Chün had eight sons. They were the first to create song and dance. (*Shan hai ching, Hai nei ching*, SPPY 18.7b)

Ti Chün gave birth to San Shen [Three-Body]. San Shen gave birth to Yi Chün. Yi Chün was the first to create Ch'iao Ch'ui [Skilled Artisan], who was the first to bring down to the people here below the hundred skilled crafts. Hou Chi was the one who sowed the hundred grains, and Chi's grandson was called Shu Chün, who was the first to make the ox-drawn plow. The Ta Pi Ch'ih Yin were the first to create a kingdom [*kuo*]. Yü and Kun were the first to distribute the land, and to define equally the Nine Provinces. (*Shan hai ching, Hai nei ching*, SPPY 18.7b–8a)

3

Saviors

There is a certain correlation between the mythical figures of the last chapter and those discussed here in the sense that both culture bearers and saviors benefit mankind, the first by teaching skills and functions through the paradigm of divine discovery, the second by delivering humankind from some form of disaster or suffering. The difference between the two lies in the context and method of the beneficial act. The mythical accounts in this chapter mainly narrate the intervention of a god, demigod, suprahuman hero, or heroic human on behalf of humans at a time of trouble or impending disaster.

The readings in this chapter focus on natural disaster, such as the absence of sunlight or rain, cosmic disorder, such as the collapse of part of the universe, a deluge, or extinction from solar disorder, or the threat of starvation and the depredations of a monster.

The word *savior* belongs by convention to Christian religion with the meaning of a mesocosmic figure, the Christ, who, although innocent, offers himself in sacrifice in order to redeem humanity. Although this soteriological dimension is absent from Chinese mythical accounts, the concept of deliverance from evil or harm, usually in its physical manifestation rather than the spiritual, is inherent in many Chinese myths. Although the word *savior* is avoided by Western mythologists in general because of its Christological aspect, it is used here in its neutral meaning of 'deliverer or rescuer', with an altruistic and divine coloration in the term.

Chu Lung, Torch Dragon

This brief narrative of Chu Lung, Torch Dragon, from *The Classic of Mountains and Seas* brings into play several mythic motifs: a god who is part-human, part-serpentine in shape; the name of a god denoting a mythical creature; the cyclical pattern of light and dark; the homologic alloform of two eyes for the sun; strangely shaped eyes; mythic geography; a god's power over the elements of wind and rain; the emblematic color scarlet; and the use of the celestial number nine. The chapter of the *Classic* from which the reading below is taken describes the great expanse to the north, and it probably dates from the first century A.D. By Han times, a cosmological Theory of the Five Elements had been formulated into a system of universal correspondences, in which major aspects of the world, such as the cardinal points, seasons, colors, the five elements of wood, metal, water, earth, and fire, and so forth each had its own attributes. According to this system, the cardinal point of the north had the attributes of the dark Yin cycle, the color black, the season of winter, the element of water, the number six, and the musical note Yü. Various systems of correlations prevailed in the Han period, but this is the most typical (Fung Yu-lan 1953, 2:7–23). Thus the northern region described in the narrative suffers from extreme darkness, which the presiding deity, Chu Lung, alleviates with the divine light from his strangely vertical eyes.

The earliest commentator of the *Classic*, Kuo P'u (A.D. 276–324), in his elucidation cites two riddles from the "Li Sao" section of the *Songs of Ch'u* which appear to be answered by the Chu Lung myth: "Where does the sun not reach to? How does Chu Lung illumine it?" (Yuan K'o 1980.1, 439). It is interesting that these riddles in the fourth-century B.C. text are immediately followed by a reference to the sun goddess, Hsi-Ho. The juxtaposition of the myths of Chu Lung and Hsi-Ho in "Questions of Heaven" suggests that the Chu Lung myth may have represented an alternative etiological myth of sunlight and darkness and that Chu Lung may be a vestige of an earlier sun god. If so, Chu Lung has a parallel function to Hsi-Ho, the charioteer of the sun and mother of the sons in the earliest solar myths.

Beyond the northwestern sea, north of Scarlet River, is Pied-Tail
Mountain. It has a god with a human face and a snake's body, and it
is scarlet. His vertical eyes are straight slits. When he closes his eyes
it grows dark. When he looks out it grows bright. He neither eats
nor sleeps nor rests. Wind and rain visit him. This god shines on the
nine darknesses. He is called Torch Dragon [Chu Lung]. (*Shan hai
ching, Ta huang pei ching,* SPPY 17.7a–b)

Nü Kua Mends the Sky

In the etiological myths presented in chapter 1, Nü Kua appeared
in her role as creatrix of humans. It was pointed out there that in Han
iconography the goddess was shown with her attributes of a measuring
rope and a pair of compasses. This constructive function of the goddess
is exemplified in the myth of Nü Kua repairing the damaged cosmos
and so saving the world from extinction. The methods she uses are primordial metallurgy and dam building. In the following reading from
Huai-nan Tzu, the cause of the cosmic disaster is said to be that "the four
poles collapsed," that is, the earthly supports holding up the sky gave
way. In some versions of the sky-earth myth, these supports are envis-
aged as pillars, or poles, or mountains. In another chapter of *Huai-nan
Tzu,* however, it is related that a primeval titan, Kung Kung, collided
with a mountain named Pu-chou supporting the sky when he fought
the god Chuan Hsu and caused it to break, with disastrous cosmic con-
sequences. Thus Kung Kung plays the role of the marplot in this other
version. It will be recalled that the text of the *Huai-nan Tzu,* compiled
circa 139 B.C., constitutes a collection of chapters by divers hands, representing different perspectives of a generally Taoistic persuasion, and as
such constitutes a valuable source of versions of myths. The Nü Kua
narrative, therefore, relates the version that all four sky-earth poles collapsed, whereas the Kung Kung version relates that only one support
was damaged. It will become evident in the discussion of the Kung
Kung myth in chapter 4 that in the minds of commentators the two
myths gradually became confused and merged into a new syncretic version. Moreover, whereas in the Nü Kua version the cataclysm is
righted, in the Kung Kung version the damage is permanent, and the
cosmic flaw serves as an etiological myth to explain why Chinese rivers
flow toward the east, following the list of the earth due to Kung Kung's
belligerent blunder.

The second part of the Nü Kua myth narrative from *Huai-nan Tzu*

Figure 4. Nü Kua on the left, holding her compass, Fu Hsi on the right holding his carpenter's square. Funerary stone bas-relief, Wu Liang Shrine, Chia-hsiang county, Shantung province, A.D. 151. From Feng and Feng, *Research on Stone Carving* (1821) 1934, chap. 4.

reflects basic concepts of Taoist philosophy. It presents an idealized image of the world after the saving intervention of the goddess, a utopia where savage beasts "no longer have rapacious hearts" and where human beings, called "the people of Chuan"—that is, the descendants of the god Chuan Hsu—survive the disaster to live in harmony with the cosmos: "They bore earth's square on their backs and embraced the round sky." In the closing sentences of the reading, the Taoist coloration becomes more pronounced with such terminology as "the Way of the True Person." This philosophical orientation in the narrative results in a subversion of the myth of the goddess Nü Kua, for she is transposed from the status of an independent primeval deity to that of a lesser goddess under the power of a supreme god, named High Ancestor (T'ai-tsu), in the Taoist pantheon. The diminution of the primal myth marks the incipient phase in the Han era in which gods and goddesses of the ancient pantheon begin to be demythologized and a new pantheon begins to evolve.

In remote antiquity, the four poles collapsed. The Nine Regions split up. Heaven could not cover all things uniformly, and earth could not carry everything at once. Fires raged fiercely and could not be extinguished. Water rose in vast floods without abating. Fierce beasts devoured the people of Chuan. Violent birds seized the old and weak in their talons. Then Nü Kua smelted five-color stones to mend the blue sky. She severed the feet of a giant sea turtle to support the four poles and killed a black dragon to save the region of Chi. And she piled up the ashes from burned reeds to dam the surging waters. The blue sky was mended. The four poles were set right. The surging waters dried up. The region of Chi was under control. Fierce beasts died and the people of Chuan lived. They bore earth's square area on their backs and embraced the round sky. . . .

Ever since then, there have been no birds or beasts, no insects or reptiles, that do not sheathe their claws and fangs and conceal their poisonous venom, and they no longer have rapacious hearts. When one considers her achievement, it knows only the bounds of Ninth Heaven above and the limits of Yellow Clod below. She is acclaimed by later generations, and her brilliant glory sweetly suffuses the whole world. She rides in a thunder-carriage driving shaft-steeds of winged dragons and an outer pair of green hornless dragons. She bears the emblem of the Fortune of Life and Death. Her seat is the Visionary Chart. Her steeds' halter is of yellow cloud; in the front is a white calf-dragon, in the rear a rushing snake. Floating, drifting, free and easy, she guides ghostly spirits as she ascends to Ninth Heaven. She has audience with God inside the holy gates. Silently, solemnly, she comes to rest below the High Ancestor. Then, without displaying her achievements, without spreading her fame, she holds the secret of the Way of the True Person and follows the eternal nature of Heaven and earth. (*Huai-nan Tzu, Lan ming,* SPPY 6.7b–8a)

Hou Chi Saves Humans from Starvation

The mythic narrative of Hou Chi, the lord of millet and god of agriculture, was presented in chapter 2 to illustrate the agricultural function of the grain god who taught humans how to cultivate plants. The text is reexamined here to underscore the god's role as a savior figure. This aspect of the god is expressed within the special mythological context of the Golden Age of Antiquity ruled by the demigods Yao and Shun which the Han historian, author of the passage cited here, borrowed from *The Classic of History.* The saving role of Hou Chi is expressed through the demigod Shun who instructs Hou Chi to rescue the people from starvation. In this passage, the Han historian Ssu-ma Ch'ien presents Hou Chi as a minister of agriculture rather than as a primeval god and as a humanized hero rather than a savior deity.

Hou Chi of the Chou was named Ch'i, the Abandoned. . . . When Ch'i was a child, he looked imposing, as if he had the bold spirit of a giant. When he went out to play, he liked planting hemp and beans, and his hemp and beans were very fine. When he became an adult, he also grew very skilled at plowing and farming. He would study the proper use of the land, and where valleys were suitable he planted and he reaped. Everyone went out and imitated him. Emperor Yao heard about him and promoted Ch'i to master of agriculture, so that the whole world would benefit from him and have the same success. Emperor Shun said, "Ch'i, the black-haired people are beginning to starve. You are the Lord Millet [Hou Chi]. Plant the seedlings in equal measure throughout the hundred valleys." He gave Ch'i the fiefdom of T'ai with the title of Lord Millet, and he took another surname from the Chi clan. (*Shih chi, Chou pen chi,* SPPY 4.1a–b)

Figure 5. a, the demigod Yao; inscription reads, "The God Yao, Fang Hsun, was humane like Heaven itself, and wise like a divine being; to be near him was like approaching the sun, to look at him was like gazing into clouds"; *b,* the demigod Shun; inscription reads, "The God Shun, Chung Hua, plowed beyond Mount Li; in three years he had developed it"; *c,* the demigod Yü with his water-control rod; inscription reads, "Yü of the Hsia was skilled in charting the earth; he explored water sources and he understood the Yin [cosmic principle]; according to the seasons he constructed high dikes; then he retired and created the physical punishments"; *d,* King "Chieh [last ruler] of the Hsia," holding a sickle-lance, supported by his two favorites, Wan and Yen. Funerary stone bas-relief, Wu Liang Shrine, Chia-hsiang county, Shantung province, A.D. 151. From Feng and Feng, *Research on Stone Carving* (1821) 1934, chap. 3.

Shun, the Filial Son

There is general agreement among the Chou texts that Shun was the second of the three demigod rulers of the Golden Age of Antiquity—Yao, Shun, and Yü. This age was paradisiacal, not in the material sense but in the sense of having perfect government. Two mythopoeic trends are discernible in the texts that narrate the deeds and speeches of these mythical rulers: one concerns the myth of the perfect ruler, the other the myth of the hero. Myths of Yao are sparse, and details of him are few, but myths and details about Shun and Yü are plentiful. In the Shun myths the first motif of the perfect ruler is expressed in several ways: the ruler's severe testing of his successor (Yao's tests of Shun); the ruler's choice of a successor unrelated to himself (Yao's passing over his ten sons in favor of Shun, and Shun's later passing over his nine sons in favor of Yü); the ruler's abdication in favor of a better person; and the enlightened reign of an ideal sage-ruler. These motifs became powerful political myths that influenced philosophers and political theorists in the late Chou and Han eras.

The primary sources for these myths of Shun are the "Canon of Yao," chapter 1 of *The Classic of History,* and the Confucian philosophical work *Mencius.* In *The Heir and the Sage,* Sarah Allan explores the twin aspects of hereditary rule and individual virtue in several mythic paradigms, including the Yao and Shun myth of succession, utilizing structuralist theories of Lévi-Strauss (Allan 1981).

The second trend, in which classical narratives relate the acts of Shun the hero, is more recognizable as the stuff of mythology. They include accounts of Shun's marriage to Yao's two daughters, the three trials Shun endured at the hands of his blind father and step-brother, Shun's reward of the good and his punishment of evil, and so forth. These accounts appear in "Questions of Heaven," *Mencius,* the *Historical Records* of Ssu-ma Ch'ien, and numerous texts of the late and post-Han eras. The earliest accounts are typically fragmented and do not constitute sustained narratives.

Overarching these two mythic trends in the accounts of Shun is a third major theme, Shun's filial piety. This tradition is mainly based on the heroic narrative of the three trials of Shun, in which he refuses to rebuke or punish his father and step-brother despite their attempts to murder him. The moral attribute of filial piety was developed and enhanced by writers of the Confucian school of philosophy, especially by Meng Tzu (latinized as Mencius), who made Shun the exemplar of

Confucian moral principles. By the early Han period, *The Classic of History*, the *Analects* of Confucius and his school, and the *Mencius* came to form part of the Confucian canon, and Shun thereby became irrevocably identified as an orthodox Confucian hero.

The four readings in this section recount different aspects of the Shun cycle of myths. They appear in the chronological order of the dating of their texts. The first, from "Questions of Heaven," refers to the story of Shun's third trial at the hands of his father, Ku Sou, whose name means 'the Blind Man,' and his half-brother, Hsiang (whose name, among various meanings, denotes 'Elephant'). The father's blindness is a mythic motif indicating his moral darkness. This has a parallel in some narratives which relate that Shun had double pupils, signifying acute mental and moral vision. (The narratives of this and other trials of Shun are presented together in chap. 4.) The reference to dog's mess in the first reading here denotes a charm against the power of alcohol.

The second reading is from the *Mencius*, dating from the fourth century B.C. It relates two of the trials of Shun, in which the hero shows mercy and filial love in the face of evil. The third reading, from the post-Han text *Biographies of Women*, briefly mentions the two brides of Shun (here he is named Yu Yü). In the earlier narratives these brides, daughters of Yao, are not named, but latter accounts tended to supply biographical data.

The fourth reading is from *Historical Records*. Its narrative is based on the myth of Shun's marriage and follows the account of Shun in *The Classic of History*, in which Shun the demigod is demythologized and humanized. The narrative tells of Yao's mark of favor in giving his daughters in marriage to Shun, and it prefigures the account of Yao's choice of Shun as successor. It is possible to hypothesize that this myth may be interpreted at one level as a myth of political intermarriage in which a ruler's successor is not his hereditary heir but an outsider who is integrated into the ruler's family through marriage and entourage affiliations. The underlying pattern of this myth may serve the function of explaining and transmitting a form of social structure which may have existed in prehistoric times.

> Shun served his brother, but his brother still wronged him. Why was his body unharmed after he had bathed in dog's mess? (*Ch'u Tz'u, T'ien wen*, SPTK 3.20b)

> Shun's parents sent him to repair the shed. Then they took the ladder away, and the Blind Man set fire to the shed. They sent Shun to

dredge the well. They went out after him and covered over the well and blocked it. Hsiang said, "I was the one who thought up the plot to kill Shun. His cattle and sheep are for you, Father and Mother, and also his granary. His spears are for me, as well as his lute and his bow. His two wives must also take care of my rooms." Hsiang entered Shun's house and there he found Shun sitting on the bed playing the lute. Hsiang was ashamed and said, "I was trying to do the best for you." Shun said, "I try to do the best for my people. You can help me in my work of governing." (*Meng Tzu*, SPTK 9.3b–4b)

Yu Yü's two consorts were the two daughters of Emperor Yao. The oldest was O-huang; the next oldest was Nü-ying. (*Lieh nü chuan, Yu Yü erh fei*, SPPY 1.1a)

Shun's father, Ku Sou, was blind, and when Shun's mother died, Ku Sou [the Blind Man] remarried and Hsiang was born to him. Hsiang was arrogant. Ku Sou loved his second wife and child and often felt like killing Shun. . . .

By the time Shun was twenty, he had won a reputation for filial piety. By the time he was thirty, Emperor Yao was making inquiries about who might be employed in his administration. The Four Peaks unanimously recommended Yü Shun as a man who was worth employing. Yao therefore gave his two daughters in marriage to Shun so that they would look after Shun's household. He ordered his nine sons to be his [Shun's] retainers so that they would look after his public business. . . . Then Yao presented Shun with fine linen clothes and a lute, and he had a granary built for him, and he gave him cattle and sheep. (*Shih chi, Wu ti pen chi*, SPPY 1.17b, 1.18a, 1.18b)

The Burial Place of Shun

There are several mythic accounts of the death and burial place of Shun. The major traditions, which include the *Historical Records* of the first reading below, locate his grave in Ts'ang-wu (modern Hunan province), where he is said to have died on a royal tour. The second reading, from *The Classic of Mountains and Seas*, points to two mythic motifs. One concerns the name Shu Chün, who may be identified as Shang Chün, Shun's eldest son, whom Shun rejected as his successor because he thought him unworthy. (A late text identifies him as Hou Chi's grandson.) The other concerns the creatures guarding Shun's grave. Most are aggressive hunting birds. The Shih-jou beast is said elsewhere in the same text to be the guardian of the earthly paradise of K'un-lun. The elephant is of special interest, since it might refer to the name of Shun's brother, Hsiang. The distinguishing feature of the elephant is its trunk, and this may have some mythological relationship with the name of the shrine set up to Hsiang, called Nose Pavilion. The story behind the names Hsiang and Nose Pavilion has not survived in classical or traditional texts. The first reading, from *Historical Records*, dates from the late second century B.C.; the second and third, from *The Classic of Mountains and Seas* and from *Disquisitions* respectively, date from the first century A.D.; and the fourth is from Chang Shou-chieh's eighth-century A.D. commentary on the Han *Historical Records*, purporting to cite a lost Han text, *A General Treatise on Geography*.

While Shun was conducting a royal progress through his southern dominions, he passed away in the wilds of Ts'ang-wu. (*Shih chi, Wu ti pen chi,* SPPY 1.23b)

East of Scarlet River are the wilds of Ts'ang-wu where Shun and Shu Chün are buried. Therefore there are the Wen-pei bird, the Li-yü bird, the Ch'iu-chiu bird, the Ying-eagle, the Ku-eagle, the Wei-wei serpent, the bear, the P'i-bear, the elephant, the tiger, the panther, the wolf, and the Shih-jou beast. (*Shan hai ching, Ta huang nan ching,* SPPY 15.1a–b)

According to legend, Shun is buried at Ts'ang-wu, which Hsiang plowed for him. (*Lun heng, Ou hui,* SPTK 3.3b)

The Spirit of Nose Pavilion is in Ying-tao district, sixty leagues north. An old legend says that Shun is buried on Chiu-yi [Nine-Doubt Mountain] and that Hsiang came to the place. People later set up a shrine, which they called the Spirit of Nose Pavilion. (Chang Shou-chieh's commentary on *Shih chi, Wu ti pen chi,* citing *K'uo ti chih, Shih chi,* SPPY 1.23b)

Yi Shoots the Ten Suns to Avert Disaster

The central myth of Yi the Archer revolves around his heroic feat of saving the world from being destroyed by a solar conflagration. This myth belongs to a nexus of solar myths figuring Hsi-Ho, the world-tree called Leaning Mulberry, and the pool where the suns were rinsed after each day's journey, especially the ten suns born of Hsi-Ho. The Yi myth narrates how the ten suns all came out together and threatened to annihilate the world. The first reading, from *The Classic of Mountains and Seas,* relates that Yi was given a sacred bow and arrows by the god Ti Chün to shoot the suns down. Ti Chün ordered Yi to rescue humans from disaster. Thus Ti Chün is connected with this nexus of solar myths, as he is through his consort, Hsi-Ho, mother of the suns.

The second reading, from *Huai-nan Tzu,* gives a slightly different version of this myth. Here Yi is a minister under the demigod Yao, who orders him to kill six monsters and to shoot down the ten suns. For this act Yao is rewarded with the title of Son of Heaven, or supreme ruler. Other versions state that it was Yao himself, not Yi, who shot the suns (Wang Ch'ung, *Disquisitions,* SPTK 11.15b). The Yao tradition did not, however, survive in mythography, and it was Yi the Archer who came to be identified with the act of deliverance.

Despite the profound significance of the myth, and although nearly all the Chou texts recite it — for example, "Questions of Heaven," *Analects, Mencius, Chuang Tzu, Kuan Tzu, Mo Tzu, Hsun Tzu, Han Fei Tzu,* and *Annals of Master Lü* — the Yi solar myth achieved far less importance in the continuum of the mythological tradition than the comparable myth of Yü controlling the flood. Perhaps this is partly because, in terms of diurnal reality, the myth of the flood and its control was more nearly relevant to the lives of the people than the less than real myth of the unnatural phenomenon of solar disaster. Another factor in this question of dominant motifs is the presentation of Yi the Archer in the totality of classical mythic narratives. Although in the solar myth he is portrayed positively as a hero, in others, such as the story of his attempt to usurp the Hsia government, he is projected negatively as a degenerate villain. This ambiguity of presentation prevented Yi from attaining the same status as Yü, who, according to all the myths in the Yü cycle, never committed any wrong.

Ti Chün presented Yi with a vermilion bow and plain-colored arrows with silk cords in order that he should bring assistance to the land below. So Yi was the first to bring merciful relief to the world below from all its hardships. (*Shan hai ching, Hai nei ching,* SPPY 18.7b)

When it came to the era of Yao, the ten suns all rose at once, scorching the sheaves of grain and killing plants and trees, so that the people were without food. And the Cha-yü Dragon-Headed beast, the Chisel-Tusk beast, the Nine-Gullet beast, the Giant-Gale bird, the Feng-hsi wild boar, and the Giant-Head long-snake all plagued the people. So Yao ordered Yi to execute the Chisel-Tusk beast in the wilds of Ch'ou

Hua, to slaughter the Nine-Gullet beast near Hsiung River, to shoot down with his corded arrows the Giant-Gale at Ch'ing-ch'iu Marsh. He ordered him to shoot the ten suns up above and to kill the Cha-yü Dragon-Headed beast below, to behead the Giant-Head long-snake at Tung-t'ing, and to capture the Feng-hsi wild boar at Mulberry Forest. The myriad people were overjoyed and decided on Yao as their Son of Heaven. And so for the first time in the whole world, there were roads and signposts in the broadlands and in the narrow defiles, in the deep places and on level ground both far and wide. (*Huai-nan Tzu, Pen ching,* SPPY 8.5b–6a)

Kun and the Flood

Of all Chinese mythical figures, Kun constitutes the perfect paradigm of the savior. The narratives in which he features, moreover, are rich in motifs. These include his mythical name, derived from a fabled fish; his descent from the god Chuan Hsu; his role as trickster figure in the theft from God of the gift of self-renewing soil; his desire to save the world from the flood; his ritual execution by Chu Yung, the fire god; the mythical location of his place of execution, Feather Mountain; Kun's incorrupt corpse; the birth of Kun's son, Yü, from the belly of Kun's corpse (variants say *fu* 'again' or *p'i* 'stubborn' for *fu* 'belly'); his metamorphosis into a yellow bear (variants say a yellow dragon or turtle); Kun's resuscitation by shamans; his fine harvest of black millet in what had been an arid heath (the context of this motif is not known); and his role as a failed hero.

The main sources for these motifs are "Questions of Heaven" and *The Classic of Mountains and Seas,* and they are represented in the three readings that follow. They portray Kun sympathetically as the hero who failed in his mission. A separate tradition based on *The Classic of History,* however, presents him as an evildoer whom Yao has executed. Karlgren has noted that in this context *The Classic of History* is "a scholastic endeavour to make history out of a deluge legend" (1946, 303). In the historicizing method of *The Classic of History,* the myth of Kun is reworked and demythologized. Kun's crime of stealing the gift of God's divine soil is transformed in *The Classic of History* to his failure to control irrigation works and to his consequent disturbance of the natural order, known as the harmony of the Five Elements. Aspects of this negative portrayal of Kun and the historicization of the myth also appear in late Chou texts, such as *Chronicle of Tso* and *Discourses of the*

States (ibid., 250). Another strand in *The Classic of History* also depicts Kun as a rebel who turned against Yao and Shun because he was not appointed as one of the Three Excellencies in government. This theme of Kun the rebel is corroborated in *Annals of Master Lü* (Yuan K'o and Chou Ming 1985, 242). Thus two equally strong traditions of Kun the failed hero and Kun the criminal developed along parallel lines in classical mythography. The tradition based on "Questions of Heaven" and *The Classic of Mountains and Seas* clearly represents the more authentically mythological matter, rather than the humanizing historicization of the *History* and the *Annals,* and so those texts are cited here.

It is worth examining the motif of the self-renewing soil (*hsi-jang*) by comparing it with the earth-diver creation motif of North America. (Besides my rendition of *hsi-jang* as 'self-renewing soil', the term has also been rendered as 'breathing earth' [Eberhard 1968, 354]; 'swelling mold' [Bodde 1961, 399]; 'idle soil' [Greatrex 1987, 267 n. 11]; and 'living earth', or 'breathing earth' [Mathieu 1989, 96 n. 1, 101 n. 6]). In the earth-diver myth various creatures are sent down from the sky to earth to dive into a flood of water to secure a small particle of soil that will be used to form the earth. All the creatures fail except the last one, who re-emerges from the flood half-dead, "bringing up the tiny bit of mud which is then put on the surface of the water and magically expands to become the world of the present time" (Wheeler-Voegelin as quoted by Dundes 1984, 277).

> If Kun was not fit to control the flood, why was he entrusted with this task? They all said, "Do not fear! Try him and see if he can accomplish it." When the bird-turtles joined together, how did Kun follow their sign? If [Kun] completed his task as it was willed, why did God punish him? He lay exposed on Feather Mountain for a long time, but why did he not decompose for three years? Lord Yü issued from Kun's belly. How did he metamorphose? (*Ch'u Tz'u, T'ien wen,* SPTK 3.5b–6b)

> When Kun came to the end of his journey to the west, how did he pass through the heights? He turned into a yellow bear. How did the shamans restore him to life? They both planted black millet and the arid heath became a tilled area. Since they planted at the same time, why did Kun's grow so tall and lush so fast? (*Ch'u Tz'u, T'ien wen,* SPTK 3.16b–17b)

Floodwater dashed up against the skies. Kun stole God's self-renewing soil in order to dam the floodwater, but he did not wait for God's
official permission. God ordered Chu Yung to kill Kun on the approaches to Feather Mountain. Yü was born from Kun's belly. So in
the end, God issued a command allowing Yü to spread out the self-
replacing soil so as to quell the floods in the Nine Provinces. (*Shan
hai ching, Hai nei ching*, SPPY 18.8b–9a)

Yü Controls the Flood

The myth of Yü and the flood is the greatest in the Chinese tradition. This is not just because the narratives tell how he managed to control the flood, but also because numerous myths, legends, and folk tales
became attached to his name. In every case, Yü is depicted as a hero, self-
lessly working on behalf of humankind, and succeeding in his task.

Yü is the third and last ruler of the mythical Golden Age of Antiquity, following Yao and Shun, and having been chosen by Shun as successor in lieu of Shun's own nine sons. Yü is also distinguished as the
founder of the mythical Hsia dynasty. He was also descended from the
god Chuan Hsu, through his father, Kun, and was miraculously born
from his father's corpse. In the historicizing account of *The Classic of
History,* the mythical Yü appears as master of works for Emperor Yao.

In the third and last reading on the preceding myth of Kun, it was
related that after Kun's death and Yü's birth, Yü was ordained by God
to continue his father's work, and he was allowed to use the stolen self-
renewing soil. In the first reading on the Yü myth, from "Questions of
Heaven," the text emphasizes that although Yü continued the labors of
his father, he embarked on a quite different plan of building channels
for the flow of flood water and reconstructing earth's boundaries. This
account is echoed in the second reading from *The Classic of History.* Several other major texts — such as *Mencius, Mo Tzu, Shih Tzu,* and *The Classic of Poetry* (poems 210, 244, 301, and 304), and *Chronicle of Tso* — uniformly praise Yü as the hero who saved the world from the flood. The
third reading in this section, from *Shih Tzu* (fourth century B.C.), underscores the hero's selfless devotion to duty.

The fourth reading is from *Annals of Master Lü.* It ends with a passage similar to the *Shih Tzu* account. The *Annals* is ascribed to the third-
century B.C. politician Lü Pu-wei; it is an eclectic work of philosophy,
literature, and mythology. The *Shih Tzu,* a century earlier, is a miscellany of textual fragments reconstructed into a short text. The graphic

descriptions of Yü in these two texts serve to exemplify Yü's role as the savior who is the servant of the people.

Of the mythical account of Yü's control of the flood in *The Classic of History* Karlgren notes: "There are scores of names of rivers, mountains and localities, and the chapter ["The Tribute of Yü"] gives in fact a rough geography of the world with which the Chinese had some contact—by sight or hearsay—in the early half of the Chou dynasty" (Karlgren 1946, 302). Karlgren's dating of this text in around 600 B.C. is debatable, and modern scholarship would move its date closer to around the fourth to the third century B.C., in respect of its authentic parts. When he speaks of "a rough geography," Karlgren means, as his footnote to this passage makes clear, mythogeography as well as verifiable geography.

In the linked myths of Kun and Yü, a pattern of binary opposites is readily discernible: Kun must die for Yü to be born; Kun must fail for Yü to succeed; Kun is blamed as a wrongdoer (in some versions), while Yü is glorified as a hero; Kun incurred the anger of God, whereas Yü was favored by God; and finally, the father's work is completed by his son. The Kun-Yü myth of the deluge is ideally suited to a structural analysis on the basis of the mediation of binary opposites, using the methodology of Lévi-Strauss in "The Story of Asdiwal" (1968, 1–47).

> If Kun was not fit to control the flood, why was he entrusted with this task? They all said, "Do not fear! Try him and see if he can accomplish it." . . . Lord Yü issued from Kun's belly. How did he metamorphose? Yü inherited his legacy and continued the work of his father. Why was his plan different, even though the work was already in progress? How did he dam the floodwaters at their deepest? How did he demarcate the Nine Lands of the earth? Over the rivers and seas, what did the Responding Dragon fully achieve and where did he pass? What plan did Kun devise? What did Yü succeed in doing? (*Ch'u Tz'u, T'ien wen*, SPTK 3.5b–7b)

> The Nine Provinces were standardized. The four quarters were made habitable. The Nine Mountains were deforested and put down for arable land. The sources of the Nine Rivers were dredged. The Nine Marshes were banked up. The Four Seas had their concourses opened freely. The Six Treasuries were well attended to. All the soils were compared and classified. Their land values and revenues were carefully controlled. (*Shang shu, Yü kung*, SPPY 6.16b)

In ancient times, Dragon Gate had not been cleft open, Lü-liang had not been bored through, and the river passed above Meng-men, its waters greatly swollen and its current irregular, so that it destroyed all in its path, the hills and high mounds, and this was what was known as the Flood. Yü channeled the river and sluiced off the Great River. For ten years he did not visit his home, and no nails grew on his hands, no hair grew on his shanks. He caught an illness that made his body shrivel in half, so that when he walked he could not lift one leg past the other, and people called it "the Yü walk." (*Shih Tzu*, SPPY 1.16b)

When Yü went east as far as the region of the Leaning Tree, the sun was rising over Nine Fords and the plains of Ch'ing-ch'iang, a place where the trees are densely clustered and where the mountains brush against the sky. He went through the districts of Bird Valley, Green Mound, through the Land of the Black-Teeth. He went south as far as the Lands of Crossed Toes, Sun-p'u, and Hsu-man, and the mountains of Nine Brilliances with their cinnabar grain, lac trees, and seething rivers that rush and roar. He went to the regions of the Feathered Men and Naked People, and the district of Never Die. He went west as far as the Land of the Three Perils, below Mount Sha-man, to the people who drink dew and sip air, to the Banked Gold Mountain, to the districts of the Odd Arm and the One Arm Three Face. He went north as far as the Land of Jen-cheng and near Hsia-hui, to the top of Heng Mountain, to the Land of Dogfight, to the wilds of K'ua-fu, to the place of Yü Ch'iang with its immense rivers and mountains of massive rocks. There was nowhere he neglected to travel. He was anxious for the black-haired people. His face became pitch black, his bodily orifices and his vital organs did not function properly, his steps were faltering. As a result, he sought out wise men, for he wished to discover everything about the advantages of these lands. It was a laborious task. (*Lü-shih ch'un-ch'iu, Ch'iu jen*, SPTK 22.8b–9b)

K'ai Receives the Music of Heaven

The myth of K'ai might appear out of place in a chapter about saviors, but there are two important reasons for its inclusion here. The first is that a textual variant in a Han version of an ancient text, *Explanations of Divination in "The Storehouse of All Things"*, refers to K'ai's attempt to steal (*ch'ieh*) the music of the gods. *The Storehouse of All Things* is an anonymous work, no longer extant except in fragments, dating from the late Chou to Han era, and it belongs to the category of divinatory books such as *The Classic of Change*. By contrast, the myth of K'ai in a late chapter of *The Classic of Mountains and Seas* (first century A.D.) uses the more neutral word *received* instead of *stole*. If the version in the *Explanations* is correct, it would mean that K'ai, the grandson of Kun, repeated Kun's theft (*ch'ieh*) from God, even at the risk of ritual execution. This version fits the savior pattern of the myth. It also casts K'ai in the role of a trickster figure in myth.

Whichever version is taken to be correct, both texts contain the important motif of music as the source of divine harmony. K'ai's act of ascending the highest point on earth to sing the music of the gods close to Heaven itself may be interpreted as a mimesis of divine harmony and power.

K'ai's association with music is linked to the circumstances of his birth. He was the son of Yü, and at his birth he had been named Ch'i, meaning 'to open'. His title, Hsia-hou, in the first reading below, from *The Classic of Mountains and Seas,* signifies his succession to Yü, founder of the Hsia, and it means 'Lord of the Hsia'. When K'ai's father was going to marry the T'u-shan girl, he leapt for joy and accidentally drummed with his feet on a stone. The girl saw Yü metamorphosed into a bear and fled in shame, carrying her son in her womb. She turned to stone, and her son was born from her north side when Yü pursued her and ordered her to give him their son. The name *K'ai* also means 'to open'. So the birth of K'ai, or Ch'i, was flawed by his father's error, and that flaw became his gift of music to the world.

The second reading is a good example of the way in which a philosopher appropriates a myth to illustrate his ideas and in so doing subverts that myth. Its author, Mo Tzu (ca. 479–ca. 381 B.C.) belonged to the utilitarian and logical traditions of classical thought. His philosophical method is adversarial in the sense that he expounded his ideas by means of a fundamental critique of Confucian concepts. He launched a polemical attack on the financial and material expense of ritual ceremony, a key element in Confucian educational and social theory, with its associated aspects of ceremonial music and dance. The chapter of *Mo Tzu* from which the reading is taken is entitled "Against Music," and since the written word for 'music', *yueh,* is a pun for 'pleasure', *lo,* Mo Tzu's attack on extravagant music carries a puritanical connotation. The *Wu kuan* mentioned in the text either refers to the five sons of K'ai, or it may mean "The Martial Kuan," the title of a lost chapter of *The Classic of History.*

> Beyond the sea to the southwest, south of Scarlet River and west of Drifting Sands, there is a man called Hsia-hou K'ai who wears a green snake in his pierced ears and rides a pair of dragons. K'ai went up to Heaven three times as a guest. He received the "Nine Counterpoints" and the "Nine Songs," and he brought them down to earth. This Plain of Heavenly Mu is sixteen thousand feet high, and it was here that K'ai first came to sing the "Nine Summons." (*Shan hai ching, Ta huang hsi ching,* SPPY 16.7b–8a)

> The *Wu kuan* says: "Ch'i then became immoral and dissipated, and he spent a great deal of time idly enjoying music. And he went out to eat and drink in the plains to a loud ra-ra! and clang-clang! as flutes and chimes played violently. He would get soaked with wine and went out more and more often to eat in the plains. The splendid Wan Dance was degraded. This show was heard up in great Heaven, and Heaven refused to have anything further to do with him." This was not pleasing to Heaven above, nor did it benefit the people below. So Mo Tzu says that if gentlemen truly wish to benefit the world and eliminate disaster, they must prohibit things like music. (*Mo Tzu, Fei yueh,* 1, SPTK 8.19a–b)

At Mulberry Forest They Pray for Rain

There is a general acceptance that a complex interrelationship exists between myth and ritual. The ritual-dominant Cambridge school, exemplified by Jane Ellen Harrison, Gilbert Murray, and G. M. Cornford, held that myth derived from earlier ritual, and they distinguished between the two in these terms: "The primary meaning of myth . . . is the spoken correlative of the acted rite, the thing done" (Harrison 1963, 328). The extremist ritological viewpoint holds that a myth is not a myth unless it is rooted in a rite. The middle view today is that a myth need not be enacted in a rite or have a verifiable link with a rite for it to exist per se. As Eliade pointed out in the context of Greek mythology, "we do not know a single Greek myth within its ritual context" (1984, 138).

The two readings that follow relate similar versions of a ritual ceremony to invoke rain. The first is from the *Annals of Master Lü;* the second is a passage alleged to be from the text of *Huai-nan Tzu* but does not appear in extant editions. The rite of rainmaking was enacted by the mythical first ruler of the Shang dynasty, T'ang the Conqueror. It is both penitential and sacrificial; the severe drought was believed to be due to a crime or fault committed on earth, and this crime could be expiated only by human sacrifice. The second reading, in fact, indicates that prior to the royal rite human sacrifice had already been offered, but without success. In both texts the king performs the ceremonial act of cutting off his hair and fingernails, a mimesis of the ritual of animal sacrifice. Thus the king is both priest and sacrificial victim. In another version of the rite in *Shih Tzu* (fourth century B.C.), the king is described being tightly bound with white rushes and driving to the open-air altar in a plain carriage drawn by white horses, for white was the symbolic color of death (Yuan K'o 1957, 289 n. 14). The kingly hero, who is a good man according to all accounts, is rewarded for his saving act with a heavy fall of rain. The narratives of the rainmaking rite belong to a cycle of myths figuring T'ang the Conqueror. (For a survey of these narratives in various classical works, see Mathieu 1989, 140 n. 1.) They uniformly project him in a positive way as a great hero who enjoyed a favored relationship with Heaven and who acted as the humble servant of the people.

> Long ago, when T'ang had conquered the Hsia and ruled the world, there was a severe drought and the harvests failed for five years. So T'ang went in person to pray at Mulberry Forest, saying, "If I, the One Man, have sinned, do not visit your punishment upon the myriad people. If the myriad people have sinned, let me alone take the blame. Do not let the demons and spirits of Almighty God harm the lives of my people simply because of my own stupid mistakes." Then he cut off his hair, rubbed his hands smooth, and offered himself as a sacrificial beast to enable him to seek the blessing of Almighty God. And then the people rejoiced, for then there was a heavy fall of rain. (*Lü-shih ch'un-ch'iu, Shun min*, SPTK 9.3b–4a)

> In the era of T'ang there was a severe drought for seven years, and divination was made for humans to be sacrificed to Heaven. T'ang said, "I will make a divination myself, and I will offer myself as a sacrifice on behalf of my people. For is this not what I ought to do?" Then he ordered an official to prepare a pile of kindling and logs. He cut off his hair and fingernails, purified himself with water, and laid himself on the woodpile in order to be burnt as a sacrifice to Heaven. Just as the fire was taking hold, a great downpour of rain fell. (Li

Shan's commentary on Chang Heng's *Ssu hsuan fu*, citing *Huai-nan Tzu*, in a passage not extant, *Wen hsuan*, KHCP 15.310)

The Virgin Brides and the River God

The myth of the river god demanding a ransom of virgin brides each year merges with historical actuality in this account from Ying Shao's second-century A.D. account in *Explanations of Social Customs*, which relates an event that took place in the third century B.C. The action is set in the reign of King Chao Hsiang of Ch'in (306–251 B.C.), when the king sent Li Ping to govern the region of Shu (modern Szechwan) following the Ch'in conquest of Shu. The narrative is full of colorful detail: the cunning hero pitted against an elusive and greedy deity, the poignancy of the two beautiful virgins, the god's contempt for the hero, the hero's challenge, the battle between god and man, metamorphosis of the god and the hero into blue oxen, and the happy resolution. The historical Li Ping is also famous for having channeled the Min River into two canals flowing around Ch'eng-tu City, besides his innovations in transport and irrigation.

The hero's cunning defeat of the god is presented in such a way that the power and authority of the god is diminished, while the efficacy of human authority, especially bureaucratic authority, is enhanced. The result is that, although the mythic narrative appears to relate to a god, the belief system that created the divinity, that of conquered Shu, has been weakened.

The narrative may be examined from another perspective. It is worth posing the question from a sociological and ethnological standpoint whether the myth of the local river god in Shu who demanded a bounty of two virgins each year may have served as a rationale of and a justification for a communal custom in the region. For it is implied in the narrative that prior to Li Ping's arrival in Shu from Ch'in, the local authorities in Shu paid the family of the two virgins a huge sum of money as compensation for their loss. This annual exchange would have brought a financial benefit to the local community and would also have served as a justification for culling unwanted daughters by drowning them. In other words, were the death of two virgins a year by drowning and the compensation money for their possession by a river god a local racket? If so, Li Ping appears to have understood this immediately, since he substituted his own two daughters as the "victims" of the alleged river god.

Lai Whalen has drawn similar conclusions in his analysis of a parallel narrative about another river god and his quota of virgin brides. There the deity is Ho-po, Lord of the [Yellow] River, and the official is the famous Confucian sage Hsi-men Pao of the late fifth century B.C. His ruse was to throw a seventy-year-old witch and her acolytes into the river to tell the river god that the bride chosen was not beautiful enough for him (Lai Whalen 1990, 335–50; also see Mathieu 1989, 181–83).

Malinowski and Lévi-Strauss have shown that such reconstructions of the "social charter" are often possible from mythic narratives, and it may be that in the case of the river god and the brides a specific social practice is the underlying concern of the myth.

> After King Chao of Ch'in had attacked and conquered Shu, he appointed Li Ping as prefect of the Shu commandery. There was a river god who took two young virgins as his brides every year. The head officer of the region declared, "You will have to hand over a million in cash to pay for the brides' dowry." Ping said, "That won't be necessary. I have young daughters of my own." When the time came, he had his daughters beautifully dressed and made up, and he led them away to be drowned in the river. Li Ping went straight up to the throne of the local god, poured out wine as an offering, and said, "Up till now, I have continued our family line into the ninth generation. Lord of the River, you are a mighty god. Please show your august presence to me, so that I may humbly serve you with wine." Ping held the goblet of wine forward. All the god did was to ripple its surface, but he did not consume it. Ping said in a thunderous voice, "Lord of the River, you have mocked me, so now I intend to fight you!" He drew out his sword, then suddenly he vanished. A little later two blue oxen were fighting on the sloping riverbank. After a few moments, Ping went back to his officers and ordered them to help him: "The ox facing south with white tied around his saddle will be me with my white silk ribbon." Then he returned to the fray. The Keeper of Records promptly shot dead with his arrow the ox facing north. With the Lord of the River dead, there was no more trouble ever again. (*T'ai-p'ing yü-lan*, citing *Feng su t'ung-yi*, SPTK 882.4a–b)

4

Destroyers

The gods and suprahumans who bear gifts of culture and well-being to humans can also be plague bearers, bringing war, drought, and chaos in their wake. While the culture-bearing gods enhance the life of humans with peace, food, clothing, and shelter, there are those gods whose wilful violence wreaks havoc on that order and security. In ancient myths the greatest gods, such as Zeus (Jupiter), Thōrr, Perún, and Indra, possess within their divinity the inherently positive forces for peace besides the negative forces of destruction. There are lesser gods, however, whose function is wholly negative. Such are the plague-ghosts, the sons of the god Chuan Hsu, and the war bringer, Ch'in P'i, and drought bearer, Drum, who are described in the readings in this chapter. The spirits of gods executed for a crime, they are like the Harpies, who defile and torment the living.

Some mythic narratives relate the violent conflict of the gods, who challenge one another for supreme power, the *Ti* or *Shen*, meaning god-head. Such is the marplot, Kung Kung, whose martial fury goes beyond control, causing a disruption in the cosmic order. There is also the myth of paradisiacal loss, or the myth of the separation of sky and earth. Then there are the contests between suprahumans and heroes, such as the quarreling brothers Yen Po and Shih Ch'en, and the enmity Hsiang has for his older half-brother, the good and virtuous Shun.

Nearer to historical time are the myths of Yi the Archer, King Chieh of the Hsia, King Kai of the Shang, and King Chou of the Shang, who caused the downfall of their dynastic line and the ruin of their royal house. Several mythic narratives depicting such flawed mythical figures constitute what Jaan Puhvel terms "nadir episodes," which show them to be venal, sacrilegious, unjust, cowardly, and treacherous (1987, 243).

Crimes of the Gods

The two readings below, from *The Classic of Mountains and Seas,* narrate myths of crimes committed by lesser gods and their punishment by God. Their crime was the murder of a sky god, Pao Chiang (or Pao Tsu), and their punishment is ritual execution. Their evil lives on after them when they turn into monster birds bringing war and drought. The identity of lesser gods such as these is uncertain. The names Drum and Bell, in the first reading, refer to the primary musical instruments of ancient China. Ch'in P'i is named K'an P'i in *Chuang Tzu;* he is said there to have entered the western paradise of K'un-lun (Watson 1968, 81). In *Huai-nan Tzu* and elsewhere, his name is variously written as Ch'in Fu or Ch'in P'i with a fish radical instead of the usual bird radical. *Ch'in* means 'the sound of a bell', and *P'i* means 'an osprey'. In his interesting discussion of myth and ritual in the Han, Derk Bodde examines numerous plague demons that were exorcized in seasonal rites (1975, 75–138).

The second reading, though from the same *Classic*, dates from the first century B.C. (the first reading dates from about the third century B.C.). It gives a graphic account of the punishment by ritual exposure on a mountaintop for the crime of murder committed by the lesser god Erh-fu, or Double Load, and his officer, Peril. Their victim was Cha Yü (also pronounced Ya Yü). It is not clear who this figure was, but in another passage of the *Classic,* it is related that six shamans kept Cha Yü's body from decaying on Mount K'un-lun, waving branches of the drug of immortality over it. Edward H. Schafer's valuable survey of ritual exposure focuses on historical cases rather than mythical accounts, although the two clearly overlap (1951, 130–84).

> Another four hundred and twenty leagues to the northwest is Bell Mountain. His son was called Drum. In appearance his face was like a human and he had a dragon's body. He and Ch'in P'i murdered Pao Chiang on the south side of K'un-lun Mountain. God therefore exe-

cuted them on the east of Bell Mountain, which is called *Yao*-Jade Cliff. Ch'in P'i turned into a huge osprey. He looked like a vulture and had black markings and a white head, a red beak and tiger's claws. His call was like that of the dawn goose. When he appears there is a great war. Drum also turned into a *chün*-bird. He looked like a kite with red feet and a straight beak, and he had yellow markings and a white head. His call was like that of a goose. Any place where he appears suffers from severe drought. (*Shan hai ching, Hsi tz'u san ching*, SPPY 2.15a–b)

Double Load's officer was called Peril. Peril and Double Load murdered Cha Yü. God therefore chained him on Su-shu Hill. He fettered his right foot and tied both hands behind his back with his hair, binding him to a mountaintop tree. This was on Mount K'ai-t'ou's northwest side. (*Shan hai ching, Hai nei hsi ching*, SPPY 11.1a–b)

The Links between Earth and Heaven are Severed

The myth of the separation of the sky and earth has a worldwide distribution. It is often associated with the myth of world parents and related as the separation of the sky-father from earth-mother. The myth also incorporates the theme of the demarcation between the sphere of the gods and the world of humans. The motif of the separation of sky and earth is listed as motif number A625 in Stith Thompson's *Motif-Index* (1955, 1:128–29), and it is found in ancient Greece, India, eastern Indonesia, Tahiti, Africa, and native North and South America (Dundes 1984, 182). The myth also exists in China in several versions. It is possible to conjecture that the late-dated P'an Ku myth is a version of this myth, and the demigod may be seen as the firstborn of his sky and earth parents, when the sky and earth gradually separated from each other. This myth was presented in chapter 1.

A different myth of the separation between sky and earth occurs in numerous classical myths, and three versions are related in the following readings. The first is from a first-century A.D. chapter of *The Classic of Mountains and Seas*. It tells of a monstrously deformed god, Chuan Hsu, who presides over the pivot of the sky. His grandchildren are Ch'ung and Li, whom he orders to keep the mass of the sky and the matter of the earth physically apart, Ch'ung by pushing the sky up, Li by pressing earth down.

The second reading is from *Discourses of the States*, and the third from *The Classic of History,* which both date from the late Chou period. In these two versions the myth is called "severing the links between earth and Heaven." Both versions are extremely convoluted and incorporate several major themes: the proper ministration of the relationship between gods and humans, political control, cosmic harmony, and paradisiacal loss.

Discourses of the States, as its title proclaims, contains political and philosophical discourse and speeches purporting to have been delivered by historical personages of the different states of the Chou dynasty. Its sophisticated style clearly marks it as later than the era of the personages it claims to portray, and it probably dates from about the fifth to the third century B.C. Although the speeches are idealized reconstructions rather than a historical record, the text is valuable for mythology because it contains versions of important myths. The myth of the separation of the sky and earth is related in the chapter of *Discourses* entitled "Discourses of Ch'u," because the Ch'u people are believed to have descended from Ch'ung and Li, and ultimately from Chuan Hsu, the three central figures of the myth. The myth is placed in three different periods. First there was the primeval era, when gods and humans did not intermingle but communicated with one another through a small number of humans with special powers who were called *hsi* and *wu,* that is, male and female shamans. Second, there was the era of Shao Hao, when gods and humans intermingled and ordinary people usurped the special functions of the *hsi* and *wu.* Third, there was the era of Chuan Hsu, Shao Hao's successor, who ordered two officers, Ch'ung and Li, to keep the affairs of Heaven and the affairs of earth under separate control. This command of Chuan Hsu became known as "severing the links between earth and Heaven." The eras in which these events occurred were characterized by an initial period of paradisiacal grace, when there were no natural calamities; a period when the cosmic order was disrupted; and a final period when order was restored.

The version in *The Classic of History* narrates the myth from a totally different perspective, although the context is similar. Again, this text belongs to the same period as the *Discourses,* and it is also characterized as a collection of idealized reconstructions of political and philosophical discourse which is valuable for its mythological material, no matter how distorted it may be. The account of the separation of the sky and earth occurs in the opening passage of the chapter entitled "The Punishments of [the Prince of] Lü." This purports to be a formal record of the archaic discourse of an ancient king of the Chou dynasty on the nature of law and punishment for the benefit of his official, the Prince of Lü, whom he had appointed as one of the highest-ranking ministers of state. The king relates the history of rebellion and evil deeds from primeval times, when Ch'ih Yu was the first rebel, to the era of Yao, Shun, and Yü. He traces the evolution of evil and characterizes it as an infectious sickness in the body politic. The evil of Chi'h Yu was passed on to the Miao people, who oppressed the population with harsh and indiscriminate punishments. The people became demoralized and were infected by the same lack of virtue as their leaders. God intervened to assuage the people, and he exterminated the Miao. He also commanded Ch'ung and Li to "sever the links between earth and Heaven," because the Miao had violated their sacred trust and had used their supernatural powers for evil purposes. Thus the account of the myth is framed within a narrative told by a king in antiquity.

The three versions of the myth in *The Classic of Mountains and Seas*, *Discourses of the States*, and *The Classic of History* are widely disparate, although they draw on the same mythological matter. The version in the first text below, with its brief narrative and lack of explanatory background, closely coincides with the worldwide motif. The other two versions clearly show signs of distortion of a basic myth for the purposes of political philosophy and legal theory. This is most noticeable in the version in the third reading, from the *History*, which eliminates the central god, Chuan Hsu, and transforms the mythical figures of Ch'ung and Li into human types serving mundane goals of sociopolitical administration and control. Both the version in the *Discourses* and the one in the *History* may be said to represent a formulation of a political myth which seeks to demonstrate the proper method of social control. The version in the *Discourses* (the second reading below), especially in its last section, may also be construed as a mythologem of the separation between sacral and temporal powers. While the first version of the myth focuses on the physical aspects of sky and earth, the second version expresses major concepts noted by G. S. Kirk concerning the myth of the separation of sky and earth: the idea of a Golden Age and the relationship between gods and humans (1970; 209, 226–38).

In the vast wastes there is a mountain. Its name is Sun-and-Moon Mountain and it is the pivot of Heaven. The Wu Chü Gate of Heaven is where the sun and moon set. There is a god with a human face and no arms. His two feet are doubled up behind the top of his head. His name is Hsu. Chuan Hsu gave birth to Old Child; Old Child gave birth to Ch'ung and Li. The god ordered Ch'ung to raise his hands up against Heaven and he ordered Li to press down against earth. Under the earth Yi was born and he lived at the west pole. Through him the movements and rotation of the sun, moon, and stars were set in motion. (*Shan hai ching, Ta huang hsi ching*, SPPY 16.4b–5a)

King Chao [of Ch'u, 515–489 B.C.] asked Kuan She-fu, "Is it really true as the *History of the Chou* says that Ch'ung and Li caused Heaven and earth to be kept apart? If they had not done that, the people would still be able to ascend to Heaven, wouldn't they?" He replied, "No, it wasn't like that. In ancient times gods and humans did not intermingle. But among the people there were some who were gifted with clear vision, who were single-minded, and who possessed the power of absolute reverence and authority. Such was their knowledge that they could correlate the affairs of the world on high and the world below. Such was their wisdom that they could illuminate the remote and reveal what was clear. . . . Therefore the shining gods descended to the people, to the males known as *hsi*-shamans and to the females known as *wu*-shamans. It was they who arranged the positions of the gods and their due sequence at ceremonies. . . . Thus the offices in charge of the functions of Heaven and earth, and of gods and humans, were named the Five Offices. . . . Humans and gods were treated as separate entities. . . . Therefore the gods sent down their blessings on humans, and they received their offerings, and no calamities were visited upon them. When it came to the period of decline under Shao Hao, the Nine Li disrupted the cosmic powers, and gods and humans intermingled and became indistinguishable, and it became impossible to determine who were mortal creatures. Everyone performed sacrifices with offerings as if they were shaman officials, and they lost their essential sincerity of faith. . . . Blessings no longer came down to them and calamities were visited upon them. Chuan Hsu succeeded him [Shao Hao], and then he ordered Ch'ung, the Principal of the South, to control Heaven in order to assemble the gods in their proper place, and he ordered Li, the Fire Principal, to control earth in order to assemble the people in their proper places. He made them go back to old established customs and not usurp powers or commit sacrilege. This was termed to "sever the links between earth and Heaven." Later the San Miao repeated the disruption of the cosmic powers as the Nine Li had done. Therefore Yao protected the descendants of Ch'ung and Li, who had not forgotten the old ways, and ordered them to supervise them. Right up until the era of the Hsia and the Shang, therefore, the descendants of Ch'ung and Li arranged Heaven and earth in their due spheres and kept their functions and sovereigns separate. (*Kuo yü, Ch'u yü*, SPTK 18.1a–3a)

The king said, "We have been taught from antiquity that Ch'ih Yu was the first to bring disorder and that this extended to the people who had been at peace. They all became thieves, bandits, hawkish people, traitors, looters, forgers, and murderers. The Miao people did not apply the restraints of training but subdued them through punishments. They devised the five severe punishments, which they called the Law. They executed the innocent and began to carry to excess punitive mutilations of amputating the nose, legs, and testicles and branding with pitch. All these were designated as punishment, and everyone received the same equal punishment, no distinction being made among those who had been pronounced guilty. The people were stirred up and affected one another with their wrongdoing, becoming troublesome and disorderly. They lost their innate good faith and broke their vows and covenants. All those who had received these severe punishments from tyrannical rule protested aloud their innocence before the Almighty. God Almighty looked down upon his people, and there was no fragrant virtue but the stench coming from those punishments. The August God felt sorrow and pity for the innocent who had been so severely chastised. His vengeance on the harsh tyrants was their own severe chastisement: he exterminated the Miao people and extinguished their line forever. Therefore he ordered Ch'ung and Li to sever the links between earth and Heaven, so that no gods descended or humans ascended. (*Shang shu, Lü hsing*, SPPY 19.10a–11b)

The Sons of Chuan Hsu

In the previous section the first reading related that the god Chuan Hsu had a son named Old Child. Another text, *Chronicle of Tso,* which dates from five centuries earlier, tells that Kao Yang, Chuan Hsu's other name, had eight talented sons known as the Eight Fortunate Ones (*Pa k'ai*). The *Chronicle* also relates that Chuan Hsu had an untalented son named T'ao Wu, the Block, who, with three others, Hun Tun (Chaos), Ch'iung Ch'i (Gargoyle), and T'ao T'ieh (Glutton), made up the Four

Ominous Ones (*Ssu hsiung*) (Karlgren 1946, 255–56, 247–49.) The first reading below is from a first-century A.D. text by Wang Ch'ung. It further relates that Chuan Hsu had three other sons who were plague-ghosts when they died in childbirth. The author, Wang Ch'ung, cites as his source one of the ancient books of ritual, and, although his account is late, his recording of known myths is usually reliable. The second reading is from *The Classic of Spirits and Strange Beings*, attributed to the famous Han author Tung-fang Shuo, but probably is later. Here the untalented son of Chuan Hsu, T'ao Wu, the Block, is fancifully described. The third reading is from a very late encyclopedic work by Ch'en Yao-wen, of which his preface is dated A.D. 1569. In this text the god goes under the name of Kao Yang.

These three readings narrate quite different myths that are linked only by the evil nature of the spirits or lesser gods descended from the otherwise benign god Chuan Hsu. The last reading shows how a classical myth can lose its identity in the later tradition and become merged with a tale relating to a popular socioreligious custom. Bodde has made a special study of demons in the Han era (1975, 85–117).

The *Rites* says, "Chuan Hsu had three sons who lived for a while and then died and turned into plague-ghosts. One lived in the Great River, and this was the Fever Ghost. One lived in Jo River and was the water goblin ghost. One lived in the palaces and houses of humans and loved scaring little children." The generation before Chuan Hsu certainly produced great numbers of sons, and there were all kinds of ghostly spirits like Chuan Hsu's ghosts. (*Lun heng, Ting kuei,* SPTK 22.14a)

In the wilds of the western region there is a beast. In appearance it is like a tiger, but it is very large. Its fur is two feet long, it has a human face, tiger's paws, and a pig's mouth and tusks, and its tail is eighteen feet long. It stirs up trouble in the wilds. One name for it is T'ao Wu and its other name is Nan Hsun. It says in the *Spring and Autumn,* "Master Chuan Hsu had a useless son whose name was T'ao Wu." (*Shen yi ching, Hsi huang ching,* HWTS 32.8b)

Master Kao Yang's son was lean and miserly. He enjoyed wearing threadbare clothes and eating rice gruel. On the last day of the first month he died in an alley. It became popular custom to cook rice gruel and throw threadbare clothes outdoors and to offer sacrifice on this day in the alleyways, which was called "The Cortege of the Wasted Ghost." (*T'ien-chung chi,* citing *Sui shih chi,* SKCS 4.57b)

Kung Kung Butts into the Mountain

The mythical figure of Kung Kung appears in several different roles in late Chou and Han mythological accounts. According to one tradition, Kung Kung was a primeval god prior to the Flame Emperor (Yen Ti) and the Yellow Emperor and followed after Sui-jen, the Fire Driller. This tradition identifies Kung Kung as the chief protagonist in a flood myth that is quite separate from that of Yü and the flood. The Kung Kung flood myth is narrated in the first two readings in this section, of which the second, from *Discourses of the States,* presents an unfavorable portrait of the god, stating that his hydraulic work caused cosmic disruption and made the people miserable in their suffering. The third reading depicts Kung Kung in his role as warrior, a mighty titan who fights Chuan Hsu for the godhead (*Ti*). This passage from *Huai-nan Tzu* gives another reason for Kung Kung's cosmic blunder, which differs from the account of cosmic disorder in the Nü Kua myth (chap. 3). In the narrative presented here, Kung Kung damages Pu-chou Mountain, one of the earthly pillars supporting the canopy of the sky. Elsewhere in *Huai-nan Tzu* it relates that Chuan Hsu killed Kung Kung because he "caused a flood disaster." The myth of Kung Kung and the flood parallels that of Yü and the flood and at the same time that of Nü Kua.

It is feasible to identify Kung Kung as the marplot of classical myth, one who spoils the order of the world. In his study of this mythical figure, William G. Boltz makes a number of interesting points. He defines Kung Kung as "a personification of the Flood itself" (1981, 147–48). Furthermore, utilizing Lévi-Strauss's theory of binary opposites, Boltz contrasts Kung Kung personifying chaos with Yü personifying order, and he interprets the Yü flood myth as "'Order' vanquishing 'Chaos'" (1981, 144–45). He also usefully analyses the various written forms of the god's first name, Kung, and its phonetic correlatives, which signify 'quarrelsome' and 'flooding waters'. Usually, phonological equations in mythology are of dubious value, but certainly in this case the name appears to be significant.

Ever since the era of the Fire Driller, there has never been one who did not consider managing the empire to be of great importance. When Kung Kung was king, water covered seven-tenths of the world and dry land consisted of three-tenths. He took advantage of the natural strengths of the earth and he controlled the world within those narrow confines. (*Kuan Tzu, K'uei to,* SPTK 23.3b)

Long ago, Kung Kung abandoned this Way. . . . He wanted to dam the hundred rivers, reduce the highest ground, and block up the low-lying ground, and so he damaged the world. But August Heaven opposed his good fortune and the common people refused to help him. Disaster and disorder sprang up everywhere and Kung Kung was destroyed. (*Kuo yü, Chou yü,* 3, SPTK 3.6b)

Long ago Kung Kung fought with Chuan Hsu to be God. In his fury he knocked against Pu-chou Mountain. The pillar of Heaven broke and the cord of earth snapped. Heaven tilted toward the northwest, and that is why the sun, moon, and stars move in that direction. Earth had a gap missing in the southeast, and that is why the rivers overflowed and silt and soil came to rest there. (*Huai-nan Tzu, T'ien wen,* SPPY 3.1a–b)

The Myths of Hun Tun

The inclusion of the Hun Tun myth here amply illustrates the polyfunctionality of the mythic material. In the various accounts, Hun Tun is an apertureless god, an avian god without facial features, an anthropomorphized human rebel, or a minor deity, and also a cosmogonic concept. Thus it is difficult to place such a figure. That Hun Tun appears among destroyers is prompted by the best-known mythic narrative, in which he is not so much a destroyer as destroyed. N. J. Girardot has examined the many-faceted Hun Tun myth, especially from the perspective of early Taoist philosophy and in its numerous metaphorical associations (1983).

The mythic traditions of Hun Tun are contradictory. One of the earliest accounts occurs in the Taoist philosophical text *Chuang Tzu* (fourth century B.C.), where he appears as the god of the central region, who has no facial apertures, and who is killed by two busybody gods after they bore holes for his eyes, ears, nostrils, and mouth. Clearly, the author of *Chuang Tzu* has used a preexisting strand of myth to illustrate the dangers of misguided charity and interventionist political policies and the benefits of a laissez-faire policy. A quite different presentation of the myth of Hun Tun appears in *The Classic of Mountains and Seas,* in a chapter postdating *Chuang Tzu* by about a century. This narrative provides a detailed description of the deity which concurs with the *Chuang Tzu* portrayal in one important respect, that Hun Tun has a featureless head. It would seem that a mythical figure named Hun Tun, which is written in at least four ways, belongs to a shadowy mythological tradition of which only faint traces appear in late Chou sources.

In both texts, Hun Tun is depicted as a benign or neutral figure. In two other late Chou works, however, Hun Tun is a negative figure. In *Chronicle of Tso,* Hun Tun is labeled as the first of the Four Ominous Ones, along with Ch'iung Ch'i (Gargoyle), T'ao Wu (the Block), and T'ao T'ieh (Glutton) (Karlgren 1946, 247). In *The Classic of History,* Hun Tun is one of the "Four Evil Ones" exiled by Shun for being rebellious and barbarous (Girardot 1983, 123).

A separate tradition concerns not so much a featureless deity or an anthropomorphized criminal as an abstract concept or a descriptive expression of featurelessness, shapelessness, and lack of definition. In this sense, the binome *hun-tun* is used as an adjective or adverb in a medley of affiliated terms, such as *hun-tun* written with various graphs, *hun,* or *tun,* or *hun-hun,* or *tun-tun,* and so forth. For example, in the Taoist text *The Classic of the Way and the Power,* the term *hun-ch'eng* appears, denoting 'confusedly formed', but the compound *hun-tun* never occurs. It is in the *Huai-nan Tzu* that the multiple forms of *hun-tun* and its synonyms are linked cosmogonically to the primordial state at the moment of creation. For example, in "Explanations," chapter 14 of that text, there is an opening evocation of primordial chaos: "In the gaping, undifferentiated void, sky and earth were an unmarked mass in confusion [*hun-tun*] which had not yet been created" (SPPY 14.1a).

Thus the ancient myth of the god Hun Tun vestigially described in the late Chou works *Chuang Tzu* and *The Classic of Mountains and Seas* evolved in the early Han era into an abstract concept that was adapted to depict a cosmogonic myth. For this reason it has often been translated as 'chaos'.

By the late Han period the mythical Hun Tun was restored to divine status, although rewritten as T'un Hun, but he was demoted from a prime deity to a minor one. In his "Table of Personages Ancient and Modern," the historian Pan Ku (A.D. 32–92) ranked T'un Hun eleventh in a secondary list of deities subsumed under the major god T'ai Hao (Karlgren 1946, 230). Even later in the mythographic tradition, Huang-fu Mi (A.D. 215–282) ranked Hun T'un (*sic*) as a major god, coming tenth after Fu Hsi and Nü Kua (Karlgren 1946, 234).

Since the Hun Tun narratives in *Chuang Tzu* and *The Classic of*

Mountains and Seas are recognizably mythological in substance and style, and since they are both authentic texts of the late Chou era, they are presented in sequence in the readings.

> The god of the south sea was Shu [Brief], the god of the north sea was Hu [Sudden], and the god of the center was Hun Tun [Confused]. Shu and Hu occasionally used to go together to Hun Tun's land, and Hun Tun received them very cordially. Shu and Hu planned how to repay his generosity. They said, "All humans have seven openings with which to see, hear, eat, and breathe. Only this one has not got any." So they tried chiseling him. Each day they chiseled one opening. On the seventh day, Hun Tun died. (*Chuang Tzu, Ying Ti Wang*, SPPY 3.19a–b)

> Three hundred and fifty leagues farther west is called Sky Mountain. There is a lot of gold and jade, and it has green realgar. Ying River springs from there and then flows southwest to empty into T'ang Valley. There is a god [*shen*] there. His appearance is like a yellow bag, and he is red like a cinnabar flame. He has six feet and four wings. Hun Tun has no face or eyes. This one knows how to sing and dance. He is, in fact, Ti Chiang [God River]. (*Shan hai ching, Hsi tz'u san ching*, SPPY 2.22b–23a)

The Shen Star and the Ch'en Star

The number of stars counted by ancient Chinese astronomers is considerable. Shih Shen's "Astronomy," of the early fourth century B.C., listed 122 constellations with 809 stars, and other astronomers counted others to make a total of 284 constellations with 1,464 stars by Ch'en Ch'o's time (fourth to fifth century A.D.). Most of the stars charted by Shih Shen and others, however, had no name (Maspero 1929, 269–319). Chinese stellar myths are few compared with the numbers of stars listed in the ancient works on astronomy.

The paucity of Chinese stellar myths contrasts with the Greco-Roman tradition, which has 45 major ones. Those of Orion the Gigantic Hunter, the Pleiades, Ganymedes-Aquarius, and Hesperus the Evening Star are among the oldest. The Chinese myth of the Shen and Ch'en stars has some parallels with Western myths. It is also one of the oldest of the Chinese stellar myths, though it cannot be dated textually as early as the Orion myth mentioned by Homer circa 700 B.C. The Shen and Ch'en myth parallels that of Orion in the sense that the Orion star is in eternal pursuit of the Pleiades or their mother, Pleione, for Shen and Ch'en were originally brothers who ceaselessly quarreled and had to pursue separate paths for eternity.

The context of this narrative, from the *Chronicle of Tso*, demonstrates the early Chinese belief in the baneful influence of the stars. The Lord of Chin was ill and Tzu Ch'an was asked to visit him. Tzu Ch'an explained that his illness was caused by the two spirits of the stars. In this account the god Kao Hsin is Ti K'u's other name.

In the Han dynasty, poets used this stellar myth as a romantic metaphor for lovers suffering from estrangement. Lines from a ballad by Ts'ao Chih (A.D. 192–232) illustrate this literary mythopoeia: "In the past you covered me with fond love, / We were in harmony like harp and lute. / Why, my love, do you reject me? / Why are we estranged like Shang from Shen?" (Birrell 1986, 70; *Shang* means 'the Ch'en star').

> Long ago Kao Hsin had two sons. The elder was called Yen Po; the younger was called Shih Ch'en. They lived in a vast forest. They could not bear each other and every day they looked out for a fight with shield and dagger-ax and made attacks on each other. The Lord God was displeased and moved Yen Po to Shang-ch'iu, putting him in charge of the Ch'en star. The Shang people followed him, and that is why Ch'en is the Shang star. And he moved Shih Ch'en to Ta Hsia, putting him in charge of the Shen star. The people of T'ang [Yao] followed him and so they became subjects of the Hsia and the Shang. (*Tso chuan, Chao kung* First Year, SPPY 15.7b–8a)

Yi Shoots the Lord of the River

Yi the Archer has already been encountered in his most famous role as the hero who saved the world from being incinerated by the ten suns. It was also suggested earlier that the mythical figure of Yi is presented ambiguously in mythic narratives, compared with the positive portrayal of figures such as Shun and Yü. Yi's function as heroic savior is countered by a separate tradition of Yi the villain. Yi is known by various names: Yi Yi or Yi of the East People, Yi Yi or Yi the Good, or Lord Yi of the Hsia.

The earliest accounts of Yi's decline from good to evil occur in the *Chronicle of Tso* and in "Questions of Heaven" (the first reading below), where his crimes are listed as the excessive pursuit of pleasure, an unprovoked attack on the river god of Lo River and the theft of his wife, and the usurpation of the Hsia royal house. Classical commentators of the second and third centuries A.D., such as Wang Yi (second and fourth readings), Ju Ch'un (third reading), and Kao Yu (fifth reading), embroider the myth of Yi's crimes of murder and adultery in their explications of passages in "Questions of Heaven" and in *Huai-nan Tzu* (seventh and tenth readings) and the commentary on it (ninth reading). Yet even while recounting his crimes, these commentators retain a sympathy for Yi and explain away his wrongdoing. The most damning accusation against Yi, however, in terms of the later historical record was that he caused the downfall of the glorious Hsia dynasty, which had been founded by Yü the Great. The narrative in the *Chronicle* (the eleventh and last reading below) clearly removes Yi from the primeval solar myth and humanizes him as a political personage who, like many other villains in the *Chronicle*, meets with a grisly death. The *Chronicle* dates from about the fourth century B.C.

The myth of the death of Yi comes in two versions, one from the aforementioned *Chronicle,* which historicizes Yi, the other from late Chou texts such as *Mencius* and *Hsun Tzu* (eighth and sixth readings). Both contain numerous mythic motifs.

> God sent down Yi Yi to drive away the evils besetting the Hsia people, so why did he shoot down the Lord of the River and take his wife, Lo-pin? (*Ch'u Tz'u, T'ien wen,* SPTK 3.15b)

> Lo-pin was a water nymph and she was called Fu-fei. . . . Yi also dreamed that he had an affair with Fu-fei, the goddess of Lo River. (Wang Yi's commentary on *Ch'u Tz'u, T'ien wen,* SPTK 3.15b)

> Ju Ch'un says that Fu-fei, the daughter of [?Fu] Hsi, died by drowning in Lo River and then she became a goddess. (Li Shan's commentary on *Lo shen fu,* citing *Han shu yin yi, Wen hsuan,* SPTK 19.14b)

> The Lord of the River turned into a white dragon and played on the riverbank. When Yi saw him, he shot him with his arrow, aiming for his left eye. The Lord of the River went up to complain to God in Heaven: "Kill Yi because of what he has done to me!" God in Heaven said, "Why were you shot by Yi?" The Lord of the River said, "When I transformed myself into a white dragon I came out to play." God in Heaven said, "If you had kept to the river depths as a god, how could Yi have committed this crime against you? Today you became a reptile, so you were bound to be shot at by someone. Of course he

is in the right—what was Yi's crime in this case?" (Wang Yi's commentary on *Ch'u Tz'u, T'ien wen*, SPTK 3.15b)

The Lord of the River killed people by drowning them, so Yi shot him in the left eye. (Kao Yu's commentary on *Huai-nan Tzu, Fan lun*, SPPY 13.22a)

Yi and Feng Men were the best archers in the world. (*Hsun Tzu, Cheng lun*, SPPY 12.9b)

In archery contests of one hundred shots, the most skilled archers were always Yi and Feng Meng. (*Huai-nan Tzu, Shui lin*, SPPY 17.4a)

Feng Meng learned archery from Yi and acquired an exhaustive knowledge of Yi's style of shooting. He realized that only Yi in the whole world was better than he, so he killed Yi. (*Meng Tzu, Li Lü*, 2, SPTK 8.8b)

"Club" is the large stick that he [Feng Meng] made out of peach wood to batter Yi to death with. From that time on demons are terrified of peach wood. (Hsu Shen's commentary on *Huai-nan Tzu, Ch'üan yen*, SPPY 14.1b)

Yi rid the world of evil, so when he died he became the god Tsung Pu. (*Huai-nan Tzu, Fan lun*, SPPY 13.22a)

Long ago, when the Hsia was beginning to decline, Lord Yi moved from Ch'u to Ch'iung-shih and, relying on the people of Hsia, replaced the Hsia government. He took advantage of his archery skills, neglecting public affairs and indulging in hunting game in the fields. He discarded the ministers Wu Lo, Po Yin, Hsiung K'un, and Mang Yü, employing instead Cho of Han. Cho of Han was a treacherous young retainer of the house of Po Ming, and the Lord of Po Ming had dismissed him. But Yi Yi trustingly received him into his entourage and appointed him as his prime minister. Cho practiced flattery at court and bribery in society at large. He deceived the people and encouraged Lord Yi to go hunting. He devised a plot to deprive Yi of his state. Society and the court all acquiesced to Cho's command. But Yi still refused to mend his ways. One day, on his return from the hunt, his clansmen all assassinated him, and they cooked his corpse in order to serve it to his sons to eat. But his sons could not bear to eat him, and they were all put to death at Ch'iung-men. (*Tso chuan, Hsiang kung* Fourth Year, SPPY 29.12b–13a)

The Three Trials of Shun

The mythical figure of Shun was discussed earlier in his primary roles as sage-ruler and exemplar of filial piety. Here attention is focused on the ways in which the myth of Shun is reworked into legend and folklore in Han and post-Han sources. The readings illustrate the heroism of Shun in countering his evil family and his conversion of their enmity into virtuous behavior. In the previous discussion, passages were drawn from "Questions of Heaven" and *Mencius,* both dating from the fourth century B.C. A different selection of narratives is presented here by way of contrast between early and late versions. It will be evident, for example, that the third reading, from the Han historian Ssu-ma Ch'ien, closely follows the version of the myth in *Mencius.* The first reading purports to be a lost fragment of *Biographies of Women,* ascribed to Liu Hsiang (79–8 B.C.), and the second reading is from the text proper of the *Biographies.*

> The *Biographies of Women* tells how the Blind Man and Hsiang plotted to kill Shun. They ordered Shun to repair the granary. Shun told his two women. The two women said, "This time it can only mean they are going to destroy you; this time it can only mean they are going to burn you to death. Take off your top garment and go out wearing the bird-patterned coat." When Shun was putting the granary in order, they immediately removed his ladder and the Blind Man set fire to the granary. But Shun had already flown away. Later they ordered him to dig a well. Shun told his two women. The two women said, "This time it can only mean they are going to destroy you; this time they are going to bury you alive. You take off your top garment and go out wearing your dragon-patterned coat." Shun went out to dig the well. They spied on his movements and then began burying him alive. But Shun had escaped and disappeared. (Hung Hsing-tsu's commentary on *Ch'u Tz'u, T'ien wen,* citing a passage in *Lieh nü chuan* not in extant editions, *Ch'u Tz'u pu chu,* TSCC 3.81)

> The Blind Man also invited Shun to drink strong liquor, so as to kill him. Shun told his two women. So the two women gave Shun a lotion to bathe himself with in the pool. Then he went off and drank the liquor all day without getting drunk. Shun's younger sister took pity on him and restored peace and harmony to her in-laws' home. (*Lieh nü chuan, Yu Yü erh fu,* SPPY 1.1b)

The Blind Man and Hsiang were delighted, imagining that Shun was now dead. Hsiang said, "I was the one who thought of it first." When Hsiang divided Shun's possessions with his father and mother, he said, "I will take Shun's two daughters of Yao and his lute. I shall give you, Father and Mother, the cattle and sheep and the granary." Hsiang immediately settled in at the palace residence and was beating time on the lute when Shun came and saw him there. Hsiang was amazed beyond belief. He said, "When I thought about you, Shun, I was very sad and anxious about you." Shun said, "All right. I hope you will always continue to be like that." Shun once again served under the Blind Man and he loved his younger brother and cared for him with devotion. (*Shih chi, Wu ti pen chi,* SPPY 1.19a)

King Kai Loses His Oxen

King Kai was the seventh Shang king descended from Hsieh, the mythical founder of the Shang dynasty. He was also known as King Hai, or Wang-tzu Hai or Heir Apparent Hai. In a later tradition he was known as the First Herdsman. Although the main account of the myth of King Kai in "Questions of Heaven" is so textually corrupt that the narrative is garbled, it is possible to elicit its basic outline from the reconstructed text of Yuan K'o (1980.2, 220–22) and, to some extent, from later fragments.

The first reading is from "Questions of Heaven" and is in the typical format of serial questions that are phrased substantively enough for a narrative to emerge. This narrative, insofar as it can be pieced together, is a tale of treachery, fornication, and murder played out in the context of two tribes of herdsmen. King Kai was the royal guest of the ruler of Yu-yi, whose name was Mien-ch'en. Implicit in the elusive narrative is the idea that Mien-ch'en allowed King Kai to pasture his herds and flocks in the rich valley of the Yellow River. When King Kai performed a warrior dance for his hosts, he inflamed Mien-ch'en's wife with passionate desire. They had an affair, and she became pregnant, her condition euphemistically expressed as: "Why did her smooth flanks and firm flesh grow so plump?" As a result of this breach of trust and diplomatic scandal, the Shang suffered a decline during the successive reigns of Shang kings, their perverse sexual mores contrasting with the strict virtue of their forebear King Chi.

The myth of King Kai is taken up with the second reading, from the commentary of Kuo P'u of the fourth century A.D. on *The Classic of*

Mountains and Seas. It relates that the ruler of the Yu-yi people, King Mien-ch'en, killed King Kai (referred to here as Prince Hai of the Yin, or Shang), and exposed his corpse in retribution for violating his wife. King Kai's successor, King Shang Chia-wei, the eighth Shang king, avenged him by killing Mien-ch'en.

The third reading, from *The Classic of Mountains and Seas* itself, returns to the classical mythological tradition with the motif of divine intervention by a river god and with an early account of the foundation myth of the Yao minority people of South China.

The basic outline of the myth of King Kai that emerges thus far is clearly insufficient to explain the myth in a convincing way. One small clue is, however, contained in a recurring feature of the first and third readings below which might be explored in the search for the underlying significance of the myth. This recurring element is the pastoral way of life of the king and his people and the particular pastoral mode expressed in the two narratives. The first reading states that the king lost his "herdsmen, cattle, and sheep" when he visited the king of a neighboring tribe but that he managed "to lead back his herds and flocks." The passage also says that relations between the two tribes remained precarious for some generations. The third reading indicates that King Kai (here named Hai) "entrusted his herds" to the neighboring tribe, but they "killed King Hai and stole his herd of domesticated cattle." If these accounts are compared with the brilliant comparative analysis of the "myth of the first cattle raid" by Bruce Lincoln, who found convincing parallels between the pastoral culture of the Masai tribe of East Africa in modern times and the Indo-Iranian pastoral culture as recorded in the ancient textual tradition, a strong argument appears to emerge for interpreting the myth of King Kai as the "myth of the first cattle raid" in the Chinese tradition. Lincoln shows that underlying such a myth is the socioeconomic value and importance of cattle in the pastoral cultures of the Masai and the ancient Indo-Iranians:

> Cattle have an enormous importance and constitute the measure of wealth, while supplying the basis for exchange relations. This value is no doubt largely based on their role as the chief source of food — furnishing milk, milk products, meat, and even blood for drinking. The value, however, goes beyond mere food production, since their skin furnishes leather for clothing, blankets, and thongs; their bones furnish material for tools; their dung furnishes fuel for fires; and their urine is commonly used as a disinfectant. . . .

Their importance transcends their worth in hard economic terms, however, for cattle come to play a major role in social transactions. They serve as bridewealth and wergeld, in the belief that only cattle can fully make up for the loss of a valued human member of society. . . . it would seem that the greatest desire of any herdsman is the possession of many cattle.

This longing for cattle has produced an interesting development: the organized theft of cattle from neighboring tribes. Warfare becomes strictly the quest for cattle, and virtually no other booty is taken. (Lincoln 1981, 6–7)

Lincoln's comparative analysis of two socioeconomic structures widely divergent in historical terms but remarkably similar in their thought patterns provides a valuable basis for viewing the garbled account of King Kai as a prototype of the pastoral myth of the first cattle raid in the Chinese tradition.

Kai maintained the power passed down by Chi, his father having been well endowed with goodness. Why then did he die in the end at Yu-yi, together with his herdsmen, cattle, and sheep? When he danced with shield and plumes, why did someone desire him? Why did her smooth flanks and firm flesh grow so plump? Where did the young herdsmen meet up with him? When they bludgeoned his bed, he had already got up, so how did he meet his fate? Heng maintained the power passed down by Chi. How did he manage to lead back his herds and flocks? Why did he go back and seek to gain from them with his attractive gifts, and not go straight back home? Hun Wei was descended from Heng and Kai, but the Yu-yi were restless. Why did the people grow troublesome and unruly, and their womenfolk and children become so immoral? Hsuan and his brother were both sexually corrupt; they endangered the life of their brother. Why is it that, even though times had so changed for the worse that they committed acts of treachery, their descendants met with good fortune? (*Ch'u Tz'u, T'ien wen*, SPTK 3.22a–24a)

The Yin [Shang] Prince Hai was a guest at Yu-yi, but he committed fornication there. The ruler of Yu-yi, Mien-ch'en, killed him and threw him away. That is why Shang Chia-wei of the Yin availed himself of the army of the Lord of the River and attacked Yu-yi and destroyed it. Then he killed its ruler, Mien-ch'en. (Kuo P'u's commentary on *Shan hai ching, Ta huang tung ching,* citing *Chu shu chi nien,* SPPY 14.4b)

There is a man called King Hai who held a bird in his two hands and then ate its head. King Hai entrusted his herds to Yu-yi and the Lord of the river domesticated his cattle. The people of Yu-yi killed King Hai and stole his herd of domesticated cattle. The Lord of the River mourned Yu-yi. Then the people of Yu-yi left the region in secret and made their kingdom among wild beasts, which people took for their food. This kingdom is called the Yao people. (*Shan hai ching, Ta huang tung ching,* SPPY 14.4b–5a)

King Chieh of the Hsia and the Two Suns

The late Chou texts refer in a piecemeal way to sixteen kings of the Hsia, the mythical dynasty much spoken of in the classical tradition, but for which no evidence as yet exists. The early texts all agree that the founder of the Hsia was the mythical figure Yü, and most agree that the last ruler of the legendary Hsia was King Chieh. In the later mythological tradition the rulers between Yü and Chieh were arranged in chronological sequence to produce a noble line of descent from the demigod Yü. A typical chronology is provided by Ssu-ma Ch'ien, which is discussed in some detail by Karlgren (1946, 314–15). None of these Hsia rulers can be historically attested.

Throughout the late Chou texts the figure of King Chieh is portrayed as an evil tyrant who brought about the fall of the legendary house of the Hsia. He is usually contrasted unfavorably with King T'ang the Conqueror, who led the Shang people to victory over the Hsia. The two figures of the tyrant and the good king interact in binary opposition, symbolizing the powers of evil and the forces of good. The struggle between the two mythical figures assumes an epic dimension in the classical texts, and the theme became a major paradigm of political theory in the course of Chinese history. It was expressed in terms of a cyclical pattern of dynastic change in which a bad last ruler of a dynasty is defeated in a just war by the virtuous first ruler of a new dynasty (Meskill 1965, 1; Allan 1981, 81–89).

The colorful account of King Chieh the Tyrant and his defeat by the good King T'ang describes several other protagonists, such as the lovely Mo Hsi, King Chieh's one-time favorite who was cast aside for two new favorites, Wan and Yen, and so schemed to bring about his downfall. For his part, King T'ang's charisma attracted the finest men to assist him in his campaign against the Hsia. One such person was Yi Yin, a major mythical figure and a famous hero. Thus the protagonists on the side of the tyrant are females, while those on the side of the good king are virtuous males, a dichotomy that reinforces the structure of binary sexual opposition, Yin and Yang, in this mythologem.

The Chou texts and later narratives were unanimous in their condemnation of King Chieh, accusing him of sexual excess, tyranny, and extravagance. The details of his crime become more picturesque as the mythological and legendary tradition lengthens. Like Caligula in ancient Rome, King Chieh is depicted as a ruler who enjoyed observing the suffering of others as they froze or drowned or were chased by ravening tigresses through the marketplace. King Chieh's extravagance is illustrated in the second reading in this section by his wasteful use of precious jewels, such as the *t'iao*-bloom jade, to carve the names of female favorites, and, in another context, his fondness for massing thirty thousand female singers for day-long concerts. Like Yi the Archer, King Chieh refused to take advice from wise counselors, but followed the advice of courtiers who pandered to his whims. In the end his weaknesses, especially his love of women, facilitated the successful ruse by which King T'ang and Yi Yin destroyed him.

The fall of the Hsia is dramatically presaged in two solar myths. The first reading, from *The Classic of History*, relates one such omen, which echoes a proverb preserved in the *Record of Ritual*, in the chapter entitled "The Questions of Tseng Tzu": "The sky does not have two suns, a knight does not serve two rulers, a household does not serve two masters, and one cannot respect two superiors." The other solar myth is related in the third reading, from *The Treatise on Research into Nature*, third to fifth century A.D. It tells of the simultaneous rising and setting of two suns in the sky, an omen that is interpreted as the dynastic ascendancy of the Shang and the decline of the Hsia. This portent ironically echoes the blasphemy of King Chieh when he swore: "When that sun dies, you and I, we'll all perish!" Like many tyrants in myth and history, King Chieh senses his own impending doom and seeks to bring down destruction on the whole world.

The second reading is taken from the compendium of historical records and documentation compiled by Ma Su in the seventeenth century, *Hypotheses on History*. This work contains a great number of valuable mythological fragments from classical times which do not always appear in the extant editions of the texts they are cited from. In this instance, Ma Su is citing from the *Bamboo Annals,* an anonymous text purporting to record ancient history. The passage narrates the causes of the fall of the Hsia, namely, the revenge of the king's castoff favorite, Mo Hsi, and the guile of his opponent's minister, Yi Yin, a double agent who poses as a Hsia ally while remaining loyal to the Shang king.

> The king of the Hsia completely depleted his country's energies, and with his system of punishments he slaughtered his people in the city of the Hsia. So great numbers of people showed disrespect toward him and the king was displeased. He said, "When that sun dies, you and I, we'll all perish!" (*Shang shu, T'ang shih,* SPPY 8.1b)

> Lord Chieh ordered Pien to attack the Min mountain people. The Min mountain people presented Chieh with two girls, one named Wan, the other named Yen. The lord found the two girls very beautiful . . . and carved their names on *t'iao*-bloom jade. . . . He discarded his former favorite mistress, named Mo Hsi, on Lo River. She plotted with Yi Yin and then they caused the Hsia to be destroyed. (Subcommentary, *Yi shih,* citing *Chu shu chi nien,* PCTP 14.3a)

> In the era of King Chieh of the Hsia, the king's clansman, Fei Ch'ang, was going along by the river when he saw two suns, one rising in brilliant light from the east, the other sinking with fading light in the west, and he heard a sound like a sudden boom of thunder. Ch'ang asked P'ing Yi, "Which sun means the Yin, and which sun means the Hsia?" He answered, "The sun in the west means the Hsia, the sun in the east means the Yin." At this, Fei Ch'ang promptly moved his clan and went over to the Yin [Shang]. (*Po wu chih, Yi wen,* SPPY 10.1a)

King Chou of the Shang Imprisons King Wen
of the Chou Dynasty

The myth of the cyclical pattern of dynastic history is repeated in the narratives below of the epic contest between King Wen and King Wu of the Chou and their enemy, King Chou of the Shang. The "last bad ruler" of the Shang, King Chou, and the "first good rulers" of the Chou dynasty, Wen and Wu, interplay in binary opposition to create a dynamic myth of good versus evil. The myth of King Chou of the Shang differs from the usual paradigm of the "last bad ruler" in the sense that his portrayal is not always entirely negative. Ssu-ma Ch'ien's portrait of him, for example, is subtle and sympathetic, suggesting that

King Chou began his career as an attractive, intelligent, heroic, and charismatic ruler who gradually succumbed to depravity by weakly refusing to accept valid criticism and good counsel. In this respect the portrait of King Chou resembles that of Yi the Archer. In her study of mythic patterns in the transfer of power, Sarah Allan presents a detailed structural analysis of King Chou of the Hsia (1981, 103–8).

King Chou was a man with remarkable qualities, and he was most discerning, besides being forceful and quick-witted. When he received counsel from his officials and when he gave them audience, he showed a very keen mind. His natural strength exceeded that of other men, and a blow from his fist could fell wild animals. He was sufficiently clever to be able to oppose official censure, and with his eloquence he was able to gloss over his mistakes. He boasted of his abilities to his courtiers, and he was loud in his praise of his own reputation to everyone. He made everyone detest him. He was far too fond of drink and he was overindulgent in listening to music. He was amorous with the ladies, but his favorite was Ta Chi, and he did everything Ta Chi told him to do. Then he made his music master, Ch'üan, compose some new love music and Pei-li dances, which were a very effete style of music. He increased taxation in order to fill the treasury at Stag Terrace and filled to overflowing the granary at Great Bridge. He collected great numbers of dogs, horses, and rare animals, which filled the palace buildings. He enlarged the park terraces at Sha-ch'iu and housed there great numbers of wild beasts and the winged birds he had caught. He was negligent in his duties toward the ghosts and gods. He had a large ensemble of musicians to entertain him at Sha-ch'iu, and he made men and girls parade naked together, holding drinking parties through the long nights. The people felt resentful toward him, and there were some who plotted sedition among the nobility. (*Shih chi, Yin pen chi,* SPPY 3.8b–9a)

King Wen cultivated the Way and his virtue, and the people grew close to him. King Wen had two sons, the Duke of Chou and King Wu, and they were all wise men. At that time, Ch'ung-hou Hu and King Wen both ranked among the nobles, but the former could not match King Wen in virtue, and so he was always jealous of him. Then he slandered King Wen to King Chou saying, "Ch'ang, the Lord of the West, is a sage, and his oldest son, Fa, and his next son, Tan, are also both sages. These three wise men have hatched a plot and they are going to take advantage of you, so you had better think carefully what you intend to do about them." King Chou made use of his advice and imprisoned King Wen at Yu-li, and he chose a day when he would execute him. Then King Wen's four ministers, T'ai Tien, Hung Yao, San Yi-sheng, and Nan-kung-kua, went to visit King Wen. King Wen winked and slid his right eye round, indicating that King Chou was overly fond of the ladies, and he patted his belly with his archery bow to hint that King Chou was greedy for rare valuables. Then he tottered feebly on his feet, meaning that his ministers should be very quick in supplying King Chou's wants. So they traveled all over the country and went to every local area, and they found two beautiful girls, a large water-cowrie, and a white horse with a red mane. They went to present these to King Chou, displaying them in the central courtyard. When King Chou saw them, he looked up to Heaven and sighed, "How lovely they are! Who do they belong to?" San Yi-sheng hurried into the courtyard and said, "They are the prize possessions of the Lord of the West, and they are for his ransom because he has been condemned to death." King Chou said, "How very generous he is to me!" Then he promptly released the Lord of the West. King Chou said to Yi-sheng, "The man who acted in secret against the Lord of Ch'i has a long nose and a disfigured ear." When Yi-sheng went back to his own country he told King Wen about this description of the traitor, and so they knew that Ch'ung-hou had betrayed him. (*Ch'in ts'ao, Chü yu ts'ao,* TSCC 1.5)

5

Miraculous
Birth

An important mythologem is the manner of birth of mythical characters. The narratives relate many different forms of miraculous birth, such as the virgin birth of the divine founders of the Shang and Chou people. There are several accounts of birth from a divinely bestowed egg, a form of ornithomorphous hierogamy, as in the case of the founders of the Shang and Ch'in people, and also King Yen of Hsu. It is noteworthy that although there are numerous accounts of virgin births, the offspring are always male, which perhaps suggests that by the time the myths were recorded, they were cast in the idiom of a patriarchal society. The Country of Women is the only myth that narrates the survival of female infants, the males being left to die in infancy. Although the miraculous conception through a bird's egg is a recurring motif, gods and heroes are born from other things, for example, Ch'i, the son of Yü, who was born from a mother metamorphosed into a stone, and Yi Yin who was born from a dead mother metamorphosed into a hollow mulberry tree. Besides myths of virgin birth, there are mythical accounts of men born from a male, as in the case of Yü, who was born from his father's corpse, and the Country of Men, whose inhabitants give birth to male children through the center of their body. Another birth motif is the miraculous conception through bathing in a sacred pool, as with Chien Ti and the Country of Women.

Mythologists posit several theories for the multiplicity of miraculous birth in myth narratives. Certainly, the major factor would seem to be gender competition in accounts of the founding of a people, a family line, a cult, or a dynasty (Doty 1986, 126). Another factor is Raglan's hero pattern, in which the hero possesses several attributes, such as divine birth, survival of exposure as an infant, and the aid of the natural or supernatural worlds (Puhvel 1987, 162, citing Raglan 1937). The mythologem of miraculous birth has also attracted the attention of Freudian theorists, such as Otto Rank, who argued that these accounts often represent the hero's revolt against his father's domination, or the hero's revenge and retaliation against his parents (Rank 1909 as cited in Doty 1986, 144). The mythic narratives in this chapter cover a wide range of variants in motif, which often find parallels in mythologies worldwide.

Ti K'u

There are many radical differences between gods of Indo-European and Chinese mythologies, but none is so striking as in the matter of divine sexuality. Gods of the Indo-European tradition, such as the sky god, Zeus, had innumerable loves and children, and this love was not of the decorous kind pictured in late Western classical art but a savage lust inspired by demonic energy. The loves of Zeus are exemplified by his desire for Europa, whom he captivated and carried away by approaching her from the sea in the shape of a mild and playful bull; similar was his desire for Leda, whom he approached in the shape of a swan. By Zeus, Europa and Leda had Minos, Rhadamanthys, Sarpedon, Helen, and Polydeuces. By contrast, the gods of the Chinese tradition, such as Ti K'u, were less fortunate. Ti K'u was husband to two goddesses who bore two sons by virgin birth. Ti K'u is a significant figure in myth because of his role as husband of the goddess Chien Ti, who bore Ch'i, or Hsieh, the founder of the Shang people, and also as husband of the goddess Chiang Yuan, who bore Hou Chi, founder of the Chou people. Both births were by miraculous conception, not through Ti K'u. Thus Ti K'u is connected, if not paternally, then by affiliation, to the founding myths of the first two historically verifiable dynasties of China.

The first of the following readings is from the reconstructed fragments of *The Genealogical Records of Emperors and Kings* by Huang-fu Mi (A.D. 215–282). This Chin dynasty author was the transmitter and reformulator of late myths and legends about primeval deities. As his title indicates, he created "official" biographies of the gods, supplying details of forebears, circumstances of birth, marriage, and offspring. Most of his material is of late mythographic vintage and cannot be corroborated by the early texts. It serves, however, as a fine example of the fashion for mythopoeia in post-Han intellectual circles.

The second reading is from the late Chou *Annals of Master Lü*. It purports to be an account of the origin of "Northern Music." The figures in the pretty drama are the major protagonists in the third reading, which is an account of the founder of the Shang people from the *Historical Records* of Ssu-ma Ch'ien. Several mythic motifs come into play here: music and a feast are often associated with love and nuptials; God is referred to as Ti; a bird, which is a swallow in the first version, a black bird in the second; the divine egg miraculously fertilized; the act of bathing, which often denotes regeneration or fertilization; the son who becomes a hero and brings order and peace to the world; the son born by parthenogenesis.

Attention has been drawn frequently to the unique demythologizing and humanizing style of *The Classic of History*, which, it will be recalled, begins in time with Yao. The account in *Historical Records*, in the third reading, is based on that in *The Classic of History*, which makes Ch'i or Hsieh a humble minister of the Golden Age ruler Shun and an assistant to Yü in controlling the flood, who is rewarded with the Shang fiefdom by Shun. The "five social relationships" are those between ruler and minister, father and son, older brother and younger brother, husband and wife, and friend and friend.

> When Ti K'u was born, there was a divine miracle. He uttered his own name, "Ch'ün." (*Ti wang shih-chi*, TSCC 3701.8)

> The Yu-Sung clan had two glamorous daughters. They built a nine-story tower for them. When they ate and drank, drum music was always played for them. God ordered a swallow to go and look at them, and it sang with a cry like "Yee-yee!" The two daughters fell in love with it and each tried to be the one to catch it. They covered it with a jade box. After a moment they opened it up and looked at it. The swallow had laid two eggs. It flew away to the north and never came back. The two daughters composed a song, a line of which went, "Swallow, Swallow, you flew away!" This is, in fact, the first composition in the style of Northern Music. (*Lü-shih ch'un-ch'iu, Yin ch'u*, SPTK 6.6b)

Yin Hsieh's mother was called Chien Ti. She was the daughter of the Yu-Sung clan and the second concubine of Ti K'u. Three of them went to bathe. They saw a black bird drop its egg. Chien Ti picked it up and swallowed it. Then she became pregnant and gave birth to Ch'i. Ch'i grew up and gave meritorious service in helping Yü control the floodwater. Emperor Shun therefore gave this command to Ch'i: "The people do not have close family relationships, and the five social relationships are in disorder. You will serve as my director of retinue." He gave him the Shang fiefdom and conferred on him the surname Tzu-shih. Hsieh flourished in the reigns of Yao T'ang, Yü Shun, and Yü the Great. His accomplishments were well known among the people, and so the people became peaceable. (*Shih chi, Yin pen chi,* SPPY 3.1a–b)

Chiang Yuan Gives Birth to Hou Chi

The earliest accounts of the virgin birth of Hou Chi occur in lines from two hymns in *The Classic of Poetry*, for which the latest date of compilation is circa 600 B.C. Poem 245, "She Who First Gave Birth to Our People," and poem 300, "The Sealed Palace," relate the myth in slightly differing versions. The latter is briefer, poem 300 being a poetic chronology of the Chou noble house of the prince of Lu, said to have been descended from Hou Chi and the founding rulers of the Chou, King Wen and King Wu. Poem 245 gives a fuller version of the myth and focuses more closely on the birth and life of the god Hou Chi. Both of the readings below were discussed in chapter 2, but here only the first half of poem 245, which narrates the birth myth and the three trials of the divinely born infant-hero, is presented (the first reading), as is the case in the prose version of the myth by Ssu-ma Ch'ien (the second reading).

It is worth enumerating the mythic motifs in these accounts: the ancestry of Chiang Yuan, her relation to the god Ti K'u, her erotic experience in the fields (in the prose version), the fertility motif of God's footprint, the miraculous birth without pain or injury, the three trials of the child god, signs of the protective presence of God in the people living close to nature and in the creatures of nature, and the mythic name Ch'i, the Abandoned.

It is always rewarding to compare two versions of a myth, whether they are of the same date or, as in this case, separated by five hundred years. Ssu-ma Ch'ien clearly rationalizes the mythic narrative of poem

245, on which he must have based his own account, and inserts explanatory data, such as names and Chiang Yuan's motivation for infanticide, but the historian excludes the fertility rite and Chiang Yuan's barrenness and the inauguration of the new temple rite to Hou Chi with its paean of praise to the glorious line of the Chou. With the advent of the Han empire, the mythic account, told by the court historian, has shifted away from a belief in the divine descent of the god Hou Chi and his people, the Chou, to a historicizing and humanizing biographical mode that subverts the mythic themes.

> She who first gave birth to our people
> Was Chiang Yuan.
> And how did she give birth to our people?
> She performed the Yin and Ssu sacrifices well
> So that she might not be without child.
> She trod in the big toe of God's footprint
> And was filled with joy and was enriched;
> She felt a movement and it soon came to pass
> That she gave birth and suckled
> The one who was Hou Chi.
>
> She fulfilled her due months
> And her firstborn came forth,
> With no rending or tearing,
> Without injury or harm.
> And this revealed the miraculous,
> For did not God give her an easy birth,
> Was he not well pleased with her sacrifice?
> And so she bore her child with comfort.
>
> She laid it in a narrow alley
> But ox and sheep suckled it.
> She laid it in a wood on the plain
> But it was found by woodcutters on the plain.
> She laid it on chill ice
> But birds covered it with their wings.
> Then the birds went away
> And Hou Chi wailed,
> Really loud and strong;
> The sound was truly great.

Then he crawled in truth;
He straddled and strode upright
To look for food for his mouth.
He planted large beans,
And the large beans grew thick on the vine;
His ears of grain were heavy, heavy,
His hemp and wheat grew thick;
The gourd stems were laden with fruit.
(*Shih ching*, 245, *Sheng min*, SPPY 17.1.1a–7a)

Hou Chi of the Chou was named Ch'i, the Abandoned. His mother, the daughter of the Yu-t'ai clan, was called Chiang Yuan. Chiang Yuan was Ti K'u's first consort. Chiang Yuan went out to the wild fields and she saw the footprints of a giant. Her heart was full of joy and pleasure, and she felt the desire to tread in the footprints. As she trod in them there was a movement in her body as if she were with child. She went on until her due time and gave birth to a baby boy. Because she thought he was unlucky, she abandoned him in a narrow alley. All the horses and cattle that passed by avoided treading on him. She moved him into woods, but she happened to meet too many people in the mountain woods. She moved him away and abandoned him on the ice of a ditch, but flying birds protected him with their wings and cushioned him. Chiang Yuan thought he might be a god, so she took him up at once and brought him up until he was fully grown. Because she had wanted to abandon him at first, his name was Ch'i. (*Shih chi, Chou pen chi*, SPPY 4.1a–b)

P'an Hu

The god Ti K'u, known by his other name, Kao Hsin, also features in the P'an Hu dog myth, and again he plays no biological role in the account of a miraculous birth. The theme of barrenness recurs in this narrative, this time in the person of a woman beyond childbearing age, "an old wife" of Ti K'u or Kao Hsin. The myth is preserved in the form of a folk tale, one of a collection compiled by Kan Pao in the fourth century A.D. Shorn of its fictional elements, the kernel is basically an etiological myth, that is, it relates the founding of a new people and a new social order. The dog myth contains two covert taboos: bestiality (copulation between a human and an animal) and sibling incest. Derk Bodde agrees with Wolfram Eberhard that this account constitutes an ancestral myth of the Miao and Yao tribes of South China (Bodde 1961, 383; Eberhard 1968, 44–46). It should be noted that although the names of the mythical P'an Hu and the cosmological demigod P'an Ku are phonetically similar, and although both myths appear to derive from South China, there is no connection between the two in terms of substance, motif, or meaning.

Kao Hsin had an old wife who lived in the royal palace. She developed an earache. After some time the doctor cleared her ear out to cure her and he removed a knob-worm as big as a cocoon. After the wife had gone out, she put it in a gourd basket and covered it with a plate. Soon the knob-worm changed into a dog and it had five-color markings. So it was named P'an Hu, Plate-Gourd, and she looked after it.

At the time the Jung-wu were powerful and successful and frequently invaded the border region. So he [Kao Hsin] dispatched generals to attack and quell the invasion but they could not capture or defeat them [the invaders]. So [Kao Hsin] issued a proclamation that if anyone in the world could capture the head of the commander in chief of the Jung-wu, he would be rewarded with a thousand catties of gold and would have the fiefdom of ten thousand households, and he would have the hand of his own daughter in marriage. Some time later, P'an Hu carried in his jaws a head he had captured and he carried it to the tower of the royal palace. The king examined it, and it turned out to be the very head of the commander of the Jung-wu. What was to be done about it? His courtiers all said, "Plate-Gourd is an animal, so he cannot have an official rank or a wife. He should not have the reward, even though he deserves it." His youngest daughter heard them and entreated the king, saying: "Your Majesty did promise me to him before the whole world! Plate-Gourd came with the head in his jaws and saved your kingdom from disaster. This was decreed by Heaven. How can it just be due to the wisdom and power of a dog? The king must weigh his words carefully; the chief earls must attach importance to their good faith. You cannot cancel an agreement that was pledged before the whole world just because of a girl's body—that would mean catastrophe for your kingdom." The king became alarmed and agreed with what she said. He ordered his youngest daughter to be a dutiful wife to Plate-Gourd.

Plate-Gourd led the girl up South Mountain. The grass and trees were thick and bushy and there was no trace of human footprints.

Then the girl took her clothes off and became bonded to him as his servant, wearing clothes that she made as best she could, and she followed Plate-Gourd up the mountain. (*Sou shen chi,* TSCC 14.91)

Po Yi

The mythical figure of Po Yi, and his numerous namesakes, was discussed in chapter 2 with a special emphasis on his culture-bearing function of domesticating birds and beasts. Here he is examined in his role as the hero descended from a god through virgin birth in the generation of his grandmother, Nü-hsiu. The myth of this miraculous birth bears a strong resemblance to the myth of Chien Ti, consort of Ti K'u, mother of Hsieh (or Ch'i), the founder of the Shang people. The motif of ornithomorphous hierogamy had become a convention in Han biographies of gods, demigods, and heroes. Both of the accounts of Chien Ti and Nü-hsiu swallowing a divine egg and becoming pregnant come from the pen of Ssu-ma Ch'ien and have to be considered late mythological versions. The Han historian's tendency to rationalize and make consistent the protean stuff of myth is also evident in his fusion of two mythical Po Yi figures, one being the ancestor of the Ch'in people, the other a minister of Shun responsible for forestry and animal husbandry. As Karlgren noted, "it would seem that Si-ma [Ch'ien] has confused two different sets of legends. . . . But there is, as we have seen, not the slightest support for all this in the pre-Han sources" (1946, 260, 261). In this version of the myth, Po Yi's name was originally Ta Fei, and this itself suggests that yet another fusion of mythical figures may have occurred.

> The ancestor of the Ch'in people was a descendant of the god Chuan Hsü. His granddaughter was called Nü-hsiu. When Nü-hsiu was weaving, a black bird dropped an egg. Nü-hsiu swallowed it and gave birth to Ta Yeh. Ta Yeh took the daughter of the Shao-tien as his wife, and her name was Nü-hua. Nü-hua gave birth to Ta Fei, who controlled the inundated earth with Yü. Once he had completed his work . . . he aided Shun in taming birds and beasts. (*Shih chi, Ch'in pen chi,* SPPY 5.1a–b)

Kun and Yü

The myths of Kun and Yü were related in chapter 3, with a focus on their function of saving the world from disaster. This chapter deals with the miracle of Yü's birth. Unlike other birth myths, in that of Yü's birth no female plays a role, and even female products, such as an egg, are absent. The birth of Yü is entirely a masculine event; he has no mother and he is born from the corpse of his executed father. The myth relates that his father, Kun, was executed for the theft of the self-renewing soil from God. From his unpromising beginning as the child of an executed criminal, Yü becomes a hero recognized and favored by God, who allows him to use his stolen gift to control the flood. Both of the readings of this myth exemplify the authentic narrative style of archaic myth. The first is from "Questions of Heaven," the second from *The Classic of Mountains and Seas,* circa the first century A.D. There is little or no logical explanation in these accounts and no sentiment, but there are the elements of savage action, abrupt accounts of metamorphoses, and an ending that resolves the conflict among Kun, God, and humankind.

There are several different versions of Kun's death in the late Chou texts. *Discourses of the States* and *Chronicle of Tso* relate that he turned into a bear, as does "Questions of Heaven." Other versions state that he became a dragon or turtle. A separate passage in the *Chronicle of Tso* recounts that Yao was the executioner, and another version that it was Shun.

If [Kun] completed his tasks as it was willed, why did God punish him? He lay exposed on Feather Mountain for a long time, but why did he not decompose for three years? Lord Yü issued from Kun's belly. How did he metamorphose? (*Ch'u Tz'u, T'ien wen,* SPTK 3.6a–b)

Floodwater dashed up against the skies. Kun stole God's self-renewing soil in order to dam the floodwater, but he did not wait for God's official permission. God ordered Chu Yung to kill Kun on the approaches to Feather Mountain. Yü was born from Kun's belly. So in the end, God issued a command allowing Yü to spread out the self-replacing soil so as to quell the floods in the Nine Provinces. (*Shan hai ching, Hai nei ching,* SPPY 18.8b–9a)

Yü, the T'u-shan Girl, and Ch'i

The account of the birth of Yü's son, Ch'i, is similarly archaic in form and content. The laconic narrative contains several motifs that have resonances with other myths of deities and heroes. Yü's metamorphosis into a bear links him with his father's dead spirit (in that version of the Kun myth which relates that Kun's corpse turned into a bear). The motif of food and drum music connect this myth with the narrative of Chien Ti, marking the Yü episode as his nuptial feast with the woman who was to bear his son. His son is conceived by an error, when Yü makes a sound like a drumbeat as his feet pound a stone in rhythmic ecstasy before his marriage. It is worth noting that ancient Chinese drums were made of stone, among other materials. The second metamorphosis in the narrative when T'u-shan girl turns into a stone links the birth of Ch'i to music and connects it to the myth of Ch'i (known as K'ai) receiving the gift of music from God. Other motifs are the godlike command of Yü that his son be brought forth from his mother's stone womb, and the miraculous splitting of the stone mother to reveal the child god. There is also the linked motif of Yü's error of pounding the stone and his later lameness, called "the Yü walk."

The source of this myth is significant for mythography. It is said by the T'ang classical scholar and commentator Yen Shih-ku (A.D. 581–645) to be a reference he located in a text from *Huai-nan Tzu*, compiled circa 139 B.C. That text, however, does not appear in the extant editions of *Huai-nan Tzu*. The only reference the latter makes to the Yü/Ch'i myth is: "Yü was born of a stone." Embroidered versions of the metamorphosis of the T'u-shan girl into stone begin to appear in the writings of Han commentators such as Kao Yu (third century A.D.), and Ying Shao (second century A.D.). The fourth-century commentator of *The Classic of Mountains and Seas,* Kuo P'u, however, specifies that the mother of Ch'i (K'ai) metamorphosed into stone and gave birth to Ch'i on the mountain (Mathieu 1989, 125). Thus the tradition of Ch'i's miraculous birth is confirmed by at least the early fourth century A.D. and probably derives from an earlier tradition.

The question the mythographer and mythologist must decide, therefore, is whether to reject the text of the myth supplied by Yen Shih-ku because it does not appear in extant editions of the putative source, or whether to accept it as authentic on the assumption that Yen was citing an edition of *Huai-nan Tzu* which is no longer extant but was available to him in the early T'ang dynasty. It will be recalled that most extant editions of the classics were fixed in orthodox versions in the Sung dynasty, four centuries after Yen. Karlgren concluded in "Legends and Cults in Ancient China" that because Yen appears only to refer to the text in question rather than citing it verbatim, and because Han and post-Han commentators in general fail to cite the passage, it must be rejected as a valid mythic text of the late second century B.C. (1946, 310). On the other hand, Wolfram Eberhard, in his critical review of Karlgren's methodology in that article, countered Karlgren's rejection of the Yen Shih-ku passage with this general principle of mythographic methodology: "All Ethnologists and Sociologists accept the fact that a myth, a custom or a cult reported earlier than a second myth, custom or cult, must not be *a priori* older or more primitive than the second; otherwise no Ethnology would be possible! A myth reported only in a later text, may very well represent a form, reflecting quite an early state of development" (1946, 360). Additional support for Yen's text of the myth resides in its intrinsic style: its syntax is archaic, it lacks consecutive narrative links, it is laconic, and it lacks the explanatory material typical of later narratives. Of course, the text could be a forgery of the early T'ang era, but stylistically it is quite different from the T'ang mode of narrative.

When Yü was controlling the floodwaters and was making a passage through Mount Huan-yuan, he changed into a bear. He spoke to the T'u-shan girl: "If you want to give me some food, when you hear the sound of a drumbeat, come to me." But Yü leaped on a stone and by mistake drummed on it. The T'u-shan girl came forward, but when she saw Yü in the guise of a bear she was ashamed and fled. She reached the foothills of Mount Sung-kao, when she turned into a stone and gave birth to Ch'i. Yü said, "Give me back my son!" The stone then split open on its north flank and Ch'i was born. (Yen Shih-ku's commentary on *Han shu, Wu-ti chi*, referring to a nonexistent passage in *Huai-nan Tzu*, SPPY 6.17b–18a)

Ti Chün and His Wives

The god Ti Chün is a shadowy figure. He is linked to solar and lunar myths of the birth of the ten suns and the birth of the twelve moons through his two consorts, Hsi-Ho and Ch'ang-hsi (first and second readings). As in the case of Ti K'u, these myths appear to recount virgin births. Ti Chün, in his function of the god who came down to his two altars on earth, is also linked (third reading) to the ornitholog-

ical myth of the bird of paradise called Hsiang-ch'i-sha, translated by
Mathieu as birds that throw back sand facing each other (1983, 1:541, 542
n. 3). (The fourth reading explains the names of these birds of paradise.)
The god is also linked to solar myth through Yi the Archer, for it was
Ti Chün who gave Yi the vermilion bow and plain arrows to shoot
down the ten suns. Yuan K'o notes that in the great repository of classical myth, *The Classic of Mountains and Seas*, Ti Chün is one of the
supreme gods, but in the evolution of myths he became a faded deity.
Since this *Classic* is the only early text to mention the deity Ti Chün,
and then only in fragments, it constitutes a valuable document for this
mythical figure (Yuan K'o 1980.2, 107). Ti Chün is also made famous
through his descendants, who, according to the same *Classic*, founded
various countries and brought the gift of culture to these regions. The
fifth reading mentions a local site named after the god. Some examples
of these were presented at the end of chapter 2. It would seem that Ti
Chün and his descendants belong to a quite separate mythological tradition, perhaps reflecting regional variation and cultural differentiation
at the time of the compilation of the chapters of the *Classic* which preserve the mythic narratives, that is, circa the first century A.D.

The five readings that follow are from these later chapters of *The
Classic of Mountains and Seas*. In the first passage the figure of Hsi-Ho
appears. She was discussed in chapter 1 as a goddess connected with the
etiological myth of sunrise and sunset. Several traditions prevail in
respect of the identity and the gender of the deity. *The Classic of History*,
for example, presents Hsi-Ho as one person, a male who was astronomer and cult master in charge of the calendar and solar divination.
Other texts, following *Major Tradition of the "Ancient History,"* present
Hsi and Ho as two males, the eldest brothers of two families who were
astronomical cult masters. A third tradition, deriving from *Songs of
Ch'u* (*Li sao* and "Questions of Heaven"), refers to Hsi-Ho in the singular as the charioteer of the sun, without specifying the gender. The
Huai-nan Tzu indicates that the charioteer of the sun is female, without
naming her. A fifth tradition, which has its source in *The Classic of
Mountains and Seas*, narrates that Hsi-Ho is the mother of the ten suns,
who looks after them following their day's journey through the sky,
and that she is the consort of Ti Chün.

The mythical figure of Ch'ang-hsi is as shadowy as Ti Chün. Two
traditions exist: (1) Ch'ang-hsi is identified as the male Shang Yi, astronomer and cult master who divined by the moon, according to *Annals of
Master Lü;* (2) Ch'ang-hsi is identified in *The Classic of Mountains and Seas*

(the second reading) as the mother of the twelve moons, who cares for them after their passage across the nocturnal world, and she is the consort of the god Ti Chün. Yet the identification of the two mythical figures as male court astronomers bears the hallmark of the historicizing impulse of texts like *The Classic of History* and has little to do with mythology. The number of the suns and moons engendered by Hsi-Ho and Ch'ang-hsi corresponds to the ten days of the week in antiquity and the twelve months of the year.

If the myths of Hsi-Ho and Ch'ang-hsi are removed from their Chinese context and compared with other mythologies, the goddess Hsi-Ho finds no counterpart among Hellenic or Roman gods of the sun Helios, Apollo, Phaeton, or Sol, but she does find an echo in the sun goddess of Japan, Amaterasu, though this goddess is authenticated only by late texts in the Japanese tradition. Ch'ang-hsi, on the other hand, has many female counterparts in the moon goddesses Phoebe, Diana, and Luna.

> Beyond the southeast sea, around Kan River there is the kingdom of Hsi-Ho. There is a girl named Hsi-Ho. She is just now bathing the suns in Kan Gulf. Hsi-Ho is Ti Chün's wife. She gave birth to the ten suns. (*Shan hai ching, Ta huang nan ching,* SPPY 15.5a)

> There is a girl. She is just bathing the moons. Ti Chün's wife, Ch'ang-hsi, gave birth to the twelve moons. She is just beginning to bathe them. (*Shan hai ching, Ta huang hsi ching,* SPPY 16.5a)

> Among the five-colored birds there is the Spit-the-Other-with-Sand, which made only Ti Chün a friend out of all those on earth below. This brilliantly plumaged bird presides over the emperor's two altars on earth. (*Shan hai ching, Ta huang tung ching,* SPPY 14.5b)

> Birds of five colors have three names: one is Huang Niao [Divine Bird], one is Luan Niao [Luan Bird], and one is Feng Niao [Phoenix Bird]. (*Shan hai ching, Ta huang hsi ching,* SPPY 16.2b)

> [Wei-] ch'iu is three hundred leagues in circumference. South of this mound is Ti Chün's bamboo grove. The bamboos are so big that each could be made into a boat. (*Shan hai ching, Ta huang pei ching,* SPPY 17.1a)

King Yen of Hsu

King Yen is a shadowy mythical figure who is said to have ruled in the Chou era, in the tenth century B.C. according to one tradition, in the seventh century B.C. according to another. The name of his kingdom, Hsu, was the name of one of the mythical provinces demarcated by Yü the Great which was traditionally located in the modern region of Shantung. The text of the reading, however, appears to place his kingdom in the Yangtze region. Eberhard more specifically situated the kingdom of Hsu in Hsu-chou, northern Kiangsu province (1968, 411). Yen's reign was characterized by remarkable political success, so the myth records, so that he attracted the enmity of the Chou ruler, who was overlord of a loose federation of states or kingdoms (*kuo*), including Hsu, and the southern kingdom of Ch'u, which was sent to vanquish Hsu.

The first reading is from *The Treatise on Research into Nature,* dating between the third and fifth century A.D. and was no doubt in part based on much earlier texts, such as *Shih Tzu* (fourth century B.C.) and *Hsun Tzu* (third century B.C.), which are the third and second readings below. The narrative in the *Treatise* contains several mythic themes. King Yen is projected as a hero miraculously born from an egg that was dropped by an elegant palace lady, who abandoned it out of shame; it was later hatched by a poor spinster. The egg motif is here linked to the dog motif, since it is a dog that finds the abandoned egg. The name of the dog, Ku-ts'ang, which means Wild Goose in the Blue Sky, connects the dog ornithologically with the divine egg, a connection with divinity, too, when the dog metamorphoses into a dragon, a creature of the skies. The name of the king's reign, Kung, after the miraculous discovery of a bow (*kung*) and arrow, also has a mythic resonance. King Yen's own name is circumstantial, deriving from his miraculous birth from an egg hatched at bedtime (*yen*). There is a mythic correlation, too, between the dog in this myth and the dog P'an Hu, since both narratives give an account at their close of the foundation of a new people and a new region. Thus the long myth of King Yen of Hsu embodies several major mythic themes: miraculous birth, the life and trials of the hero, mythical names, a divine dog metamorphosed into a dragon, discovery of divine weapons, the mercy and justice of a true leader, and the foundation of a new state.

The annals of King Yen of Hsu say that an attendant in the palace of the ruler of Hsu became pregnant and gave birth to an egg, but because she thought it was unlucky, she abandoned it by the riverside. A woman who lived on her own had a dog called Ku-ts'ang. He was out hunting on the riverside when he found the abandoned egg.

So he put it in his mouth and brought it home. The woman who lived all alone thought it was very strange, so she covered the egg to keep it warm. Later on it hatched and produced a baby boy. The time of its birth was bedtime, and so it was called Yen [Bedtime].

The attendant in the palace of the ruler of Hsu heard about it and went to reclaim him. The child grew up to be merciful and wise and succeeded the ruler of the kingdom of Hsu. Later, when the dog Ku-ts'ang was on the point of death, he grew horns and nine tails and, in fact, turned out to be a yellow dragon. King Yen then buried him. (In the region of Hsu you still today see burial clothes made of dog skin.) When King Yen had established his kingdom, his mercy and justice became well known. He conceived the idea of making a journey by boat to the sovereign state [of Chou], so he cut a watercourse between the states of Ch'en and Tsai. While the canal work was in progress, they found a scarlet bow and a scarlet arrow. He considered this to mean that he had won special favor from Heaven. So he took as the name of his reign Kung [Bow] and proclaimed himself King Yen of Hsu. The nobles of the Yangtze and Huai river areas all submitted to his authority. Thirty-six states in all submitted to him. When the king of Chou heard of this, he dispatched an envoy riding in a four-horse carriage. In one day he reached Ch'u state and ordered Ch'u to attack King Yen. Being a merciful man, King Yen could not bear to harm his people by fighting, and so he was defeated by Ch'u. He fled to P'eng-ch'eng in Wu-yuan district near the east hills. Those of his people who followed him numbered several tens of thousands. Later these hills were named Hsu Hills after him. People erected a stone house on the hilltop for the spirit of the place, and the people worshiped there. (Today it all still exists.) (*Po wu chih, Yi wen,* SPPY 8.3a–b)

In appearance, King Yen of Hsu had eyes that could not look down. (*Hsun Tzu, Fei hsiang,* SPPY 3.2a)

King Yen of Hsu had muscles but he had no bones. . . . King Yen of Hsu loved anything unusual. He dived deep into rivers and caught strange fish, and he went far into the mountains and caught strange animals. He laid many of them out on display in the courtyard. (*Shih Tzu,* SPPY 1.2a, 1.3b)

Yi Yin Is Born of a Hollow Mulberry Tree

Yi Yin is the great hero who aided T'ang the Conqueror in his epic struggle to defeat the last tyrannical ruler of the Hsia and found the Shang. If Yi Yin were an historical figure, his dates would be around 1766 B.C., that is, the traditional date (not historically verified) for the accession of T'ang, the founding king of the Shang. Yi Yin appears in most of the important late Chou texts, such as *Annals of Master Lü, Mo Tzu,* "Questions of Heaven," *Mencius, Hsun Tzu, Shih Tzu,* and elsewhere. In all of these he is portrayed sympathetically as the hero who rose to fame from humble circumstances. *Mencius,* for example, even elevates Yi Yin to the status of the exemplar of the good minister who exiles a "bad ruler" (the son of T'ang the Conqueror), making Yi Yin the archetypal Confucian hero.

The reading that follows is from the *Annals of Master Lü,* of the third century B.C. The narrative establishes the heroic character of Yi Yin from his miraculous birth to the beginning of his illustrious career with T'ang the Conqueror. It explains how Yi Yin acquired his name from Yi River (*yin* means 'chief'), how T'ang obtained Yi Yin's services through a ruse, and how Yi Yin in his initial career delighted his ruler with his superb cooking. It is noteworthy that in the version in *Mencius,* Yi Yin's early job is as a farmer, not as a chef (D. C. Lau 1970, 146). Other fragments of myth exist, however, which relate that Yi Yin was not so much a chef as ceremonial bearer of the sacrificial vessel (*ting*) used for cooking food for the gods (Allan 1981, 92 n. 18). If one probes deeper into this motif, it is possible to surmise that Yi Yin's specialized ritual knowledge brought him to the attention of T'ang, who sought to endow his rule with authority and legitimacy through proper socio-ritual observance. The motif at once denotes the humble status of Yi Yin and points to a sitiogonic myth.

The passage contains numerous other motifs: an abandoned baby who turns out to be a hero; a flood; a cradle of hollow mulberry; dead wood preserving new life; the mythical significance of mulberry, a world-tree associated with the rising sun; the oracular dream; the divine command not to look back home; punishment for disobeying the command; metamorphosis; the lowly cook as foster parent; the mortar presaging the hero's early career as a cook. Many of these motifs are to be found in hero myths and apocalyptic myths worldwide, such as Moses in the bulrushes and Lot's wife turned to salt, to draw on but one Western source.

The account clearly divides into two sections: the first contains the motifs that herald the coming of the great man; the second deals with a special rite. The mythic first half does not inform this rite; the rite does not enact the myth. The rite essentially has to do with the act of transference as Yi Yin moves from one social order, the Yu Shen, to another, the household of T'ang, the royal house. The rite has nothing to do with Yi personally, for he is said to be "a good man." The text says that this rite "cleansed him of evil," perhaps indicating the presence of a social taboo in respect of Yi Yin's association with another social group or class. Whether such a taboo operates because he will be preparing food for the future king, or for the king's gods, or whether it is because of his strange parentage, or because of his being an outsider is not made clear. The purification rite is considered a necessary stage before embarking on the great task awaiting him in the heroic service of T'ang the Conqueror.

A daughter of the Yu Shen clan was picking mulberry [leaves] when she found a baby in a hollow mulberry tree. She presented it to her lord. The lord ordered his cook to bring the child up. When he inquired how this had happened, someone said that the baby's mother had lived near Yi River and that after she became pregnant a spirit told her in a dream, "If your mortar bowl leaks water, hurry to the east, but don't look back." Next day she did see her mortar bowl leak water, so she told her neighbors and hurried ten leagues to the east. But she looked back at her city—there was nothing but water. Her body then transformed into a hollow mulberry tree, which is why they called the baby Yi Yin. This is the reason why Yi Yin was born of a hollow mulberry tree. He grew up and became a good man. T'ang the Conqueror heard about him and sent a messenger to ask if the Yu Shen clan would let him have Yi Yin, but the Yu Shen clan refused. Yi Yin, for his part, wanted to serve in the household of T'ang the Conqueror. T'ang therefore asked the Yu Shen for a bride for him to marry. The Yu Shen clan was delighted and they made Yi Yin a guarantor to escort the bride. . . . When T'ang the Conqueror acquired the services of Yi Yin, they cleansed him of evil in the temple: they incensed him with *huan-wei* grass and bound some *wei* plants and set fire to them; they smeared him with the blood of a sacrificial ox and pig. The next day T'ang the Conqueror formally presided at court and gave Yi Yin an audience. He delighted T'ang the Conqueror with tasty dishes cooked to perfection. (*Lü-shih ch'un-ch'iu, Pen wei,* SPTK 14.3b–4a, 14.5a)

6

Myths of
the Yellow
Emperor

The god called the Yellow Emperor played a minor role in the early tradition, but he gradually acquired a complex biography, an elaborate genealogy, and a cycle of folkloristic legends that gave him an exalted status in the divine pantheon. Although later tradition made the Yellow Emperor the supreme deity of the Taoist pantheon, when philosophical Taoism had acquired a more religious coloration and was espoused by imperial rulers, and although traditional histories have presented this god as the pacific culture bearer, the early tradition clearly shows that the Yellow Emperor (Huang Ti) is first and foremost a warrior-god who successfully fought against a series of enemies — the Flame Emperor, Ch'ih Yu the god of war, the Four Emperors, the hero Hsing T'ien, and the one-legged god K'uei, besides many other lesser known mythical figures. When the warrior function of the Yellow Emperor is compared with gods in mythology worldwide, his battles are violent but not frenzied, purposeful but not mindless, pacific in motive but not anarchic in the way that Thōrr, Indra, and Odin are in their warrior function. In addition to his functions as warrior and peacemaker, this god also had the function of culture bearer in later local traditions. For the Han historian Ssu-ma Ch'ien, the Yellow Emperor symbolized the fountainhead of Chinese culture and civilization.

The Battle between the Yellow Emperor and the Flame Emperor

The first two readings, from the early and later tradition, narrate the battle between the Yellow Emperor and his brother, the Flame Emperor, Yen Ti. Each ruled half the world but fought for total supremacy. Georges Dumézil has shown that the concept of dual sovereignty is a major motif in myth and is epitomized in Indo-European mythology by the Indic gods Mitra and Varuna (cited in Littleton 1973, 64–65). In other traditions the contest for total supremacy by brothers is illustrated by the myths of Romulus and Remus and Cain and Abel, in which, like the Flame Emperor, Remus and Abel are killed. As such, the motif of dual supremacy and the motif of fraternal enmity characterize the narrative of the two Chinese gods and fit the paradigm of binary opposition.

A second major motif in the narrative of the hostility between the two brothers is the elemental dualism of fire and water. As Puhvel notes, "Fire and water are archetypally antithetical in the physical world and in human perception alike. In the former their incompatibility is relentless, but in the mind of mythopoeic man it has created its own dialectic of conflict resolution that is reflected in ancient tradition" (1987, 277). By tragic necessity, the antithetical weapon of water controlled by the Yellow Emperor conquers the elemental weapon of fire. The myth is narrated in *Annals of Master Lü* and *Huai-nan Tzu* of the third and second centuries B.C. A variant occurs in the third reading, from *New Documents* (second century B.C.), which says that the weapons were not elemental fire and water but clubs.

The fourth reading is from the *Lieh Tzu*, which is a late text but incorporates early myth material. It probably dates from the fourth century A.D. In this text the image of the all-conquering warrior-god is underscored by his control of the natural world, so that besides the element of water, the god has power over spirits and the most violent of the birds and beasts.

Because the fighting had gone on for a long time, the Yellow Emperor and the Flame Emperor used the elements of water and fire. (*Lü-shih ch'un-ch'iu, Tang ping*, SPTK 7.3a)

Because the Flame Emperor used fire to destroy him, the Yellow Emperor finally captured him. (*Huai-nan Tzu, Ping lueh*, SPPY 15.1b)

The Flame Emperor had the same father and mother as the Yellow Emperor, and he was his younger brother. Each possessed one half of the universe. The Yellow Emperor followed the Way, but the Flame Emperor refused to obey. So they fought on the Waste of Cho-lu. Blood flowed in streams from their clubs. (*Hsin shu*, SPTK 2.3a)

When the Yellow Emperor and the Flame Emperor fought on the Wastes of P'an-ch'üan, all the bears, grizzly bears, wolves, panthers, cougars, and tigers were in his [the Yellow Emperor's] vanguard, while the eagles, fighting pheasants, falcons, and kites served as his banners and flags. (*Lieh Tzu, Huang ti*, SPPY 2.22a)

After three battles, he [the Yellow Emperor] succeeded in fulfilling his ambition. (*Ta Tai Li chi, Wu ti te*, SPTK 7.1b)

Ch'ih Yu Attacks the Yellow Emperor

The next two narratives, both from late chapters of *The Classic of Mountains and Seas* (first century A.D.), deal with the battle between the Yellow Emperor and the god of war, Ch'ih Yu. The name Ch'ih is based on the word for a reptile (*ch'ung*), a flying creature that belongs to air, water, and earth. Besides his other functions as the god of war and inventor of military weapons, Ch'ih Yu is a rain god with power over the Wind God (Feng Po) and the Rain Master (Yü Shih). But the Yellow Emperor has control over superior forces, the Responding Dragon (Ying lung) and Drought Fury, his daughter, who can both afflict the world with severe drought by withholding water and rain.

In one version of this war of the gods, the battlefield is said to be Cho-lu, the same place-name as the arena of the fighting between the Yellow Emperor and the Flame Emperor. Karlgren has shown that certain place-names are mythopoeic in the sense that they are used in several different narratives "simply because they have a *nimbus*, which lends glory to the myth in question" (1946, 210). These are names like Ch'iung-sang or Exhausted Mulberry, Ming-t'iao, and Cho-lu.

The two readings from *The Classic of Mountains and Seas* on the Ch'ih Yu/Yellow Emperor myth demonstrate another mythographic point: that the same source may present different versions of a myth. In the first reading the battle is said to be between Ch'ih Yu and the Yellow Emperor, who is aided by Responding Dragon and Drought Fury. In the second, the executioner is said to be Responding Dragon, and neither the Yellow Emperor nor Drought Fury appears. In this version,

Figure 6. Responding Dragon executes the God of War, Ch'ih Yu, after his battle with the Yellow Emperor. Funerary stone bas-relief, Wu Liang Shrine, Chiahsiang county, Shantung province, A.D. 151. From Feng and Feng, *Research on Stone Carving* (1821) 1934, chap. 3.

Ch'ih Yu is linked with K'ua-fu, who, according to several mythic narratives, was killed because he dared to challenge the power of the sun in a race against time. Paired in this way, Ch'ih Yu and K'ua-fu are gods executed by Responding Dragon for the crime of hubris.

The latter version is a valuable document insofar as it combines aspects of myth and of ritual. The myth of Responding Dragon in his function of drought bringer may be viewed as "the spoken correlative of the acted rite," in this case, the rite of rainmaking.

In the great wilderness there is a mountain called Pu-chü, where rivers and seas flow in. There are the Related Brothers Mountains and there is the Terrace of Kung Kung. Bowmen did not dare to go north of it. There was someone dressed in green clothes named the Yellow Emperor's daughter, Drought Fury. Ch'ih Yu took up arms and attacked the Yellow Emperor, so the Yellow Emperor commanded the Responding Dragon to launch an attack against him in the wilderness of Chi Province. The Responding Dragon stored up all the water. Ch'ih Yu asked the Wind God and the Rain Master to release a cloudburst. Then the Yellow Emperor sent down the Daughter of Heaven named Drought Fury and the rain stopped. Then he killed Ch'ih Yu. (*Shan hai ching, Ta huang pei ching,* SPPY 17.4b–5b)

In the northwest corner of the vast wilderness there is a mountain called Cruel-Plow Earth-Mound. The Responding Dragon lived at its southern boundary. He killed Ch'ih Yu and K'ua-fu. He did not succeed in getting back up to the sky, so there were frequent droughts on earth. But during these droughts someone assumed the guise of the Responding Dragon and so they managed to receive a heavy rainfall. (*Shan hai ching, Ta huang tung ching,* SPPY 14.6a–b)

The Yellow Emperor Captures the K'uei Monster

The warrior god's battle with the god K'uei is also recounted in *The Classic of Mountains and Seas* (in a first-century A.D. chapter): K'uei is a one-legged storm god of mountain and water. He is killed by the Yellow Emperor, who uses his hide as a war drum to bring the world to order through terror. With its typical rationalizing logic, *The Classic of History* historicizes this god as Yao's humanized, and sanitized, master of music, with a magical talent (his vestigial divinity) for making animals dance. This version of the K'uei myth is the subject of a classical joke: when Confucius was asked if "K'uei really only had one foot?" (*K'uei yi tsu*), he avoided the mythological account with the punning reply, "One K'uei was enough!" (*K'uei yi tsu yeh*). The purely mythical, unhistoricized figure of K'uei is, however, attested by an early text that predates *The Classic of Mountains and Seas* and *The Classic of History*. In the *Chuang Tzu,* K'uei is mentioned as a storm god with one leg who lives in the mountains (Watson 1968, 183, 203).

In the eastern seas there is Flowing Waves Mountain. It sticks up seven thousand leagues from the sea. There is a beast on its summit which looks like an ox with a blue body, and it has no horns and only one hoof. When it comes in and out of the water there are severe storms. Its light is like the sun and moon; its voice is like thunder. Its name is K'uei. The Yellow Emperor captured it and used its hide for a drum. When he struck it with a bone from the thunder beast the sound was heard for five hundred leagues, and it made the world stand in awe. (*Shan hai ching, Ta huang tung ching,* SPPY 14.6b)

The Yellow Emperor Conquers the Four Emperors

A further aspect of the Yellow Emperor cycle of myths is his battle with the Four Emperors, which is preserved in *The Myriad Sayings of Master Chiang*, dating from the third century A.D. The mythic text states the ambiguity inherent in a warrior-god who hates war: "He took no pleasure in war or aggression" but who nevertheless goes on "to destroy the Four Emperors." This ambiguity may simply mean that the warrior-god must use destructive force to bring about constructive peace. Yet, when this account is compared with earlier mythic texts from *Huai-nan Tzu, Annals of Master Lü*, and *The Classic of Mountains and Seas* concerning battles with the Flame Emperor and Ch'ih Yu, it is clear that a moralizing element has crept in. Master Chiang, or Chiang Chi, clearly felt that the primeval violence of the Yellow Emperor had to be toned down and explained in palatable terms for the more cultivated society of the Wei dynasty, in which he lived and wrote. By a late tradition, the Four Emperors are T'ai Hao, god of the east, with the emblematic color green; the Flame Emperor, god of the south, with the color scarlet; Shao Hao, god of the west, white; and Chuan Hsu, god of the north, black. If this tradition is to be believed, the Flame Emperor rose again and had to be killed twice.

At the beginning of the Yellow Emperor's era he cared for his own person and loved his people. He took no pleasure in war or aggression. But the Four Emperors each took the name of their regional color and gathered together to plot against him. Each day they threatened him near his city walls, refusing to remove their armor. The Yellow Emperor sighed and said, "If the ruler on high is in danger, the people beneath will be unstable. If the ruler suffers the loss of his kingdom, his officers will 'marry' themselves off to another kingdom. Because of this kind of damage, it is the same as harboring bandits, isn't it? Today I stand at the head of the people, but you four robbers oppose me and cause my army to be on the alert constantly."

Then he moved his army over to the fortified walls in order to destroy the Four Emperors. (*Chiang Tzu wan chi lun, Huang Ti wei ssu tao*, SYTS 1.4a)

The Yellow Emperor Loses the Black Pearl

The *Chuang Tzu*, the earliest verifiable work of philosophical Taoism, is a valuable source of primal myth, but its value is seriously diminished by the practice of its author, Chuang Chou, or Master Chuang, of utilizing myth for the purpose of propounding and illustrating his philosophical beliefs, in so doing often distorting those myths. This tendency is exemplified by Chuang Tzu's treatment of the mythical figure of the Yellow Emperor. The only reference to the god as a warrior occurs in a negative critique of his battle with Ch'ih Yu (Watson 1968, 327). Most of the other references to the Yellow Emperor in *Chuang Tzu* are ambiguous or negative, since he casts him in the role of a lesser god and as a demythologized figure who subserviently seeks the Truth from wiser Taoists or innocents (ibid., 119, 266). Therefore, while Chuang Tzu subverts the classical mythological tradition for polemical and satirical purposes, he embarks on a new mythopoeic course, creating his own myths.

The first reading on the myth of the Yellow Emperor's black pearl is a prime example of this mythopoeia. In it the philosopher argues that knowledge, sensory excellence, and technical debating skills are the marks of civilized behavior, which has to be learned, whereas inborn nature or instinct, characterized as Shapeless, belongs to a higher order of human existence. The myth of the instinctual versus the civilized has been explored brilliantly by Lévi-Strauss in his analyses of the Bororo myths of Central Brazil, in which he establishes his paradigmatic paradox of *le cru: le cuit* 'the raw: the cooked', or the primitive and civilized (Lévi-Strauss 1970).

The second reading is a variant text of the black pearl myth. It comes from a T'ang source, *Seven Tomes from the Cloudy Shelf*, a Taoist text. The third reading is from a Sung dynasty account of the eleventh century A.D.

The Yellow Emperor was traveling north of Scarlet River. He climbed up the Mound of K'un-lun and gazed south. On his way back he dropped his black pearl. He told Chih [Knowledge] to look for it, but he could not find it. He told Ch'ih Kou [Wrangling Debate] to look for it, but he could not find it. So he told Hsiang-kang [Shape-less] to do so, and Hsiang-kang found it. The Yellow Emperor said, "That's amazing! How was Hsiang-kang the one who was able to find it?" (*Chuang Tzu, T'ien-ti,* SPPY 5.2b–3a)

He [the Yellow Emperor] made Kang-hsiang search for it and he found it. Later, because the daughter of the Meng clan, the Lady Chi-hsiang, stole the black pearl, he [Kang-hsiang] drowned in the sea and became a god. (*Yün chi ch'i ch'ien, Hsien-yüan pen chi,* SPTK 100.23a)

According to ancient history, when the daughter of Chen Meng's clan stole the Yellow Emperor's primeval pearl, he sank into the river and drowned. He changed into the god of this place. Today he is the god of the River Tu-miao. (Chang T'ang-ying's commentary on *Shu t'ao wu,* HH 1.9b)

The Yellow Emperor Questions the Dark Lady on the Art of War

The last reading is a fragment from the fourth to the fifth century preserved in a Sung dynasty encyclopedia. The narrative underscores the Yellow Emperor's function as a warrior god, but it demythologizes the god by making him subservient to a newly invented Taoist god-dess. To borrow Puhvel's phrase, the Dark Lady is "a latter-day mani-pulative invention," designed to enhance the new deity of the post-Han neo-Taoist pantheon.

The Yellow Emperor and Ch'ih Yu fought nine times, but for nine times there was no winner. The Yellow Emperor returned to T'ai Mountain for three days and three nights. It was foggy and dim. There was a woman with a human head and bird's body. The Yellow Emperor kowtowed, bowed twice, and prostrated himself, not dar-ing to stand up. The woman said, "I am the Dark Lady. What do you want to ask me about?" The Yellow Emperor said, "Your humble ser-vant wishes to question you about the myriad attacks, the myriad victories." Then he received the art of war from her. (*T'ai-p'ing yü-lan,* citing *Huang Ti wen Hsüan nü chan fa,* SPTK 15.9b)

7

Myths of
Yi the Archer

In the late Chou period several traditions were established concerning the mythical figure of Yi, and in the Han and post-Han periods Yi attracted different mythical accounts, many of which incorporate other figures. Yi is variously known as the East Barbarian, Yi the Good, Lord Yi, and Yi, Lord of the Hsia. The East Barbarians (Yi) are identified as the proto-Yueh people of Southeast China. The ethnographer Wolfram Eberhard linked the main solar myth of Yi the Archer with the Yao people of South China (1968, 86). Given the wealth of material in the Yi cycle of myths, it is not surprising to find numerous inconsistencies and contradictions in these traditions. For example, the classical texts set the deeds of Yi in the era of Ti Chün prior to the Golden Age of Yao, Shun, and Yü, but some texts also place him in the era of Yao. Furthermore, the greatest act in the whole of the Yi cycle of myths, averting solar disaster, is also attributed to Yao, for example, in *Disquisitions* by Wang Ch'ung of the first century A.D. (Huang Hui 1938, II.511).

Moreover, so ambiguously are Yi's exploits recounted that he is precariously poised between the archetypal and antithetical roles of heroic savior and criminal villain. In his eufunctional role of saving the world from the ten suns at the command of Ti Chün, Yi is favored by the god, and in other versions by Yao. In his negative manifestation, Yi is depicted as a murderer, adulterer, and usurper. In this dysfunctional role, he falls from grace with the gods, but, more important, he loses the good will and trust of human beings. Although the functional ambiguity of Yi is clearly and frequently expressed in the early texts, exegetes and commentators of the late Han and post-Han eras invariably sympathized with him and identified him as a positive hero. Thus commentators such as Wang Yi (A.D. 89–158), Kao Yu (fl. A.D. 205–215), and Ju Ch'un (fl. A.D. 198–265) explain away and rationalize Yi's actions and even go as far as to condone his crimes. In the literary mind and in popular imagination, the mythical figure of Yi remains Yi the hero and savior rather than Yi the antihero and usurper.

Yi Shoots the Ten Suns to Avert Disaster

The first and second readings relate the solar myth of Yi the Archer. The first is from a late chapter of *The Classic of Mountains and Seas*, dating from the first century A.D. The second, from *Huai-nan Tzu* (second century B.C.), elaborates Yi's heroism by relating how he killed six monsters.

> Ti Chün presented Yi with a vermilion bow and plain-colored arrows with silk cords in order that he should bring assistance to the land below. So Yi was the first to bring merciful relief to the world below from all its hardships. (*Shan hai ching, Hai nei ching,* SPPY 18.7b)

> When it came to the era of Yao, the ten suns all rose at once, scorching the sheaves of grain and killing plants and trees, so that the people were without food. And the Cha-yü Dragon-Headed beast, the Chisel-Tusk beast, the Nine-Gullet beast, the Giant-Gale bird, the Feng-hsi wild boar, and the Giant-Head long-snake all plagued the people. So Yao ordered Yi to execute the Chisel-Tusk beast in the wilds of Ch'ou Hua, to slaughter the Nine-Gullet beast near Hsiung River, to shoot down with his corded arrows the Giant-Gale at Ch'ing-ch'iu Marsh. He ordered him to shoot the ten suns up above and to kill the Cha-yü Dragon-Head beast below, to behead the Giant-Head long-snake at Tung-t'ing, and to capture the Feng-hsi wild boar at Mulberry Forest. The myriad people were overjoyed and decided on Yao as their Son of Heaven. And so for the first time in the whole world, there were roads and signposts in the broadlands and in the narrow defiles, in the deep places and on level ground both far and wide. (*Huai-nan Tzu, Pen ching,* SPPY 8.5b–6a)

The Rock of the Nine Suns

The next two readings narrate the Wu Chiao myth. The first is from an early fourth-century A.D. source and points up the remarkable potency of the Yi solar myth. The second reading is from a twelfth-century miscellany. The name Wu Chiao is an oxymoron representing the antagonistic elements of fire and water: Wu is the infinite power and capacity of a divine sea, Chiao is the fabled fiery furness of rock which is where the suns shot down by Yi fell from the sky. The rock of Wu Chiao is thought to be the Kuroshio Current, or else Mount Min in northern Szechwan (Greatrex 1987, 185 n. 10).

> Wei-lü is where the waters of the seas empty out. It is also called Wu Chiao, and it is in the center of the great ocean. The Wei is at the very end of all rivers; that is why it is called Wei [Tail]; *lü* means 'massed'; it is where water masses together, and that is why it is called *lü*. East of Leaning Mulberry there is a rock that is forty thousand leagues all round and forty thousand leagues thick. Although the seas and rivers empty into it, it never fails to consume all the water, and that is why it is called Chiao [Consume]. (Kuo Ch'ing-fan citing Ssu-ma Piao's commentary on *Chuang Tzu*, *Ch'iu shui*, *Chuang Tzu chi shih*, SHCSK 6.2.3b)

> Wu Chiao is east of Pi Sea. It has a rock that stretches forty thousand leagues across, and it is forty thousand leagues thick. It lies at the tail end of all flowing rivers; that is why it is called Wei-lü. According to *The Classic of Mountains and Seas,* in the era of Yao the ten suns all rose at once, so Yao ordered Yi to shoot down nine suns, and they fell onto Wu Chiao. (*Chin hsiu wan hua ku* referring to *Chuang Tzu su,* HHSC 1.5.3b)

Yi Shoots the Lord of the River

The readings that follow narrate the myth of Yi's crimes of murdering the Lord of the River, Ho Po, and appropriating his wife. The first reading below is from "Questions of Heaven." The second and fourth are from Wang Yi's commentary on that text. The third reading is a citation by the famous T'ang commentator Li Shan (d. A.D. 689) of the third-century A.D. commentator Ju Ch'un, who mythopoeically links the goddess of Lo River, Fu-fei, with the god Fu Hsi. The fifth reading, by the third-century A.D. commentator Kao Yu, seeks to condone Yi's murder of the river god by stating that the Lord of the River had himself been killing humans.

The final reading, from *Chronicle of Tso,* deals with the myth of Yi the usurper. In a historicizing mode it removes the hero from the context of gods, suprahumans, and demigods and fixes him firmly among human beings. Here, Yi's crimes are directed not against deities but against the state. Thus Yi the demigod becomes Yi the human opportunist who usurps the Hsia state and embarks on a career of misrule and indulges in a reckless private life. The primary motif of Yi's skill in archery is subordinated to the demands of the humanizing narrative and is transmuted into Yi's excessive fondness for sport at the expense of affairs of state. Yi is consequently made to fit the paradigm of "the bad ruler." Yi's death is similarly narrated without regard for the mythological tradition, since the manner of his political assassination is identical to that of many other victims of palace intrigue recounted in the *Chronicle.*

> God sent down Yi Yi to drive away the evils besetting the Hsia people, so why did he shoot down the Lord of the River and take his wife, Lo-pin? (*Ch'u Tz'u, T'ien wen,* SPTK 3.15b)

> Lo-pin was a water-nymph and she was called Fu-fei. . . . Yi also dreamed that he had an affair with Fu-fei, the Goddess of Lo River. (Wang Yi's commentary on *Ch'u Tz'u, T'ien wen,* SPTK 3.15b)

> Ju Ch'un says that Fu-fei, the daughter of [?Fu] Hsi, died by drowning in Lo River and then she became a goddess. (Li Shan's commentary on *Lo shen fu,* citing *Han shu yin yi, Wen hsuan,* SPTK 19.14b)

> The Lord of the River turned into a white dragon and played on the riverbank. When Yi saw him, he shot him with his arrow, aiming for his left eye. The Lord of the River went up to complain to God in Heaven: "Kill Yi because of what he has done to me!" God in Heaven said, "Why were you shot by Yi?" The Lord of the River said, "When I transformed myself into a white dragon I came out to play." God in Heaven said, "If you had kept to the river depths as a god, how could Yi have committed this crime against you? Today you became a reptile, so you were bound to be shot at by someone. Of course he is in the right—what was Yi's crime in this case?" (Wang Yi's commentary on *Ch'u Tz'u, T'ien wen,* SPTK 3.15b)

> The Lord of the River killed people by drowning them, so Yi shot him in the left eye. (Kao Yu's commentary on *Huai-nan Tzu, Fan lun,* SPPY 13.22a)

Figure 7. Yi the Archer and the world-tree, Leaning Mulberry. Funerary stone bas-relief, Wu Liang Shrine, Chia-hsiang county, Shantung province, A.D. 151. From Feng and Feng, *Research on Stone Carving* (1821) 1934, chap. 3.

The Prince of Chin said, "What happened to Lord Yi?" Wei Chiang replied, "Long ago, when the Hsia was beginning to decline, Lord Yi moved from Ch'u to Ch'iung-shih and, relying on the people of Hsia, replaced the Hsia government. He took advantage of his archery skills, neglecting public affairs and indulging in hunting game in the fields. He discarded the ministers Wu Lo, Po Yin, Hsiung K'un, and Mang Yü, employing instead Cho of Han. Cho of Han was a treacherous young retainer of the house of Po Ming, and the Lord of Po Ming had dismissed him. But Yi Yi trustingly received him into his entourage and appointed him as his prime minister. Cho practiced flattery at court and bribery in society at large. He deceived the people and encouraged Lord Yi to go hunting. He devised a plot to deprive Yi of his state. Society and the court all acquiesced to Cho's command. But Yi still refused to mend his ways. One day, on his return from the hunt, his clansmen all assassinated him, and they cooked his corpse in order to serve it to his sons to eat. But his sons could not bear to eat him, and they were all put to death at Ch'iung-men." (*Tso chuan, Hsiang kung* Fourth Year, SPPY 29.12b–13a)

Feng Meng Kills Yi

This demythologized version of Yi's death contrasts strongly with the accounts of Yi's murder by Feng Meng (also known as Feng Men). These accounts have the authentic ring of myth. They mostly occur in late Chou texts, such as *Hsun Tzu* and *Meng Tzu* (the first and third readings below), and in Han texts, such as *Huai-nan Tzu* (the second reading below). These versions of Yi's death introduce the mythic theme of envy and rivalry in the figure of Feng Meng. It is interesting that when the two champion archers meet in mortal combat, Feng Meng does not use the weapon in which he is inferior but a crude, primeval club.

The motif of peach wood, from which the club is made, is explained by its connection with exorcism. In the *Chronicle of Tso* several accounts of exorcism mention its use (Bodde 1975, 134). The symbolic function of peach wood is clarified by James R. Hightower in his analysis of a Han text by Han Ying (fl. 157 B.C.): "As the word [*t'ao* = peach] is a homophone of 'to expel' [*t'ao*], peach wood was used to expel noxious influences" (Hightower 1952, 337 n. 2). Thus the phonetic interpretation and the mythical context combine to reveal the significance of this motif, and it occurs in the same way in the myth of Saint Shu and Yü Lü and the Giant Peach Tree related in chapter 14.

Yi and Feng Men were the best archers in the world. (*Hsun Tzu, Cheng lun,* SPPY 12.9b)

In archery contests of one hundred shots, the most skilled archers were always Yi and Feng Meng. (*Huai-nan Tzu, Shui lin,* SPPY 17.4a)

Feng Meng learned archery from Yi and acquired an exhaustive knowledge of Yi's style of shooting. He realized that only Yi in the whole world was better than he, so he killed Yi. (*Meng Tzu, Li Lü*, 2, SPTK 8.8b)

"Club" is a large stick, that he [Feng Meng] made out of peach wood to batter Yi to death with. From that time demons are terrified of peach wood. (Hsu Shen's commentary on *Huai-nan Tzu, Ch'üan yen*, SPPY 14.1b)

Yi rid the world of evil, so when he died he became the god Tsung Pu. (*Huai-nan Tzu, Fan lun*, SPPY 13.22a)

Ch'ang O Escapes to the Moon

The myths centering on Yi discussed thus far include several other mythical figures—Ti Chün, Yao, the six monsters, the Lord of the River, Lo-pin, his wife (identified, probably mistakenly as Fu-fei, goddess of Lo River, who in turn is mistakenly identified as Fu Hsi's daughter), God in Heaven, Cho of Han, and Feng Meng. But the best-known myth centers on the figure of Heng O, also known as Ch'ang O, who was Yi's wife. She stole the elixir of immortality given to him by the Queen Mother of the West and she was metamorphosed on the moon. She is not the moon goddess as such but is said to be the "essence of the moon." Her lunar role is parallel in some respects to that of Ch'ang-hsi, the mother of the twelve moons and consort of Ti Chün. Although there is a myth that explains the disappearance of the nine suns, leaving just one, through the heroism of Yi the Archer, no myth exists for the eventual disappearance in myth narratives of the eleven moons to leave one. Michel Soymié has noted that the moon myth in China is not so developed or familiar as that of the sun (1962, 292). The demigod Yi is linked, however, to a major solar myth and a major lunar myth in the classical narratives, just as Ti Chün is through somewhat different narratives.

The earliest account of Heng O/Ch'ang O introduces the motif of a toad, the creature she metamorphosed into on the moon. This motif denotes immortality because of the toad's sloughing off of its skin and its apparent rebirth. The moon, with its phases of growth, decline, and rebirth has the same denotation. These two motifs of the cycle of eternal return have parallels worldwide, as James G. Frazer has shown in "The Story of the Cast Skin" (in "The Fall of Man" [1984, 88–95]). In Han iconography the toad on the moon is often depicted dancing on its hind legs while pounding the drug of immortality in a mortar. This and other lunar motifs in Han iconography have been discussed extensively by Michael Loewe (1979, 53–55, 127–33).

Another worldwide motif that occurs in the Ch'ang O moon myth is the theft of a gift of the gods and the punishment of the thief. This motif has already been discussed with reference to Kun, and also to K'ai, or Ch'i. Ch'ang O, or Heng O, fits this pattern of the trickster in several respects: she stole the gift of the drug of immortality from Yi the Archer, who had received it from the Queen Mother of the West; she metamorphoses into an ugly creature with the saving grace of immortality.

Although her punishment is not specified but only surmised from the context of the myth, the theme of punishment is clearly expressed in the final reading. It concerns another mythical figure on the moon, Wu Kang. The text is from *A Miscellany from Yu-yang* by Tuan Ch'eng-shih (d. A.D. 863). This work contains much early material. It relates the fate of Wu Kang, an alchemist seeking the elixir of immortality, who was punished for making an error against the unseen world of the spirits. He is condemned to chop down a tree on the moon which forever grows again. The repeated action of his punishment is reflected in the name of the tree: *kuei* 'cassia' is a pun for *kuei* 'to return', signifying his eternal return in an eternal act of atonement. The brilliant red of the cassia perhaps mockingly reflects the color of cinnabar, the alchemist's stone. In contrast to the sun, which in some versions has only a single bird in it, the moon is cluttered with mythical figures: Heng O/Ch'ang O, the toad, a hare, the mortar and pestle, Wu Kang and his ax, and the cassia tree. In later iconography, the moon was furnished with a jade tree, a jade palace. and other accouterments denoting neo-Taoist symbolism.

> Yi asked the Queen Mother of the West for the drug of immortality. Yi's wife, Heng O, stole it and escaped to the moon. She was metamorphosed on the moon and became the striped toad Ch'an-ch'u, and she is the essence of the moon. (Subcommentary of *Ch'u hsueh chi*, citing *Huai-nan Tzu*, SPCY 1.4a)

> In those days people said that there was a cassia on the moon and the striped toad, Ch'an-ch'u. That is why books on marvels say that the cassia on the moon is five thousand feet high, and there is someone under it who is always chopping the tree but the gash in the tree soon becomes whole. This man's family name is Wu, and his given name is Kang, and he is from the West River area. They say that because he made a mistake in his quest for immortality, he was exiled and forced to chop the tree. (*Yu-yang tsa-tsu*, *T'ien chih*, SPTK 1.8b)

8

Myths of
Yü the Great

Of all the major primeval figures, including the Yellow Emperor, Yi the Archer, and Yao and Shun, Yü the Great has attracted the most mythological stories and legends. Unlike Yi the Archer, Yü is not an ambiguous figure; he is consistently presented as a beneficent demigod, savior of humankind, and, in some early traditions, the exemplar of the dutiful minister who put public duty before private interests.

It will be apparent from earlier readings and in discussions thus far that there are four flood myths in the Chinese tradition. The first has Kung Kung as its central figure and is narrated in *Kuan Tzu, Kuo yü*, and *Huai-nan Tzu*. In a second flood myth, Nü Kua plays the major role. The third is the Kun flood myth, and the fourth is the Yü myth.

Yü Controls the Flood

Yü is mainly associated with the Kun-Yü tradition of the flood myth which is told in many versions in most of the early texts. The first two readings from the "Questions of Heaven" and *The Classic of Mountains and Seas*, focus on the myth of the orphaned son born by a miracle who carried on the work of his disgraced and executed father. The third reading, from *The Classic of History*, underscores the topographical reconstruction and hydraulic work of the hero as he controls the world flood. In this version, Yü appears not so much a demigod as a human-ized minister of Shun. The fourth reading, from *Shih Tzu,* corroborated in *Chuang Tzu,* chapter 33, gives a graphic account of the physical extremes Yü suffered when delivering the world from the misery of the flood. Yü's heroic labors are the subject of a joke in the *Chronicle of Tso,* when Duke Ting, Prince of Lu quipped in the year 540 B.C., "If it had not been for Yü, we would just be fishes!" (*Chao kung* First Year, Couvreur 1914, 3.19).

If Kun was not fit to control the flood, why was he entrusted with this task? They all said, "Do not fear! Try him and see if he can accom-plish it." . . . Lord Yü issued from Kun's belly. How did he metamor-phose? Yü inherited his legacy and continued the work of his father. Why was his plan different, even though the work was already in progress? How did he dam the flood waters at their deepest? How did he demarcate the Nine Lands of the earth? Over the rivers and seas what did the Responding Dragon achieve, and where did he pass? What plan did Kun devise? What did Yü succeed in doing? (*Ch'u Tz'u, T'ien wen,* SPTK 3.5b–7b)

Floodwater dashed up against the skies. Kun stole God's self-renew-ing soil in order to dam the floodwater, but he did not wait for God's official permission. God ordered Chu Yung to kill Kun on the ap-proaches to Feather Mountain. Yü was born from Kun's belly. So in the end, God issued a command allowing Yü to spread out the self-replacing soil so as to quell the floods in the Nine Provinces. (*Shan hai ching, Hai nei ching,* SPPY 18.8b–9a)

The Nine Provinces were standardized. The four quarters were made habitable. The Nine Mountains were deforested and put down for arable land. The sources of the Nine Rivers were dredged. The Nine Marshes were banked up. The Four Seas had their concourses opened freely. The Six Treasuries were well attended to. All the soils were compared and classified. Their land values and revenues were care-fully controlled. (*Shang shu, Yü kung,* SPPY 6.16b)

In ancient times, Dragon Gate had not been cleft open, Lü-liang had not been bored through, and the river passed above Meng-men, its waters greatly swollen and its current irregular, so that it destroyed all in its path, the hills and high mounds, and this was what was known as the Flood. Yü channeled the river and sluiced off the Great River. For ten years he did not visit his home, and no nails grew on his hands, no hair grew on his shanks. He caught an illness that made his body shrivel in half, so that when he walked he could not lift one leg past the other, and people called it "the Yü walk." (*Shih Tzu*, SPPY 1.16b)

The Signs of Yü's Divine Favor

The many and diverse accounts of Yü are rich in mythic themes. The flood myth, of course, has numerous parallels in traditions worldwide, but the Chinese flood myth is distinctive in the sense that the flood is eventually controlled not by a supreme deity but by a demigod with a nature nearer to the human than the divine. Kun's theft of the miraculous substance from God and the subsequent punishment of the altruistic thief also has parallels, such as Prometheus's theft of fire and Tantalus's theft of the food of the gods. The first reading, from "Questions of Heaven," relates the myth of divinely endowed creatures, such as the Responding Dragon and the turtle, who help Yü by signaling a passage through the floodwater. The second reading, from a fourth-century A.D. text, elaborates this myth. There is also Yü's miraculous birth from the belly of his father's corpse and the birth of his own son from a mother turned to stone, and these miracles mark Yü as the hero favored by God and nature. Yü's metamorphosis into a bear echoes that of his dead father (following one of several versions of Kun's metamorphosis).

> How did he dam the floodwaters at their deepest? How did he demarcate the Nine Lands of the earth? Over the rivers and seas what did the Responding Dragon fully achieve and where did he pass? What plan did Kun devise? What did Yü succeed in doing? (*Ch'u Tz'u, T'ien wen*, SPTK 3.6b–7b)

> Yü exhausted his strength in cutting dikes and ditches and in conducting the courses of rivers and leveling mounds. The yellow dragon dragged its tail in front of him, while the dark tortoise carried green mud on its back behind him. (*Shih yi chi*, HWTS 2.2b)

Yü's Function as Warrior

A further image emerges from the narratives of Yü the warrior in his punishment of Fang-feng, Kung Kung, Hsiang Liu, and the Wu-chih-ch'i beast. In this punitive aspect, his function of warrior-god most nearly coincides with the warrior function of the Yellow Emperor. The chastisement of the god Fang-feng is linked to the story of the first assembly of the gods, told in the first reading, from a first-century A.D. text. The second reading, from a late Chou era text circa the fifth century B.C., purports to cite Confucius's (551–479 B.C.) explanation of the Fang-feng myth. According to this account, the god must have been a giant.

The third reading, from a second-century B.C. text, recounts how Kung Kung caused an inundation that disturbed the cosmos. The fourth reading, from a philosophical work of the Confucian school dating from the third century B.C., tells briefly how Yü punished the marplot Kung Kung to save the people.

The fifth reading is linked to the myth of Yü's punishment of Kung Kung. The account, from a second-century B.C. chapter of *The Classic of Mountains and Seas,* states that the poisonous monster Hsiang Liu was Kung Kung's official. The execution of this nine-headed, serpentine monster is one of the tasks of Yü in the concatenation of stories in the myth of Yü and the flood.

The sixth reading illustrating the warrior function of the demigod Yü is notable more for its literariness than for its mythological form. It is from Li Kung-tso's narrative "Prefect Li T'ang." It relates Yü's struggle with the Wu-chih-ch'i beast in his effort to control the flood. It is the first written occurrence of this legend. Probably based on the classical myth of K'uei, the one-legged storm god, it constitutes an interesting example of fiction based on myth, which itself inspired numerous pieces of mythopoeic literature. The Yuan dynasty dramatist Wu Chang-ling, for example, cast Wu-chih-ch'i in the role of the sister of the legendary character of the Monkey King, whereas the Ming novelist Wu Ch'eng-en (ca. 1506–ca. 1582), converted Wu-chih-ch'i into Monkey, Sun Wu-k'ung (Lu Hsün 1964, 109–10).

> From the beginning, Yü was so anxious for the people that he rescued them from the flood. He reached Great Yueh. He went up Mao Mountain and held a major assembly [*k'uai-chi*]. He rewarded the virtuous and gave fiefdoms to the meritorious. He changed the name of Mao Mountain to K'uai-chi. (*Yueh chueh shu, Wai chuan chi ti,* SPPY 8.1a)

> Confucius said, "I have heard this said about it. Long ago, Yü assembled all the gods on the Mountain of K'uai-chi. Fang-feng arrived too late. Yü killed him and beheaded his corpse. One joint of his

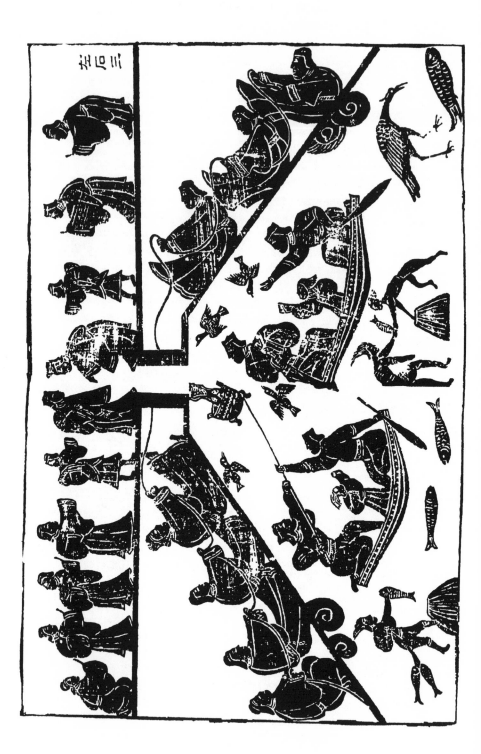

skeleton filled up a whole cart because it was so huge!" (*Kuo yü, Lu yü, 2,* SPTK 5.13b–14a)

In the era of Shun, Kung Kung stirred the floodwater to make crashing waves, so that they rose as far as K'ung-sang [Hollow Mulberry]. (*Huai-nan Tzu, Pen ching,* SPPY 8.6a)

Yü achieved success in his labors. He curbed the inundation and so he rescued the people from disaster, and he exiled Kung Kung. (*Hsun Tzu, Ch'eng hsiang,* SPPY 18.3b)

Kung Kung's official was called Hsiang Liu. He had nine heads, so he ate from nine mountains at the same time. Whatever Hsiang Liu knocked against became marshy or a ravine. Yü killed Hsiang Liu. His blood stank, so that it was impossible to plant the five grains. Yü excavated the area and filled it three times, but it leaked three times. He therefore created out of that place a terrace for the gods north of K'un-lun and east of Jou-li. This Hsiang Liu had nine heads with human faces and a snake's body, and he was green. (*Shan hai ching, Hai wai pei ching,* SPPY 8.1b–2a)

When Yü was controlling the floods, he came to T'ung-po Mountain three times, and each time there were terrifying windstorms and rolling thunder, so that the rocks roared and the trees groaned. The Five Lords [var. The Earth Lord] blocked the rivers and the Old Man of Heaven summoned his army, but to no avail. Yü grew angry and ordered all the spirits to assemble before him, and he entrusted his command to K'uei-lung. T'ung-po and the thousand rulers bowed low and sought his orders. Yü then imprisoned Master Hung-meng, Master Chang-shang, Master Tou-lu, and Master Li-lou. And he hunted down the river god of the Huai and Wo rivers, whose name was Wu-chih-ch'i.

This god was expert in formal rhetoric and could distinguish between the shallows and deeps of the Yangtze and Huai rivers and between the proximity and distances of plains and lowlands. He was shaped like an ape with an upturned snout and a high forehead. He

Figure 8 (opposite). The unsuccessful attempt by the First Ch'in Emperor (r. 221–210 B.C.) to recover one of the nine sacred cauldrons of Yü from the river; a dragon's head appears in the tilting cauldron. Funerary stone bas-relief, Wu Liang Shrine, Chia-hsiang county, Shantung province, A.D. 151. From Feng and Feng, *Research on Stone Carving* (1821) 1934, chap. 4.

had a green body and a white head with metallic eyes and snowy teeth. His neck stretched out for a hundred feet. He was stronger than nine elephants. He lunged out with his fists and leapt about in a sudden frenzied rush, so swift and fast that now you'd hear him, now you wouldn't, now you'd see him, now you wouldn't.

Yü handed him over to T'ung-lü but he could not control him. He handed him over to Wu-mu-yu but he could not control him. He handed him over to Keng-ch'en and he was able to control him. The Ch'ih-p'i and Huan-hu, wood demons and water sprites, mountain trolls and rock monsters rushed forth screaming in a circling mass numbering several thousand. Keng-ch'en chased him with his spear. Then he chained his neck with a huge rope and threaded a metal bell through his nostril, and he banished him to the south of Huai River to the foothills of Tortoise Mountain. So Huai River was able to flow peacefully out to sea for ever more. Afterward, people made images of the monster, and they no longer suffered from the stormy waves of Huai River. (*T'ai-p'ing kuang chi, Li T'ang,* citing *Jung-mo hsien t'an, JMWH* 467.2b)

Yü Measures the Whole World

A theme of special significance in the Chinese mythological tradition concerns mythological geography. Some early accounts of Yü's divinely inspired flood control work throughout the area first demarcated by him as the Nine Provinces constitute the beginning of Chinese geography. The term, *geography,* in its basic meaning of the delineation of the land or the earth, may be said to form the substance of such accounts. The earliest texts on water control and on cartography occur in two chapters of *Kuan Tzu,* dating from the seventh century B.C., "A Consideration of Land" and "Maps," besides the later texts of *The Classic of History, Chou Ritual,* and *Intrigues of the Warring Sates* (Rickett 1965, 72–82, 232–35).

The best account of this pseudo-geography occurs in a long narrative in *The Classic of History,* in the chapter entitled "The Tribute of Yü," and a similar one occurs in *Mencius* (3.11) and elsewhere. Some of the place-names in these texts are recognizable, such as the Yangtze, Huai, Han, and Yellow rivers, as well as the names of some early states and principalities. But the majority belong to mythology rather than to the science of geography based on a real knowledge of the world. The reports of Han travelers and post-Han surveyors were the first to provide proper information based on firsthand accounts. A fine example is chapters 61 and 96 of Pan Ku's *History of the Han* (first century A.D.), which record diplomatic and military expeditions to the western regions of Central Asia (Loewe and Hulsewé 1979). For the rest, as Karlgren forcefully emphasizes, the attempts by Han and post-Han commentators on the late Chou classics to identify mythological place-names, especially in the pseudo-geographical accounts of Yü controlling the flood, are quite "void of value" (1946, 208). Nevertheless, the chapter entitled "The Tribute of Yü" and other related texts on the flood myth are of major importance in terms of mythological material. It may be argued, moreover, that these major myths stimulated a curiosity and intellectual interest in formulating a more scientific foundation for the science of geography in later times.

Apart from "The Tribute of Yü" and the account in *Mencius*, a mythic narrative of Yü the World Measurer appears in *Huai-nan Tzu*, a motif that has its Vedic parallel in Vishnu (Puhvel 1987, 183). This valuable account constitutes a prototype of mathematical geography. In classical Chinese mythology the earth was conceived of as a square, seagirt plane vaulted by the sky (and, in some accounts, with the Yellow Springs below). In the second-century B.C. *Huai-nan Tzu* account, Yü orders two officers, whose names signify 'building' and 'design', to measure the longitude and latitude of the square earth and to fathom all stretches of water. The measurements are different in various versions of the myth (for a résumé see Mathieu 1989, 108 nn. 1–2).

> Yü then commanded T'ai Chang to pace out from the east pole as far as the west pole, making 233,500 leagues and 75 paces. He commanded Shu Hai to pace out from the north pole as far as the south pole, making 233,500 leagues and 75 paces. Of all the vast waters to the deepest abyss from twenty-four feet and higher he fathomed 233,559 stretches of water. Yü then dammed the vast waters with self-renewing earth, and these banks became famous mountains. (*Huai-nan Tzu, Chui hsing,* SPPY 4.2a)

Yü Casts the Nine Cauldrons

Another significant myth in the Yü cycle is the forging of the nine metal cauldrons. There are several versions as to the identity of the divine forger, but the Yü version is more generally accepted as orthodox. In *Mo Tzu*, however, it is Yü's son K'ai, also known as Ch'i, who is said to play that role in conjunction with one Fei Lien (Yi-pao Mei 1929, 212–13). The reading presented in this section is from the *Chronicle of Tso,* dating from the fourth century B.C., as with the *Mo Tzu.* Its narrative contains several motifs: Yü as the divine smith, the divine wisdom of Yü in teaching humans how to distinguish between harmful and benign gods, the symbolic value of representing images of gods on the nine cauldrons, the number nine, which reflects the celestial sphere, and the moral value of the cauldrons in gauging the rise or decline of sovereign power. This moral worth of the cauldrons is expressed metaphorically through their weight. For example, in the third-century B.C. text *Intrigues of the Warring States,* it was stated that the victorious Chou people waged their war against the Shang, conscious of the Chou's moral supremacy; it was also stated that the Chou "captured the nine cauldrons [from the Shang] and it took ninety thousand men to haul one cauldron" (Crump 1970, 38). Conversely, when in turn the Chou were overthrown by the Ch'in, it was stated that "in the nineteenth year of King Nan of the Chou, King Chao of the Ch'in captured the nine cauldrons. Then one cauldron flew into Ssu River and the other eight went into the territory of Ch'in" (*Historical Records,* official commentary on the "Basic Annals of the Ch'in," SPPY 5.26b). Thus the divinely forged cauldrons of Yü passed from dynasty to dynasty, becoming heavy with moral virtue and light with moral turpitude. K. C. Chang has observed that the nine cauldrons "became a symbol of legitimate dynastic rule," being "symbols of wealth . . . symbols of ritual . . . and symbols of the control of metal" (1983, 95–97). The function of Yü as the divine smith links him to Nü Kua when she repaired the cosmos and to Ch'ih Yu, inventor of metal and weapons.

The myth of Yü and the nine sacred cauldrons is also connected with another important motif, Yü's role as dynastic founder of the Hsia, and this brings him into the nexus of founding myths. (The Yü cycle has been identified by Eberhard with the Yueh culture of Southeast China [1968, 348–62].) This in turn is linked to Yü's prominent role in the important myth of the Golden Age, when first Yao, then Shun, and lastly Yü ruled the world with suprahuman wisdom. Unlike the Golden Age of Greek myth, when humans enjoyed a long life free from disease, toil, and old age, the Chinese myth presents a utopia of peace and good government, when rulers were benevolent and just.

[The prince of Ch'u asked Wang-sun Man of the royal state of Chou about the size and weight of the nine cauldrons. Wang-sun Man gave this reply.]

Long ago, when the aspect of the Hsia showed virtue, people from distant areas made illustrations of objects and creatures and made tributary offerings of metal to the nine regional stewards. So he [Yü] forged cauldrons in the image of these creatures. He took precautionary measures against all living things on behalf of the people, to make sure that they knew which were the malign spirits. Therefore, when the people went on rivers or entered marshes, or went on mountains or into forests, they never came across adverse beings; neither goblins or trolls could ever run into them. They also enjoyed the grace of harmony between Heaven above and earth below, and received blessings from Heaven. Chieh [of the Hsia] was wicked, so the cauldrons and their sovereign power passed over to the Shang for six centuries. Chou [last ruler of the Shang] was a harsh despot, so the cauldrons passed over to the Chou. If the virtue of the ruling house is pure and true, even though the cauldrons might be small, they weigh heavily. If the ruling house is perverted and prone to instability, even though the cauldrons may be large, they are lightweight. Heaven protects pure virtue and keeps it safe. (*Tso chuan, Hsuan kung* Third Year, SPPY 21.8b–9a)

Yü collected metal from the nine regional stewards and forged the nine cauldrons. (*Han shu, Chiao ssu chih,* SPPY 25.1.21a)

Yü and the T'u-shan Girl

Although the main stories of the myth of Yü and the flood are written in the heroic mode and accentuate the labors of the demigod and his selfless devotion to duty, an account from the earliest phase of the mythological tradition portrays the hero's lyrical and romantic character. This does not mean that the rougher, more abrupt, and brutal mythic elements are absent, as the third reading shows.

The first reading, from the fourth-century B.C. text "Questions of Heaven," is one of the few mythic narratives that tell of physical desire. Its final wording is, however, garbled, and the translation must be considered as only a tentative rendition of its obscurities. The second reading, from about the first century A.D., provides an explanation for Yü's romantic interlude: that time and youth and virility were running out.

The account establishes that the mating was for dynastic rather than passionate considerations. This account moves from the mythic mode of "Questions of Heaven" to a legendary one. The third reading bears all the hallmarks of a mythological account, referring as it does to metamorphosis, bestiovestism, divine error, and miraculous birth. The motifs and the textual source were discussed in full in chapter 5.

> Yü labored with all his strength. He came down and gazed at the earth below. How did he get the T'u-shan girl and lie with her in T'ai-sang? His consort became his mate and her body gave forth a child. Why did they hunger for the same food, when they had satisfied their hunger for the food of love at dawn? (*Ch'u Tz'u, T'ien wen*, SPTK 3.13b–14a)

> By the age of thirty, Yü still had not married. On his travels he reached T'u-shan. Because he was afraid that time was running out, he abandoned his vow. So he announced, "If I am to marry, let there be an omen." Then a white fox with nine tails came in front of Yü. Yü said, "White is the color of my robes, and the nine tails are the emblem of a ruler. A song of the T'u-shan goes:
>
>> The white fox loiters and prowls,
>> His nine tails are firm and bushy.
>> My home is welcoming,
>> The guest who comes will be king.
>> His family will succeed, his house will succeed.
>> I will make you wealthy,
>> For this is a time when Heaven favors a man.
>> We should go ahead right now!
>
> "Now I understand!" exclaimed Yü. So Yü married into the T'u-shan, and he called his bride Nü-chiao. (*Wu Yueh ch'un-ch'iu, Yueh wang Wu Yü wai chuan*, SPPY 6.2b)

> When Yü was controlling the floodwaters and was making a passage through Mount Huan-yuan, he changed into a bear. He spoke to the T'u-shan girl: "If you want to give me some food, when you hear the sound of a drumbeat, come to me." But Yü leaped on a stone and by mistake drummed on it. The T'u-shan girl came forward, but when she saw Yü in the guise of a bear she was ashamed and fled. She reached the foothills of Mount Sung-kao, when she turned into a stone and bore Ch'i in her womb. Yü said, "Give me back my son!" The stone then split open on its north flank and Ch'i was born. (Yen

Shih-ku's commentary on *Han shu, Wu-ti chi*, referring to a nonextant passage in *Huai-nan Tzu*, SPPY 6.17b–18a)

The Deities Help Yü to Control the Flood

The transformation of myth to legend and the use of mythic material for literary purposes are most clearly evident in the late narratives of the myth of Yü and the flood. In the transition from myth to literature, the eternal verities of myth become the impermanent values of fiction, poetry, and drama as style and value alter from age to age. The most interesting contribution to this aspect of the literary use of myth is Eric Gould's *Mythical Intention in Modern Literature* (1981), which explores motifs borrowed from the Western classical tradition of myth in modern works such as the novels of James Joyce and D. H. Lawrence and the poetry of T. S. Eliot. In the Chinese tradition this transmutation from myth to literature is exemplified by the account of the myth of Yü and the flood in *Researches into Lost Records,* dating from the fourth century A.D. It is particularly manifest when compared with similar mythic narratives of a much earlier period, some eight centuries earlier in the case of "Questions of Heaven," or three centuries earlier in the case of chapter 18 of *The Classic of Mountains and Seas,* which were the first readings in this chapter. In the later, literary miscellany of *Researches,* several legendary features are added to the basic myth: a dark cavern, a hoglike beast, a bright pearl, a green dog, metamorphoses from animal to human shape, a multiplicity of minor deities, a jade tablet and a river chart, divine genealogy, and so forth. Moreover, when compared with the earlier texts, this later account reveals a number of sophisticated stylistic features: an integrated, consecutive narration, color motifs, similes, dialog, besides magic and precious substances. The shift in Yü's role from demigod to human hero, aided by the gods rather than acting as a god, marks the transmutation from myth to literature.

Another such account that is notable for its literariness rather than its mythological form is the narrative of Tu Kuang-t'ing (A.D. 850–933). Tu's account in *A Record of Immortals, Compiled in Yung-ch'eng* reveals several elements in the evolution from classical myth to literary fiction. Tu's mythopoeic inventions include the dominant role of a goddess named Jasper Lady, her miraculous birth, her five metamorphoses, Yü's inability to change shape, the five sorcery arts of the goddess, the arcane text charting river courses, and various Taoistic motifs. The most important element is the shift in emphasis to Yü's subservient role toward the goddess compared with his dominant, masculine role in classical narratives. This marks the evolution from myth to religion, as new legendary personages from the Taoist pantheon color the account with quasi-religious terminology.

Yü forged the Mountain of Dragon Pass and then called it Dragon Gate. He came to an empty cavern several tens of leagues deep and so pitch black that he could go no further. So Yü carried a fire torch on his back and went forward. There was a beast that looked like a hog, and it held a night-shining pearl in its mouth, the light of which was like a torch. There was also a green dog, which barked and ran on ahead. Yü reckoned that he must have gone ten leagues, and he lost track of whether it was day or night. Suddenly he was aware that it was gradually getting a bit lighter, and he noticed the hog and the dog coming toward him, and as they did, they changed into human form, both wearing dark clothes. He also noticed a god with a serpent's body and a human face, and so Yü had a talk with him. The god at once showed Yü a chart of the Eight Trigrams spread out on top of a bench of gold. And there were eight gods in attendance on all sides. Yü said, "Hua Hsu gave birth to a sage-child—was it you?" He answered, "Hua Hsu is the goddess of the Nine Rivers and she gave birth to me." Then he reached for a jade tablet and handed it to Yü. It was one foot, two inches long, and it contained all the numbers of the twelve hours, which would enable Yü to make calculations of Heaven and earth. As soon as Yü held the tablet, he brought order to the flooded land. The god with the serpent's body was [Fu] Hsi the August. (*Shih yi chi*, HWTS 2.2b–3a)

Lady Yun-hua was the twenty-third daughter of the Queen Mother and the younger sister of Princess T'ai-chen. Her personal name was Yao-chi, Jasper Lady. She had been granted the techniques of causing whirlwinds, fusing substances, creating myriad visions, refining divine beings, and flying away in different shapes and forms. She happened to be roaming away from the area of the east sea and was passing by the river when Mount Wu came into view. Its peaks and cliffs jutted out sharply, and wooded ravines were darkly beautiful, with gigantic rocks like an earthly altar. She lingered there for a long while. At that time, Yü the Great was controlling the floods and was living near the mountain. A great wind suddenly came, making the cliffs shudder and the valleys collapse. There was nothing Yü could do to prevent it. Then he came upon the lady, and bowing to her, he asked her for her help. She at once commanded her handmaid to bring Yü the *Book of Rules and Orders* for demons and spirits. Then she ordered her spirits K'uang-chang, Yü-yü, Huang-mo, Ta-yi, Keng-ch'en, T'ung Lü, and others, to help Yü to hew rocks in order to clear the spurting waves and to dredge blocked riverbeds to conduct water through the narrow places, so as to ease the flow of water. Yü bowed to them and thanked them for their help.

Yü wished to visit the lady on the summit of the soaring pinnacle, but before he could look around, she had turned into a rock. Now she suddenly flies around, dispersing into light cloud, which grows dense, then stops, and condenses into an evening shower. Now she turns into a roving dragon, now into a soaring crane. She takes on a thousand appearances, ten thousand shapes. It was impossible to approach her. Yü suspected she might be a treacherous phantasm, not a true immortal, so he asked T'ung Lü about her. Lü said, " . . . Lady Yun-hua is the daughter of the Mother of Metal. . . . Hers is not a body that dwelt naturally in the womb, but it is the vapor from the pale shadow of West Hua. . . . When she comes among humans, she turns into a human, among animals she turns into an animal. Surely she is not limited to the shape of clouds or rain, or a dragon, or a stork, or a flying swan, or wheeling phoenix?" Yü thought what he said was right.

Later on, when he did go to visit her, he suddenly saw a cloudy tower and a jade terrace, a jasper palace with jade turrets, which looked magnificent. Standing on guard were spirit officers whose names were unknown: lions held the gates, horses of Heaven made way, vicious dragons, lightning animals, eight guards stood by the palace pavilions. The lady was sitting quietly on the jasper terrace. Yü bowed his head very low and asked about the Way. . . . Then the lady ordered her handmaid, Ling Jung-hua, to bring out a small cinnabar-red jade box. She opened it and lifted up a priceless document in a distinguished script and presented it to Yü. Yü bowed low as he accepted it and then he left. He also gained the help of Keng-ch'en and Yü-yü, so that in the end he managed to direct the waves and contain the rivers, and he succeeded in accomplishing his task. He made fast the Five Peaks and demarcated the Nine Provinces. Heaven therefore conferred on him the Black Jade insignia and made him the True Man of the Purple Palace. (*T'ai-p'ing kuang chi,* citing *Yung-ch'eng chi hsien lü,* JMWH 56.347–49)

9

Goddesses

There are fewer goddesses in the classical Chinese pantheon than gods, and, with a few exceptions, goddesses are not equal in importance to the gods in terms of function, cult, or continuity of mythological tradition. Of the nineteen goddesses who feature in various myths throughout this book, ten are the focus of particular attention here. The most ancient in the textual tradition are Chiang Yuan, Nü Pa or Drought Fury, and Weaver Maid, who are mentioned in separate poems in *The Classic of Poetry,* circa 600 B.C. Chien Ti, Nü Kua, Fu-fei, and the T'u-shan girl also belong to the old mythology and appear in the fourth-century B.C. texts "Questions of Heaven" and *Li sao* of *Songs of Ch'u.* Next in the textual chronology are Heng O/Ch'ang O, Hsi-Ho, Ch'ang-hsi, the Queen Mother of the West, Woman Ch'ou, and Ching Wei, who appear in *The Classic of Mountains and Seas* and *Huai-nan Tzu,* dating between the third and second centuries B.C., except for Ch'ang-hsi and Hsi-Ho, whose myths are narrated in late chapters of the *Classic,* dating from the first century A.D. O-huang and Nü-ying, the Hsiang queens who were wives of Shun, are first mentioned by name as the daughters of Yao in the sixth century A.D., although the two daughters of Yao are mentioned but not named in the late Chou *Classic of History.* The Dark Lady and Huang O first achieve importance in the period from the fourth to the sixth century A.D. The earliest reference to the

Goddess of Salt River is in the late classical era, but this account is probably based on an earlier oral tradition. Jasper Lady appears in the tenth century, being an amalgam of goddesses in the ancient Ch'u tradition of the "Nine Songs" of *Songs of Ch'u,* and in rhapsodies of the Han and post-Han eras, notably those epideictic evocations of goddesses by the pseudonymous Sung Yü, which were probably written in the third or fourth century A.D.

From a mythographic standpoint, of course, the first mention of some goddesses in a late textual source does not mean that they cannot belong to a much earlier oral tradition. Conversely, some deities, for example, O-huang and Nü-ying, who are identified as the daughters of Yao in the sixth century A.D., may originally have been independent divinities localized in the Yangtze region, a localization the author of our reading from the *Commentary on the Classic of Rivers* makes clear, since he refers to them by the name Hsiang, a tributary of the Yangtze.

The goddesses mentioned throughout this book do not include some well-known deities. Excluded are the goddesses Hsiang Chün or Princess of the River Hsiang, Hsiang Fu-jen or Lady of the River Hsiang, and Shan kuei or Mountain Wraith, who all appear in the "Nine Songs," dating from the fourth century B.C., in *Songs of Ch'u.* A second omission is the earth deity Hou-t'u, who is invoked in Han hymns. Mountain goddesses who appear in literary evocations in rhapsodies attributed to Sung Yü, a Ch'u author of the early third century B.C., are also excluded. These rhapsodies belong to pseudepigraphic literature, that is, anonymous pieces ascribed to a well-known name. A hiatus of seven centuries divides the era of the putative Sung Yü from these lyrically erotic rhapsodies, and their style is radically different from that of literary pieces known to date from the third century B.C. The main reason for their exclusion is that they belong to the literary tradition rather than mythological sources. They do not impart a myth; rather, they express religious, ritual, and imaginative verities.

The gender of some divinities is often obscured by their title. For example, the name of the earth deity is Hou-t'u: *Hou* signifies a hallowed title, such as Divine Lord or Divine Lady, or Lord or Empress, attached equally to females and males; *t'u* means earth or soil. Sinologists have been divided on the issue of the gender of Hou-t'u. Burton Watson favors the traditional rendition, "Earth Lord" (1961, 2, 59). Edouard Chavannes and Michael Loewe prefer the rendition "Earth Queen" (Chavannes 1910, 521–25; Loewe 1974, 28, 170–72). More recently, Rémi Mathieu has agreed with Chavannes and Loewe (1989, 195), and Wolfgang Münke has explored the issue (1976, 142–43). In a Han hymn recorded in Pan Ku's *History of the Han* of the first century A.D., which the historian dates from the reign of the Han Emperor Wu (141–87 B.C.), the earth deity is lauded thus: "Empress Earth is the rich Old Woman" (*Hou-t'u fu-wen*) (Birrell 1993, 35, 183 nn. 37–38). In the same set of hymns, a deity who is linked to the deity of Heaven, and who is therefore likely to be the earth deity, is praised thus: "Old Goddess is richly endowed" (ibid., 38). The female gender of Hou-t'u has, however, recently been rejected by David R. Knechtges, who, referring to the Han hymn, states that "the rich Old Woman . . . has nothing to do with the female sex" (1990, 312). He bases his evidence for this assertion on the opinion of a thirteenth-century A.D. commentator of the Han hymn, Wu Jen-chieh (d. ca. 1200), who claimed that *fu-wen* 'rich old woman' is a variant or corruption of *fu-yun* 'rich and fecund' (ibid.). Nevertheless, his argument on this point must be seen in the light of textual evidence proper. For it is well known that medieval commentators amended and manipulated classical textual readings in the name of variants, corruptions, or rare glosses to suit their argument, opinion, or point of view. A textual rule holds, however, that if the original, earliest text reads convincingly, it should remain intact; whereas if that text is garbled, then amendments are clearly allowable. In the case of the text of the Han hymn, preserved in an important traditional history, it clearly indicates a female gender for Hou-t'u, who must therefore be rendered as Empress Earth, or a similar feminine title. It is most likely that late commentators such as Wu Jen-chieh preferred to conceive of Hou-t'u as a male deity, and their preference, or prejudice, has filtered down to modern research and translation. Edward H. Schafer draws the same conclusion concerning the diminution of the role of the goddess Nü Kua in the T'ang dynasty (1973, 29).

The concept of Hou-t'u as a female deity certainly accords with similar deities in mythologies worldwide. Just as early textual evidence supports the view that the Chinese earth deity was female, so, too, it could be shown that the corn deity, Hou Chi, might be female, Empress Millet. Thus she would parallel the corn goddess, Demeter or Ceres, in the Greco-Roman tradition. The comparative method, however, is a double-edged sword here, and it could be equally argued that Hou Chi has his counterpart in the male Eleusian Triptolemus sent by Demeter to teach humans the art of agriculture.

It will be noted that several goddesses bear the name O or Huang, which are used as a prefix or suffix, and are known as stopgap names or quasi-names. They are similar to the Greek name Hera, meaning Lady, to the name Eurydice or Wide-Judging, and Creusa or Princess, the feminine of Creon, Prince or Ruler. Such stopgap names are often applied to more than one mythical figure, such as O-huang, who is either the daughter of Yao or the wife of Ti Chün. Other goddesses have in their name the prefix Nü or Woman, such as Nü Kua, Nü Ch'ou, Nü Pa (Drought Fury), Nü Chiao, Nü-ying, and so on. Karlgren took the curious position, no doubt influenced here by paternalistic traditionalism, that Nü Kua might be a male deity, arguing that the word Nü in Nü Kua "does not necessarily indicate a lady" but could just form part of the general clan name Nü Kua (1946, 229). Yet when one analyses the function and role of deities having the prefix Nü in their names, one finds all of them to be distinctively female. Furthermore, no clearly male mythical figure bears the prefix Nü in his name. The only conclusion to be drawn is that deities bearing that prefix in their name must be female.

Although male deities predominate in the classical Chinese pantheon, female ones are often more mythologically significant in terms of their function and role. Nü Kua, for example, is both the creator of human beings and the savior of the threatened cosmos. Ch'ang-hsi is the mother of the moons; Hsi-Ho is the charioteer of the sun and the mother of the suns. Ch'ang O is another lunar deity. The Queen Mother of the West is ruler of the western paradise and a punishing goddess; she is also the deity who grants mortals the gift of immortality. Woman Ch'ou (Nü Ch'ou) and Drought Fury (Nü Pa) are the baneful demons of drought. Fu-fei is the river goddess of the Lo. Ching Wei is a doomed goddess, as is the star-goddess, Weaver Maid. The T'u-shan girl gave birth to the demigod Ch'i/K'ai. Chiang Yüan and Chien Ti were the ancestral goddesses of the Shang and Chou peoples. Thus the functions and roles of these female deities are diverse and significant: creation, the motion of celestial bodies, nature spirit, local tutelary spirit, mother of a god, consort of a demigod or a god, harbinger of disaster, donor of immortality, bringer of punishment, and dynastic foundation.

Nü Kua

The earliest references to Nü Kua are sparse and enigmatic. The "Questions of Heaven" asks, "Who shaped the body of Nü Kua?" indicating that she was unusually formed. The question also implies that

Nü Kua, the greatest primeval cosmogonic deity, was not the ultimate creator, since she was formed before she created humans. In this respect, the creatrix is similar to those other cosmogonic gods of mythology worldwide who create the world and humankind not *ex nihilo* but from preexisting matter and from a preexisting state. The *Huai-nan Tzu* relates that in the beginning of time, Nü Kua made "seventy transformations," but it is not clear if this refers to her creative powers of changing and renewing the cosmos or to her own sacred metamorphoses. *The Classic of Mountains and Seas* mentions "ten spirits whose name is 'The Bowels of Nü Kua,'" which strangely describes a deity whose bodily form exists disparately, but in aggregate, in other supernal beings. These early traditions about Nü Kua always treat her as an independent deity and a major cosmogonic goddess.

In the Latter Han era, however, the process of relegating her to a minor role began with Pan Ku's incorporation of Nü Kua as one of a number of minor deities subsumed under the major god T'ai Hao, whom he mistakenly identified as Fu Hsi (Karlgren 1946, 230). Later in the Han period, Nü Kua's divinity was further eroded when she lost her independent status and became linked to Fu Hsi as his consort, making a divine pair, like Zeus and Hera. In Han iconography she is represented with a body of a serpent entwined with Fu Hsi's serpentine form. Edward H. Schafer offered a plausible explanation of the diminution of Nü Kua in the postclassical tradition: "Her gradual degradation from her ancient eminence was partly due to the contempt of some eminent and educated men for animalian gods, and partly due to the increasing domination of masculinity in the elite social doctrine" (Schafer 1973, 29).

The mythic motifs and themes in the readings have already been discussed in chapters 1 and 3.

> People say that when Heaven and earth opened and unfolded, humankind did not yet exist. Nü Kua kneaded yellow earth and fashioned human beings. Though she worked feverishly, she did not have enough strength to finish her task, so she drew her cord in a furrow through the mud and lifted it out to make human beings. That is why rich aristocrats are the human beings made from yellow earth, while ordinary poor commoners are the human beings made from the cord's furrow. (*Feng su t'ung-yi,* CFCE 1.83)

> In remote antiquity the four poles collapsed. The Nine Regions split up. Heaven could not cover all things uniformly, and earth could not

carry everything at once. Fires raged fiercely and could not be extinguished. Water rose in vast floods without abating. Fierce beasts devoured the people of Chuan. Violent birds seized the old and weak in their talons. Then Nü Kua smelted five-color stones to mend the blue sky. She severed the feet of a giant sea turtle to support the four poles and killed a black dragon to save the region of Chi. And she piled up the ashes from burned reeds to dam the surging waters. The blue sky was mended. The four poles were set right. The surging waters dried up. The region of Chi was under control. Fierce beasts died and the people of Chuan lived. They bore earth's square area on their backs and embraced the round sky. . . .

Ever since then, there have been no birds or beasts, no insects or reptiles, that do not sheathe their claws and fangs and conceal their poisonous venom, and they no longer have rapacious hearts. When one considers her achievement, it knows only the bounds of Ninth Heaven above and the limits of Yellow Clod below. She is acclaimed by later generations, and her brilliant glory sweetly suffuses the whole world. She rides in a thunder-carriage driving shaft-steeds of winged dragons and an outer pair of green hornless dragons. She bears the emblem of the Fortune of Life and Death. Her seat is the Visionary Chart. Her steeds' halter is of yellow cloud; in the front is a white calf-dragon, in the rear a rushing snake. Floating, drifting, free and easy, she guides ghostly spirits as she ascends to Ninth Heaven. She has audience with God inside the holy gates. Silently, solemnly, she comes to rest below the High Ancestor. Then, without displaying her achievements, without spreading her fame, she holds the secret of the Way of the True Person and follows the eternal nature of Heaven and earth. (*Huai-nan Tzu, Lan ming,* SPPY 6.7b–8a)

Draught Ox and Weaver Maid

The earliest reference to the star goddess, Weaver Maid, occurs in poem 203 of *The Classic of Poetry* (see the first reading below), where she is personified as a hapless weaver. Draught Ox is also mentioned in the same poem and is juxtaposed with Weaver Maid. But the two stars are not linked in the poem, although the later tradition makes them lovers and then mates. Unlike other stellar myths, such as the Ch'en and Shen stars, and Fu Yueh, no myth exists to explain whether Weaver Maid and Draught Ox were metamorphosed into stars from suprahuman or human form, or whether the movement and pattern of the stars to which their names became attached inspired their stellar personifications. Weaver Maid and Draught Ox stars are the equivalent to stars in Vega and Altair. Michael Loewe has shown that in the Han period, Weaver Maid star formed a triangle of three stars and Draught Ox star formed a straight line of three stars (1979, 112).

The primary intent of the reference to the stars in the poem from the *Classic* is to illustrate the themes of negative capability, failure, and uselessness. For although the weaver weaves, she never finishes her cloth, and although the ox is a powerful draught animal, it is not yoked to a carriage. It was in the Han era that the juxtaposition of the two star deities prompted mythopoeic poets to link the two romantically as unhappy lovers. The most famous expression of this occurs in poem 10 of the "Nineteen Old Poems" of the Han era: "Tears she sheds fall like rain. / River Han clear and shallow, / Away from each other—how much longer?" (Birrell 1986, 40, ll. 6–8). Mythopoeia has supplied a romantic liaison between the stars, and a reason for their separation is evident in the flooding waters of the River Han or Sky River, which flows between them and ebbs only once a year for them to meet. In the course of time, new legendary details were added, such as the sentimental feature of magpies flocking to form a bridge for the lovers on the seventh night of the seventh month. From the sixth century A.D. the figure of Weaver Maid rather than Draught Ox dominated the myth and legends of the two star gods. The second reading, from *Material Appended to the "Erh ya" [Dictionary]* by Lo Yuan (A.D. 1136–84), reflects this development. In this text, the star goddess is given a divine genealogy, and she is more fully personified compared with her portrayal in *The Classic of Poetry*. Moreover, her place in the sky is localized; the purpose of her weaving is explained; the context of her marriage to the star god is given; the figure of God supersedes that of Draught Ox (making the father-figure more significant than the lover-husband); and a reason for her punishment is provided. Draught Ox never became a major mythical figure but played a minor role in stellar myth. It is possible that originally the star god was not human but a beast and that in postclassical mythography the implication of bestiality made him a taboo figure. His other name is River Drum.

> In the sky there is Han River;
> It looks down and is so bright.
> And at an angle is the Weaver Maid;
> All day long she makes but seven moves;

Though she makes seven moves
She does not finish her pattern.
Dazzling is the Draught Ox,
But he is not yoked to a carriage.
(*Shih ching*, 203, SPPY 13.7a–b)

East of Sky River is Weaver Maid, daughter of God in Heaven. Year by year she toils and slaves with loom and shuttle till she finishes weaving a celestial robe of cloudy silk. God in Heaven pitied her living alone, and allowed her to marry Draught Ox west of the river. After they married she neglected her weaving work. God in Heaven grew angry and punished her by ordering her to return to the east of the river, letting her make one crossing each year to be with Draught Ox. (*Erh ya yi*, TSCC 13.147)

The Hsiang Queens

A similar romantic tradition grew up around the two daughters of Yao (*Erh nü*), who became the wives of Shun. When Shun died on a tour of the realm at a place called Ts'ang-wu (probably in Hunan province), his wives drowned in Hsiang River. They became spirits of the river and were known by the river's name. But long before this myth evolved, local river goddesses of the Hsiang, the main river of ancient Ch'u, were already being worshiped and hymned, as attested by the Ch'u "Nine Songs" (Hawkes 1985, 104–9). Perhaps the earliest text to equate the two daughters of Yao with the Hsiang River goddesses was chapter 5 of *The Classic of Mountains and Seas* (third century B.C.), which is the third reading here. The later author of the *Commentary on the Classic of Rivers*, Li Tao-yuan (d. A.D. 526), incorporated local lore into his notes based on a Han book on China's rivers, and in his chapter on Hsiang River he added the legend that forms the first reading. It would seem that by his day the ancient river goddesses hymned in the Ch'u "Nine Songs" had lost their mythological and religious individuality and had become absorbed into a confused amalgam of river spirits of the Hsiang. Li Tao-yuan makes it clear that the haunt of the drowned wives of Shun was the area of Lake Tung-t'ing (Hunan), into which several rivers drain, including the Hsiao and Hsiang rivers. By the Ming dynasty the lore of the two spirit queens had become so well known and well loved that their name was given to a species of bamboo. The second reading is from the Ming text *A Botanical Treatise* by Wang

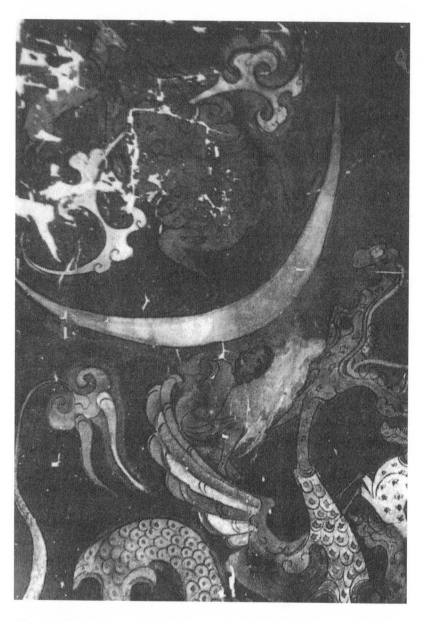

Figure 9. Ch'ang O ascending to the crescent moon, with the elixir-bearing toad and hare. Funerary Ch'u silk painting, Tomb of the wife of the Marquis of Tai, Ma-wang-tui, Ch'ang-sha, Hunan province, circa 190 B.C. From Wen-wu, *The Western Han Silk Painting* (1972), detail from Fig. I.

Hsiang-chin (1561–1653). A biography full of mythical, legendary, and fictional elements appears in *Biographies of Women* (*Lieh nü chuan*, SPPY 1.1a–2a).

> They say that when Shun the Great made a royal tour of his territories, his two queens followed the expedition. They drowned in Hsiang River, and their spirits wandered over the deeps of Lake Tung-t'ing and appeared on the banks where the Hsiao and Hsiang rivers meet. (*Shui ching chu, Hsiang shui*, SPTK 38.14a)

> The local speckled bamboo are very beautiful, and in the Wu area the speckled bamboo is called the Hsiang queens' bamboo. The speckles on it are like tear stains. (*Ch'ün fang p'u, Chu p'u*, CFPCS 5.139)

> A further 120 leagues southeast is the mountain called Tung-t'ing. On the mountaintop there is a lot of yellow gold, and at the base a lot of silver and iron. The mountain trees are full of *tzu*-trees, pear trees, tangerine trees, and pomelos, and there are many plants — *chien*-fragrant grass, *mi-wu* grass, *shao-yao* peony, and *ch'ung-ch'iung* grass. The god's two daughters live on the mountain. They often wander over the depths of the river in the breezes blowing from the Li and Yuan rivers where they meet in the deep waters of the Hsiao-Hsiang confluence in the region of Kiukiang. And every time the waters of these rivers ebb and flow, there is always a raging wind and driving rain. And there are many strange spirits who look like humans and wear snakes on their head, and they hold snakes in their left and right hands. And there are many strange birds there. (*Shan hai ching, Chung tz'u shih-erh ching*, SPPY 5.41b–43a)

Woman Ch'ou

The three narratives of Woman Ch'ou (Nü Ch'ou) from *The Classic of Mountains of Seas* are rich in mythic motifs. They display the incongruities, oddness, and paradox of authentic myth. The first two readings date from the first century A.D., the third from the second century B.C. The first narrative relates that "there are two people in the sea," but, paradoxically, only Woman Ch'ou is mentioned. Her attribute of a crab may be explained as a symbol of regeneration and as a creature that knows the ways of the sea and the lie of the land. Since the crab periodically sheds its shell and reveals fresh skin underneath, there is a widespread belief that it never dies (Malinowski 1954, 129; Frazer 1984,

90). The *Huai-nan Tzu* links the regenerative power of the crab with the moon, stating that the crab waxes and wanes with the moon (Mathieu 1983, I: 497 n. 3, citing *Huai-nan Tzu* 4.5b). The name Ch'ou signifies the second of the Twelve Earthly Branches of the ancient calendrical system, and also a period of time, the nocturnal hours between 1.00 and 3.00 A.M.

Further paradox is evident in the second and third readings, which relate that the goddess's name was Woman Ch'ou Corpse, stating that "Woman Ch'ou Corpse was born." Besides this corpse deity, the *Classic* describes or refers to ten other corpse deities. The paradox signifies life in death and death in life. Woman Ch'ou's function is to counter the effects of drought by self-immolation, from which she is reborn because she never truly dies. Her deformity from being scorched by the sun she hides with her sleeve, or in the variant, with her right hand. Her rebirth is marked by the green clothes she wears, a color emblematizing life and cyclical renewal: green signifies water, vegetal growth, and so life itself. It is emblematic of the thing desired. The same *Classic* relates that the other drought deity, Drought Fury or Nü Pa, was "dressed in green clothes." Like Drought Fury, Woman Ch'ou is virginal, as are other generative deities in mythology. The last reading narrates, "Where the ten suns are up above, Woman Ch'ou lived there on the top of the mountain," thus linking the goddess to the nexus of solar myths, in which Ti Chün, Yi the Archer, Hsi-Ho, and K'ua-fu play a role. Commentators have sought to establish that this and similar mythic narratives point to the practice of sacrificing shamanesses to the sun in times of drought, interpreting the myth in sociological terms (Mathieu 1989, 49 n. 1). Yet the mythic motifs are so complex and profound that such a reading would seem to be too narrow.

> There are two people in the sea. Her name is Woman Ch'ou. Woman Ch'ou has a large crab. (*Shan hai ching, Ta huang tung ching*, SPPY 14.5a)

> There was a person who wore green clothes and hid her face with her sleeve. Her name was Woman Ch'ou Corpse. (*Shan hai ching, Ta huang hsi ching*, SPPY 16.4a)

> Woman Ch'ou Corpse was born, but the ten suns scorched her to death. That was north of the Land of Men. She screened her face with her right hand. Where the ten suns are up above, Woman Ch'ou lived there on the top of the mountain. (*Shan hai ching, Hai wai hsi ching*, SPPY 7.2b)

Figure 10. The Queen Mother of the West, with *sheng* head-dress, seated on her leopard throne, attended (*clockwise*) by the nine-tailed fox, the kneeling hare offering an elixir, two officials, the trance-dancing toad, a crouching suppliant, the three-legged crow of the sun, and a standing guard. Rubbing from a funerary carved brick, 38 cm. high, 18 cm. wide. Latter Han, Ch'eng-tu, Szechwan Provincial Museum Collection. From Shih Yen, *Chung-kuo tiao-su shih t'u lu*, vol. 1 (Shanghai: Shanghai Jenmin mei-shu), 1983, 248.

The Queen Mother of the West

The Queen Mother of the West is not a primeval cosmogonic deity but a goddess who appears comparatively late in the mythological tradition during the late Chou and early Han periods. The name West Mother (*Hsi-mu*), however, appears very early in Chinese culture, being inscribed on Shang oracle bones (thirteenth century B.C.) in the context of animal sacrifice. The Queen Mother of the West is first mentioned in *Chuang Tzu* in the fourth century B.C., together with primeval deities such as Fu Hsi, the Yellow Emperor, Chuan Hsu, and some lesser gods, but this is only a scant reference. She is not mentioned in any other

Chou text. In one late text, *Hsun Tzu* of the third century B.C., the name refers only to the western kingdom.

The first readings relate myths about the goddess and describe her attributes. Of these four readings from *The Classic of Mountains and Seas,* the first and third date from the third century B.C.; the second is from the second century B.C., the fourth from the first century A.D. The goddess portrayed in the narratives appears like the Greek goddess, Artemis, a "lady of wild things," and a "lion unto women" (Rose 1970, 127). Like Artemis, she is a goddess of the wilds, far from human habitation and cultivation. The Queen Mother of the West is a deity who presides over a mountain wilderness in the west and lives among wild beasts. In these accounts she is described as a human with unkempt hair, a panther's tail, and tiger's fangs, and she has a retinue of feline beasts and birds that bring her messages and food. Her only civilizing features are the symbolic *sheng* head ornament she wears, a sort of crown, and her staff, a sort of scepter. Her mountain realm is designated as being in the west, and it is said to be the sacred mountain range of K'un-lun. This is an *axis mundi,* a holy place poised equally between sky and land, Heaven and earth, and is visited by gods. It is a paradise for mortals who have been favored with the gift of eternal life and those who have a communion with the gods. Like Artemis, too, whose name means Slaughterer or Butcher, the Queen Mother of the West's other attribute is that she is a plague bringer and an avenging goddess.

In her later manifestation, the Queen Mother of the West, like the monstrously ugly Gorgo, who in early myth was hairy and wild, is represented as a beautiful female divinity. This is well illustrated by the fifth reading, a long narrative from *The Chronicle of Emperor Mu,* which is believed to date from the fourth century B.C. but is probably a post-Han fictional romance. The narrative depicts the Queen Mother of the West in her civilized aspect, behaving like a dignified queen in her exchange of diplomatic gifts and polite courtesies with King Mu, the fifth king of the Chou dynasty (trad. 1001–947 B.C.). Many legends are attached to his name, such as the anecdote preserved in *Lieh Tzu* about the inventor Master Yen. The *Lieh Tzu* contains a chapter entitled "King Mu of Chou," which relates many of these traditional tales. The text of *The Chronicle of Emperor Mu* purports to be much earlier than *Lieh Tzu,* a fourth-century A.D. forgery. The *Chronicle* was allegedly discovered in A.D. 281 when a graverobber named Pu Chün stole treasures from the grave of King Hsiang of the Wei state, a late Chou ruler who died between 319 and 296 B.C. The style of the *Chronicle,* however, bears many resemblances to the fictional romances combining poetry and prose which began to be popular in the Six Dynasties era, circa the fourth to fifth century A.D., and the story of the discovery in the tomb might well be apocryphal (see Mathieu's study of the text and translation, 1978).

It is clear from the mythic narratives of the Queen Mother of the West that, like many other mythical figures, she is polyfunctional and ambiguous. Moreover, her attributes and functions evolve over the centuries in accordance with the changing values of myth in society. Thus she moves with relative ease from the role of wild and savage deity, the avenging goddess, to cultured and humanized queen, the audience-granting monarch. It is in her latter role and function that she is generally recognized by most Sinologists. Yet this is a role described in such a late mythic narrative, *The Chronicle of Emperor Mu* [of the Chou], dating between the third and fourth century A.D., that it cannot serve as the pristine image of the goddess. In his recent article on the Queen Mother of the West (*Hsi wang mu*), Riccardo Fracasso summarized the views and speculations of several Sinologists concerning the elusive and enigmatic function of the goddess in the earliest extended narrative, that is, the first reading below, from *The Classic of Mountains and Seas,* a passage dating from the late Chou period (ca. third century B.C.). In this text the Queen Mother of the West is stated to be "the official in charge of vile plagues sent from Heaven, and of the five dread evils." This translation disguises the fact that it allows of several renditions and interpretations, ranging from the goddess's power over the stars Li and Wu ts'an, to her power over the disasters visited by Heaven on earth for crimes, or to her control of baneful spirits. Fracasso concludes his summary of these versions and views of the meaning of the phrase "T'ien chih li chi wu ts'an" by drawing a significant parallel between the Tibetan goddess Kha la me 'bar ma, with her attendant "masters of illnesses" and "masters of epidemics" (Fracasso 1988, 15, 32, citing Wojkowitz 1977, 269–73, 303, 308). In my view his mythic parallel convincingly elucidates the Queen Mother of the West's earliest role as an avenging goddess, awesome in her divine power.

The major attribute of the Queen Mother of the West is her power to confer immortality, and it is this that comes into play in the later mythological and literary tradition. She is pictured in traditional iconography holding her staff (scepter or wand) in her left hand and a basket of the peaches of immortality in the other. The peaches were fabled to ripen only once in every three thousand years. The fruit may be mythically linked to the giant cosmic peach tree, which serves as a massive sky-ladder three thousand leagues across for the gods to descend and ascend (see chap. 14). Her function of bestowing immortality, however, was a late invention and is not mentioned in early texts. Even in the *Chronicle* she only expresses a wish to the earthly ruler, "May you never die," and "For you alone does Heaven wait"; otherwise, the account is devoid of the trappings of immortality which characterize later texts. The earliest textual reference to the goddess's power to confer immortality occurs is *Huai-nan Tzu*, in the narrative about Ch'ang O, who stole the drug of immortality from Yi, who had obtained it from the goddess. In later texts, such as *The Old Fable of [Emperor] Wu of the Han* and *The Inner Chapters of Emperor Wu of the Han*, the royal visit of a Chinese king or emperor to the goddess is elaborated, but the theme shifts from immortality to longevity, showing that the potency of the myth of immortality was commencing to wane.

Another three hundred and fifty leagues west is a mountain called Jade Mountain, which is where the Queen Mother of the West dwells. In appearance the Queen Mother of the West is like a human, with a panther's tail and a tiger's fangs, and she is a fine whistler. In her tangled hair she wears the *sheng* crown. She is the official in charge of vile plagues sent from heaven, and of the five dread evils. (*Shan hai ching, Hsi tz'u san ching,* SPPY 2.19a–b)

The Queen Mother of the West reclines on a bench throne and wears the *sheng* crown on her head and holds her staff in her hand. South of her are three bluebirds who gather food for the Queen Mother of the West north of K'un-lun void. (*Shan hai ching, Hai nei pei ching,* SPPY 12.1a)

Another two hundred and twenty leagues west are the mountains of San-wei, where the three bluebirds live. This mountain is one hundred leagues around. (*Shan hai ching, Hsi tz'u san ching,* SPPY 2.22a)

There are three bluebirds with scarlet heads and black eyes. One is called the Greater Blackfeather, one is called the Lesser Blackfeather, and one is called the Bluebird. (*Shan hai ching, Ta huang hsi ching,* SPPY 16.3b)

On the lucky *chia-tzu* day the emperor was the guest of the Queen Mother of the West. Then, bearing the white jade tablet and the dark jade disc of monarchy, he had an audience with the Queen Mother of the West. As a token of good will, he presented her with a brocade sash embroidered in a hundred colors and a [textual lacuna] embroidered in three hundred colors. The Queen Mother of the West accepted them with repeated bows of thanks. On the [textual lacuna] *yi-ch'ou* day, the emperor held a banquet in honor of the Queen Mother of the West beside Jasper Pool. The Queen Mother of the West sang an unaccompanied song for the emperor which went:

> White clouds in the sky,
> Hilly mounds rise up through them.
> Miles of road far ahead,
> Mountains and streams crossing it.
> May you never die
> So you can return to us again.

The emperor answered her with a poem that went:

> I must go home to my land in the east
> To govern all the Hsia in peace.
> When the myriad people are settled and at peace
> I will want to visit you.
> Within three years
> I will return to your wilds.

The Queen Mother of the West sang another ditty for the emperor which went:

> Ever since I went to this land in the west
> I have lived in these wilds.
> Tigers and panthers form my pride,
> Crows and jays nest with me.
> I enjoy my life and will not move.
> I am the Emperor of Heaven's daughter.
> How I pity all humankind
> For they are parted from you.
> Blow the panpipes, beat the panpipe tongues!
> Let your mind soar on high,
> Master of humankind,
> For you alone does Heaven wait.

Then the emperor drove his horses and ascended Mount Yen. Then he recorded an inscription on a rock on Mount Yen and planted a locust tree there with a sign inscribed "the Queen Mother of the West's Mountain." (*Mu T'ien-tzu chuan*, SPPY 3.1a–2a)

Ch'ang O

The mythical figure of Ch'ang O, or Heng O, has been discussed in the context of the myths of Yi the Archer. The motifs of the narratives will be summarized here. The earliest reference to this deity in *Huai-nan Tzu* uses the name Heng O. Rémi Mathieu notes that the name Heng violated the taboo name of Emperor Wen of the Han (r. 180–157 B.C.) and was replaced by Ch'ang, although in the late Han period the name Heng was restored (1989, 56 n. 2). She is not the only lunar goddess; there is a mythic narrative that relates that Ch'ang-hsi gave birth to the twelve moons and cared for them after their passage across the sky. The *Ch'ang* of Ch'ang O is written with the female radical, *Ch'ang* of Ch'ang-hsi without, but the two names are the same; the *hsi* of Ch'ang-hsi is the same as in Hsi-Ho, and in Fu Hsi. The two major motifs in the Ch'ang O narratives are her theft and her metamorphosis. Her theft is not of the altruistic kind exemplified by Kun; but, like Kun, she belongs to the trickster category of figures in mythology. Her metamorphosis into a toad may be read as her punishment by a higher god. This reading is the earliest reference to the Queen Mother of the West's role as donor of immortality.

> Yi asked the Queen Mother of the West for the drug of immortality. Yi's wife, Heng O, stole it and escaped to the moon. She was metamorphosed on the moon and became the striped toad Ch'an-ch'u, and she is the essence of the moon. (Subcommentary of *Ch'u hsueh chi,* citing *Huai-nan Tzu,* SPCY 1.4a)

Jasper Lady

The goddess Jasper Lady, Yao-chi, is a late invention whose name is derived from Taoistic epithets based on a jadelike substance, believed to be the purest and most refined of mundane things. In this she resembles divine women described in post-Han rhapsodies. Similarly, her image is based on mythopoeic evocations of the fertility goddess of Mount Kao-t'ang and Mount Wu, place-names that are mentioned in the reading that follows. The reading consists of a long narrative from *A Record of Immortals, Compiled in Yung-ch'eng* by Tu Kuang-t'ing (A.D. 850–933). It relates how the powerful goddess Jasper Lady helped Yü to control the flood. Without her aid, the narrative persuades, Yü would not have succeeded; Yü's role is to be helpless and subservient before the divine woman.

Tu Kuang-t'ing lived in Ch'eng-tu (Szechwan province) in the late T'ang era and was a Taoist priest who wrote many pieces on magic and alchemy. His most famous work is the fictional tale (*ch'uan-ch'i*) "The Man with the Curly Beard," which deals with the legendary theme of the foundation of the T'ang dynasty. The title of the miscellany from which the narrative of Jasper Lady is taken contains the mythic place-name Yung-ch'eng, which evokes a place in western Shu (Szechwan) where the Queen Mother of the West was believed to live. Numerous fictional elements appear in Tu's tale which are typical of a T'ang romance: an opening genealogy of the goddess which is further elaborated in the narrative; miraculous conception; magical techniques and metamorphoses; atmospheric place-names; literary references; descriptions of nature; a supernatural storm; arcane scripture; a bejeweled fairy palace; the color motifs of cinnabar, signifying immortality; black, symbolizing here the occult; and purple, emblematic of the Taoist pantheon. It is clear from Tu's treatment of the ancient demigod Yü and his elevation of the newly invented Taoist deity Jasper Lady, together with his inclusion of Taoist motifs, that he has utilized mythological themes and figures for the purposes of fiction and, in so doing, has subverted their ancient values and meaning in order to subordinate them to the interests of Taoist belief prevalent in the medieval age of the late T'ang period.

Lady Yun-hua was the twenty-third daughter of the Queen Mother and the younger sister of Princess T'ai-chen. Her personal name was Yao-chi, Jasper Lady. She had been granted the techniques of causing whirlwinds, fusing substances, creating myriad visions, refining divine beings, and flying away in different shapes and forms. She happened to be roaming away from the area of the east sea and was passing by the river when Mount Wu came into view. Its peaks and cliffs jutted out sharply, and wooded ravines were darkly beautiful, with gigantic rocks like an earthly altar. She lingered there for a long while. At that time, Yü the Great was controlling the floods and was living near the mountain. A great wind suddenly came, making the cliffs shudder and the valleys collapse. There was nothing Yü could do to prevent it. Then he came upon the lady, and bowing to her, he asked her for her help. She at once commanded her handmaid to bring Yü the *Book of Rules and Orders* for demons and spirits. Then she ordered her spirits, K'uang-chang, Yü-yü, Huang-mo, Ta-yi, Keng-ch'en, T'ung Lü, and others, to help Yü to hew rocks in order to clear the spurting waves and to dredge blocked riverbeds to conduct water through the narrow places, so as to ease the flow of water. Yü bowed to them and thanked them for their help.

Yü wished to visit the lady on the summit of the soaring pinnacle, but before he could look around, she had turned into a rock. Now she suddenly flies around, dispersing into light cloud, which grows dense, then stops, and condenses into an evening shower. Now she turns into a roving dragon, now into a soaring crane. She takes on a thousand appearances, ten thousand shapes. It was impossible to approach her. Yü suspected she might be a treacherous phantasm, not a true immortal, so he asked T'ung Lü about her. Lü said, " . . . Lady Yun-hua is the daughter of the Mother of Metal. . . . Hers is not a body that dwelt naturally in the womb, but it is the vapor from the pale shadow of West Hua. . . . When she comes among humans, she turns into a human, among animals she turns into an animal. Surely she is not limited to the shape of clouds or rain, or a dragon, or a stork, or a flying swan, or wheeling phoenix?" Yü thought what he said was right.

Later on, when he did go to visit her, he suddenly saw a cloudy tower and a jade terrace, a jasper palace with jade turrets, which looked magnificent. Standing on guard were spirit officers whose names were unknown: lions held the gates, horses of Heaven made way, vicious dragons, lightning animals, eight guards stood by the palace pavilions. The lady was sitting quietly on the jasper terrace. Yü bowed his head very low and asked about the Way. . . . Then the lady ordered her handmaid, Ling Jung-hua, to bring out a small cinnabar-red jade box. She opened it and lifted up a priceless document in a distinguished script and presented it to Yü. Yü bowed low as he accepted it and then he left. He also gained the help of Keng-ch'en and Yü-yü, so that in the end he managed to direct the waves and contain the rivers, and he succeeded in accomplishing his task. He made fast the Five Peaks and demarcated the Nine Provinces. Heaven therefore conferred on him the Black Jade insignia and made him the True Man of the Purple Palace. (*T'ai-p'ing kuang chi*, citing *Yung-ch'eng chi hsien lü*, JMWH 56.347–49)

The Goddess of Salt River

The myth of the Goddess of Salt River derives from fragments of a text entitled *The Origin of Hereditary Families*, which dates from the

Ch'in/Han era, circa late third to early second century B.C. These fragments were collated and edited, and also in part reconstructed, by Ch'in Chia-mo and other Ch'ing scholars to form a consecutive narrative about the larger myth of the origins of the Pa tribe of Szechwan. The mythological genealogy of the Pa is related in the first reading, which comes from *The Classic of Mountains and Seas,* in a late chapter dating from the first century A.D. The second reading is from Ch'in Chia-mo's reconstructed text.

The myth of the goddess forms a part of the narrative of the trials and ultimate success of the hero, the Lord of the Granary, who was of the Pa tribe. It relates the aggressive encounter between the hero and the goddess, which constitutes one of the hero's trials before he becomes leader of his people and ruler of a new city-kingdom. The goddess is cast in the role of a malign deity whose evil is foiled by the resourceful hero. In its colorful drama and its depiction of the hero as a cunning adversary, the myth is reminiscent of myths of Odysseus, who defeated his enemies by his cunning, resourcefulness, and courage. The cunning of the Lord of the Granary is evident in the gift he offers the goddess: it is a green silk cord, which she accepts, through his wily flattery, as a decorative girdle, but which in the end ensnares her, because it is also a hunting weapon.

It is significant that both protagonists have the element of food in their name, that is, salt (*yen*) and grain > granary (*lin*). This nominally makes the account a sitiological myth. Since the larger mythic narrative of the Lord of the Granary relates how he became chief of the tribe and then went on to found a new city, it is possible that the underlying structure of the submyth of his encounter with the goddess could be read as a contest between a matriarchal community, Yen-yang, which was rich in the resources of fish and salt, and a dynamically expanding patriarchal tribe seeking conquest of rich land and peoples beyond its frontiers.

> In the southwest is Pa country. Ta Hao gave birth to Hsien-niao. Hsien-niao gave birth to Ch'eng-li. Ch'eng-li gave birth to Hou-chao, and Hou-chao was the founder of the Pa people. (*Shan hai ching, Hai nei ching,* SPPY 18.4a)

> The ancestor of the Lord of the Granary originally came from Wu Tan. The Man tribe of Pa commandery and Nan commandery originally had five surnames: the Pa clan, the Fan clan, the Shen clan, the Hsiang clan, and the Cheng clan. They all came from Mount Wu-lo

Chung-li. On this mountain there were two caves, one scarlet and one black, like cinnabar and lacquer. The children of the Pa clan were born in the scarlet cave, and the children of the other four surnames were all born in the black cave. Before there were chieftains, they were all subjects of the spirits and gods. The Lord of the Granary's given name was Wu-hsiang; his surname was that of the Pa clan. He set out together with the Fan clan, the Shen clan, the Hsiang clan, and the Cheng clan—five surnames in all—and they all competed for divine power to rule. Then they all together threw their swords at a rock and agreed that whoever could hit the target would be elevated to be their lord. When the son of the Pa clan, Wu-hsiang, was the only one to hit the target, they all sighed. Then he ordered each clan to sail in an earthenware boat, carved with designs and painted, and to float the boats in the river. They made an agreement that whoever could stay afloat would become their lord. The other clans all sank, and Wu-hsiang's was the only one to stay afloat. So they unanimously made him their chieftain. He became the Lord of the Granary. Now he sailed the earthenware boat from Yi River to Yen-yang. At Salt River there is a goddess. She said to the Lord of the Granary, "This land is vast, and there is all the fish and salt that come from it. I wish you would stay here and live among us." The Lord of the Granary refused. At nightfall the Salt Goddess suddenly came to sleep with him. At dawn she turned into a flying insect and flew in a swarm with other insects. They blotted out the sunlight and the world grew pitch black for more than ten days in a row. The Lord of the Granary could not make out which was east or west for seven days and seven nights. He ordered someone to hold a green silk cord and present it to the Salt Goddess. He said to her, "This will suit you if you wear it as a fringed belt. If we are to live together, then please accept it from me." The Salt Goddess accepted it and wore it as a fringed belt. At once the Lord of the Granary stood on a sunlit rock, and aiming at the green cord she wore, he shot arrows at her. He hit her and the Salt Goddess died. Then the sky cleared far and wide. The Lord of the Granary then ruled over Yi City, and the four clan names submitted to him. (Ch'in Chia-mo's reconstructed text, *Shih pen, Shih hsing,* 1:93–94)

IO

Immortality

In early Chinese mythology the dividing line between immortality and mortality is often blurred, and there are degrees of both states. The great primeval gods are presumed to be immortal. Yet the Flame Emperor, brother of the Yellow Emperor, besides Ch'ih Yu and K'ua-fu, are all killed and die a death, though parts of them live on in a meta-morphosed state. Metamorphosis is also the final destiny of other mythical figures who have died by execution or drowning, such as Kun, who becomes a bear (variants: turtle, dragon), Kang-hsiang, who becomes a river god, and Ching Wei, who turns into a bird. In the myth of the cosmological human body, P'an Ku is transformed into the universe at the moment of death. Some mythical figures exist on the border between life and death, such as Woman Ch'ou, who was born a corpse, and the hero Hsing T'ien, who continues to fight after his head has been lopped off. Clearly, the terms *mortality* and *immortality* are inappropriate for the nebulous existence and transformational powers of the gods known as Ti, Huang, Shen, Ling, Kuei, and Po, terms for divine beings, besides variously named elves, goblins, and monsters.

The more usual meaning of the word *immortality* in mythology has to do with attaining the divine state of a god by shuffling off mortal coils. The earliest reference to immortality occurs in *Chuang Tzu*, with a description of a holy human, *shen jen;* or perfect man, *chih jen;* or sage, *sheng jen.* *Chuang Tzu*'s description goes as follows:

> He said there is a Holy Man living on faraway Ku-she Mountain, with skin like ice or snow, and gentle and shy like a young girl. He doesn't eat the five grains, but sucks the wind, drinks the dew, climbs up on the clouds and mist, rides a flying dragon, and wanders beyond the four seas. By concentrating his spirit, he can protect creatures from sickness and plague and make the harvest plentiful. (Watson 1968, 33)

Several themes emerge here: a hermit existence on a mountain, which denotes proximity to Heaven; dietary abstention; transformed gender behavior; pure elements as food; the technique of riding the dragon; ability to travel at will; transcendental meditation; ability to perform miracles (basically to do with sickness and food); and bringing benefits to humankind. Although this account belongs to the realm of philosophy, it has obvious overtones of myth and local cult religion.

The passionate pursuit of the idea of physical immortality in humans is discernible in the late Chou and Ch'in dynasties, and is epitomized by the fascination with elixirs and paradisiacal worlds which characterized the short reign of the First Emperor of the Ch'in Dynasty, Ch'in Shih Huang Ti (221–210 B.C.). He was the first ruler to appropriate for himself the sacred titles of Huang and Ti, which previously had been applied only to gods. He sent adepts and magicians in search of the isles of the immortals, Fang Wu, Ying-chou, and P'eng-lai (Graham 1981, 176–77). In the Han era the cult of immortality, or deathlessness, became particularly identified with the philosophical school of Taoism, which by the early Han period had incorporated from the philosopher Yang Chu (ca. 350 B.C.) concepts of nurturing life, longevity, and self-preservation. Thus two strands of thought emerge in the Han era: the pursuit of deathlessness and the art of longevity. The first could be acquired through a gift from a god, such as the Queen Mother of the West, or through self-cultivation leading to sainthood, or through alchemical potions and pills. Longevity could be sought through diet, drugs, meditation, breathing exercises, and sexual rites. But in the Han period a shift in belief is noticeable: less emphasis was placed on the pursuit of immortality, and more interest was paid to the idea of longevity, living one's life span to the full. This conceptual shift indicates that belief in the primeval and ancient deities was diminishing and that the values of primitive mythology were being eroded.

The Mountain Paradise of K'un-lun

The first reading that follows is from *The Classic of Mountains and Seas*, a chapter dating from the first century B.C. It presents one of the earliest and most elaborate descriptions of the earthly paradise of K'un-lun, and as such it constitutes a valuable mythological text. The passage is full of mythic themes and motifs to do with immortality. The highest mountains of K'un-lun in the west were believed to form an epicenter of the universe, an *axis mundi,* where Heaven and earth meet in a perfect equipoise. Like Mount Olympus, it is the place where the gods descend from the sky to that part of the human world which most nearly replicates the paradisiacal state of Heaven. The *Classic* contains numerous other references to earthly places favored by the gods, such as God's City, God's Resting Place, God's Bedroom, and so forth. The K'un-lun earthly paradise has a sky-ladder in the form of a giant tree, the Tree Grain, so that earthly beings who have achieved a near perfect state and the heavenly gods may commune. Idealized concepts of size, space, and distance are conveyed through mystic numbers, especially the cosmic number nine representing the heavens and the number eight representing the mythic ideal of harmony, and also through detailed measurements of the gigantic and the profound. The color motif of scarlet predominates in the descriptive passage, emblematic of immortality. The pure substance of jade is associated with the divine, being the finest stone known to humans.

This earthly paradise is guarded from intrusion by a fierce array of mythical beasts, such as the K'ai-ming, which, with its nine heads and feline body, recalls the fabled nine-tailed fox, and the nine-headed Hsiang Liu monster slaughtered by Yü. Other guardian beasts are serpents, the dragon, felines, and birds of prey. Polycephality is repeated in the three-headed man guarding a tree of life, and the six-headed hawk. The Shih-jou is a mythical beast symbolizing renewal of life; elsewhere in the *Classic* it is described as a creature that looks like a lump of liver and that eats itself but then grows again. Besides the mythical birds and beasts, there are twelve fabled trees, including the Never Die tree, trees of precious jewels, and unknown trees with fabulous names.

The text moves from a general description of this earthly paradise to a detailed account of a rite enacted by six shamans (*wu*). They are guarding the corpse of the mythical figure Cha Yü, who was murdered by two lesser gods, and are keeping it from corruption. (The myth of Cha Yü appears in chap. 4.) In his study of the shaman tradition in ancient China, Chow Tse-tsung lists three sets of shamans' names, including the set in this reading, and these three sets overlap. They number twenty-two individual shamans. Basing his research on ancient dictionaries, inscriptions, and textual sources, Chow interprets the names of the six shamans in the reading as follows: P'eng denotes a "drum sound"; Ti means "needling with a stone" or a "thorn," "pierce," or "a straight root," or "slander," hence "to invoke curses"; Yang "refers to the sun," but can also mean the "moon," or a "lunar eclipse"; Li means "treading on" or "stepping on"; Fan "may have symbolized the square object used in such a [shamanistic] dance"; and Hsiang denotes "a drum and drumstick" (Chow Tse-tsung 1978, 72–83). Schafer noted that the name Fan, identified as a female shaman, is engraved on Shang oracle bones in connection with a rain ceremony or with ritual exposure (1951, 132, 184). The six shamans in the reading are custodians of the secret of preserving life. They are probably thought of as being immortal themselves, but this is not overtly stated. Although the word *wu* usually applies to female shamans, the gender of the six shamans in this reading is not given or implied. A curious omission from this text is the Queen Mother of the West, who elsewhere in the *Classic* is said to be the presiding deity of Jade Mountain in the K'un-lun void.

This narrative of the mountain paradise in the west is a valuable document for mythology because of all these themes and motifs. It is also important for its account of the shamanistic rite of preserving a corpse, the body of the god Cha Yü. The narrative may represent the vestige of an archaic rite of inducing deathlessness which was enacted in the age of belief in immortality.

> Within the seas the K'un-lun wastes are in the northwest, and this is God's capital city on earth below. The K'un-lun wastes are eight hundred leagues square and eighty thousand feet high. On top there is the Tree Grain; it is forty feet tall and five spans wide. On all sides there are nine wells with well-sills made of jade. On all sides there are nine gates, and at the gates there is the K'ai-ming beast on guard. The dwelling place of the gods is on a cliff with eight nooks. The boundary of the Scarlet River has a cliff on the ridge which no one could ascend unless he were the Good Archer. . . . The gulf south of K'un-lun is two thousand, four hundred feet deep. The body of the K'ai-ming beast is mostly that of a tiger, and it has nine heads, all of which have human faces that look eastward. It stands on top of K'un-lun. To the west of the K'ai-ming are the male and female phoenix

and the *luan*-bird. They all carry a serpent on their head and tread a
serpent underfoot, and there is a scarlet snake on their breast. North
of the K'ai-ming there is the Shih-jou creature, the pearl tree, the
patterned-jade tree, the *yü-ch'i* tree, and the Never Die tree. The male
and female phoenix and *luan*-bird all wear armor plate on their heads.
And there are the Li-chu bird, the giant Grain Tree, the cypress, the
Sweet Water, and the Wise Man tree, the Man-tui, also called the
T'ing-tree-cross-fanged. To the east of the K'ai-ming there are Shaman P'eng, Shaman Ti, Shaman Yang, Shaman Li, Shaman Fan, and
Shaman Hsiang, who bear the corpse of Cha Yü, each holding the
drug of immortality to protect him. Cha Yü has a serpent's body and
a human head. He was killed by Double Load and his officer. There
is also the Fu-ch'ang tree. On its crown there is a three-headed man
who watches over the red *lang-gan* jade tree. To the south of the K'ai-
ming beast there is the Tree Bird with its six heads, and the scaly dragon, the cobra, the serpent, the long-tailed ape, the panther, the *niao-
chih* tree, Splendid Pool tree, the hummingbird, the *shun*-hawk, and
the Shih-jou creature. (*Shan hai ching, Hai nei hsi ching,* SPPY 11.2b–5b)

The Island Paradises in the East

A different paradise from mountainous K'un-lun is described in the
reading below, from the late text *Lieh Tzu,* circa fourth century A.D.
Here the paradise is in the east and consists of islands inhabited by
immortals known as *hsien* and *sheng,* or transcendent beings. These
terms emerged in the post-Han era, and a considerable literature — part
mythological, part legendary, part lore, and part fiction — grew up
around the concept of the *hsien*-immortal. Examples among a proliferation of such books are *Biographies of Immortals* (*Lieh hsien chuan*) and *Biographies of Holy Immortals* (*Shen hsien chuan*), ascribed to Liu Hsiang (79–8
B.C.) but now thought to date from the fourth to the fifth century, and
to Ko Hung (A.D. 254–334). *Lieh Tzu* belongs to this category of books.
Purporting to be the work of Lieh Tzu, or Lieh Yü-k'ou, a mythical
figure who features frequently in the fourth-century B.C. text *Chuang
Tzu* as a sorcerer and a perfect man, the text of *Lieh Tzu* is now believed
to be a forgery by the Chin dynasty author Chang Chan (fl. A.D. 370).

The long narrative from *Lieh Tzu* contains numerous themes: concepts of infinity and perfect equilibrium, epitomized by Kuei-hsu, a
bottomless pool; isles of the immortals; fruit of the tree of immortality,
or the Tree of Life; the crime of a titan and his punishment by God; and

an explanation for the size of titans and giants. The account is set *in illo tempore,* before the gods Fu hsi and the Farmer God. Despite the proliferation of mythological motifs, the narrative style betrays the late provenance of the text and its trend toward legend rather than primeval myth. The story has a sophisticated framework: it consists of a series of imaginary discussions between T'ang the Conqueror of the Shang/Yin, who poses several questions about the origins of things, and one Chi of the Hsia, who replies with lengthy explanations.

Emperor T'ang of the Yin dynasty asked another question: "In nature, what are the giant and minute things, the longest and the short, similar and different kinds?" Chi of the Hsia dynasty said: "To the east of Po Sea, countless thousands of millions of miles away, there is a vast pool, a truly bottomless valley. Its bottomless depth is called Kuei-hsu. All the waters of the Eight Sides and the Nine Wilds and the courses of Heavenly Han flow into it, yet it neither increases nor decreases. There are five mountains in it. One is Tai Yü. The second is Yuan Chiao. The third is Fang Hu. The fourth is Ying-chou. The fifth is P'eng-lai. These mountains are thirty thousand leagues high and around, and their flat crests are nine thousand leagues across. Each mountain is seventy thousand leagues apart, yet they are neighbors. The terraced viewpoints on them are all of gold and jade. The birds and beasts on them are all pure silky white. The pearly garnet trees all grow densely; their blossom and fruit are richly flavored. Whoever eats them will never grow old or die. The people living there are all immortals and sages. They are innumerable as they flit to and fro all day and all night. But the bases of the five mountains are not firmly secured, and they constantly ebb and flow with the waves of the tides, unable to pause even for a short while. The immortals and sages hated this and complained about it to God in Heaven. God feared they might drift into the West Pole and lose the dwellings of the host of immortals and sages. So he commanded Yü Ch'iang to use fifteen giant sea turtles to bear the mountains on their raised heads. By alternating three to a group they took turns every sixty thousand years. For the first time the five mountains stood still. But in the Dragon Earl's kingdom there was a giant who, by just lifting his feet a few steps, reached the place where the mountains stood. With each single throw of his line, he caught six of the giant sea turtles in succession. He bundled them onto his back and hurried back to his own country, where he burned their shells to tell his fortune.

As a result, the two mountains Tai Yü and Yuan Chiao drifted toward the North Pole and sank in the vast ocean. The immortals and sages who scattered in exile numbered in their millions. God in Heaven was very angry and he shrank the Dragon Earl's kingdom to narrow confines and shrank the Dragon Earl's people to a small size. Right up until the time of Fu Hsi and the Farmer God, the people of that kingdom were still only a hundred feet tall. (*Lieh Tzu, T'ang wen,* SPPY 5.3b–5b)

The Myth of P'eng-tsu's Longevity

The two readings below narrate the myth of P'eng-tsu, which combines both themes of immortality and longevity. The first is a brief passage from "Questions of Heaven," which states that P'eng K'eng "received the gift of eternal life" from God. It is intimated that this was a reward for P'eng K'eng's special sacrificial offering, but because the mythical context is not known and is not referred to in any other text, it remains obscure. The brief passage mentions both longevity and immortality, which are different concepts. A text also dating from the fourth century B.C., *Chuang Tzu,* refers to one P'eng-tsu, Ancestor P'eng, who was long-lived rather than immortal, living from the twenty-sixth to the seventh century B.C. (Watson 1968, 82 n. 12).

The ambiguous mythic narrative in "Questions of Heaven" is later reinterpreted to mean a myth of longevity, as in such texts as Ko Hung's *Biographies of Holy Immortals,* from which the second reading is taken. Ko Hung was an alchemist and philosopher of the Chin dynasty and was the author of *Master Embracing-Simplicity (Pao-p'u Tzu),* his sobriquet. This work is a quintessential expression of fourth-century A.D. belief in immortality, longevity, and supernatural beings. In it, Ko Hung explains the methods and techniques for acquiring immortality, with several recipes for drugs and potions. One of his recipes for making gold is: a pound each of red bole, saltpeter, mica, calcareous spar, and red hematite, plus half a pound of sulphur and a quarter-pound of malachite, all blended with vinegar, to produce a lining for the alchemical receptacle; then mix a pound of mercury, half a pound each of cinnabar and amalgam (mainly lead); process, heat, and stir, and "it will immediately turn into gold" (Ware 1981, 274–75). Ko Hung assures his devotees that one pound of this gold will cure many illnesses and make the "Three Worms cry for mercy" in the body. Three pounds consumed will ensure longevity as long as nature itself. One pill placed in the mouth of a corpse, plus some spit from the mouth of the living, will ensure that the body will return to life immediately (ibid., 275–77).

The reading on the P'eng-tsu myth is a shortened version of the original, and it opens with the account of the long-lived *hsien,* or transcendental being. The graph for the name P'eng is the same as that of Shaman P'eng (Wu P'eng) in the first reading, on the K'un-lun paradise. It is ironic that P'eng-tsu's description of his state of longevity consists of the typical list of complaints of any very old person, except that in this case P'eng-tsu lived to be almost eight hundred years old and had suffered the loss of one hundred and five relatives, including parents, wives, and children. The parallel between P'eng-tsu and Methuselah is often drawn because of the similarity of their age. It is noteworthy that in recent times the myth of longevity has been immortalized by medical science, since the name the Methuselah gene has been given to a gene identified in some human beings as a longevity gene.

> When P'eng K'eng poured out pheasant soup, how did God enjoy his sacrificial offering? He received the gift of eternal life, so how did he achieve such longevity? (*Ch'u Tz'u, T'ien wen,* SPTK 3.32b)

> P'eng-tsu's surname was Chien. He was named K'eng at his death. He was the great-great-grandson of Chuan Hsu. At the end of the Yin [Shang] he was already 767 years old, but he never declined into old age. . . . Therefore the king ordered an imperial concubine to ride in a closed carriage and go to P'eng-tsu to question him about the Way. When she arrived, she bowed several times and asked about his methods for extending one's life span and about longevity. P'eng-tsu said: ". . . I had been orphaned while I was still in my mother's womb. Then I was born, and at three years of age I lost my mother. I suffered during the revolt of the T'ai Jung and was exiled in the western regions for over one hundred years. In addition, I was a widower at an early age. I buried forty-nine wives and lost fifty-four children. I have frequently experienced sorrow and tragedy. My good Humor in my guts has been broken, my cold flesh and my hot flesh are not glossy and smooth, and both the blood circulating through my body and my still blood have grown dry. I am afraid that I am not long for this world. My knowledge is shallow and inadequate. I am not able to put it into words for you. . . . " And then he was gone, and no one knows where he went. Over seventy years later I heard that someone had caught a glimpse of him out west in the kingdom of Flowing Sands. (*Shen hsien chuan,* HWTS 1.7b–11b)

Metamorphoses

Like their Greco-Roman counterparts, many Chinese mythical figures become metamorphosed into plants, birds, and animals, or objects such as a dead tree or stone. As Daphne turned into laurel and the sisters of Phaeton into amber-dropping trees, so Ch'ih Yu's fetters turned into a grove of maple trees and Yi Yin's mother turned into a dead and hollow mulberry tree. As Ganymede (or Deucalion) and Orion turned into the constellations of Aquarius and Orion, so Fu Yueh became a star, and the two quarreling brothers Yen Po and Shih Ch'en became stars that never crossed paths. As the nymph Psamathe turned into a seal, so Ch'ang O became a toad on the moon. Birds are the most frequent form of metamorphosis, possibly because their winged flight more vividly suggests aerial divinity. Semiramis, who became a dove, Ceyx and Alcyone, who turned into birds, Leda, who metamorphosed into a swan, Nemesis, who became a goose, and Philomela, who turned into the nightingale—all have their counterparts in Chinese gods and goddesses: Ching Wei and Tan Chu became birds, and the emperor of Shu, Tu Yü, was associated with the nightjar's call.

The correlation between deity and metamorphosed state in the Greco-Roman tradition is often wittily realized. Syrinx turns into a reed as she flees from Pan, who makes a musical instrument from her new form. Narcissus turns into a delicately beautiful water flower, the narcissus, after he drowns while admiring his reflection in the water. To Philomela is given a nightingale's poignant eloquence to requite her muteness when Tereus raped her and cut her tongue out to prevent her from denouncing him. Such symbolic correlations are not always present or so clearly expressed in Chinese myths of metamorphoses, perhaps partly because the meaning of the metamorphosed state is not yet known. There are some parallels, however, such as the metamorphosis of Ch'ih Yu's (? bloodstained) fetters into a red-leafed maple tree, or the girl who was turned into a silkworm jointly with the horse she had promised to marry but did not, and the pregnant mother who became a hollow mulberry tree floating her infant on a river.

The theme of punishment occurs in many Chinese myths of metamorphosis. Ch'ih Yu was punished by the Yellow Emperor, Tan Chu by his father, Yao. Yi Yin's mother was punished because she disobeyed the command of a spirit in her dream not to look back on her flooded city, and Ch'ang O because she stole the Queen Mother of the West's drug of immortality given to Yi the Archer. Tu Yü, Emperor Wang of Shu, was punished because he had ravished his prime minister's wife, and Kun was executed because he stole from God. Although the significance of maple, a hollow tree, a bird, and a toad is known in these instances, more often it is not. For example, the meaning of the metamorphosis of Kun and Yü into a bear is unclear because their ursinity and, in the case of Yü, his bestiovestism have yet to be convincingly interpreted. It could well be that ursinity may be deciphered in terms of the bear cult to be found among Siberian tribes or the Ainu of Japan, but a specific link has yet to be established (Bodde 1975, 78, 81, 122). The link between bestiovestism and totemism in archaic times, moreover, has been rejected by Karlgren (1946, 251).

P'an Ku Is Transformed into the Universe

The clearest correlation between the nature of the god and his metamorphosed state is to be seen in the late myth of P'an Ku, which is a major etiological myth of the cosmological human body. The significance of this correlation has been analyzed in chapter 1, utilizing the terminology of Doty (1986, 115–17) and Lincoln (1986, 5–20).

When the first born, P'an Ku, was approaching death, his body was transformed. His breath became the wind and clouds; his voice became peals of thunder. His left eye became the sun; his right eye became the moon. His four limbs and five extremities became the four cardinal points and the five peaks. His blood and semen became water and rivers. His muscles and veins became the earth's arteries; his flesh became fields and land. His hair and beard became the stars; his bodily hair became plants and trees. His teeth and bones became metal and rock; his vital marrow became pearls and jade. His sweat and bodily fluids became streaming rain. All the mites on his body were touched by the wind and were turned into the black-haired people. (*Wu yün li-nien chi*, cited in *Yi shih*, PCTP 1.2a)

The Monster Fish Changes into the Monster Bird

The K'un fish, the mythical creature that turned into the P'eng bird, belongs to a very early mythological tradition predating the fourth-century B.C. text *Chuang Tzu*. This is evident because the central passage of the next reading was cited by Chuang Tzu from a preexisting book, *Tall Stories from Ch'i* (*Ch'i hsieh*), a book of marvels originating in the northeastern state of Ch'i (Shantung province). That book has not survived, but the vestigial myth is preserved in Chuang Tzu's philosophical work, in the first of seven chapters known to be authentic. The myth of the K'un fish become P'eng bird remained vestigial and was not developed in the later tradition. Perhaps this is because the myth became fixed in amber by being incorporated into the conceptual framework of this original and witty philosopher of the school of Taoism. Chuang Tzu uses the device of changing visual perspective, when the P'eng bird high in the sky looks down at miniscule objects in the world below, to propound difficult concepts of relativity, subjectivity, and objective reality. That Han exegetes glossed *k'un* as 'fish roe', thus accentuating the dichotomy between the miniscule, k'un, and the gigantic, P'eng, between the microcosm and the macrocosm, adds a further dimension to the interpretation of the myth.

In North Gloom there is a fish. Its name is K'un. K'un is countless thousand leagues big. It changes into a bird, and its name is P'eng. P'eng's back is countless thousand leagues broad. When it is aroused and flies, its wings are like clouds suspended in the sky. When the seas roll back their waves, this bird migrates to South Gloom. South Gloom is the Pool of Heaven. The book *Tall Stories from Ch'i* is about wonders. *Tall Stories* says, "When the P'eng bird migrates to South Gloom, the water is dashed up across three thousand leagues. Rolling on the whirlwind, it rises ninety thousand leagues high." Only when it has gone for six months does it rest. Are those horses of the wild? Or is it fine dust? Or is it just creatures blown into one another by the bird's breath? The blue, blue sky—is that its real color, or is it because it is so distant and infinite? From where this bird looks down, it must look just like that. (*Chuang Tzu, Hsiao-yao,* SPPY 1.1a–2a)

The Death of Ch'ih Yu

Myths of Ch'ih Yu in his function as the god of war and the warrior-god who challenged the Yellow Emperor for supremacy have been presented and discussed in chapters 2 and 6. It is sufficient here to draw attention to the major mythic motifs surrounding the death of the god. First there is the analogous metamorphosis of his wooden fetters into a grove of maple trees. The maple motif may signify the color of the god's blood following his execution, and it may be emblematic of his function as the god of war. The first reading is from a first-century A.D. chapter of *The Classic of Mountains and Seas* and is the earliest expression of the god's metamorphosis. It is elaborated in the second reading, a T'ang version of the myth, in *Seven Tomes from the Cloudy Shelf* by Wang Ch'üan. The color motif predominates in later versions. Shen Kua of the eleventh century mentions red salt known as "Ch'ih Yu's Blood" in his miscellany *Essays Written from Dreaming Pond* (the third reading below), whereas the fragmentary third-century A.D. text *Imperial Survey* refers to a scarlet vapor known as "Ch'ih Yu's Banner." This fourth reading records antiquarian information concerning mythical sites and the supposed burial place of the god.

> In the middle of the vast wilderness . . . there is Sung Mountain, and on it there is a scarlet snake named Birth Snake. There is a tree growing on the mountaintop called the maple. The maple tree is the wooden fetters and manacles left behind by Ch'ih Yu, and that is why it is called the maple tree. (*Shan hai ching, Ta huang nan ching,* SPPY 15.3b–4a)

> The Yellow Emperor killed Ch'ih Yu on the mound of Li Mountain. He threw his fetters on the summit of Sung Mountain in the middle of the vast wilderness. His fetters later turned into a grove of maple trees. (*Yun chi ch'i ch'ien, Hsien-yuan pen chi,* SPTK 100.18b)

Hsieh-chou is a salt marsh. The color of the salt is bright red. The popular name for it is "Ch'ih Yu's Blood." (*Meng-ch'i pi-t'an chiao cheng*, CH 3.127)

The mound of Ch'ih Yu is in T'ung-p'ing commandery in Shou-ch'ang county in the city of K'an-hsiang. It is seventy feet high. The people always worship at it in the tenth month. There is a scarlet vapor from it like the roll of blood-red silk. The people call it "Ch'ih Yu's Banner." Shoulders-and-Thighs Mound is in Shan-yang commandery in Chü-yeh county in the city of Chung-chü. It is the same in size as the K'an mound. Legend has it that, when the Yellow Emperor fought with Ch'ih Yu at the Cho-lu wilderness and the Yellow Emperor killed him, his body changed places, and that is why he was buried in another place. (*Huang lan, Chung-mu chi*, TSCC 1.3)

The Myth of Yao's Son Tan Chu

Several fragments narrating the myth of Tan Chu, Cinnabar Crimson, illustrate the phenomenon in mythography of the tendency toward a tenuous, and spurious, linkage between one mythical figure and several unrelated ones. In this case the mythical Tan Chu, who was also known as Yao's unworthy son, is linked through color motifs in his name to the Land of Huan-chu, Rousing Crimson, and to the mythical bird Chu (a phonetic pun), and also by extension to Huan Tou, an official of Yao, and to the land of Huan-t'ou. The readings present the myth of Tan Chu, Cinnabar Crimson, besides these tenuous connections. This law of mythographic fallacy is typical of the false associations that are sometimes adduced to a famous mythical figure.

The basic narratives of the Tan Chu myth occur in *Chuang Tzu* and *The Classic of History*, which form the fifth and second readings respectively. These relate that Yao killed his eldest son and that Tan Chu was a degenerate youth. The Tan Chu myth fits the recurring pattern in early texts of myths relating to Yao and Shun, who are both said to have passed over their eldest son in favor of a man unrelated to them and to have ceded him succession to the throne. In these cases the eldest son is labeled "unworthy" or "worthless," and it is not only he but also their many other sons who are passed over in the succession. This myth has traditionally been presented in socioethical terms as a eufunctional paradigm of the sage-ruler ceding to an unrelated man on the basis of merit. The most recent exposition of this interpretation, bolstered with

Lévi-Straussian structural analysis, is Sarah Allan's work *The Heir and the Sage* (1981, 27–68).

If the myth is subjected to an alternative mode of analysis, however, it suggests a quite different underlying pattern. Taking what Malinowski termed the "sociological charter" as a conceptual framework, the myth of Tan Chu sent into exile, or even killed by his father, Yao, allows of a fresh interpretation. The myth might represent the vestige of a social custom in archaic society of transmitting succession outside the lines of kinship. As such, the motif of the "unworthy eldest son" who has to be punished by exile or death would constitute a rationale for what may have been an unpopular custom. It is significant that the mythologem of passing over the eldest son to an unrelated heir, the unworthy displaced by the worthy, died out with the succession of Yü's son after Yü died. The myth survived, however, as a potent element in ethical philosophy in the sociopolitical debates of the late Chou period.

> Yao took the daughter of the San-yi clan as his wife and gave her the name Nü-huang. (*Ta Tai Li chi*, SPTK 7.5b)

> There was nothing to match the pride of Tan Chu. All he did was take an insolent delight in frivolity and behave as an arrogant tyrant. He did not care whether it was day or night—it was all the same to him. He would go boating even when there was no water. He and his friends would indulge in sexual frolics in his house, and so his line of succession was abolished. (*Shang shu, Yi Chi*, SPPY 5.6b)

> Yao's son was not a good son. Shun had him banished to Cinnabar Gulf to serve as overlord of it, which is why Yao's son was called Tan Chu, Cinnabar Crimson. (*T'ai-p'ing yü-lan*, citing *Shang shu yi p'ien*, SPTK 63.3b)

> Yao fought a battle on the bank of Cinnabar River, and as a result he subjugated the Southern Man tribe. (*Lü-shih ch'un-ch'iu, Chao shu*, SPTK 20.9b)

> Yao killed his eldest son. (*Chuang Tzu, Tao chih*, SPPY 9.22b)

> The land of Huan-t'ou is to the south of it. The people there have human faces and a bird's wings, and a bird's beak, which is useful for catching fish. One idea is that it is east of Pi-fang. Another that it is the Land of Huan-chu [Rousing Crimson]. (*Shan hai ching, Hai wai nan ching*, SPPY 6.2a)

Huan Tou was Yao's official. He committed a crime and threw himself into the South Sea and killed himself. Yao felt pity for him and made Huan Tou's son live in South Sea and offer sacrifice to his father. In paintings he is represented as an immortal. (Kuo P'u's commentary on *Shan hai ching, Hai wai nan ching,* SPPY 6.2a)

Chü Mountain looks out over Liu-huang country to the west, faces Mount Chu-p'i to the north and Mount Ch'ang-yu to the east. Ying River flows out from it and runs southeast to Scarlet River. There is a great amount of white jade and cinnabar grains on Chü Mountain. There is a beast on it which looks like a sucking-pig. There is an ogre on it which makes a noise like a dog barking; its name is Li-li. The district where it appears will achieve great things. There is a bird on it. In appearance it is like an owl with human hands, and its call sounds like "Bee!" Its name is Chu. It is named after its own call. The district where it appears always drives away its good men. (*Shan hai ching, Nan tz'u erh ching,* SPPY 1.4b–5a)

Ch'ang O Becomes a Toad in the Moon

The myth of Ch'ang O's metamorphosis into a toad in the moon will by now be familiar from earlier chapters. The brief passage is rich in motifs: the trickster figure, theft from a god, punishment by metamorphosis, the regenerative powers of the toad and the moon, the drug of immortality, and the related mythical figures of Yi the Archer and the Queen Mother of the West.

Yi asked the Queen Mother of the West for the drug of immortality. Yi's wife, Heng O, stole it and escaped to the moon. She was metamorphosed on the moon and became the striped toad Ch'an-ch'u, and she is the essence of the moon. (Subcommentary of *Ch'u hsueh chi,* citing *Huai-nan Tzu,* SPCY 1.4a)

Yi Yin's Mother Changes into a
Hollow Mulberry Tree

The myth of Yi Yin has been discussed in chapter 5. The narrative is full of important motifs: miraculous birth; an abandoned baby boy; a hollow mulberry, which has links with the motif of the cosmic tree, Leaning Mulberry; the mother's prophetic dream; the mortar bowl, which replicates the image of the floating hollow tree and presages Yi

Yin's upbringing and early career as cook; metamorphosis as a punishment for disobeying the spirit world; and the naming of the foundling after the river where he was discovered. These motifs conjoin to create the major motif of the hero.

> A daughter of the Yu Shen clan was picking mulberry [leaves] when she found a baby in a hollow mulberry tree. She presented it to her lord. The lord ordered his cook to bring the child up. When he inquired how this had happened, someone said that the baby's mother had lived near Yi River and that after she became pregnant a spirit told her in a dream, "If your mortar bowl leaks water, hurry to the east, but don't look back." Next day she did see her mortar bowl leak water, so she told her neighbors, and hurried ten leagues to the east. But she looked back at her city — there was nothing but water. Her body then transformed into a hollow mulberry tree, which is why they called the baby Yi Yin. (*Lü-shih ch'un-ch'iu, Pen wei,* SPTK 14.3b–4a)

Fu Yueh Turns into a Star

The mythical figure of Fu Yueh is first mentioned in the fourth-century B.C. text *Chuang Tzu,* as a sage who became a minister to the historical Shang emperor Wu Ting (ca. 1200–1181 B.C.) and then turned into a star as a reward for his wise and humane government (the second reading below). The third-century B.C. Confucian philosopher *Hsun Tzu* notes Fu Yueh's strange appearance in his chapter entitled "Against Physiognomy" (the first reading). With Ssu-ma Ch'ien's account in the third reading, mythic motifs give way to legendary embellishment as Fu Yueh becomes the archetypal unknown man who is selected by an omen to lead the kingdom to greater glory. The same pattern is noticeable in the myths of Shun, Yi Yin, and the Great Lord Chiang.

> In appearance, Fu Yueh's body was like an erect fin. (*Hsun Tzu, Fei hsiang,* SPPY 3.2b)

> Fu Yueh achieved the Way and became prime minister for King Wu Ting, and his rule extended over the whole world. He ascended to East Tie, mounted Winnower Star and Tail Star, and joined the ranks of the countless stars. (*Chuang Tzu, Ta tsung shih,* SPPY 3.6a–b)

> Wu Ting dreamed one night that he had acquired a sage called Yueh. Taking note of the appearance of the person he had seen in his dream, he then scrutinized all his assembled ministers and all his officials,

but none of them was the man in his dream. So he ordered all his officers to conduct a search in the outlying areas of his realm, and they found Yueh on Fu Gorge. At that time, Yueh was part of a prisoners' chain gang doing construction work on Fu Gorge. He appeared before Wu Ting. Wu Ting said, "This is the man I dreamed of." He took him aside and had a discussion with him, and it turned out that Yueh was a sage. He promoted him to the rank of prime minister and the Yin [Shang] kingdom enjoyed excellent government. (*Shih chi, Yin pen chi,* SPPY 3.7a–b)

Tu Yü and the Call of the Nightjar

The narrative of Tu Yü may be said to be a singular expression of classical mythic motifs: the descent of the Shu ancestral kings from the god of sericulture, Ts'an Ts'ung; the metamorphosis of Shu kings into immortals; the descent of Tu Yü from Heaven to rule the world below; the appearance of his bride-to-be from a well; the resurrected corpse of Pieh Ling, who became Tu Yü's minister; a flood; the crime of adultery; abdication in the manner of Yao (but for a different reason); and self-punishment by exile.

The myth of metamorphosis became attached to the figure of Tu Yü; it was said that when he left his kingdom in shame and went from Shu into exile, the call of the *tzu-kuei* bird was heard, and so the deposed king became identified with the bird. Some translators render the name of the bird as the cuckoo. But although the cuckoo has the connotation of cuckoldry in Western lore and the theme of cuckoldry is present in the narrative, it has not been used to render *tzu-kuei* here for the reason that the punning intention of cuckoo-cuckoldry is not present in the Chinese text. The name *nightjar* has been used instead. This semantically neutral name also has the virtue of coinciding with the sympathetic attitude of traditional writers toward the figure of Tu Yü.

This motif-bound text contains no fewer than three metamorphoses: the kings and their people, who become immortal; the corpse of Pieh Ling, which comes back to life; and the transference of Tu Yü's spirit to the nightjar.

The text of the first reading below, *Basic Annals of the Kings of Shu,* is attributed to Yang Hsiung (53 B.C.–A.D. 18), who was a native of Shu, but it more probably belongs to the category of pseudepigraphic literature. It is almost certain, however, that the anonymous author either was a native of Shu in the post-Han era or lived there and viewed the mythology of the region with great sympathy. The second reading is from the renowned dictionary of the Han era, *An Explication of Written Characters* by Hsu Shen (ca. A.D. 100).

The first ancestor of the Shu kings was called Ts'an Ts'ung. In the next era his descendant was called Po Huo, and in the era after that his descendant was called Yü Fu. Each of these three eras lasted several hundred years. In each era they became gods and did not die, and their people followed their kings, taking another shape and vanishing like them. The king was out hunting when he came to Mount Yü, then he vanished as an immortal. Today he is worshiped in a temple to him in Yü. In those days the population of Shu grew very sparse. Later on, a man named Tu Yü descended from Heaven and alighted on Mount Chu-t'i. A girl called Li emerged from a well in Chiang-yuan and became Tu Yü's wife. Then he proclaimed himself King of Shu, with the title of Emperor Wang. He governed a city called P'i near Mount Min. The other people who had become transformed gradually reappeared. When Emperor Wang had reached an era of over a century long, there was a man in Ching called Pieh Ling whose corpse completely disappeared. People in Ching searched for it but could not find it. Pieh Ling's corpse reached Shu, where it came to life again. Emperor Wang made Pieh Ling his prime minister. At that time a huge body of water poured out of Jade Mountain, like the floods in the era of Yao. Emperor Wang was unable to control the flooding, so he ordered Pieh Ling to dredge Jade Mountain so that the people could go back to their houses free from worry. After Pieh Ling had left to control the floods, Emperor Wang had an affair with his wife. But when he realized that his virtue was not equal to the task of ruling and that he did not measure up to Pieh Ling, he abdicated the throne and handed power over to him, and then he went away (just as Yao did when he resigned in favor of Shun). When Pieh Ling came to the throne, he took the title of Emperor K'ai-ming. A son was born to Emperor Ch'i named Lu Pao, who also took the imperial title of K'ai-ming. (*T'ai-p'ing yü-lan*, citing *Shu wang pen chi*, SPTK 888.2b–3b)

Emperor Wang of Shu committed adultery with his prime minister's wife, and then, full of shame, he went into voluntary exile. He became the *tzu-kuei* bird [nightjar]. So when the people of Shu hear the call of the nightjar, they always say it is Emperor Wang. (*Shuo-wen chieh-tzu*, SPTK 1.4.5a)

The Silkworm Horse

Horse myths are not very numerous in the Chinese tradition. The counterpart of Pegasus, the winged messenger of Zeus, is the dragon that wings through the air and dives into the deep. The most famous early account of mythical horses occurs in the story of King Mu of Chou, who drove a team of eight horses to visit the Queen Mother of the West. His fabled team is described with the same fond hyperbole as the legendary Bucephalus, the favorite horse of Alexander the Great, who had the city Bucephalus built in honor of his horse after it died in battle in 326 B.C. In the Han era the myth of the horse of Heaven and the golden horse of the west seized the imagination of emperors, who sent emissaries to obtain them from Ferghana (Loewe and Hulsewé 1979, 42–43, 132–35; Birrell 1993, 40–42, 183 nn. 41–51).

The following narrative of the horse and the girl is taken from the fourth-century A.D. collection of stories *A Record of Researches into Spirits*. In terms of the mythological tradition, this is a late work, and so the text should be classified as a fictional reworking of older legendary material. The fictional elements are evident in the consecutive narrative style; the characterization of the girl, her father, the horse, and the neighbor; naturalistic dialog; realistic detail; a dramatic climax; and the setting of the narrative in the days of yore. Despite its numerous fictional aspects, however, the story reveals some vestigial mythic motifs that suggest that the account may have originated in a local mythological tradition. As in the myth of P'an Hu the dog, the animal is male. The horse also possesses supernatural intelligence and the power to metamorphose and cause bodily transformation. The metamorphosis of the girl is again a punishment, for she reneged on her trickster promise to marry the horse and also tormented him in his desire. The narrative may be classified as a vestigial etiological myth since it explains the origin of the mulberry tree. A further comparison with the myth of P'an Hu the dog reveals the presence of a similar taboo against bestiality, voiced by the "Dad" in the narrative, when he tells the girl, "Don't say anything—I'm afraid we will disgrace our family." In the best tradition of myth, however, his worst fears are realized when his daughter is changed with the horse skin (after he killed and skinned the horse) to become a silkworm that spins a gigantic cocoon. This cocoon serves as a ribald sexual emblem, since the word for the prolific cocoon silk (*ssu*) is a pun for sexual desire (*ssu*). Derk Bodde has noted that this account by Kan Pao originated in Shu (1975, 271).

There is an old story that in the period of great antiquity, there was a grown man who traveled far away and left no other person at home except his young girl and a stallion, which she looked after herself. She lived in poverty in this dismal place and she longed for her father. Then she said to the horse, "If you can coax our Dad to come home, I will marry you." When the horse received this promise from her, he tore free from his bridle and left, heading in the direction of her Dad. When her Dad saw his horse, he was amazed and delighted. So he took hold of it to ride it. His horse looked in the direction it had come from and neighed sadly without stopping. Her Dad said, "This horse is not behaving like this for nothing—is there some reason for it at home or not?" Then he hurriedly mounted his horse and returned home. He was extremely fond of his horse, so he cut an extra generous amount of grass to feed it, but the horse refused to eat it. Every time he saw the woman going in and coming out he immediately burst into a paroxysm of rage and joy. This happened on more than one occasion. Her Dad was amazed by this and questioned the girl about it in private. The girl told her Dad all about it, and he was convinced that this was the reason for it all. Her Dad said, "Don't say anything—I'm afraid we will disgrace our family—and don't keep going in and out of here." Then he took cover and killed it with his bow and arrow and put the skin out in the garden to dry. Her Dad went on his travels. The girl and a neighbor's wife were playing with the skin when the girl kicked it with her foot and said, "You're just a domestic animal, yet you wanted a human as your wife, eh? It's all your own fault you've been butchered and skinned, so why should you feel sorry for yourself. . . ?" Before she had finished speaking, the horse skin rose up with one bound, wrapped the girl up, and went away. The neighbor's wife was so afraid and alarmed she did not dare to rescue her but ran off to tell her Dad. When her Dad got back home, he searched for her but he had long since lost track of her. Several days later they found that the girl and the horse skin had completely changed into a silkworm spinning thread in the branches of a big tree. The cocoon's threads were thick and large and different from an ordinary silkworm's. The neighbor's wife took it down and looked after it. It produced several times more silk than the normal silkworm. So she called the tree the mulberry— mulberry [*sang*] stands for "mourning" [*sang*]. Because of this everyone rushed to plant from it, and what is cultivated nowadays comes from this stock. (*Sou shen chi*, TSCC 14.93–94)

12

Love

Compared with the rude promiscuity, violent couplings, and lustful passions of myths worldwide on the theme of love, the decorous tenor of this motif in the Chinese mythological tradition indicates at least two major trends in the mythographic period, namely, censorship and social mores. In comparison with mythologies worldwide, it becomes evident that although Chinese myths generally find their counterpart in other mythic systems, there is a clear distinction between Chinese and other myths on the sexual theme, for they are sanitized and domesticated for the presumed sensibilities of readers of the late and postclassical era. While evidence for censorship is not ample, there is one instance of redactors trawling the classical repertoire. This occurs in the extant text of *The Classic of Mountains and Seas.* At the end of chapters 9 and 13, two identical endnotes state that in the year 6 B.C. the officials Wang, Kung, and Hsiu corrected the text of chapters 1–9 and 10–13 of the *Classic.* The word *correct* could indicate mild editorial amendments or full-scale censorial excision of offending material. It is noteworthy that this took place in the first year of the reign of the Former Han Emperor Ai (6–1 B.C.), when the emperor, convinced of the unethical, unorthodox developments in the government office responsible for court entertainment, abolished the office *in toto* (Birrell 1993, 5). It is probable that the new broom also swept through other departments in line with the emperor's distaste for laxity and depravity. Whether there were originally no bawdy passages in the early texts of myths or, as seems more likely, such passages were bowdlerized, the result is that in classical Chinese mythology there is no goddess of love such as Aphrodite (or Venus), nor a god of love such as Eros or Cupid, nor the amorous adventures of Zeus and others. Even in texts that only imply sexual activity, such as Yü's encounter with the T'u-shan girl, the episode is hedged with ambiguity and innuendo. During the Han period, either in conjunction with puritanical censorship or in an independent evolution, new social mores dictated that narratives on the theme of love should depict courteous exchanges between lovers, as with the Queen Mother of the West and King Mu of Chou, or express the ideal values of fidelity and devotion, but in particular that they should skirt around a direct reference to physical realism and avoid prurient excess. In all this, of course, the values of the social system should be reflected in the conventional gender roles of the subordinate female and dominant male. The result is, as the readings indicate, that the mythic power of the narratives had been subdued by social philosophy current in the Han and post-Han eras.

In other, more robust mythological traditions, lustful couplings between the gods and humans usually have a procreative function. Clearly, this functional aspect is absent from most classical Chinese myths. This does not mean to say that the procreation myth per se is a minor one but that procreation results not from Olympian intercourse but through miraculous birth or following an idealized and courtly exchange of pleasantries. Examples are the birth of Ch'i in the myth of Yü and the T'u-shan girl and the birth of Shao Hao in the myth of the Son of the White Emperor and Huan O. Most conceptions in Chinese myth are divine and miraculous and are achieved without the intervention of a male. The only exceptions are Kun, who gave birth to Yü, and the fabled Country of Men, where men give birth to sons only, through their middle, back, or side. The most prestigious examples of divine procreation without sex are Chien Ti, ancestress of the Shang, and Chiang Yüan, ancestress of the Chou, who trod in a giant's footprint and swallowed a bird's egg.

The readings in this chapter illustrate typical aspects of mythic love: the battle between the sexes, the founding of the institution of marriage, married love, divine courtship, separation, and bereavement.

Nü Kua Marries Her Brother in the First Marriage

The Nü Kua text has been placed first in the readings because the goddess originally belonged to the pantheon of primeval deities as creatrix and savior of the world. But in this text, which is late in the mythographic tradition, she does not appear in her earlier emanation. The reading serves to show how a classical myth is reworked to convey new values and is thus subverted. The T'ang author Li Jung (fl. A.D. 846–874) has eliminated the two main functions of the goddess and has humanized her, relegating her to a conventionally subordinate female role and diminishing her own divinity and mythic power by making her pray to a higher god.

In this mythopoeic passage, Li Jung presents an etiological myth of the institution of marriage. The sentence "there were two people, Nü Kua, older brother and sister," is so awkward that it betrays this reworking of old mythic material. Some scholars interpret it to mean that Nü is the sister, Kua the brother. The same odd construction occurs in the Woman Ch'ou narrative: "There are two people in the sea. Her name is Woman Ch'ou." Leaving aside the question of the name or names, the narrative relates how the brother and sister invoked God to sanction their union and how permission was granted for what was the first marriage among humans. Like Adam and Eve, the first couple, who covered their nakedness with a fig leaf, the brother and sister feel ashamed of their sexual difference after carnal knowledge of each other and hide behind a fan.

Although interpretation of Li Jung's version could stop at a new etiological myth that explains the human institution of marriage sanctioned by God, the lateness of his version prompts further questions beyond the purely etiological concerning the necessity for such a new version of the myth. Li Jung's neomyth of the late T'ang era may fit the paradigm proposed by Malinowski: "myth serves principally to establish a sociological charter, or a retrospective moral pattern of behavior" (1954, 144). It is possible to conjecture that the T'ang myth may have as its underlying intent a rationale for incest between brother and sister in certain communities and in certain situations. It might belong to that category of myth which converts an overtly antisocial behavior pattern into a socially acceptable norm. Eberhard has stated of this mythic narrative, "Otherwise, cases of sibling marriage are rare in Chinese mythology" (1968, 445). Other accounts of sibling marriage occur in *The Treatise on Research into Nature*, of the third to the fifth century A.D., and in *A Record of Researches into Spirits,* of the fourth century A.D. (Mathieu 1989, 158–59). Sibling marriage is also present in the P'an Hu dog myth, when the sons and daughters of the dog and the princess intermarry to found a new race. It would seem that in times of dire need, such as floods, famine, war, or epidemics which decimate populations and reduce humans to the bare choice of survival of the human race, traditional taboos tend to be overlooked and the forbidden condoned.

> Long ago, when the world first began, there were two people, Nü Kua and her older brother. They lived on Mount K'un-lun. And there were not yet any ordinary people in the world. They talked about becoming husband and wife, but felt ashamed. So the brother at once went with his sister up Mount K'un-lun and made this prayer:
>
> > Oh Heaven, if Thou wouldst send us two forth to become man and wife,
> > then make all the misty vapor gather;
> > if not, then make all the misty vapor disperse.
>
> At this the misty vapor immediately gathered. When the sister became intimate with her brother, they plaited some grass to make a fan to screen their faces. Even today, when a man takes a wife, they hold a fan, which is a symbol of what happened long ago. (*Tu yi chih,* TSCC 3.51)

The Lord of the Granary and the Goddess of Salt River

The narrative of the Lord of the Granary and the Goddess of Salt River from *The Origin of Hereditary Families* (commentary ca. third century A.D.) contains numerous motifs based on that most enduring of myths, gender competition or, stated in more traditional terms, the battle between the sexes, which literally informs this narrative. The goddess plays the role of the trickster familiar to many mythologies, especially Old Man Coyote of the Crow Indians (Lowie 1935, 111). In this role she is comparable to Ch'ang O of the lunar myth. Like other trickster tales worldwide, the myth of the Goddess of Salt River is a humorous account, in which the hero, the Lord of the Granary, outwits the tricky goddess by playing on her feminine weakness of vanity and by using the cunning ruse of offering her an intimate love token, a waist girdle, which turns out to be a hunting weapon. Other motifs are the metamorphosis of the goddess into a swarm of insects; the darkening of the world as she blots out the sun; the sunlit rock from which the hero shoots his fatal arrow; and the restoration of the world to goodness and light. The sitiological motif in the names of the two protagonists, grain and salt (*Lin* and *Yen*), suggests that the underlying intent of this section of the account might be construed as the desire of the ruler of a territory rich in the natural resources of salt and fish to acquire territory rich in grain, or vice versa. In primitive economies salt was a prerequisite for the preservation and preparation of staple foods. One last motif is discernible in this narrative, that is, the vestige of a local sun myth in which a goddess possesses power over the sun. If this surmise is correct, it parallels other sun myths in the Chinese tradition, such as that of Hsi-Ho, in which a female deity predominates. The theme of gender competition mentioned at the outset also implies that the myth might also be read as an evolving contest for supremacy between a matriarchal and patriarchal society.

> So they unanimously made him their chieftain. He became the Lord of the Granary. Now he sailed the earthenware boat from Yi River to Yen-yang. At Salt River there is a goddess. She said to the Lord of the Granary, "This land is vast, and there is all the fish and salt that come from it. I wish you would stay here and live among us." The Lord of the Granary refused. At nightfall the Salt Goddess suddenly came to sleep with him. At dawn she turned into a flying insect and flew in a swarm with other insects. They blotted out the sunlight and the world grew pitch black for more than ten days in a row. The Lord of the Granary could not make out which was east or west for seven days and seven nights. He ordered someone to hold a green silk cord and present it to the Salt Goddess. He said to her, "This will suit you if you wear it as a fringed belt. If we are to live together, then please accept it from me." The Salt Goddess accepted it and wore it as a fringed belt. At once the Lord of the Granary stood on a sunlit rock, and aiming at the green cord she wore, he shot arrows at her. He hit her and the Salt Goddess died. Then the sky cleared far and wide. (Ch'in Chia-mo's reconstructed text, *Shih pen, Shih hsing,* 1.93–94)

Draught Ox and Weaver Maid

The motifs of the stellar myth of Weaver Maid and Draught Ox were discussed in chapter 9, where attention was drawn to the evolution of the love motif of the myth.

East of Sky River is Weaver Maid, the daughter of God in Heaven. Year by year she toils and slaves with loom and shuttle till she finishes weaving a celestial robe of cloudy silk. God in Heaven pitied her living alone, and allowed her to marry Draught Ox west of the river. After they married she neglected her weaving work. God in Heaven grew angry and punished her by ordering her to return to the east of the river, letting her make one crossing each year to be with Draught Ox. (*Erh ya yi,* TSCC 13.147)

The major star myth of Weaver Maid spawned a number of subsidiary mythic narratives, of which that of the Sky River or the Sky Voyager is the most important. This narrative, along with that of Weaver Maid and Draught Ox, combines the elements of astronomy and aerial travel. The motif of an aerial voyage reflects the great interest in travel into the unknown during the Han period, itself a mark of the territorial expansion of that great dynasty. The first verifiably dated explorer was Chang Ch'ien, who was sent on a diplomatic mission by the Han Emperor Wu to secure treaties with China's western neighbors. From his travels between 138 and 122 B.C., he gathered information on the geographic, scientific, and social aspects of different ethnic regions in the Tarim Basin and brought back many exotic items, such as the grape, walnut, and hemp. A sixth-century A.D. text, *A Record of the Seasonal Customs of Ching Ch'u,* preserved in a Ming compendium, even relates that Chang Ch'ien was ordered by the Han Emperor Wu to discover the source of the "River," by which is meant the Yellow River (Yuan K'o 1980.2, 88). The earlier narrative from *The Treatise on Research into Nature,* which forms the reading here, follows the account in the *Seasonal Customs* more or less verbatim but does not have the prefatory section on Emperor Wu's command.

That the events in the account of the Sky Voyager were attached to the historical figure of Chang Ch'ien in the *Seasonal Customs* illustrates a general rule in the making of myth or legend, namely, to give greater glory to a narrative by investing it with the name of a famous person, real or imagined. The same mythopoeia revolved around the person of the Han Emperor Wu. The reading mentions by name a historical figure, one Yen Chün-p'ing, who lived in the first century B.C. He was a Taoist and an astronomer of Shu (Szechwan), who was said to sight strange stars. The text itself is attributed to the author and astronomer Chang Hua (A.D. 232–300) but is probably a pseudepigraphic work of the Six Dynasties.

In olden days it was said that Sky River was connected to the sea. Nowadays there is a man who lives on a little island. Year after year in the eighth month, a floating raft comes and goes, and it never fails to pass by at the same time. The man had a wonderful idea—he erected a soaring compartment on the raft, packed provisions, boarded the raft, and left. During ten days or more he still saw the stars, moon, and sun, but from then on it became blurred far and wide, and he could not tell whether it was day or night. He went on for ten days or more, when suddenly he came to a place where there were what seemed like inner and outer city walls and well-ordered houses, and in the distance he could see many weaver women in a palace. He saw a man leading oxen to an island bank to drink from it. The oxherd then said in surprise, "How did you get here?" The man explained all about his purpose in coming here and, for his part, asked where this place was. He answered, "Go back to Shu commandery and put your question to Yen Chün-p'ing; then you will know." In the end the man did not go farther up the island shore because he was to return according to the raft's regular time. Later on he reached Shu and asked Yen Chün-p'ing, who said, "On a certain day of a certain month in a certain year a stranger star trespassed into the Draught Ox constellation." He calculated the year and month, and it was just when this man had arrived in Sky River. (*Po wu chih, Tsa shui*, 2, SPPY 3.3a)

The Son of the White Emperor
Courts the Goddess Huang O

The love of the goddess Huang O and the Son of the White Emperor is told in a courtly narrative dating from the sixth century A.D., itself based on an account in *Researches into Lost Records* by Wang Chia, of the fourth century A.D. The courtly mode is evident in the way their love is described through indirection, and the consummation of their love, which resulted in the birth of their son, the god Shao Hao, is omitted, in keeping with the high literary mode of the Liang dynasty (Birrell 1986, 6–28). Despite this obviating style, there are clear markers of sexual desire: the love feast, outdoor scenario, music, song, and an idyllic boat journey. Moreover, the elegant but elusively phrased songs that the gods exchange contain covert declarations of love.

The child-god who was born from this love has two names apart from Shao Hao, which his mother gave him: Ch'iung Sang or Exhausted Mulberry, and Sang Ch'iu, the first being the name of the mythical place where his parents courted. Mulberry has the connotation of the Tree of Life in the east, the world-tree, Leaning Mulberry. Other names for the god Shao Hao are Metal Sky and Phoenix Bird. Metal is the element that is usually an attribute of the west, according to the traditional Five Elements theory, whereas Shao Hao is more generally believed to preside over the east. His "tomb" is now sited in the east, in Ch'ü-fu, Shantung, the birthplace of Confucius.

Shao Hao ruled by the power of metal. His mother was called Huang O. She lived in a palace of exquisite jade and she wove by night. Sometimes she sailed on a wooden raft by day to amuse herself, passing the vast and boundless reach of Ch'iung Sang. At that time there was a child-god whose appearance stood out from the ordinary. He was called the Son of the White Emperor, that is, the essence of T'ai-po. He descended from on high to the margin of a river and feasted and played with Huang O. He performed the "Easy Grace" music and had fun and games until he forgot to go home. At Ch'iung Sang there was a lone mulberry tree on the shore of the West Sea which grew straight up for eight thousand feet. Its leaves were red and its berries maroon. It bore fruit once in ten thousand years. Anyone who ate it became as old as Heaven. The prince and Huang O drifted on the sea. Their mast was of cassia, the banners were plaited with scented reeds. A pigeon made of carved jade was fixed on the masthead, for there is a saying that a pigeon knows the times of the four seasons. That is why it says in the *Spring and Autumn* records, "When midsummer comes and midwinter goes, they arrange the ordinances for this interval." Nowadays the weathercock is a vestigial symbol of this. The prince and Huang O sat down together and strummed their paulownia lute and catalpa zither. Huang O bent over her zither and sang a clear song:

> The sky is clear, the earth is wide and immense,
> Ten thousand images turn to fading, changing into nothing.
> We drift through skies so vast and gaze into space.

We ride in a light boat, companions of the sun.
We point our craft somewhere and reach Ch'iung Sang.
My heart knows such joy, yet our bliss is not yet full.

People say that where she journeyed is Sang-chung; in the "Airs of Wei" in *The Classic of Poetry* it says: "He made a date with me among the mulberries [*sang chung*]." It must refer to this. The Son of the White Emperor replied with this song:

The Four Cords and the Four Sides, it is hard to see their
  limits.
I race with light and chase shadow, and all around there's
  water.
In the quiet of the night in the royal palace she faces her
  weaving loom.
On Catalpa Peak the brilliant catalpa trees are very tall and
  straight.
We cut catalpa for instruments, to make lute and zither.
I sing a clear song and free, my joy knows no bounds.
On the vast seashore I have come to make my nest.

When Huang O gave birth to Shao Hao, she called him Ch'iung Sang and Sang Ch'iu. (*Shih yi chi*, HWTS 1.4b–5b)

The Bereavement of Shun's Wives

The legend of the consorts of Shun, who, according to a late tradition, became river goddesses after his death, was discussed in chapter 9, under the heading of "The Hsiang Queens."

They say that when Shun the Great made a royal tour of his territories, his two queens followed the expedition. They drowned in Hsiang River and their spirits wandered over the deeps of Lake Tung-t'ing and appeared on the banks where the Hsiao and Hsiang Rivers meet. (*Shui ching chu, Hsiang shui,* SPTK 38.14a)

The local speckled bamboo are very beautiful, and in the Wu area the speckled bamboo is called the Hsiang queens' bamboo. The speckles on it are like tear stains. (*Ch'ün fang p'u, Chu p'u,* CFPCS 5.139)

Yü and the T'u-shan Girl

The myth of Yü's marriage to the T'u-shan girl was discussed in chapters 5 and 8, with a special emphasis on the motifs of the necessary error of Yü's drumming on a stone, Yü's ursinic bestiovestism, the girl's metamorphosis into a stone, and the miraculous birth of the god of music, Ch'i, or K'ai. No love is expressed between the parents, and the narrative itself is typical of the primitive myths, which lack sentiment and emotion but are rich in graphic action.

> When Yü was controlling the floodwaters and was making a passage through Mount Huan-yuan, he changed into a bear. He spoke to the T'u-shan girl: "If you want to give me some food, when you hear the sound of a drumbeat, come to me." But Yü leaped on a stone and by mistake drummed on it. The T'u-shan girl came forward, but when she saw Yü in the guise of a bear she was ashamed and fled. She reached the foothills of Mount Sung-kao, when she turned into a stone and gave birth to Ch'i. Yü said, "Give me back my son!" The stone then split open on its north flank and Ch'i was born. (Yen Shih-ku's commentary on *Han shu, Wu-ti chi*, referring to a nonextant passage in *Huai-nan Tzu*, SPPY 6.17b–18a)

Han P'ing, a Husband and His Wife

The story of Han P'ing and his wife expresses the powerful mythic theme of undying love. The reading comes from the fourth-century A.D. collection of mythological, legendary, and fictional tales compiled by Kan Pao. Its date is approximate to that of a long anonymous verse narrative that has the same theme and shares many familiar features, "A Peacock Southeast Flew" (Birrell 1986, 53–62). The most obvious parallels are the enforced separation of a young married couple, their enduring love, a villainous prince (in the verse narrative a scheming mother-in-law), the wife given to another man, a double suicide, twin trees growing across their graves, mandarin ducks symbolizing married love singing a sad song over their graves, and the popular sympathy their tragic fate aroused. The similarities between the prose and poetic expressions of the love story cannot be coincidental but result from the power of its mythic theme. This is attested by the continued reworking of the story in later centuries. The same story is included in the tenth-century compendium *Atlas of the Whole World in the T'ai-p'ing Era* (A.D. 976–984), compiled by Yueh Shih (A.D. 930–1007), but it contains additional decorative detail about the wife's suicide leap: "The rags that came away in their hands turned into butterflies" (Yuan K'o 1980.2, 281). The story was also dramatized in the Yuan dynasty, and the Ming dynasty author Ch'en Yao-wen inserted a song Han P'ing sang before committing suicide:

> On South Mountain there is a crow;
> On North Mountain they set their snares.
> Crows by nature fly high;
> What use are those snares now!
> Crows and magpies fly in pairs,
> They would not be happy with a phoenix mate.
> My wife is an ordinary girl,
> She is not happy with the Sung prince.
>   (*T'ien-chung chi,* citing *Chiu kuo chih,* SKCS
>   18.7ıb)

The text of the love narrative from Kan Pao's collection follows.

Prince K'ang of the Sung had a manservant called Han P'ing. Han P'ing married a daughter of the Ho family, who was so beautiful that Prince K'ang took her away from him. P'ing deeply resented this, so the prince imprisoned him and punished him by making him do early morning labor on the city wall. His wife sent P'ing a letter in secret, which was worded to disguise her meaning: "When the rain pours in torrents and the river rises and gets deeper, our hearts will come together at sunrise." When the prince received her letter, he showed it to his courtiers, but none of the courtiers could decipher its meaning. His official Su Ho gave this solution: "'When the rain pours in torrents' means to grieve and pine; 'the river rises and gets deeper' means to be unable to go out or come in; 'our hearts will come together at sunrise' means a death wish." Not long afterward, P'ing committed suicide. Then his wife secretly made her clothes worn and rotten. When the prince went up the tower with her, she threw herself from the tower. The courtiers grabbed her, but her clothes missed their grasp and she fell to her death. A suicide note in her belt said, "The prince would have preferred me to live, but I preferred to die. I request the favor that my body be buried with P'ing." The prince was very angry and refused to grant her wish. He ordered a countryman to bury her so that the burial mounds would face each other at some distance from each other. The prince said, "You went on loving each other as husband and wife. If you can make your burial mounds come together I will not stand in your way." When everyone was asleep, two huge catalpa trees grew up at the edge of the two burial mounds. In ten days they had grown to full size. They bent their trunks across toward each other, so that the roots were entwined below and the boughs embraced above. And there were two mandarin ducks, a male and a female, which remained perched on top of the trees. They refused to leave at night or by day but entwined their necks and sang sadly, so that people were very moved. The people of Sung felt sorry for them and ever after called these trees the "loving-you tree." (*Sou shen chi,* TSCC 11.77–78)

13

Heroes

The mythical figure of the hero has been encountered in previous chapters in the different roles as savior, culture bearer, warrior, and founder of a new race, tribe, or dynasty. Figures such as Shun closely resemble Raglan's model of the hero with twenty-two stereotypical biographical features (1937). The powerful and successful Yellow Emperor, who combines both military and civil roles of warrior and culture bearer, is one of the great heroes in the pantheon. Of the demigods Yao, Shun, and Yü in the Golden Age, the mythical qualities of the hero are most fully realized in the narratives of Yü, who overcame a multiplicity of heroic tasks while confronting the overwhelming disaster of the flood. In the human sphere the Lord of the Granary and Li Ping fit the heroic paradigm, with the added element of humor, which is so lacking in the Yü stories.

Another aspect of the hero type which complements the dynamic and positive function of the all-conquering, successful, and dominant mythical hero, such as the Yellow Emperor, Shun, or Yü, is the failed hero, a god, demigod, or human who struggles in a fair contest for supremacy but loses against a more formidable contender. The failure is not projected as a monster or villain but is treated sympathetically in the myths. The term *the nobility of failure* was coined by Ivan Morris in his analysis of Japanese heroes in myth, legend, and history (1975). The term admirably characterizes role models in the Chinese tradition, such as the Flame Emperor, Ch'ih Yu, Yi the Archer, Kun, and Tan Chu, whose myths fit the paradigm of the failed hero. They are gods and demigods whom the communal memory stubbornly refuses to vilify, rubbish, and expunge from myth, legend, and folktale.

The mythical and legendary heroes presented here performed acts of heroism which were inspired by such diverse motives as revenge, hubris, military courage, idealism, nobility of spirit, and patriotism. Many were immortalized in a narrative poem entitled "On Reading *The Classic of Mountains and Seas*" by T'ao Yuan-ming, also called T'ao Ch'ien (A.D. 365–427); heroes such as K'ua-fu, Ching Wei, Hsing T'ien, Cha Yü, and Kun were all lauded in his literary appreciation of the *Classic* (Davis 1983, 1:160–64; *Chien chu T'ao Yuan-ming chi,* SPTK 4.18a–24a).

Ching Wei Dams the Sea

The myth of Ching Wei combines the diverse themes of pathos, pluck, and the refusal to accept defeat. Nü Wa, the Lady Beautiful, was one of the three daughters of the Flame Emperor. After she drowned in the east sea, she metamorphosed into the Ching Wei, Spirit Guardian bird. In some versions she mated with a sea swallow. The myth of Ching Wei does not explain why she is doomed to the futile task of damming the vast east sea with pathetically tiny bits of wood and pebble. It could be that she was punished for trespassing, for "playing in the east sea" without permission, thus violating the territorial prerogative of the sea god; or her act may be construed as a token of her revenge against the sea god in whose waters she drowned. Certainly, the motif of metamorphosis is linked to the theme of punishment in mythic narratives. The revenge motive was, in fact, accepted by the earliest commentator on the mythic narrative, which appears in an early chapter of *The Classic of Mountains and Seas* (third century B.C.). Kuo P'u's interpretation is supported by the goddess's other names: the Oath Bird, Resolve Bird, and Victim Bird. The first two express her vow for revenge, while the third denotes her fate. It is significant that just as the Flame Emperor was conquered by his brother, the Yellow Emperor, using the element of water against his fire, so the goddess Nü Wa, the Flame Emperor's daughter, was overcome by the hostile element of the east sea. Although it is tempting to adduce the motif of punishment for this myth, it is not so explicit as in the myths of Kun or Ch'ih Yu.

Another two hundred leagues to the north is a mountain called Fa-chiu, and on its summit there are numerous *che*-thorn trees. There is a bird in them. Its appearance is like a crow, and it has a colorful head, a white beak, and scarlet feet. Its name is Ching Wei; its name is from its call. It is the Flame Emperor's younger daughter, who was called Nü Wa. Nü Wa was playing in the east sea when she sank and failed to resurface. So she became the Ching Wei [Spirit Guardian]. She is forever carrying in her beak wood and stones from the western hills to dam up the east sea. (*Shan hai ching, Pei tz'u san ching,* SPPY 3.16b)

K'ua-fu Races the Sun

The name K'ua-fu means Boastful Father or Braggart Man, and it is one of the few names in Chinese mythology which clearly describes the theme associated with the mythical figure. This theme is hubris, the sin of pride in challenging a greater power than oneself and treating that power or authority with contempt. The myth of hubris is usually accompanied by the motif of nemesis. The first text below narrates that K'ua-fu was a lesser god who lived on a mountain near the sky, the name of which is the Perfect City Which Bears Heaven (*Ch'eng-tu tsai t'ien*). It denotes a sacred height, an *axis mundi,* which Eliade terms the celestial archetype of the holy city (1971, 7–9). Thus K'ua-fu is at the epicenter of Heaven and earth, with control over the powers of each sphere.

The conventional genealogy of K'ua-fu gives his descent from Hou-t'u, Empress Earth. The color motif in the yellow snakes he wears is emblematic of the yellow earth. Snakes held by deities in their hands or worn in their ears or on their head signified the gods' power over the kinetic forces and mysterious design of the cosmos. The two readings from *The Classic of Mountains and Seas* tell how K'ua-fu challenged the power of the sun to a race against time. As the sun went down, K'ua-fu caught up with it but was consumed by thirst and died. After he died, his stick was metamorphosed into Teng Grove. His death from thirst was the punishment analogous to his crime of hubris. The first reading is from a first-century A.D. chapter of the *Classic;* the second is from a first century B.C. chapter.

A separate tradition relating to K'ua-fu's death is based on yet another account in the *Classic* which relates more clearly the theme of punishment. It tells how the Responding Dragon, which had power over water and could cause severe drought, killed him. In that passage the death of K'ua-fu is linked to the death of Ch'ih Yu, and both gods were executed because they were judged to be rebels. Metamorphosis into wood also links the myths of these two gods.

Kuo P'u responded ambiguously to the mythical figure of K'ua-fu in his commentary, saying, "Divine was K'ua-fu! But he was difficult to understand." T'ao Yuan-ming applauded K'ua-fu's audacity in his narrative poem: "His divine strength was very wonderful. . . . / His merits were accomplished after his death" (Davis 1983, 1:160–61).

> In the great wilderness there is a mountain called the Perfect City Which Bears Heaven. There is a man who wears two yellow snakes in his ears and holds two yellow snakes in his hands. His name is K'ua-fu. Empress Earth gave birth to Hsin, and Hsin gave birth to K'ua-fu. K'ua-fu's strength knew no bounds. He wanted to chase the sun's shadow and he caught up with it at Yü valley. He decided to drink from the river, but there was not enough, so he decided to walk toward the Great Marsh. But he did not reach it and he died in this place. (*Shan hai ching, Ta huang pei ching*, SPPY 17.4a)

> K'ua-fu and the sun had a race. The sun went in. K'ua-fu was so thirsty he wanted to have a drink. He drank from the river and the Wei, but the river and the Wei were not enough. He went northward to drink from the Great Marsh, but he did not reach it, and he died of thirst on the way. His abandoned stick turned into Teng Grove. (*Shan hai ching, Hai wai pei ching*, SPPY 8.2b)

Hsing T'ien Dances with Shield and Battle-Ax

The myth of the failed hero Hsing T'ien relates how this lesser god challenged God (Ti) for the godhead, or divine rule (Shen), but he lost. The brief narrative does not explain who the warrior god Hsing T'ien was, nor his place in the pantheon. His name has several variants: Hsing T'ien or Punished by Heaven, Hsing T'ien or Formed by Heaven, and Hsing Yao or Form Prematurely Dying. The confusion in his name is matched by that of the battlefield, Ch'ang-yang, which is written either as Eternal Sunlight or as Eternal Ram. The translation of mythical names is notoriously difficult, and the renditions here are only approximate. A. R. Davis discussed fully the variants of the names, noting of T'ien (Heaven) and Yao (Prematurely Dying) that their written forms are very similar (2:129). The name of this hero becomes significant in terms of his myth if it is taken as Hsing T'ien, meaning Punished by Heaven, for this would constitute an epithet applied to the mythical figure after his death and would explain the reason for his death. In this case, Hsing T'ien would belong to the group of heroes such as Ch'ih Yu and K'ua-fu who were punished for the crime of hubris.

Although the mythical figure of the warrior-god, such as Ch'ih Yu, Kung Kung, the Flame Emperor, and the Yellow Emperor, occurs frequently in Chinese mythology, the motif of gruesome violence is rare. The presence of the motif in the Hsing T'ien myth allows of comparison with similar instances in mythology worldwide, especially in the narratives of Odinic warriors. Hsing T'ien's bizarre war dance after he has been decapitated is unusual in the Chinese repertoire for its reference to the headless hero using his nipples and navel to serve as replacement eyes and mouth. The rarity of such motifs prompts the speculation that the Hsing T'ien myth was overlooked by the censoring redactors who otherwise managed to delete much of the typical barbarism of mythological narrative. As such, sex and gruesome violence, and coupling and nudity were linked as taboo topics in the minds of officials such as Wang, Kung, and Hsiu, who are known to have "corrected" the text from which the following reading is taken, in *The Classic of Mountains and Seas*, first century B.C.

The myth of Hsing T'ien is particularly interesting because it anticipates the concept in medical science of bodily transplants. In the frenzy of battle the warrior-god substitutes part of his torso to make good the loss of his sight and speech, so that he is able to continue his furious battle. That he eventually died is indicated by a fragment in *Huai-nan Tzu:* "In the west is the corpse of Hsing's remains" (Yuan K'o and Chou Ming 1985, 64). Kuo P'u wrote this appraisal of the hero: "Though transformed, he did not submit," and T'ao Ch'ien wrote this epitaph for the dead god: "His fierce spirit will live for ever" (Davis 1983, 1:161–62).

> Hsing T'ien and God came to this place and fought for divine rule. God cut off his head and buried it on Ch'ang-yang mountain. Hsing T'ien made his nipples serve as eyes and his navel as his mouth, and brandishing his shield and battle-ax, he danced. (*Shan hai ching, Hai wai hsi ching,* SPPY 7.2a)

The Foolish Old Man Moves a Mountain

The sophisticated fictional techniques of the long account of the Foolish Old Man, Yü-kung, from the fourth-century A.D. text *Lieh Tzu* indicate that the myth is late in the tradition, and this is confirmed by the absence of early classical texts referring to or narrating this myth. The myth shares with that of Ching Wei the theme of seemingly futile effort. Unlike the earlier myth of the goddess metamorphosed into a bird, the *Lieh Tzu* narrative contains many complex motifs and themes. To the basic theme of futility are harnessed those of commitment to an ideal and faith in one's beliefs and goals. The thematic framework is based on Taoist concepts and philosophical attitudes familiar from *Chuang Tzu,* such as the relativity of values and role reversals, so that the Foolish Old Man proves to be wise while the Wise Old Man in the story turns out to be wrong. While the myth has enduring appeal due to the theme of adherence to an ideal, it lacks the poignancy and individual heroism of the myths of Ching Wei and Hsing T'ien. The reason is that the philosophical thrust of the narrative requires that the hero win in his struggle, and his eventual triumph is achieved by the device, literal in this case, of *deus ex machina.*

The two mountains T'ai Hsing and Royal House are seven hundred leagues square and eighty thousand feet high and were originally in the south of Chi Province and north of Ho-yang. The Foolish Old Man of North Mount was almost ninety years old, and he lived opposite these mountains. He thought it a painful burden that the northern edge of the mountains should make his journeys back and forth such a long way around. So he gathered his household and put this plan to them: "You and I will use our utmost strength to level out a narrow pass, which will go through to Yü in the south and go as far as the south side of Han River. How about it?" They all agreed with his plan. His wife expressed her doubts, saying, "With your strength you couldn't even destroy the hillock of K'uei-fu, so how could you destroy T'ai Hsing and Royal House mountains? And where would you put the soil and stones?" They all said, "We'll throw them on the tail end of Po Sea north of Yin-t'u." Then leading his son and grandson, the three men carrying poles, he broke up rocks and furrowed the soil, and they transported them in baskets and hods to the tail end of Po Sea. A neighbor, the widow Ching-ch'eng, had a son left to her who was just losing his milk teeth, and he leaped up and went to help them.

The seasons had changed from cold to hot when they all came back home for the first time. The Wise Old Man of the River Bend laughed at the Foolish Old Man and said, "Well, you aren't very smart. How can you, with your last bit of strength and in your declining years, ever break up even one hair of this mountain, let alone the earth on it?" The Foolish Old Man of North Mount gave a long sigh and said, "Your mind is thick, you just can't understand — you're not nearly as good as the widow's weak young boy. Even if I die, there'll be my son, who will carry on, and my son has had my grandson born to him too, and that grandson will also have a son born to him, and his son will have a son born to him as well, and that son will have his grandson too. Son after son, grandson after grandson forever and ever. This mountain won't get any bigger, so why do you fret that eventually it won't be flattened?" The Wise Old Man of the River Bend was lost for an answer. The snake-holding god heard of this and, feeling concerned that this would never come to an end, reported it to God. God was moved by his faith in his ideal and ordered the two sons of K'ua-o to carry the two mountains on their backs, placing one in Shuo to the east, and placing one in Yung to the south. Ever since then, from south of Chi Province to the south side of Han River there is not a single bank to interrupt the flat ground. (*Lieh Tzu, T'ang wen,* SPPY 5.8a–9b)

K'ai Receives the Music of Heaven

The myth of K'ai, or Ch'i, son of Yü, has been discussed in several chapters, where it has been noted that a textual variant of *steals* instead of *receives* alters the interpretation, making K'ai a hero who dares to offend God in order to bring the harmony of Heaven down to earth. The reading comes from a first-century A.D. chapter of *The Classic of Mountains and Seas.*

Beyond the seas to the southwest, south of Scarlet River and west of Drifting Sands, there is a man called Hsia-hou K'ai who wears a green snake in his pierced ears and rides a pair of dragons. K'ai went up to Heaven three times as a guest. He received the "Nine Counterpoints" and the "Nine Songs," and brought them down to earth. This Plain of Heavenly Mu is sixteen thousand feet high and it was here that K'ai first came to sing the "Nine Summons." (*Shan hai ching, Ta huang hsi ching*, SPPY 16.7b–8a)

The Death of Po Yi and Shu Ch'i

Po Yi and Shu Ch'i are famous exemplars of political idealism. Princes of the kingdom of Ku-chu, they went into self-imposed exile when each refused to ascend the throne after the death of their father. In exile from their homeland, they sought refuge with a nobleman of the Chou people, named Ch'ang, Lord of the West. This was a critical moment in politics because Ch'ang, and later his son, Fa, were campaigning against the Shang ruler, King Chou, who had been tyrannically oppressing his people. Ch'ang became known as King Wen of the Chou after the conquest of the Shang was completed by Fa, who became King Wu of the Chou. Unfortunately for the exiles Po Yi and Shu Ch'i, their loyalty lay with the Shang, and they voiced objections to the military campaigns of the Chou. Refusing "to eat the corn of Chou," they fled once more, this time to a mountain wilderness. In the end, their political idealism led them to die of starvation.

In the philosophical writings of Confucius and Mencius, Po Yi and Shu Ch'i became heroic exemplars of the Confucian ideals of nonviolent political engagement and of political integrity. The philosopher Chuang Tzu is ambiguous in his treatment of the two princes. On the one hand, he depicts them as Taoist exemplars of the virtue of avoiding social and political contamination by abstention from high office. On the other, he condemns them for bringing about their own death (Watson 1968, 321–22, 78–79, 329).

Sarah Allan discusses the myth of Po Yi and Shu Ch'i, and the related figures of the Chou kings Wen and Wu, from the perspective of the transfer of rule from Shang to Chou. She notes that in the version of the myth in "Questions of Heaven," King Wu went into battle against the Shang king bearing the corpse of his father, King Wen. In the first reading below, from *Historical Records*, however, Ssu-ma Ch'ien relates that King Wu bore only the spirit tablet of his father as he launched his final campaign. The Han historian also explains why Po Yi and Shu Ch'i refused to acknowledge King Wu as a legitimate ruler: first, he showed a lack of filial piety in not burying his father before going to war; second, he committed the crime of regicide in killing King Chou of the Shang; third, Po Yi and Shu Ch'i objected to this breach of hereditary rule (Allan 1981, 107, 111–17). The second reading is from an early text, which is no longer extant, cited by Ma Su in *Hypotheses on History*, preface dated A.D. 1670. The title of the early text is *Biographies of Great Men*.

Po Yi and Shu Ch'i were the two sons of the ruler of Ku-chu. Their father wanted to make Shu Ch'i his heir. When their father died, Shu Ch'i ceded the throne to Po Yi. Po Yi declined and said, "It was Father's wish." Then he fled from the kingdom. Shu Ch'i was also unwilling to accede, so he ran away from the kingdom too. Then the kingdom made the middle son the successor to the throne. Then Po Yi and Shu Ch'i heard that Ch'ang, the Lord of the West, had a good reputation for caring for the aged and they asked themselves whether it would be a good idea to go and make their home there. When they arrived, the Lord of the West had died, and King Wu was bearing his wooden tablet of royal authority inscribed with the name "King Wen," for he was moving to the east to attack King Chou. (*Shih chi, Po Yi lieh chuan,* SPPY 61.2a–b)

When King Wu of the Chou attacked the Shang King Chou, Po Yi and Shu Ch'i did not follow him but retired and went into hiding on Mount Shou-yang. There they gathered edible ferns for food. Wang Mo-tzu came into the mountains and rebuked them, saying, "You refused to eat the corn of Chou state, yet you have hidden away in the mountains of Chou and you are eating Chou ferns. Why is that?" So the two men refused to go on eating ferns, and at the end of seven days, Heaven sent them a white deer to give them milk. The two men thought to themselves that this deer would make an excellent meal. The deer realized their intention and refused to come back to them. So the two sons passed away from starvation. (*Yi shih,* citing *Lieh shih chuan,* PCTP 20.37b)

Kan Chiang and Mo Yeh Forge Swords

In those of the early texts that date from the fourth to the second century B.C., such as *Chuang Tzu, Annals of Master Lü, Huai-nan Tzu,* and *Intrigues of the Warring States,* the myths of sword casting and of the two famous swords named Kan Chiang and Mo Yeh are only glancingly mentioned in terms of these names. It is only in the first century A.D. that the fully developed myth of the two sword makers Kan Chiang and Mo Yeh first appears in *Spring and Autumn Annals of Wu and Yueh* compiled by Chao Yeh (fl. ca. A.D. 40). Wu and Yueh were ancient states famous for their fine swords. The sudden appearance of this fully fledged myth has led Lionello Lanciotti to believe that "the origin of that group of legends is not purely Chinese" (1955, 106–7). He went on to suggest that the written characters for the name Mo Yeh had several variants and were undoubtedly originally the transliteration of a foreign name.

The narrative of the legendary sword makers of Wu state, Kan Chiang and his wife, Mo Yeh, belongs to the considerable lore of metallurgy, sword making, and magic swords in antiquity. For example, according to an early tradition, the sword that was used to cut open the corpse of Kun to release his son Yü was a Wu sword (*The Storehouse of All Things*, TSCC 1.1b). The lore of myth and legend derives in part from the fact that sword making was a noble but dangerous profession. As the reading illustrates, this profession engendered its own mythic tradition, its own ritual, and its own identity as a mining community. The idea of a separate mining community is expressed in the central and final passages, which speak of hill-mining and a group of three hundred children from miners' families assisting in the metallurgical process. The evidence for a special ritual for the smelting process occurs several times in the text: adherence to cosmological conjunctions of Yin and Yang and the proper season, attendance upon the witness of the gods, the wearing of white hemp and grass (white symbolizing the element of metal and the color of death), human sacrifice with the ritual of cutting off nails and hair, and the naming of swords after their makers. The multiplicity of rituals referred to in the text suggests that the process of smelting ore often failed. (It is clear from the text that the metal used was iron ore rather than bronze.) That the tradition of metallurgy inspired its own lore is indicated by the opening reference to a master sword maker, and later in the text by the reference to the authority of this master in connection with a tradition of ritual self-sacrifice. Moreover, as Lanciotti suggested, Kan Chiang's revelation of the secret of his master's ritual self-sacrifice only after he has failed in smelting indicates that Kan Chiang belongs to "a dynasty of smiths with secret doctrines" (1955, 110).

The tragic heroism of the wife, Mo Yeh, who throws herself into the furnace as sacrifice to the gods of metallurgy, is prompted by the villain of the story, King Ho Lü of Wu. Elsewhere, however, King Ho Lü (r. 514–496 B.C.) is portrayed as a great military leader who conquered the great state of Ch'u and was an expert on metal weaponry. Mo Yeh's suicide is only hinted at in the text. It is suggested by the verb *t'ou* 'to throw'. This verb is frequently used in the context of women who commit suicide by throwing themselves into a river or off a tower, or, as in this case, into a fire. The same verb *t'ou* is used in the story of the suicide of Han Ping's wife recounted in chapter 12. Some scholars, however, prefer to read the Mo Yeh passage not as suicide, the ultimate sacrifice to the gods, but as a ritual act of throwing only her hair and nail clippings into the furnace, a mimetic act of animal sacrifice in antiquity. It will be recalled, nevertheless, that in the mythic narrative "At Mulberry Forest They Pray for Rain," in chapter 3, the Shang ruler, T'ang the Conqueror, performed this ritual too but then placed himself on top of a sacrificial pyre.

Kan Chiang came from Wu state. He had studied under the same master as Ou the Smith and both of them could make swords. When Yueh state had previously sent three swords of fine workmanship as a gift, [King] Ho Lü acquired them and prized them. That is why the state ordered their sword maker to make two more fine swords. One was called Kan Chiang, the second was called Mo Yeh. Mo Yeh was Kan Chiang's wife. When Kan Chiang made swords, he selected the purest iron from the five mountains and the finest gold in the six cosmic points. Then he waited for Heaven's proper time and attended on earth's due season, when Yin and Yang would be in conjunction and all the gods would be present to observe.

But the breath of Heaven descended, and the result was that the molten essences of gold and iron would not fuse and refused to liquify. Kan Chiang did not know why this had happened. Mo Yeh said, "Your reputation for skilled sword making came to the attention of the King, and he ordered you to make swords for him. But three months have passed and they are still unfinished. Perhaps there is a meaning in the failure with the smelting?" Kan Chiang said, "I do not know what the reason is." Mo Yeh said, "In the transformation process between gods and humans, a human is required before success can be achieved. You, sir, are now making swords. Do you think you will be successful after the gods have taken their human [offering], or if they haven't?" Kan Chiang said, "Some time ago, when my master was smelting and the gold and iron substances would not fuse, both he and his wife got into the smelting oven together, and afterward the smelting was successful. From that time on, whenever people have gone mining for ore for smelting, they have worn white hempen clothes and a robe made of sweet grass. Otherwise they would not dare to smelt gold on the mountain. Do you think I should have done the same just now when I was making the swords and the transformation process failed?" Mo Yeh said, "If your former master realized that he had to have his body burned up in the furnace to achieve success, where is our difficulty?" So Kan Chiang's wife cut off her hair and clipped her nails and threw herself into the fire. Then he made all the boys and girls, three hundred of them, pound the furnace pipes and bank up the charcoal. Then the gold and iron liquified and so the swords were made. The Yang sword was called Kan Chiang, the Yin sword was called Mo Yeh. The Yang one was decorated with a tortoise design, the Yin one with an inscription. Kan Chiang hid the Yang sword and took away the Yin sword and presented it to Ho Lü, the King of Wu, who treasured it dearly. (*Wu Yueh ch'un-ch'iu, Ho Lü nei chuan*, SPPY 4.1b–2a)

The potency of the myth of the two swords is evident from its literary elaboration in later centuries. The following poem by Pao Chao (A.D. ?412–?466) expresses the romanticized aspect of the myth, and it was included in the famous early medieval anthology of love poetry, *New Songs from a Jade Terrace*, compiled circa A.D. 539–545:

> A pair of swords about to part
> First cried out in their case.
> In night's smoky rain they became one,
> Then they took different forms.
> The female sank in Wu River water,
> The male flew into Ch'u city.
> Wu River is deep, fathomless,
> Ch'u city has forbidding portals.
> Once Heaven parted from Earth
> Wasn't that worse than Light gone from Dark?
> Magic things do not part forever,
> One thousand years and they reunite.
>   (Birrell 1986, 119, amended)

Eyebrows Twelve Inches Apart

Although there is a strong case for arguing that Chao Yeh's text indicates that Mo Yeh committed suicide, Kan Pao's fourth-century A.D. text reveals that Mo Yeh is alive and well but that Kan Chiang is executed by royal command of the king of Ch'u state. The action has moved from Wu through Yueh to Ch'u. It will be recalled that in general, Kan Pao's collection of tales constitutes reworkings of old mythic material, besides legend and folklore, the intent of which was to amuse and divert readers rather than to transmit the eternal verities of myth. It is probably safer to take Chao Yeh's narrative as a version close to the authentic myth of sword making and to treat Kan Pao's tale as a fictional diversion based on an older mythical account. Certainly, his narrative is full of fictional color: the oath sworn by the father who is about to die, the numerical motif of three, repetition of speech, the riddle of the rock, the vow of revenge, the king's ominous dream, the king's ransom, the dirge of the boy hero, the miracle of his petrified corpse, the act of revenge, the three heads in the cooking pot, and the joint grave with its ironic epitaph. The piece ends with a familiar Six Dynasties touristic touch.

The account belongs to the category of revenge myth which traces its ancestry to Chou dynasty classics such as the *Chronicle of Tso,* which has a similarly grisly account of the fate of Yi the Archer and his sons. The revenge myth has its apotheosis in gruesome macho–sadistic stories of heroes in *The Water Margin* of the Ming dynasty (Plaks 1987, 304–58).

In his cogent article on this myth, Lanciotti has interpreted it as a follow-up of the narrative presented by Chao Yeh (1955, 316–22). As with the name of Mo Yeh, he noted that the young hero's name is written with many variants, suggesting that "the origin of that group of legends is not purely Chinese" (ibid., 114). The various names for the son of Kan Chiang, Ch'ih Pi, mean Red between the Eyebrows, One Inch Broad between His Eyebrows, Scarlet Nose, and Scarlet Likeness (Yuan K'o 1980.2, 277).

When Kan Chiang and Mo Yeh were in Ch'u, Kan Chiang had to make swords for the king of Ch'u. After three years they were ready, but the king was angry and decided to put him to death. The swords were male and female. Kan Chiang's wife was heavily pregnant and was due to give birth. Now Kan Chiang told his wife, "I was asked to make swords for the king, and I completed them in three years. But the king is angry with me. When I go, the king is sure to have me put to death. If you give birth to a boy, tell him when he grows up, 'As you go out of the door, look south at the hill, and where a pine tree grows above a rock, my sword lies hidden behind it.'" Then, taking the female sword with him he went to have an audience with the king of Ch'u. The king grew very angry. He ordered Kan Chiang to produce the other sword. But Kan Chiang said that there had been two swords, one male and one female; the female sword had been brought, but not the male sword. The king was enraged and promptly had him put to death.

Mo Yeh's son was called Ch'ih Pi. Later, when he had grown up, he asked his mother, "Where is my father?" His mother said, "Your father had to make swords for the king of Ch'u. He finished them in three years, but the king was very angry and killed him. When he was about to die he charged me: 'Tell your son, "As you go out of the door, look south at the hill, and where a pine tree grows above a rock, my sword lies hidden behind it."'" Then the son went out of the door, looked south, but failed to see a mountain. All he saw was a pine stump in front of the hall, and nearby was a stone sticking up. He at once cleaved open the back of the stone with an ax and found the sword. Night and day he longed to seek his revenge from the king of Ch'u. The king dreamed he saw a lad with eyebrows twelve inches apart who said he wanted to seek revenge. The king immediately offered a ransom of a thousand pieces of gold for this young boy. When the boy heard of this, he disappeared and went into the forest. He sang sadly as he walked along. A stranger who met him said, "You are very young. Why are you wailing so sadly?" He said, "I am the son of Kan Chiang and Mo Yeh. The king of Ch'u killed my father, and I want my revenge on him." The stranger said, "I have heard that the king has offered a ransom of a thousand pieces of gold for your head. If I go to the king with your head and your sword, I will get your revenge for you." The boy said, "That would be fine!" Then he slit his own throat and held out his head and his sword and gave them to him. He stood there, a petrified corpse. The stranger said, "I will not fail you." Then the corpse toppled over.

The stranger took the head and went to see the king of Ch'u. The king was overjoyed. The stranger said, "This is the head of a very brave man, so we must boil it in a large pot." They boiled the head for three days and three nights, but it would not cook through. The head bobbed about in the boiling water, its eyes glaring with rage. The stranger said, "The boy's head refuses to cook through. I would like Your Majesty to go up and look in at it yourself, then it will be sure to cook properly." The king at once went up to it. The stranger chopped the king's head off with the sword and the king's head fell into the boiling water. Then the stranger lopped off his own head and another head fell into the boiling water. The three heads all dissolved into each other, so it was impossible to tell who was who. Then they separated the flesh from the boiling water and buried it. That is why the burial ground bore the name Grave of the Three Kings. Today it is situated in the region north of Ju-nan in Yi-ch'un county. (*Sou shen chi*, TSCC 11.71–72)

The Five Brothers

This long passage that follows is from the *Gazette of Hua-yang* by Ch'ang Chü, of the fourth century A.D. It is a miscellany of interesting bits of information about Hua-yang, the area of ancient Shu (Szechwan), which included the ancient city of Ch'eng-tu. The extract bears all the hallmarks of a scissors-and-paste miscellany, for it comprises three different narratives loosely linked by the theme of Shu itself. The three accounts are: (1) an explanation of how Stalagmite Village acquired its name in the era of one of the ancestral kings of Shu; (2) an explanation of the enmity between the kings of Ch'in and of Shu in the late Chou era; and (3) an explanation of the names of a mythic peak based on the tale of the five strong men of Shu who brought five Ch'in brides to the king of Shu.

It is curious that a miscellany about the region of Shu should express a point of view critical of the place, its people, and its ruler in antiquity: the king of Shu is branded as an oversexed ruler; the soldiers of Ch'in play a scatological trick on the people of Shu, in which ox feces become "gold"; the Ch'in court hurls insults at the Shu envoys; and the five strong men of Shu suffer a drastic fate together with the brides of Ch'in. The narrative as a whole differs from others in this chapter because it expresses no praise or admiration for the heroic ideal but ridicules the Shu envoys for their pretensions to heroism in a coarse satire. Thus the extract may be read as an anti-Shu tract.

In the reign of Emperor K'ai-ming . . . there were in Shu five strong men who could move mountains and lift weights of three hundred thousand pounds. Every time a prince passed away, they would immediately set up a huge stone thirty feet long, weighing thirty thousand pounds, for the tomb's memorial stone. Today, these are like stalagmites. The area is called Stalagmite Village. . . .

In the era of King Hsien of the Chou, the king of Shu possessed the territory of Pao and Han [-chung]. As he went hunting in the valley, he happened to meet King Hui of the Ch'in. King Hui filled a wicker box with gold and sent it to the king of Shu. The king of Shu reciprocated with precious objects. But all the objects turned to clay, and King Hui became angry. But his court officials congratulated him, saying, "Heaven has singled us out for its favor. Your Majesty will take the land of Shu." King Hui was overjoyed. So they made five stone oxen, and each morning they released gold from their buttocks and announced, "Even our ox-shit is gold!" There were a hundred soldiers in charge of the stone oxen. The people of Shu were delighted with them. He [the king of Shu] ordered envoys to ask for the stone oxen, and King Hui allowed them to take them. So they sent the five brothers to receive the stone oxen. But the oxen no longer dropped gold dung and they became angry. He sent the five brothers back to return the oxen and they twitted the people of Ch'in saying, "Huh! You eastern calf-boys!" The people of Ch'in laughed at them and said, "We may be calf-boys, but we are sure going to take Shu!" . . .

King Hui knew that the king of Shu enjoyed sex, so he allowed five brides to be sent in marriage to Shu. The Shu court sent the five brothers to receive them. As they were bringing them back to Tzu-t'ung, they saw a huge snake that went into a cave. One of the men held onto its tail and tugged it, but he could not manage. The five men came and helped together, and with loud shouts they dragged the snake out. The mountain collapsed, and as it did, it crushed to death the five men and the five ladies of Ch'in with their retinue. Then the mountain formed into five peaks crowned with a flat slab of stone. The king of Shu was bitterly upset. So he climbed the mountain and officially named it Five Bride Peak. He had the words "Watching Brides Beacon" and "Longing Wives Terrace" incised into the slab of stone. Today this mountain also goes by the name of Five Brothers Peak. (*Hua-yang kuo-chih, Shu chih,* SPTK 3.2a–3b)

Li Ping Fights the Water Beast

A discussion of the Li Ping myth appears in chapter 3 under the title "The Virgin Brides and the River God," where the myth was examined from the aspect of the hero's function as the slayer of an evil monster and the underlying pattern of its "sociological charter." It is worth noting that in this narrative a hero of Ch'in is the savior of the people of Shu, thus replicating the subordinate relationship of Shu to Ch'in which was evident in the preceding text.

After King Chao of Ch'in had attacked and conquered Shu, he appointed Li Ping as prefect of the Shu commandery. There was a river god who took two young virgins as his brides every year. The head officer of the region declared, "You will have to hand over a million in cash to pay for the brides' dowry." Ping said, "That won't be necessary. I have young daughters of my own." When the time came, he had his daughters beautifully dressed and made up, and he led them away to be drowned in the river. Li Ping went straight up to the throne of the local god, poured out wine as an offering, and said, "Up till now, I have continued our family line into the ninth generation. Lord of the River, you are a mighty god. Please show your august presence to me, so that I may humbly serve you with wine." Ping held the goblet of wine forward. All the god did was to ripple its surface, but he did not consume it. Ping said in a thunderous voice, "Lord of the River, you have mocked me, so now I intend to fight you!" He drew out his sword, then suddenly he vanished. A little later two blue oxen were fighting on the sloping riverbank. After a few moments Ping went back to his officers and ordered them to help him: "The ox facing south with white tied around his saddle will be me with my white silk ribbon." Then he returned to the fray. The Keeper of Records promptly shot dead with his arrow the ox facing north. With the Lord of the River dead, there was no more trouble ever again. (*T'ai-p'ing yü-lan*, citing *Feng su t'ung-yi*, SPTK 882.4a–b)

14

Fabled Flora
and Fauna

Mythic nature manifests itself as a god-haunted world under the sway of supernatural beings. Nature is subordinated to the gods, who are immanent in sacred mountains, streams, rocks, and trees. Nature reveals the potency of the gods; they are elemental, controlling light, heat, wind, and rain; they are generative, producing irrigated fields, fertile soil, and abundant crops. And the gods can be jealous and punitive, withholding life and creative energy. Humans are in and of nature, and the gods belong to the world of nature and of humans. The two spheres of the human and the divine interact in terms of form and function. When the gods manifest themselves, they appear as half-human, half-animal beings, or as hybrid creatures. Nü Kua and Fu Hsi took on half-human, half-serpentine form. Many deities are described as having a bird's body and a human face. And the metamorphoses of gods and demigods demonstrate the easy transference from one state to another. The epitome of this interaction is the myth of the dying god P'an Ku. This interconnectedness between the gods, nature, and humans has a negative and a positive dimension. Its negative dimension is visible in its congeries of hybrid monsters and beasts such as Hsiang Liu or the Wu-chih-ch'i, who wreak havoc on the human world. Conversely, the concept of perfect harmony among the three worlds is visible in the earthly paradises of K'un-lun or the Isles of the Immortals in the eastern sea. The sky-ladder of Chien-mu or the Tree of Life, Leaning Mulberry in the east, appear at these points of perfect equilibrium, allowing a communion between gods and humans within nature.

Within mythic nature are the mythical bestiary and vegetal myths. They include divine creatures and plants that express concepts of primitive allegory. Moral significance is attached to real or imagined characteristics of animals or plants. For example, the ram of the mythical judge Kao Yao is endowed with the power of discerning guilt in humans. The Beast of White Marsh knows the mysterious workings of the universe. A plant in the courtyard of Yao had divine knowledge of the human heart and could point out flatterers at court.

A few birds and beasts came to be emblematic of deities, such as the bluebirds and hybrid panthers of the Queen Mother of the West, or the nightjar with Tu Yü, the ram with Kao Yao, the bear with Yü, and the toad with Ch'ang O. Similarly, plants came to be connected with certain deities, such as millet with Hou Chi, maple with Ch'ih Yu, and, later in the tradition, peaches with the Queen Mother of the West. This emblematic concept, however, is not a well-developed aspect of Chinese mythology, as it was in the Greco-Roman tradition, with most of the gods having their emblem or attribute drawn from nature. In general, creatures in classical Chinese mythology such as dragons, serpents, the tortoise, or bird of paradise were connected with a number of different deities and carried no specific symbolic meaning in their relationship to individual deities.

The sources for these bestial and vegetal myths constitute an early form of "unnatural natural history." The material is for the most part fragmentary. The source par excellence is *The Classic of Mountains and Seas;* other early texts, such as *Chuang Tzu, Hsun Tzu,* and *Huai-nan Tzu,* also contain a great deal of scattered narratives relating to nature myths. In the Han and post-Han periods the material proliferated. The prime examples of this valuable literature are the lexicon of Hsu Shen (ca. A.D. 100), *An Explication of Written Characters;* the miscellany of Wang Ch'ung (A.D. 27–100), *Disquisitions;* and *The Treatise on Research into Nature* of the third to fifth century. Of course, these fragmentary sources of bestial and vegetal myths are rudimentary when they are compared with the fully developed didactic genre of the European bestiary, such as Philippe de Thaon's *Bestiary* (ca. A.D. 1125) or Richard de Fournial's *Bestiary of Love* (ca. A.D. 1250) (Preminger 1965, 77). Nevertheless, the small sample of Chinese myths in this chapter should suffice to reveal the imaginative and colorful nature of this genre at an early stage in its evolution.

The Divine Light of Torch Dragon

The mythic features of the god of light, Torch Dragon, were examined in chapter 3. The god's appearance is hybrid: part-human, part-serpent; and the color motif of scarlet is emblematic of his function of bringing light to the darkened world. The reading is from a chapter of *The Classic of Mountains and Seas* dating circa the first century A.D.

> Beyond the northwestern sea, north of Scarlet River, is Pied-Tail Mountain. It has a god with a human face and a snake's body, and it is scarlet. His vertical eyes are straight slits. When he closes his eyes it grows dark. When he looks out it grows bright. He neither eats nor sleeps nor rests. Wind and rain visit him. This god shines on the nine darknesses. He is called Torch Dragon [Chu Lung]. (*Shan hai ching, Ta huang pei ching*, SPPY 17.7a–b)

The Chien-mu Sky-Ladder

The name *Chien-mu* literally means 'the Building-Tree'. This myth conforms in every respect with Eliade's paradigm of archaic cosmological beliefs that are "invested with the prestige of the Center" (1971, 12). The Chien-mu or Building-Tree is situated at the center of the world. It is an *axis mundi* where Heaven and earth meet. The first reading accentuates this belief in the idea of a perfect center, which casts no shadow and releases no echo. The text comes from *Huai-nan Tzu*. The second reading describes the holy site of the tree and its marvelous appearance. The number motif of nine appears frequently in mythic narratives and denotes the celestial sphere or aspects of the divine. The double motif of the "nine tanglewoods" and the "nine root twinings" is perhaps best explicated by a comparison with the Hungarian myth of the sky-high tree. This tree is said to have grown up to the sky and then "curved thirteen times under the firmament because it should have grown more" (Erdész, citing Lajos Ámi, 1984, 319). In the same way, the Building-Tree, or sky-ladder, continues to grow, but after reaching the sky, which it cannot penetrate, it is forced to spread under the barrier of the sky and likewise above the barrier of the ends of the earth, creating gigantic coils in the sky and huge root tangles in the earth. The text is from a late chapter of *The Classic of Mountains and Seas* (ca. first century A.D.).

The Chien-mu is in Tu-kuang. All the gods ascended and descended by it. It cast no shadow in the sun and it made no echo when someone shouted. No doubt this is because it is the center of Heaven and earth. (*Huai-nan Tzu, Chui hsing,* SPPY 4.3a–b)

Beyond the South Sea, between Black River and Green River . . . there are nine hills bounded by rivers. Their names are T'ao-t'ang Hill, She-te Hill, Meng-ying Hill, K'un-wu Hill, Black-and-White Hill, Red Gaze Hill, Ts'an-wei Hill, Wu-fu Hill, and Holy People Hill. There is a tree with green leaves, a purple trunk, black blossoms, and yellow fruit called the Chien-mu tree. For one thousand feet upward it bears no branches, and there are nine tanglewoods, while underneath there are nine root twinings. Its fruit is like hemp seed; its leaves resemble bearded grass. T'ai Hao used to pass up and down by it. The Yellow Emperor created it. (*Shan hai ching, Hai nei ching,* SPPY 18.3a–4a)

The Giant Peach Tree

Several other world-trees appear in Chinese mythology besides the Chien-mu. They are Trinity Mulberry (San-sang), Search Tree (Hsun-mu), Accord Tree (Jo-mu), and, most important, Leaning Mulberry (Fu-sang). They all form an *axis mundi.* There is also the giant peach tree, which, like the Chien-mu, grows in a convoluted tangle against the sky barrier it cannot pierce. In common with other world-tree myths, the peach tree creates a passage to the sky beyond the human world, and it carries at its crest celestial gates presided over by two punitive gods, Holy Shu (Shen Shu) and Yü Lü. The narrative is linked to the Yellow Emperor cycle of myths. The account ends with a description of a ritual derived from the myth of the guardian gods of the gates to Heaven. The ritual enacts the punitive role of the gods in order to exorcize evil from the home.

The author of the reading is Wang Ch'ung, of the first century A.D., who states in his text that he is citing *The Classic of Mountains and Seas.* In fact, this citation does not appear in extant editions of the *Classic,* but it reveals how valuable Wang Ch'ung's eclectic essays are for their preservation of otherwise lost material.

In Ts'ang Sea there is the Tu-shuo Mountain. On its summit is a huge peach tree. It twists and turns over three thousand leagues. Among its branches on the northeast side are what is called Goblin Gates through which a myriad goblins pass. On top there are two gods. One is called Holy Shu; the other is called Yü Lü. These lords supervise and control the myriad goblins. Whenever a goblin does evil, they bind him with a reed rope and feed him to tigers. Then the Yellow Emperor devised a ritual ceremony so that they could expel the evildoer in due season. They set up large peach wood figurines and painted images of Holy Shu and Yü Lü and a tiger on gates and doors and hung reed ropes from them so as to harness the evil. (*Lun heng, Ting kuei,* citing a non-extant passage from *Shan hai ching,* SPTK 22.15b–16a)

Leaning Mulberry

The solar myths attached to this world-tree were discussed in chapters 1 and 5, with the motifs of sunrise, the crow of the sun, Yi the Archer, and Ti Chün and his wife, Hsi-Ho, mother of the ten suns. The two readings are from *The Classic of Mountains and Seas,* the first from a first-century B.C. chapter, the second from a first-century A.D. chapter.

Beside T'ang Valley there is the Leaning Mulberry, where the ten suns are bathed—it is north of the land of Black-Teeth—and where they stay in the river. There is a large tree, and nine suns stay on its lower branches while one sun stays on its top branch. (*Shan hai ching, Hai wai tung ching,* SPPY 9.3a–b)

In the middle of the great wasteland, there is a mountain called Nieh-yao Chün-ti. On its summit there is a leaning tree. Its trunk is three hundred leagues tall; its leaves are like the mustard plant. There is a valley called Warm Springs Valley. Beside Yang Valley there is Leaning Mulberry. As soon as one sun arrives, another sun rises. They are all borne by a crow. (*Shan hai ching, Ta huang tung ching,* SPPY 14.5a–b)

The Vastness of K'un-lun Mountains

The motifs in this narrative were discussed in chapter 10. The reading is from a first-century B.C. chapter of *The Classic of Mountains and Seas.*

Within the seas the K'un-lun wastes are in the northwest, and this is God's capital city on earth below. The K'un-lun wastes are eight hundred leagues square and eighty thousand feet high. On top there is the Tree Grain; it is forty feet tall and five spans wide. On all sides

there are nine wells with well-sills made of jade. On all sides there
are nine gates, and at the gates there is the K'ai-ming beast on guard.
The dwelling place of the gods is on a cliff with eight nooks. The
boundary of the Scarlet River has a cliff on the ridge which no one
could ascend unless he were the Good Archer. . . . The gulf south of
K'un-lun is two thousand, four hundred feet deep. The body of the
K'ai-ming beast is mostly that of a tiger, and it has nine heads, all of
which have human faces that look eastward. It stands on top of K'un-
lun. To the west of the K'ai-ming are the male and female phoenix
and the *luan*-bird. They all carry a serpent on their head and tread a
serpent underfoot, and there is a scarlet snake on their breast. North
of the K'ai-ming there is the Shih-jou creature, the pearl tree, the
patterned-jade tree, the *yü-ch'i* tree, and the Never Die tree. The male
and female phoenix and *luan*-bird all wear armor plate on their
heads. And there are the Li-chu bird, the giant Grain Tree, the
cypress, the Sweet Water, and the Wise Man tree, the Man-tui, also
called the T'ing-tree-cross-fanged. To the east of the K'ai-ming there
are Shaman P'eng, Shaman Ti, Shaman Yang, Shaman Li, Shaman
Fan, and Shaman Hsiang, who bear the corpse of Cha Yü, each holding the drug of immortality to protect him. Cha Yü has a serpent's
body and a human head. He was killed by Double Load and his
officer. There is also the Fu-ch'ang tree. On its crown there is a three-
headed man who watches over the red *lang-gan* jade tree. To the south
of the K'ai-ming beast there is the Tree Bird with its six heads, and
the scaly dragon, the cobra, the serpent, the long-tailed ape, the panther, the *niao-chih* tree, Splendid Pool tree, the hummingbird, the
shun-hawk, and the Shih-jou creature. (*Shan hai ching, Hai nei hsi
ching*, SPPY 11.2b–5b)

The Beast of White Marsh

This account belongs to the didactic category of bestial myths. It is
taken from the *Basic Annals of Hsien-yuan,* a fanciful biography of the Yellow Emperor, compiled by the T'ang author Wang Ch'üan, who was of
the Taoist persuasion. It will be recalled that the Yellow Emperor was
adopted as the supreme deity of the Taoist pantheon in the Latter Han
era. In this narrative he is known by the name Hsien-yuan, which originally belonged to a shadowy primeval god but later became attached
to the more illustrious god, the Yellow Emperor. The format of Wang's
account is modeled on the official biography of emperors and kings to

be found in traditional histories since the Han period. Like earthly rulers, the Yellow Emperor conducts a royal tour of his realm in this episode from the biography, and in the manner of sage-rulers, he seeks wisdom from others, in this case, from a god known as the Beast of White Marsh. This god in bestial form knows the infinitesimal number of metamorphosed beings and the mystery of the cosmos. The quest of the Yellow Emperor for divine knowledge is cast in the heroic mold, and his success is crowned with the reward of the chart of the cosmos, for knowledge is power. His portrayal as a god who prays to a lesser god in the traditional pantheon exemplifies the desacralization of deities in later mythography.

> The Emperor went on a tour of inspection. In the east he came to the sea. He went up Mount Huan. On the seashore he found the Holy Beast of White Marsh which could speak and understand the natures of all living creatures. There were a total of 11,520 kinds of wandering souls that had undergone a metamorphosis. While White Marsh was talking about them, the Emperor ordered someone to write them down on a chart to show them to the whole world. Then the Emperor ordered someone to compose a written prayer to pray to him. (*Yün chi ch'i ch'ien, Hsien-yüan pen chi*, SPTK 100.23a–b)

King Mu of Chou's Fabled Horses

The myth of King Mu of Chou's visit to the Queen Mother of the West was presented and discussed in chapter 9, and the motif of the fabled horse in chapter 11. An inscription on an early Chou bronze wine vessel in the shape of a foal reveals the Chou king's interest in horse breeding; it says that King Mu handled a foal and gave its owner two colts (Hsu Cho-yun and Linduff 1988, 139, frontispiece). His legendary association with horses is confirmed by the fourth-century B.C. text "Questions of Heaven," which relates the brief mythic narrative: "King Mu was a breeder of horses" (*Ch'u Tz'u, T'ien wen*, SPTK 3.27a). The following reading is from *Researches into Lost Records*, from the fourth to sixth century (attributed to Wang Chia).

> When King Mu had been on the throne for thirty-two years, he went on a royal tour of the empire. . . . The king drove a fleet of eight horses swift as dragons. One horse was called Beyond Earth, whose hooves did not touch the ground. The second was called Windswept Plumes, which went faster than any winged bird. The third was

called Rush-by-Night, which covered ten thousand leagues in the night. The fourth was called Faster-than-Shadow, which could keep up with the journeying sun. The fifth was called Finer-than-Flashing-Light, whose coat was the sheen of dazzling light. The sixth was called Faster-than-Light, whose single bound cast ten shadows. The seventh was called Rising Mist, which rushed along on the crest of the clouds. The eighth was called Wing Bearer, whose body had fleshy plumes. (*Shih yi chi,* HWTS 3.1a–b)

The Many-Splendored Bird

The account of the Many-Splendored Bird, a mythical bird of evil omen, is from the same classical source attributed to Wang Chia (fourth century A.D.) and edited by Hsiao Ch'i, of the sixth century. Like Wang Ch'ung's account of Holy Shu and Yü Lü on the giant peach tree, this passage provides an explanation of the popular custom of exorcism through mimetic ritual. In this case it is the post-Han custom of exposing images of the ill-omened bird, the Many-Splendored Bird, outside homes in the New Year to ward off evil. Again the ritual is derived from a myth. The myth narrative purports to date from the era of Yao, but it does not even occur in any pre-Han source, and it probably belongs to the oral myth tradition of a minority tribe which became incorporated into the canon of mythological writings. The bird's features include double pupils, signifying great wisdom, as with the demigod Shun. The bird is a hybrid, combining the characteristics of aggressive birds, such as the eagle and rooster, and the bird of Heaven, the phoenix. It should be noted that although the Chinese mythical bird *feng* is rendered as 'phoenix', it does not possess the phoenix's symbolic meaning of resurrection. The *ch'i-lin* mentioned in the reading is a hybrid mythical creature that resembles a deer; it was believed to appear on earth when the ruler was a sage and governed well. *Ch'i-lin* is usually, but erroneously, translated as 'the unicorn'.

While Yao was on the throne for seventy years, every year young male phoenix flocked to him, the *ch'i-lin* roamed through the lush marshes, and eagle-owls fled to the farthest desert. There was a country called Chih-chih, which brought the Many-Splendored Bird to him in tribute. It was also known as the Double-Pupil Bird, which means that its eyes had double pupils. In appearance it was like a rooster, and its call was like that of the phoenix. It would often shed its down and feathers, flap its fleshy wings, and fly off. It could swoop down on wild beasts like a tiger or wolf and could cause unnatural disasters and all kinds of evil, but it could not be harmed itself. Sometimes, if it was offered the essence of rare red jade, it might appear several times in one year, but otherwise it would fail to appear for several years. All the people in the land swept and sprinkled their gateways and doorways hoping to make the Many-Splendored Bird come to roost. When it did not appear, the people in the land carved the likeness of the bird in wood or cast its image in metal and fixed it between their gates and doors, so that if there were any goblins or trolls, they would be repelled or vanquished. Nowadays, every New Year's morning, when people make an image of the bird carved out of wood, or cast in metal, or else painted in a picture, and then place it over the window, this is a vestige of the custom in olden days of making the bird's image. (*Shih yi chi,* HWTS 1.10b–11a)

Vegetal Myths: *Ming-chia, Sha-fu,* and *Chih-ning*

Yao was the first of the demigods in the Golden Age. In the early Confucian tradition, he became the exemplar of the wise and benign ruler who embodied humanitarian principles advocated by that philosophical school, and especially the sociopolitical principle of meritocracy. There are very few myths of Yao compared with the two other Golden Age demigods Shun and Yü. Nevertheless, his name appears in numerous accounts, even if a mythic story is not attached to it in every case. The main body of myths about Yao is contained in *The Classic of History,* a work edited in the Han period consisting of passages dating from the late Chou and the Han eras. The text combines reconstructed history from the beginning of time, which, for this *Classic,* means from the time of Yao; mythological material that has been largely rewritten and reinterpreted compared with other late Chou mythic narratives; and also political theory.

Other texts, however, have preserved fragments of myth about Yao, which, unlike *The Classic of History,* are not politicized and historicized but are recognizable as the true stuff of mythology. The first reading below is a citation by Ma Su, of the seventeenth century, of a fragment from a work dating from the late Chou era (ca. fourth to third century B.C.) entitled *Master T'ien-ch'iu.* It relates that a miraculous plant, the *ming-chia,* grew in Yao's garden, serving him as a natural calendar: it grows one petal a day from the beginning of each month until the

Figure 11. The ming-chia plant; inscription reads, "The ming-chia plant grew [lacuna] in the era of Yao." Funerary stone bas-relief, Wu Liang Shrine, Chia-hsiang county, Shantung province, A.D. 151. From Feng and Feng, *Research on Stone Carving* (1821) 1934, chap. 4.

fifteenth day, and then it sheds one petal a day until the end of the month, when it is bare again. It is also known as the Calendar Petal and the Portent Plant. The second reading is a dictionary definition of the *sha-fu* plant from Hsu Shen's lexicon of the first century A.D. According to this account, the roots of the *sha-fu* are as fine as silk thread, but its leaves are large and prolific. It can whirl about like the wind so that it drives away insects and cools food and drink in hot kitchens. Again the plant is associated with Yao. The third reading tells of the plant of omen which grew in Yao's garden. This vegetal myth fits the paradigm of the didactic mythologem. The fragment is from *The Treatise on Research into Nature* of the third to fifth century. The monograph by Hino Iwao entitled *A New Appraisal of Legendary Plants* is an important resource for the study of this group of mythic motifs (1978, 57–59).

When Yao became the Son of Heaven, a *ming-chia* plant grew in his garden and served the emperor as a calendar. (*Yi shih*, citing *T'ien-ch'iu Tzu*, PCTP 9.5b)

The *sha-fu* is a plant that foretells an omen. In the time of Yao it grew in his kitchen, and it fanned the hot atmosphere and made things cooler. (*Shuo-wen chieh-tzu*, 2, SPTK 1.1b)

In the time of Yao there was a *ch'ü-yi* plant growing in the garden. Whenever a flatterer came to court, it bent forward and pointed him out. It is also called the *chih-ning*, Point the Flatterer plant. (*Po wu chih, Yi ts'ao mu*, SPPY 4.2a)

Kao Yao Honors His Ram

Mythological material relating to the figure of Kao Yao is similar to the case of myths about Yao, in the sense that much of it is to be found in *The Classic of History*. The earliest reference to Kao Yao occurs in poem 299 of *The Classic of Poetry*, where he is a judge commended for his treatment of prisoners of war. In the chapter of *The Classic of History* entitled "Canon of Yao," Kao Yao is presented as the supreme judge who is responsible for administering punishment as a minister in the government of Yao. In another chapter of *The Classic of History*, "The Speeches of Kao Yao," the wisdom of the judge is related in formal discourse (Karlgren 1950, 7, 8–12).

The tendentious rationalizing impulse of the anonymous political theorist who wrote *The Classic of History* in the late Chou or Han period did not permit the inclusion of more recognizably mythological material about Kao Yao. Several colorful details have survived in other texts, although they are fragmentary and some are of late provenance. The first of the readings that follow is from *A Garden of Anecdotes*, of the first century B.C. The second is taken from the third-century B.C. Confucian philosopher Hsun Tzu, who refers to Kao Yao in his essay "Against Physiognomy." Another detail is given in the third passage, which draws on physiognomical correlations. It is from *The Debates in White Tiger [Hall]*, attributed to the Han historian Pan Ku (A.D. 32–92). The last reading narrates a bestiary myth about Kao Yao's percipient ram. It appears in an essay by Wang Ch'ung in which he explains the juridical custom in the Han of painting images of Kao Yao and his divine one-horned ram in the courtroom. Another Han custom was for judges to wear a cap called the *chieh-chai* cap, signifying the myth of Kao Yao's ram (Yuan K'o 1980.2, 135).

> In the era of Yao . . . Kao Yao became grand controller. (*Shuo yuan, Chün tao,* SPTK 1.6b–7a)

> In appearance Kao Yao's complexion was like a peeled melon. (*Hsun Tzu, Fei hsiang,* SPPY 3.2a)

> Kao Yao's horse muzzle means that he was perfectly truthful and the sentences he passed were clear, for he penetrated the mind and heart of humans. (*Pai-hu t'ung-yi, Sheng jen,* TSCC 3A.178–79)

> The Hsieh-chih creature has one ram's horn, and it has the ability to know who is a criminal. When Kao Yao was conducting a trial and was in doubt about who the guilty person was, he would order the ram to butt the criminal. It would butt the guilty one, but it would not butt the innocent. Now this is a case of a sage beast born in Heaven who helped provide evidence in a trial. That is why Kao Yao honored his ram, even rising from the bench to look after its needs. (*Lun heng, Shih ying,* SPTK 17.10a–b)

The Dragon and the Tortoise

The earliest version of the myth of the dragon that helped Yü to control the flood was discussed in chapter 8. The Responding Dragon appears in the myths of the deaths of K'ua-fu and Ch'ih Yu as a god in control of the element of water. The first reading below narrates the earliest version, from "Questions of Heaven." The second is from Wang Chia's *Researches into Lost Records,* some seven centuries later. His account seeks to explain a myth that by his time no longer retained mythic relevance. The alterations to the myth in this late version indicate the influence of Taoism: the Responding Dragon has become a yellow dragon, yellow being the emblematic color of Taoism; and a "dark tortoise" has been added, "dark" (*hsuan*) being a mystical epithet in Taoism. The tortoise is a symbol of longevity, which itself constitutes one of the fundamental aspirations of this philosophical and religious creed.

> How did he dam the flood waters at their deepest? How did he demarcate the Nine Lands of the Earth? Over the rivers and seas what did the Responding Dragon fully achieve, and where did he

pass? What plan did Kun devise? What did Yü succeed in doing? (*Ch'u Tz'u, T'ien wen,* SPTK 3.6b–7b)

Yü exhausted his strength in cutting dikes and ditches and in conducting the courses of rivers and leveling mounds. The yellow dragon dragged its tail in front of him, while the dark tortoise carried green mud on its back behind him. (*Shih yi chi,* HWTS 2.2b)

Carp Leap over Dragon Gate

The myth of carp turning into dragons at Dragon Gate Mountain, which another narrative relates had been forged open by Yü, has enduring appeal because it illustrates the concepts of equal opportunity for all and success through individual effort. The myth acquired the cachet of social acceptance in the elite establishment of traditional society when the success of candidates in the awesomely difficult civil service examinations became known as the divine feat of carp that had leapt the river heights and turned into dragons.

Dragon Gate Mountain is in the east region of the river. When Yü melted the mountain and hewed a gateway a league or more wide, the Yellow River flowed down the middle and a horse and carriage could not pass between the two sides of the river. Every year at the end of spring, yellow carp fight their way upstream. Those which reach it [Dragon Gate] turn into dragons. Also, Lin Teng says, "Every year below Dragon Gate in late spring, yellow carp fishes leave the sea and come to the rivers and fight to leap over Dragon Gate. In one year the carp that scale Dragon Gate number no more than seventy-two. As soon as they scale Dragon Gate, cloudy rain follows in their wake and heavenly fire ignites their tails and they turn into dragons. (*T'ai-p'ing kuang chi,* citing *San Ch'in chi,* JMWH 466.3839)

15

Strange Lands
and Peoples

An interest in geography, as defined by the Greek word meaning 'delineation of land', is apparent in several early classical Chinese texts. It is, however, usually subordinated to the main theme of a given text and presented in a fragmentary way, so that passages that might be designated as geographical are incidental to the central aim of the work. The main inspiration for such topographical writings was the myth of Yü and the flood. The most important texts dealing with this myth which incorporated geographical material are the chapter of *The Classic of History* entitled "The Tribute of Yü" (Karlgren 1950, 12–18), *Shih Tzu* (Karlgren 1946, 303), and *Mencius* (Lau 1970, 102, 113). The last two accounts are brief, but the first constitutes an extended essay that describes in detail Yü's progress through the Nine Provinces within the Four Seas, as the mythological world was known, when he channeled the flow of water and drained the flooded land. According to this account, Yü traveled over fifty rivers and numerous mountains, charting the land and noting regional variations in terms of topography, type and quality of soil, the names of local tribes, and their sources of revenue and forms of tribute. Among these peoples are the skin-wearing Niao-yi; the Lai-yi herdsmen; the Huai-yi, renowned for oyster pearls and silk; the grass-wearing Tao-yi; the Ho-yi, with their tributary gifts of metallurgical goods to the court of Yao; the felt-wearing Hsi-ch'ing people; the San Miao people, with tribute of jewels; and the felt-wearing western Jung people of K'un-lun. The details of tribute and the information conveyed about different tribal groups no doubt replicate the sort of report compiled and presented to the Chou court when the Chou dynasty was at its apogee. Thus "The Tribute of Yü" constitutes a document that is part-history, part-mythology, and part-idealized political theory.

The chapter contains many place-names that cannot be identified or located with any certainty. As Karlgren observed, the exact position of "a framework of fundamental names" in pre-Han texts is "certain beyond any doubt," but most place-names "are to a large extent quite impossible to determine exactly" (1946, 209). Thus while the chapter records some factual data relating to names of known rivers, such as the Lo, Han, Huai, and so forth, it primarily belongs to the category of pseudo-geography or mythic geography.

Chinese geography becomes less mythological and more of a scientific study in the late Han era as speculation about the old world of gods and heroes ceded from the second century B.C., to a real knowledge of the Chinese empire and its contiguous lands and peoples. The first systematic attempt to provide a specific account is the "Treatise on Geography" by Pan Ku, the Han historian (A.D. 32–92). The word for *geography* in his treatise is *ti-li,* meaning 'land patterns', or 'the earth's system'. It is a combination of descriptive and historical geography in which the author seeks to set down and identify all known place-names. Yet Pan Ku was drawing for his source material on preexisting texts with exegetical commentaries that gave traditional explanations of names and places, and many of these are flawed through a lack of hard information. Karlgren's caveat, therefore, still applies to Pan Ku's "Treatise," and the number of place-names that can be identified or localized is very small (1946, 209).

Appearing after "The Tribute of Yü" and before Pan Ku's "Treatise," with some overlapping of early and late chapters, is *The Classic of Mountains and Seas,* a work presented as a descriptive geography of the old world, its lands, and its peoples, incorporating myth, legend, and lore. In one respect its structure is similar to the format of "The Tribute of Yü," for its anonymous author charts first the mountains of the south, west, north, east, and central regions (chaps. 1–5); then the regions beyond the seas, or stretches of water, south, west, north, and east (chaps. 6–9); the regions within the seas south, west, north, and east (chaps. 10–13); the expanse of land to the east, south, west, and north (chaps. 14–17); and regions within the seas (chap. 18). Scattered among its eighteen chapters are fragmentary accounts of strange lands and peoples, noted mainly for their differences and peculiarities vis-à-vis the Chinese. While much of this material has to do with mythology and the stuff of fable, it would be unwise to discount every descriptive detail. As Malinowski has shown, sociological data probably underlie and inform a good deal of this kind of early record of things un-Chinese. Many inhabitants of countries described in the *Classic* indicate societies marked by physical deformity, such as the Linked-Chest, the Three-Headed, the One-Eyed, Forked-Tongue, Odd-Arm, One-Foot, and Dwarf People. It is not difficult to conjure up parallels known to medical science and social science, such as the condition known as Siamese twins, or the practice of inflicting mutilations on members of society, including slitting the tongue (as in Australasian bull-roaring initiation rites), or punishing by removing a finger, limb, or even an eye. Accounts of peoples known as Deep-Set Eyes and as Whites are also clearly descriptive of un-Chinese physical characteristics. The names of the Country of Men and the Country of Women denote specific social systems based on matriarchy and patriarchy at their most extreme, in which the opposite sex is eliminated at an early age. The names of some countries are manifestly phonetic, such as Chih, Ku-she, and Meng Shu (the last significantly having several variants).

In terms of methodology, *The Classic of Mountains and Seas* may be viewed as a sort of mythological Baedeker guide to the ancient world, an enclosed chart of the world as it appeared to the Chinese at various stages between the third century B.C. (chaps. 1–5), the first century B.C. (chaps. 6–13), and the first century A.D. (chaps. 14–18). Some of its fanciful accounts were put to satirical use by Li Ju-chen (A.D. 1763–ca. 1830) in *Flowers in the Mirror* (Lin Tai-yi 1965, 58–127). Most of the readings in this chapter are from the *Classic*. For a different selection of translated texts from a variety of sources, see Mathieu's *Anthologie* (1989, 149–67) and Schiffeler's *Legendary Creatures* (1978).

Pierced-Chest Country

The tradition about the Pierced-Chest Country dates as far back as the fourth-century B.C. text *Shih Tzu*, cited by Kuo P'u in his commentary to the account of this country in *The Classic of Mountains and Seas* (Yuan K'o 1980.1, 195). The entry in the *Classic* itself is very brief, and it accentuates the deformity of the people: "Hole-Chest Country is to the east of there [San Miao]. Its people have a cavity through their chest. It is also said to lie to the east of Chih Country" (ibid., 194). A longer narrative from *The Treatise on Research into Nature* (third to fifth century A.D.) forms our reading. This myth explains the origin of their deformity, and it is linked to the major myth of Yü and the flood. It is based on the episode when Yü executed Fang-feng for arriving too late for the council of the gods. In this account, Yü is firmly associated with the Hsia. The author of the *Treatise* accredits Yü with the power of performing a miracle, when he resurrects the dead with the herb of immortality.

When the account in the *Treatise* is compared with the terse record in *The Classic of Mountains and Seas*, it becomes evident that several myths are fused in the *Treatise* to form a new narrative, myths that are culled from the classical tradition and mythic motifs from the Han and post-Han repertoire. They include Yü's founding role as ruler of the Hsia era, the flood, the assembly of the gods at K'uai-chi, Yü's execution of Fang-feng, the apparition of two divine dragons, the reference to the mythic place-name T'u-shan, the revenge of the lesser gods for Fang-feng's death, the miraculous storm, double suicide, and the healing role of Yü in the miraculous revival of the two dead avengers. All these mythic and legendary strands are brought together to explain the origin of the Pierced-Chest People, and as such they constitute a new etiological myth of a country, which itself constitutes a hybrid version of the myth.

> Long ago, when Yü was bringing order to the world, he assembled all the lords in the wilds of K'uai-chi, but Fang-feng arrived too late, so he killed him. The power of the Hsia was in the ascendant, and two dragons came down to him from on high. Yü ordered Ch'eng-kuang to harness them, and he traveled beyond his territory. He toured everywhere and then came back. He reached Nan-hai and passed by Fang-feng's land. Because of the stabbing incident at T'u-shan, two gods, the officers of Fang-feng, were enraged when they saw Yü, and they pierced him. A sudden gale and storm blew up and the two dragons rose up and left. The two officers were terrified. They stabbed themselves in the heart with their daggers and died. Yü grieved over them, and so he pulled out their daggers and revived them with the herb of immortality, and they became the Pierced-Chest People. (*Po wu chih, Wai kuo*, SPPY 8.4b)

Odd-Arm Country

The same sources give the earliest accounts of this country, inhabited by people having only one arm (variant: one thigh, *Huai-nan Tzu;* Yuan K'o 1980.2, 205). The first reading below is from a first-century B.C. chapter of *The Classic of Mountains and Seas.* The version of the myth given in the second reading, from *The Treatise on Research into Nature,* sets the narrative in the era of the founder of the Shang, or Yin, named T'ang the Conqueror. The account of flying machines in the text is not the earliest, since the tradition of Mo Tzu's kite predates the *Treatise* by about seven centuries. The account in the *Treatise* is the first instance, however, of manned flight and may be said to present a mythological paradigm of future technology or a technological desideratum. At another level, the narrative may be viewed as a migration myth in the Shang era.

> Odd-Arm Country is to its north. The people there have one arm and three eyes, for darkness and for daylight. They ride on piebald horses. There is a bird with two heads, red and yellow in color, which perches beside them. (*Shan hai ching, Hai wai hsi ching,* SPPY 7.1b–2a)

> The people of Odd-Arm are clever at ways of carrying things on their shoulders. They can kill any type of bird and can make flying carriages that travel long distances in the wake of the wind. In the era of T'ang the Conqueror of the Yin [Shang], a west wind came and blew their carriages down to Yü-chou. T'ang broke up their carriages, so that his people would not see them. Ten years later an east wind came, and they made more carriages, and he sent them back home. This country is forty thousand leagues from the Jade Gate Pass. (*Po wu chih, Wai kuo,* SPPY 8.4a)

The Country of Men

The sources for the myth of the Country of Men are *The Classic of Mountains and Seas* and Kuo P'u's commentary on it. The former, dating from the first century B.C., is typically terse. The latter, postdating it by some four centuries, is more informative in the manner of later mythography. Unfortunately, Kuo P'u does not indicate the sources for his new information, but it may be assumed that it derives from a Han or post-Han account that is from a text no longer extant.

Kuo P'u's narrative is set in the time of the Shang King Ta Wu (or, Wu the Great, trad. 1637–1562 B.C.). It takes the form of the odyssey of one Wang Meng to obtain the drug of immortality from the Queen Mother of the West. The details of the narrative mark Wang Meng as an adept in the art of longevity: dietary regimen, abstention from sex, and naturist clothing. He founds a new race of people descended from males through male conception and birth.

This myth of male procreation may have its origins in puberty initiation rites and the custom of couvade, instances of which Bruno Bettelheim has documented. He explained that these rites were the performance of rebirth, in which the male initiate is seen to be born anew from a male parent. Women are banned from such ritual, emphasizing the male denial of a woman's procreative role (Bettelheim 1954, as cited by Dundes 1984, 278–79). It may be assumed, by comparison of this myth with that of the Country of Women, that most female infants in such a society were left to die, while male children were allowed to survive.

> The Country of Men lies north of Wei-niao. They are a people who wear clothes and carry a sword. (*Shan hai ching, Hai wai hsi ching,* SPPY 7.2b)

> Wu the Great, emperor of the Yin [Shang], sent Wang Meng to gather drug herbs from the Queen Mother of the West and he arrived at this land. He broke off some grain but could not enter there. He ate fruit from the trees and wore tree bark to clothe himself. All his life he never had a wife, but he produced two sons who issued from the center of his body. When their father died, these sons became the people of the Country of Men. (Kuo P'u's commentary on *Shan hai ching, Hai wai hsi ching,* SPPY 7.2b)

The Country of Women

The narratives of the myths about countries where only men and only women live appear to describe in mythic terms the existence of social systems that tolerate or emphasize only one sex. The first reading below is from a first-century B.C. chapter of *The Classic of Mountains and Seas,* and the second is Kuo P'u's commentary on that passage. The enigmatic myth of the first text is amplified and explained by Kuo P'u, who seeks to rationalize how a single-gender society is achieved: the female is mysteriously impregnated while bathing, and if she gives birth to a boy, he is left to die before he reaches the age of three. The motif of the impregnating bath is similar to that of virgin birth in the narrative of Chien Ti. The motif of abandoning a baby also occurs in the myth of Chiang Yuan and her infant, Hou Chi.

The myths of the Country of Men and the Country of Women embody the most enduring of all human concerns, since they embrace associated myths of gender competition, gender roles, virgin birth, matriarchy, patriarchy, and the social control of kinship lines. That these ancient myths remain potent in contemporary society, not the least in Western society at the end of the second millennium A.D., is evident from the modern fascination with all manner of non-natural means of reproduction, including semen banks, surrogate motherhood, *in vitro* fertilization, artificial insemination for unmarried virgins (the so-called virgin birth phenomenon), lesbian or homosexual marriage with an adopted or "inherited" child, and so forth. It is possible to conjecture that this plethora of nontraditional social experimentation derives in the main from gender competition, which in turn has been engendered by the crisis of role reversals and role challenges due to political movements and socioeconomic trends in the twentieth century.

Gender competition is particularly evident in recent social developments, with the phenomenon of the "glass ceiling" blocking female promotion and the syndrome of equal opportunity employment for women and its practical side effect of "tokenism." A recent study of contemporary Western mores and myths of sex and gender focuses on attitudes in the late nineteenth century and their aftermath in the twentieth century. The author, Elaine Showalter, comments: "The myths that interest me most are the ones that project apocalyptic anxiety on to sexual change, particularly those having to do with reproduction, both biological and creative. When people think the distinction between the sexes is dissolving or intensifying, then you get panic" (1991.1, 20).

> The Country of Women is north of Shaman-hsien. There two girls live, surrounded by water. (*Shan hai ching, Hai wai hsi ching,* SPPY 7.3a–b)

> There is a yellow pool. When the women enter it to bathe, they emerge pregnant. If they give birth to a male child, within three years it will die prematurely. (Kuo P'u's commentary on *Shan hai ching, Hai wai hsi ching,* SPPY 7.3a–b)

The Country of Meng Shu

This country is variously called Meng Shu, Meng Niao, Meng Hsi, Meng K'uei, and Meng Shuang. The multiplicity of names for a country of human-avian hybrids suggests a phonetic confusion in the transcription of a foreign name and possibly a confusion of place-names. Of the five names, Meng Niao and Meng Shuang clearly have a semantic value: *Niao* means 'a bird', and *Shuang* means 'a couple'. The words *Shu, Hsi,* and *K'uei* probably denote phonetic values. The word *Meng,* constant in all five, may signify here the idea of ferocity. The element *Niao,* meaning 'bird', correlates with the themes of three narratives, which constitute an ornithomorphous myth, a foundation myth, and a migration myth. These are the myths of Meng Niao, Meng Shu, and Meng Hsi. The myth of Meng Shuang is quite different. It relates a sibling marriage resulting in the exile of the incestuous couple from the region. The narrative appears in *The Treatise on Research into Nature* (Mathieu 1989, 158).

The first of the following readings is from a first-century B.C. chapter of *The Classic of Mountains and Seas,* which tells of a country of birds north of Mo, a Chinese transliteration of a foreign place-name, possibly in Central Asia. The second reading is from *The Treatise on Research into Nature,* of the third to the fifth century A.D., and it introduces a human feature in the description of the people. The third reading is from a tenth-century encyclopedia citing a lost text of *A General Atlas* dating from the Han period. This passage narrates a more complex myth. The ancestors of Meng Hsi are said to have emerged in the Shun era as a people skilled in domesticating birds and beasts, a skill that indicates that they were a settled community. This people migrated from their Hsia overlords, however, an exodus that, although unexplained, is marked by special favor with the escort of birds of paradise. This multilayered myth integrates the motifs of ornithomorphology, the foundation of a new people, migration, and the domestication of birds and beasts, as well as being a sitiological myth explaining how humans first began to eat eggs. This myth was also recorded in *The Treatise on Research into Nature* in a passage almost identical to the late citation from the Han work *A General Atlas* (Greatrex 1987, 132), which would seem to confirm the mythographic view that not all late citations are invalid as classical mythic texts.

Meng Niao is north of Mo Country. The birds there are speckled with red, yellow, and green, and they point toward the east. (*Shan hai ching, Hai wai hsi ching,* SPPY 11.2b)

The people of Meng Shu Country have a human head and a bird's body. (*Po wu chih, Wai kuo,* SPPY 8.5a)

In Meng Hsi people have a human head and a bird's body. Their ancestors tamed all the beasts and fowl for the Yü clan [of Shun]. In the era of the Hsia Lord, the people first started to eat eggs. When the Meng Hsi left them, male and female phoenix escorted them from there till they came to settle here. The mountains were thick with bamboo that grew eight thousand feet high. The male and female phoenix fed off the fruit of the bamboo, and the Meng Hsi ate from the fruit of the trees. It is eighteen thousand leagues from Chiu-yi. (*T'ai-p'ing yü-lan,* citing *K'uo ti t'u,* SPTK 915.9a)

Owl-Sunshine Country

The description of the inhabitants of Owl-Sunshine Country makes them appear subhuman, although the wording of the text of the first reading below, from a first-century B.C. chapter of *The Classic of Mountains and Seas,* clearly refers to humans: *ch'i wei jen,* which means "as people, they. . . ." The account, with its grotesque depiction of foreigners, belongs to the type of hyperbolic and xenophobic ridicule of alien features and behavior. The fear of these inhabitants has led the anonymous author to portray them as wild beasts. The second reading comes from the commentary of the third-century A.D. writer Liu K'uei on a contemporary prose poem. A similar description to Liu K'uei's (fl. ca. A.D. 295) occurs in the *History of the Chou,* but there it refers to a creature called the Chou-mi-fei-fei. The Chou-mi is the name of a country believed to be in the southwest; *fei-fei* describes a primate or simian and is taken to be a man-eating beast rather than a cannibalistic human (Yuan K'o and Chou Ming 1985, 293; Knechtges 1982, 388 n. 223). A variant of this myth reads Owl-Ram Country, as in the second reading.

Owl-Sunshine Country lies west of North Ch'ü. As people, they have human faces with long lips, and black, hairy bodies. Their heels grow back to front. When they see humans, they break out laughing. In their left hand they hold a bamboo cane. (*Shan hai ching, Hai nei nan ching,* SPPY 10.2a–b)

The *Erh ya* [Dictionary] says: "Owl-Ram [Country] is also Yü-yü. There they have faces like human beings, with long lips and black, hairy bodies, and their heels point the wrong way. When they see humans, they laugh. So people carry a pole in their left hand." (Liu K'uei's commentary on *Wu tu fu* by Tso Ssu, citing *Erh ya, Wen hsuan k'ao yi* 5.9a)

16

Founding
Myths

Founding myths were encountered in several narratives presented in preceding chapters. Here those separate strands will be brought together in conjunction with new material on the motif of founding a city, a dynasty, a people, or a country. The myth of the Lord of the Granary relates the institution of a city; that of the Meng Hsi (or Meng Shu) narrates the founding of a new country; that of P'an Hu recounts the foundation of a tribe; that of Po Yi traces the divine ancestry of the dynastic line of the Ch'in people; that of Ts'an Ts'ung outlines the divine ancestry of the Shu kings; and that of Hou Chi narrates the divine origins of the Chou people. In his monumental study, "Legends and Cults in Ancient China," Karlgren demonstrated that the great clans and aristocratic families of antiquity traced their descent from legendary heroes, demigods, and gods, who were regarded as the founders of their noble house and family line (1946, 213). Granet proposed a similar thesis (1959, 39, 389).

Like the founding myth of Rome, which relates that a she-wolf sacred to Mars suckled the abandoned twins Romulus and Remus, Chinese founding myths are characterized by bird and animal motifs. Chien Ti became pregnant from the egg of a dark or black bird sent by the god Ti K'u and gave birth to the Shang ancestor, Hsieh. The divinely born Hou Chi was abandoned by his mother, Chiang Yuan, but was protected by birds and beasts and became the founder of the Chou. P'an Hu was a divine dog, who founded a new people of canine and human descent. Yü changed into a bear at the moment of his courtship of and mating with the T'u-shan girl, who gave birth to Ch'i, Yü and Ch'i being the first founders of the legendary Hsia.

Other motifs characterize founding myths. The person of the founder is invested with heroic qualities that mark him as a leader of men. Such a hero is shown to be favored by God and endowed with the power of performing miracles, changing shape, invoking supernatural aid, and conquering enemies obstructing his path to triumph. This motif is illustrated by the mythic narratives of Hou Chi, T'ang the Conqueror, and King Wen and King Wu of the Chou. The founder in the heroic mold is also one who is distinguished by a gift for attracting or winning over or selecting a wise adviser, a man often identified in a divinely inspired dream and plucked out of obscurity. Such is the case with T'ang the Conqueror with his brilliant minister Yi Yin, King Wen with his supernaturally intelligent counselor, the Great Lord Chiang (also known as the Great Lord Wang), and King Wu with his resourceful younger brother and adviser, the Duke of Chou. Sarah Allan has explored this relationship between leader and adviser in *The Heir and the Sage* (1981, 91–121).

Although various myths relate the founding of a city or a dynasty or a country, it is usually impossible to identify their location or existence. The Lord of the Granary's city of Yi, for example, cannot be located. No evidence yet exists for the historicity of the Hsia. Equally, no archeological sites of ancient Hsia or early Shang cities have yet been identified. In archeological and historical terms, what was previously thought to represent Hsia culture is now more cautiously referred to as Erh-li-t'ou culture datable to the third to second millennium B.C. As far as Shang cities are concerned, the location of the ancient Shang capitals of Ao and Po, which are mentioned in Shang inscriptions, has yet to be ascertained. The archeological and historical evidence for Shang cities commences only with the late Shang capital city of Yin, the last capital of the Shang, situated near An-yang in Honan province. The Yin site yielded inscriptions identifying eight (or nine) Shang rulers from King Wu, a period dating from circa 1200–1050 B.C. This amalgam of archeological evidence and a historical written record is the earliest for the Shang state or city (Keightley 1983, 524).

No known city of ancient China's legendary Hsia, protohistorical early Shang and historical late Shang, or other city such as Yi is linked to an illustrious mythological founder, as Romulus and Remus are with Rome. On the link between mythic narratives and historical fact, Hsu and Linduff conclude in their study of the Chou that many Chinese founding myths are based on migration myths or exodus myths that tell of a leader or hero who moves to a new region and is followed by the entire population. This migration myth finds its historical expression in "the general pattern of Chou expansionism" (Hsu Cho-yun and Linduff 1988, 163).

The Founding Myth of the Shang

Several motifs appear in narratives of the founding of the Shang. The readings are taken from the main accounts in *The Classic of Poetry*, circa 600 B.C., the *Annals of Master Lü*, of the third century B.C., and the *Historical Records*, of the late second century B.C. The motif of the black bird in the poetry is taken up by the two prose narratives. They contain the motifs of a tall tower protecting the virginity of two well-born girls, a feast with drum music presaging a wedding, a swallow laying two eggs, and, in the second prose passage the fertility act of the girls bathing, pregnancy following the act of swallowing the egg of the black bird, divine birth, the hero's success in accomplishing his tasks, the gift of the territory of the Shang, and the popularity of the hero with the people.

Sarah Allan argues that "the Shang rulers had a totemic relationship with the ten suns which were also thought to be birds" (1991, 46). Her definition of totemism in this context, however, is too vague to serve as evidence for her argument: "'totemism' [is] a system of classification rather than a social institution" (ibid., 46, 172). To substantiate her argument, Allan combines the myth of the ten suns with the myth of a crow bearing the sun to the top of Leaning Mulberry each dawn. From this amalgamation of separate myths she deduces that just as there are ten suns, so there are ten birds, one in each sun, representing the power of the sun and, ultimately, representing the totemic relationship between the Shang, the ten suns, and the ten birds. The textual evidence does not support such a deduction, however, for the various versions of the myth of the suns and crow are as follows: (1) a sun bears a crow; (2) a crow bears one sun each dawn to the top of the world-tree; and (3) the crow is sometimes said to be three-legged. It should be made clear that nowhere in the classical or postclassical texts are ten crows in the ten suns ever specified or implied. Thus the transformational theory Allan uses to force the conclusion that the Shang had a totemic relationship with the ten suns believed to be birds is invalidated, since it is not justifiable to merge several myths and to inject a totally new motif (ten birds) to create a neomyth to suit one's theory. I have discussed the motifs of the readings in chapter 5.

> Heaven ordered the Black Bird
> To come down on earth and give birth to the Shang.
> (*Shih ching, Hsuan niao*, 303, SPPY 23.9a)

The Yu-Sung clan had two glamorous daughters. They built a nine-story tower for them. When they ate and drank, drum music was always played for them. God ordered a swallow to go and look at them, and it sang with a cry like "Yee-yee!" The two daughters fell in love with it and each tried to be the one to catch it. They covered it with a jade box. After a moment they opened it up and looked at it. The swallow had laid two eggs. It flew away to the north and never came back. The two daughters composed a song, a line of which went, "Swallow, Swallow, you flew away!" This is, in fact, the first composition in the style of Northern Music. (*Lü-shih ch'un-ch'iu, Yin ch'u*, SPTK 6.6b)

Yin Hsieh's mother was called Chien Ti. She was the daughter of the Yu-Sung clan and the second concubine of Ti K'u. Three of them went to bathe. They saw a black bird drop its egg. Chien Ti picked it up and swallowed it. Then she became pregnant and gave birth to Ch'i. Ch'i grew up and gave meritorious service in helping Yü control the floodwater. Emperor Shun therefore gave this command to Ch'i: "The people do not have close family relationships, and the five social relationships are in disorder. You will serve as my director of retinue." He gave him the Shang fiefdom and conferred on him the surname Tzu-shih. Hsieh flourished in the reigns of Yao T'ang, Yü Shun, and Yü the Great. His accomplishments were well known among the people, and so the people became peaceable. (*Shih chi, Yin pen chi*, SPPY 3.1a–b)

T'ang the Conqueror Attacks the Hsia

The image of the hero is more developed with the mythical figure of T'ang, a later founder of the Shang. The mythological line moves from the divine bird to the girl Chien Ti, from her to her son, Hsieh,

and then to a later Shang king, T'ang. With this mythical figure the epic
of the Shang evolves from a people descended from God to a dynasty
founded by a hero. Whereas the demigod, Hsieh, or Ch'i, belongs to
archaic mythological time, T'ang is closer to historical time. He is an
earthly ruler who wrests power from the evil tyrant, Chieh of the Hsia,
and goes on to overthrow the Hsia and establish a glorious dynasty.
T'ang's qualities as a hero are as numerous as Chieh's qualities as a villain. The *casus belli* between the two is projected in the mythic narratives
as a moral campaign, a point emphasized in the first of the following
readings, from *Annals of Master Lü*. The second reading is from *Historical Records*. The third is from a first–century A.D. chapter of *The Classic
of Mountains and Seas*. The last is from *Biographies of Women*, dating from
about the third to the fourth century.

The narratives relate that T'ang was a military hero whose army
was ready to fight and die for him, while Chieh's army refused to
engage in battle. They show that T'ang was an exemplar of moral virtue
who attracted men of worth, such as Yi Yin, and who, when he became
king, offered himself in sacrifice for rain during a drought of many
years. In many of these narratives several figures are dramatically polarized: T'ang against Chieh, Yi Yin against the favorite, Mo Hsi, and Mo
Hsi in the end against Chieh. These polarities create patterns of binary
opposition in the mythic struggle between good and evil. Sarah Allan
has analyzed this myth in *The Heir and the Sage* (1981, 77–101).

Chieh committed more and more wrongdoing and transgressed the
right way of the ruler, bringing harm and destruction to his country
and his people. So T'ang, in anxious concern for the stability of the
empire, ordered Yi Yin to go and observe the mighty Hsia. But he
was afraid that the Hsia would not trust him, so T'ang personally
shot at Yi Yin, and then Yi Yin fled to the Hsia. Three years later, he
returned and reported in Po, the Yin [Shang] capital. He said, "Chieh
used to be bewitched by Mo Hsi, and now he is in love with Wan and
Yen. He shows no pity toward the masses, and the will of the people
is that they won't endure it. Everyone from the top level of society
to the bottom loathes him. The people's hearts are full of resentment,
and they all say, 'Unless Heaven up above is without pity, the days
of the Hsia will come to an end.'" T'ang said to Yi Yin, "What you
tell me about the mighty Hsia is just what I want." T'ang swore an
oath with Yi Yin to show that they would destroy the Hsia. Yi Yin
went back again to observe the situation in mighty Hsia and learn

what Mo Hsi had to tell him. (*Lü-shih ch'un-ch'iu, Shen ta*, SPTK 15.1b–2a)

Then T'ang raised an army and took command of the nobles. Yi Yin went with T'ang's army, and T'ang himself held the great ceremonial ax, to attack K'un-wu and then to attack Chieh. (*Shih chi, Yin pen chi*, SPPY 3.3b)

There was a headless person called the Corpse of Hsia Keng, who stood holding a spear and shield. Long ago, when T'ang the Conqueror attacked Chieh of the Hsia at Mount Chang and captured Mount Chang, he cut Keng in two in front of the mountain. When Keng stood up, he was headless, so he ran away to hide his shame and then sank without a trace into Mount Wu. (*Shan hai ching, Ta huang hsi ching*, SPPY 16.7a)

Then T'ang received the mandate to rule, and he attacked the Hsia, and the battle was fought at Ming-t'iao. Chieh's army refused to do battle, so T'ang sent Chieh into exile. Chieh sailed out to sea in the same boat as Mo Hsi and his other favorites. He died on the Mountain of Nan-ch'ao. (*Lieh nü chuan, Hsia Chieh Mo Hsi*, SPPY 7.1b)

Hou Chi, Founder of the Chou

The mythic motifs of the founding of the Chou people were discussed in several early chapters. The most significant are: divine descent, miraculous birth, the trials of the hero as an infant, divine intervention through the charity of simple folk and the creatures of nature, and the success and popularity of the hero. The reading is from *Historical Records*, of the late second century B.C.

Hou Chi of the Chou was named Ch'i, the Abandoned. His mother, the daughter of the Yu-t'ai clan, was called Chiang Yuan. Chiang Yuan was Ti K'u's first consort. Chiang Yuan went out to the wild fields and she saw the footprints of a giant. Her heart was full of joy and pleasure, and she felt the desire to tread in the footprints. As she trod in them there was a movement in her body as if she were with child. She went on until her due time and gave birth to a baby boy. . . . Chiang Yuan thought he might be a god, so she took him up at once and brought him up until he was fully grown. Because she had wanted to abandon him at first, his name was Ch'i. When Ch'i was a child, he looked imposing, as if he had the bold spirit of a giant.

When he went out to play, he liked planting hemp and beans, and his hemp and beans were very fine. When he became an adult, he also grew very skilled at plowing and farming. He would study the proper use of the land, and where valleys were suitable he planted and he reaped. Everyone went out and imitated him. Emperor Yao heard about him and promoted Ch'i to master of agriculture, so that the whole world would benefit from him and have the same success. Emperor Shun said, "Ch'i, the black-haired people are beginning to starve. You are the Lord Millet [Hou Chi]. Plant the seedlings in equal measure throughout the hundred valleys." He gave Ch'i the fiefdom of T'ai with the title of Lord Millet, and he took another surname from the Chi clan. (*Shih chi, Chou pen chi,* SPPY 4.1a, 4.1b)

King Wen of the Chou

As the Shang had divine origin through miraculous conception and divine birth and emerged as a conquering people, so too did the Chou. The ancestors of the Shang and the Chou, Hsieh and Hou Chi, are parallel figures. In the same way the triumphant conquerors of the Shang and the Chou, T'ang and King Wen, are complementary hero figures. But whereas T'ang is a mythical figure, King Wen belongs to the historical era, though this does not mean that his character and his career are not imbued with mythological features. Thus both historical dynasties possess their myths of divine kingship and of temporal power. The myths surrounding King Wen emphasize his wisdom in acquiring an adviser, the Great Lord Chiang (also known as the Great Lord Wang, Lü Wang, or Wang the Counselor). He was a man chosen by God, as discovered through divination or a dream, to steer the king through successive campaigns against the Shang, whose last ruler was a tyrant. In fact, some accounts tend to portray the character of this adviser in such sympathetic terms that he threatens to upstage the heroic figure of the king himself. The first reading below, from the fourth-century B.C. text "Questions of Heaven," marks the earliest version of the mythic encounter between King Wen and the counselor. This version alludes to the fact that the future Great Lord Chiang (known as the Great Lord Wang) had the low status of a butcher. In the second reading, taken from *Historical Records,* the social status of the adviser becomes that of a fisherman. Although this appears to be lowly, it is enhanced by the noble mythos of the fisherman in the *Songs of Ch'u* (Hawkes 1985, 206–7). The third reading is a late fictional narrative, based on early mythical material, from Kan Pao's collection of the fourth century A.D. Here the adviser acquires the supernatural power to deflect a goddess's elemental force, which might otherwise have destroyed his city.

When Wang the Counselor was in the market, how did Ch'ang [King Wen] recognize him? (*Ch'u Tz'u, T'ien wen*, SPTK 3.31a)

King Wen intended to go hunting, so he had his augurer prepare divination for it. It said: "What you will catch won't be a dragon, and it won't be a hornless dragon. It won't be tiger and it won't be a bear. What you will catch is one who will help the mighty King." So King Wen drove toward the west and went hunting. It did indeed turn out that he met the Great Lord north of the River Wei. After having a discussion with him, he was very pleased and said to him, "Ever since the time of his lordship my late father, it has been said that 'when the wise man goes to the Chou, the Chou will prosper.' Are you really that man? His lordship my father was a long time hoping for you!" He therefore gave him the title of the Great Lord Wang [Hope]. Getting into the carriage, they returned together. King Wen installed him as his guiding mentor. (*Shih chi, Ch'i T'ai-kung shih chia*, SPPY 32.1b)

King Wen made the Great Lord Wang the Great Lord Governor of Kuan-tan. After a year of his being governor, even the wind did not make a noise in the branches of trees. King Wen dreamed that an extraordinarily beautiful woman was standing on the road weeping. He asked her why, and she said, "I am the daughter of the spirit of Mount T'ai, and I became the wife of the spirit of the East Sea. I want to go back home, but my road is blocked because of the governor of Kuan-tan. He is a good man, but even if he obstructs me in my journey I shall have to continue my journey, but there is bound to be a terrible storm. And then his good reputation will suffer." When King Wen woke up he summoned the Great Lord to question him. On that very same day it turned out that there was a terrible storm, but it passed by the Great Lord's city and broke out over the outskirts of the city. Then King Wen honored the Great Lord by making him his commander in chief. (*Sou shen chi*, TSCC 4.25)

King Wu of the Chou

The mythological accounts of the successful military campaigns that led to the founding of the Chou dynasty again polarize the protagonists in a great moral crusade: King Wu carries on the task of his father, King Wen, with the help of a brilliant and wise adviser, the Duke of Chou, King Wu's younger brother. The names of the two kings are also polarized: King Wen means 'King Civility', and King Wu means 'King Military'. King Wu's adversary is King Chou, the last ruler of the Shang. The readings accentuate the moral prerogative of King Wu, who is aided by supernatural powers, such as a river god, and is guided by his brother, who demonstrates resourcefulness and cunning in tactical and psychological warfare. Again, as with the Chou King Wen and his adviser, the roles of King Wu and the Duke of Chou are at times complementary, at times ambiguous. For example, in the first and fourth readings below, from two Han sources, King Wu is portrayed as a subordinate character and even appears ridiculous in his inability to lead men or to control events.

The first reading is from Wang Ch'ung's *Disquisitions*, of the first century A.D. The second is from the *Six Sword Bags*, a fragmentary work attributed to the Chou hero the Great Lord Chiang but more likely to date from the late Ch'in to early Han era (ca. late third century B.C.). The third reading is from *Huai-nan Tzu*, of the late second century B.C. The fourth is from Han Ying's commentary on and exposition of *The Classic of Poetry*, of the second century B.C. The fifth and sixth readings belong together: the fifth is a citation of an old text by Yü Shih-nan (A.D. 558–638) in his *Collation from the North Hall*; the sixth is a narrative of King Wu's divine mandate to commence his campaign against the Shang, aided by the wisdom and divine percipience of the Duke of Chou.

When King Wu of the Chou was about to attack King Chou of the Shang, he had divination made using stalks, but the result was negative, and the diviner declared, "Very bad luck." The Great Lord pushed aside the milfoil stalks and trod on the tortoises and said, "What do withered bones and dead plants know about good luck or bad luck!" (*Lun heng, Pu shih*, SPTK 24.9b)

When King Wu was going to attack the Yin, he boarded a boat and crossed the river. The troops and carriages set off and then smashed their boats up in the river. The Great Lord said, "The heir apparent will avenge his father. Today they will all die—let there be no survivors!" As the troops passed the bridges of the ferry port, they burned them all down. (*T'ai-p'ing yü-lan*, citing *Liu t'ao*, SPTK 482.1a)

King Wu went to attack King Chou. As he was crossing the river at Meng Ford, the river god, Lord Yang, made strong waves turn the current and dash against the boats. A fierce wind blew up and it grew pitch dark, so that men and horses could not see each other. Then King Wu held the yellow ax in his left hand and clenched the white command spear in his right hand. His eyes glared. Brandishing his spear, he said, "I have been entrusted with the defense of the world. Who dares to oppose my will?" At this, the wind died down and the waves subsided. (*Huai-nan Tzu, Hsien ming*, SPPY 6.1b)

King Wu went to attack King Chou. When he reached Hsing-ch'iu, his shield broke in three and the heavens poured with rain continuously for three days. King Wu's heart was filled with dread. He summoned the Great Lord and asked him, "Does this mean that King Chou cannot be attacked yet?" The Great Lord replied, "Not at all. The fact that your shield broke in three means that the army ought to be divided into three sections. The fact that the heavens poured with rain continuously for three days means that it will freshen up our troops." King Wu said, "If you are right, how will we do what you suggest?" "If people like a man, they will even like the crow on the top of his house. But if they hate him, they will also hate the very walls of his house. Let everyone slaughter the enemy! Let there be no survivors!" (*Han shih wai chuan*, TSCC 3.32)

In the capital city of King Wu of the Chou, the snow was more than ten inches deep. The Revered Father [the Duke of Chou] [textual lacuna: ? was informed of strangers] riding horse-drawn carriages. He sent a messenger to hold a vessel of rice gruel and go out to them. He opened the gates and admitted them. He said, "It is cold today, so why don't you come in for some hot rice gruel to ward off the cold?" (*Pei-t'ang shu-ch'ao*, subcommentary of K'ung Kuang-t'ao, referring to *T'ai-kung chin kuei*, KC 144.12b)

King Wu of the Chou attacked King Chou of the Shang. King Wu was establishing his capital, Lo City, but before it was completed, there were storms for over ten days with ice-cold rain and snow over ten inches deep. On the day of *chia-tzu*, just as day was about to break—no one knows who they were, but five officers riding in

horse-drawn carriages with two horsemen riding behind halted outside the royal palace gates and expressed their wish to have an audience with King Wu. King Wu was about to refuse to go out and see
them, but the Revered Father [the Duke of Chou] said, "You must
not do that. The snow is over ten inches deep, but the carriages and
riders have left no tracks. They are probably wise men." The Grand
Master and Revered Father then sent a messenger to go outside and
hold a vessel of rice gruel. He opened the gates and admitted the five
carriages and two horsemen and said, "His Majesty is in his private
rooms and does not wish to come out for the time being. But the
weather is cold, so why don't you come in for some hot rice gruel to
ward off the cold? I'm sorry, but I do not know how you gentlemen
are ranked in precedence?" The two horsemen said, "Our senior man
is the Lord of the South Sea, next is the Lord of the East Sea, then the
Lord of the West Sea, then the Lord of the North Sea, then the River
Earl with the Rain Master and the Earl of the Winds."

When they had finished their rice gruel, the messenger told the
Revered Father everything in detail. The Revered Father said to King
Wu, "You may now have an audience with your visitors. The occu-
pants of the five carriages and the two horsemen are the gods of the
Four Seas, besides the River Earl, the Rain Master, and the Earl of
the Winds. The God of the South Sea is called Chu Yung, the God
of the East Sea is called Kou Mang, the God of the North Sea is called
Hsuan Ming, and the God of the West Sea is called Ju Shou. The
River Earl's name is Feng Yi, the Rain Master's name is Yung, and the
Earl of the Winds's name is Yi. Please ask our Guest Master to sum-
mon each of them in by his name." So when King Wu was at the top
of the hall, the Guest Master stood outside the gates leading into the
lower end of the hall and called for Chu Yung to enter. The five gods
were all amazed, and they looked at one another and sighed. Chu
Yung made a deep bow. King Wu said, "You have come from far in
dire weather; what instructions do you wish to give me?" They all
said, "Heaven is going to attack the Yin dynasty and establish the
Chou dynasty. We have come here humbly to receive your com-
mands. Please advise the Earl of the Winds and the Rain Master of
your wishes, and they will each carry out their duties." (Yuan K'o,
SHHYPT 88.247-48)

The Beginning of the Yao People

The myth of the inception of the Yao people was discussed in chapter 5 with reference to the miraculous conception of P'an Hu, the divine dog. Franz Boas recorded a similar dog myth among the Dog-Rib Indians of North America (1966, 438). The narrative of the reading is from Kan Pao's collection, of the fourth century A.D.

Kao Hsin had an old wife who lived in the royal palace. She developed an earache. After some time the doctor cleared her ear out to cure her and he removed a knob-worm as big as a cocoon. After the wife had gone out, she put it in a gourd basket and covered it with a plate. Soon the knob-worm changed into a dog and it had five-color markings. So it was named P'an Hu, Plate-Gourd, and she looked after it. . . . [The king] ordered his youngest daughter to be a dutiful wife to Plate-Gourd.

Plate-Gourd led the girl up South Mountain. The grass and trees were thick and bushy and there was no trace of human footprints. Then the girl took her clothes off and became bonded to him as his servant, wearing clothes that she made as best she could, and she followed Plate-Gourd up the mountain. They entered a valley and stopped in a stone house. The king was sorrowful when he thought about it, and he sent his men to go and look out for her. But the sky at once grew stormy, the mountain ranges thundered and the clouds grew black. Those who had set out refused to go any further. After three years or so had passed, she had given birth to six sons and six daughters. After Plate-Gourd died, they paired off as mates and became husbands and wives for each other. (*Sou shen chi*, TSCC 14.91)

The Ancestor of the Shu

The myth of Ts'an Ts'ung, divine ancestor of the kings of Shu, was discussed in chapter 2. The first two readings are from *Basic Annals of the Kings of Shu*, a fragmentary text dating from the Han period. The third is from the tenth-century miscellany *A Continuation of "The Origin of Things,"* compiled by Feng Chien following on from *The Origin of Things* by Liu Ts'un, of the T'ang era. The fourth reading is from a late source of the Yuan dynasty, *A Compendium of Information on the Gods of the Three Religions* (Confucianism, Taoism, and Buddhism). This is an illustrated source book of popular hagiography recounting the lives of the gods and saints of China's three main traditions of belief.

The first ancestor of the Shu kings was called Ts'an Ts'ung. In the next era his descendant was called Po Huo, and in the era after that his descendant was called Yü Fu. Each of these three eras lasted several hundred years. In each era they became gods and did not die. Their people followed their kings, taking another shape and vanishing like them. (*T'ai-p'ing yü-lan*, citing *Shu wang pen chi*, SPTK 888.2b)

The first ancestors of Shu with the title of king were Ts'an Ts'ung, Po Huo, and Yü Fu. In the K'ai-ming reign people used to pile their hair up, and they wore their collar on the left. They did not understand writing and they did not yet have ritual or music. From the K'ai-ming reign back to Ts'an Ts'ung was an aeon of 34,000 years. (*Ch'üan Shang-ku, Ch'üan Han wen*, citing *Shu wang pen chi*, 53.5a)

Ts'an Ts'ung set himself up as king of Shu. According to tradition, he taught the people about silkworms and mulberry. He made several thousand golden silkworms. At the start of each year, he took the golden silkworms and gave the people one silkworm each. The silkworms the people raised always multiplied prolifically, so that in the end they could return the gift to the king. When he went on a royal tour of his realm, wherever he stopped on his journey, the people created a market town. Because of his legacy people in Shu hold a silkworm market every spring. (*Hsu shih shih*, citing *Hsien chuan shih yi*, *Shuo-fu* 10.45a)

The god in the green clothes is Ts'an Ts'ung. According to tradition, Ts'an Ts'ung began as the lord of Shu and later took the title of king of Shu. He always wore green clothes. When he conducted a royal tour of the city limits and countryside, he taught his people the management of silkworms. The countryfolk appreciated his kindness, and so they set up a temple to sacrifice to him. Shrines to his name spread all over the western region, and they proved without exception to have miraculous powers. He was generally called the god in the green clothes, and that is how Green-God County got its name. (*San chiao sou-shen ta ch'üan*, Lien-ching 316)

The Founding Myth of the Pa People

The founding myth of the Pa people and the migration of the Lord of the Granary to found his new city of Yi were discussed in chapter 9, and also in chapter 12 in connection with the Goddess of Salt River and his amorous encounter and battle with her. The first reading below is a narrative collated from fragments of *The Origin of Hereditary Families*, commentary by Sung Chung (ca. third century A.D.) and edited in a reconstructed text by the Ch'ing scholar Ch'in Chia-mo. The second reading is from *A History of the Chin [Dynasty]* [A.D. 265–419] by Fang Hsuan-ling (A.D. 578–648).

The ancestor of the Lord of the Granary originally came from Wu Tan. The Man tribe of Pa commandery and Nan commandery originally had five surnames: the Pa clan, the Fan clan, the Shen clan, the Hsiang clan, and the Cheng clan. They all came from Mount Wu-lo Chung-li. On this mountain there were two caves, one scarlet and one black, like cinnabar and lacquer. The children of the Pa clan were born in the scarlet cave, and the children of the other four surnames were all born in the black cave. Before there were chieftains, they were all subjects of the spirits and gods. The Lord of the Granary's given name was Wu-hsiang; his surname was that of the Pa clan. He set out together with the Fan clan, the Shen clan, the Hsiang clan, and the Cheng clan—five surnames in all—and they all competed for divine power to rule. Then they all together threw their swords at a rock and agreed that whoever could hit the target would be elevated to be their lord. When the son of the Pa clan, Wu-hsiang, was the only one to hit the target, they all sighed. Then he ordered each clan to sail in an earthenware boat, carved with designs and painted, and to float the boats in the river. They made an agreement that whoever could stay afloat would become their lord. The other clans all sank, and Wu-hsiang's was the only one to stay afloat. So they unanimously made him their chieftain. He became the Lord of the Granary. Now he sailed the earthenware boat from Yi River to Yen-yang. (Ch'in Chia-mo's reconstructed text, *Shih pen, Shih hsing* 1:93–94)

The Lord of the Granary once more sailed in his earthenware boat and went downstream till he reached Yi City. At Yi City the rocky cliffs zigzagged and the spring watercourse also meandered. The Lord of the Granary looked at what seemed like a cavern. He sighed and said, "I've just come out of a cave, if I go into another one now, what will happen?" The cliff all at once collapsed thirty feet or more across, but some steps were within reach of him. The Lord of the Granary climbed up them. On the clifftop there was a flat rock, ten feet square and five feet long. The Lord of the Granary rested on it. He threw bamboo slips to make calculations and they all touched the rock. So he established his city next to it and lived there. Later on all manner of people followed him there in crowds. (*Chin shu, Li T'e, Tsai-chi* 20, SPPY 120.1b)

The God Shao Hao Founds the Niao Kingdom

The myth of Shao Hao was discussed in connection with his mother, Huang O, and his father, the Son of the White Emperor, in chapter 12. The narratives are significant for the repetition of the bird motif (*Niao* of Niao Kingdom means 'Bird'), which itself accentuates the recurring pattern of ornithological myths in the classical repertoire. The first of the readings in this section is from a first-century A.D. chapter of *The Classic of Mountains and Seas*. The second is from *Shih Tzu*, a fourth-century B.C. text. The last is from another fourth-century B.C. text, the *Chronicle of Tso*.

The great waterfall pool beyond the eastern sea is Shao Hao's kingdom. Shao Hao had the god Chuan Hsu suckled here, and he threw away his lute and zither. (*Shan hai ching, Ta huang tung ching*, SPPY 14.1a)

Shao Hao, Master Metal Heaven, founded his city at Ch'iung Sang [Exhausted Mulberry]. The five colors of the sun's light shone down below on the radiance of Ch'iung Sang. (*Shih Tzu*, SPPY 1.16a)

Autumn. The Duke of T'an came to court and Duke Chao of Ch'in held a banquet for him. The duke asked him, "Why were Shao Hao's government officials named after birds?" The Duke of T'an said, "He was my ancestor, so I know about it. In olden times, the Yellow Emperor used an auspicious cloud as his official emblem; that is why he had a cloud minister and cloud for official titles. The Flame Emperor used fire as his official emblem, so he had a fire minister and fire for official titles. Kung Kung used water as his official emblem; that is why he had a water minister and water for official titles. T'ai Hao used a dragon as his official emblem; that is why he had a dragon minister and had the dragon for official titles. When my ancestor Shao Hao came to the throne, phoenix birds suddenly appeared. He therefore took the birds as his emblem, creating a bird minister and the birds for official titles. The Phoenix Bird clan became astronomers principal. The Primeval Bird clan became controllers of the equinoxes. The Po-ch'ao Shrike clan became controllers of the solstice. The Green Bird clan became controllers of [spring] inaugurations. The Cinnabar Bird clan became controllers of the [winter] closures. The Partridge clan became controllers of retinue. The Vulture clan became controllers of the cavalry. The Wood Pigeon clan became controllers of the K'ung-harp. The Hawk clan became controllers of crime. The Falcon clan became controllers of home affairs. The Five Pigeons became assemblymen for the people. The Five Pheasants became the five artisans principal, to create revenues from the use of tools, to regulate measures and weights, and to observe order among the people. The Nine-Tailed Birds became the nine agriculture principals, to restrain people from vice." (*Tso chuan, Chao kung* Seventeenth Year, SPPY 17.7b–9a)

Concordance of English and Chinese Book Titles

Analects: Lun yü
Ancient History: Shang shu
Annals of Master Lü: Lü-shih ch'un-ch'iu
Anthology of Literature: Wen hsuan
Atlas of the Whole World in the T'ai-p'ing Era: T'ai-p'ing huan-yü chi
The Bamboo Annals: Chu shu chi nien
Basic Annals of Hsien-yuan: Hsien-yuan pen chi
Basic Annals of the Kings of Shu: Shu wang pen chi
Biographies of Great Men: Lieh shih chuan
Biographies of Holy Immortals: Shen hsien chuan
Biographies of Immortals: Lieh hsien chuan
Biographies of Women: Lieh nü chuan
A Botanical Treatise: Ch'ün fang p'u
Chart of The Magic Art of Being Invisible: Tun chia k'ai shan t'u
The Chronicle of Emperor Mu: Mu T'ien-tzu chuan
Chronicle of the Five Cycles of Time: Wu yun li-nien chi
Chronicle of Tso: Tso chuan
Chuang Tzu, or Master Chuang: Chuang Tzu
The Classic of Change: Yi ching
The Classic of History (= Shang shu): Shu ching
The Classic of Mountains and Seas: Shan hai ching
The Classic of Poetry: Shih ching
The Classic of Spirits and Strange Beings: Shen yi ching
The Classical Pharmacopoeia of the Farmer God: Shen-nung pen-ts'ao ching
A Collation from the North Hall: Pei-t'ang shu-ch'ao
Collected Explanations of Chuang Tzu: Chuang Tzu chi shih
Commentary on the Classic of Rivers: Shui ching chu

A Compendium of Information on the Gods of the Three Religions: San chiao sou-shen ta ch'üan

A Compilation of Prose Texts from Antiquity: Ch'üan Shang-ku San-tai, etc.

Compositions for the Lute: Ch'in ts'ao

A Continuation of "The Origin of Things": Hsu shih shih

The Debates in White Tiger [Hall]: Pai-hu t'ung-yi

Discourses of the States: Kuo yü

Disquisitions: Lun heng

The Elder Tai's Record of Ritual: Ta Tai Li chi

An Encylopedia of Belles-Lettres: Yi-wen lei chü

The Erh ya [Dictionary]: Erh ya

Essays Written from Dreaming Pond: Meng-ch'i pi-t'an

Explanations of Divination in "The Storehouse of All Things": Kuei tsang ch'i shih

Explanations of Social Customs: Feng su t'ung-yi

An Explication of Written Characters: Shuo-wen chieh-tzu

The Fate of the Flowers in the Mirror: Ching hua yuan

A Garden of Anecdotes: Shuo yuan

Gazette of Hua-yang: Hua-yang kuo-chih

The Genealogical Records of Emperors and Kings: Ti wang shih chi

A General Atlas: K'uo ti t'u

A General Record of the Writings of the T'ai-p'ing Era: T'ai-p'ing kuang chi

A General Treatise on Geography: K'uo ti chih

Gossip from the Barracks: Jung-mo hsien-t'an

Han Fei Tzu, or Master Han Fei: Han Fei Tzu

Han [Ying]'s Outer Chapters on The [Classic of] Poetry: Han shih wai chuan

Historical Records: Shih chi

Historical Records of the Three Sovereign Divinities and the Five Gods: San Wu li chi

A History of the Chin [Dynasty]: Chin shu

A History of the Glory and Fall of Yueh [State]: Yueh chueh shu

History of the [Former] Han: Han shu

Hsun Tzu, or Master Hsun: Hsun Tzu

Huai-nan Tzu, or Master Huai-nan: Huai-nan Tzu

Hypotheses on History: Yi shih

Imperial Survey: Huang lan

An Imperial Survey of Writings of the T'ai-p'ing Era: T'ai-p'ing yü-lan

The Inner Chapters of Emperor Wu of the Han: Han Wu-ti nei chuan

Intrigues of the Warring States: Chan kuo ts'e
Kuan Tzu, or Master Kuan: Kuan Tzu
Lieh Tzu, or Master Lieh: Lieh Tzu
Major Tradition of the "Ancient History": Shang shu ta chuan
Master Embracing-Simplicity: Pao-p'u Tzu
Master T'ien-ch'iu: T'ien-ch'iu Tzu
Material Appended to the "Erh ya [Dictionary]": Erh ya yi
Mencius, or Master Meng: Meng Tzu
A Miscellany from Yu-yang: Yu-yang tsa-tsu
Mo Tzu, or Master Mo: Mo Tzu
The Myriad Sayings of Master Chiang: Chiang Tzu wan chi lun
New Documents: Hsin shu
The Old Fable of [Emperor] Wu of the Han: Han Wu ku shih
The Origin of Hereditary Families: Shih pen
Prefect Li T'ang: Li T'ang
Pronunciation and Meaning in the "History of the [Former] Han": Han shu
    yin yi
Prose-Poem on the Capital City of Wu [State]: Wu tu fu
Prose-Poem on the Goddess of Lo River: Lo shen fu
Prose-Poem on Rapture for Mystery: Ssu hsuan fu
"Questions of Heaven": T'ien wen
A Record of Accounts of Marvels: Shu yi chi
A Record of Immortals, Compiled in Yung-ch'eng: Yung-ch'eng chi hsien lü
A Record of Researches into Spirits: Sou shen chi
Record of Ritual: Li chi
A Record of the Seasonal Customs of Ching Ch'u: Ching Ch'u sui shih chi
Records from T'ien-chung: T'ien-chung chi
Researches into Lost Records: Shih yi chi
Seasonal Customs and Festivals: Sui shih chi
Seven Tomes from the Cloudy Shelf: Yun chi ch'i ch'ien
Shih Tzu, or Master Shih: Shih Tzu
The Six Sword Bags: Liu t'ao
Songs of Ch'u: Ch'u Tz'u
Sources for Beginning Scholarly Studies: Ch'u hsueh chi
Spring and Autumn: Ch'un-ch'iu
Spring and Autumn Annals of Wu and Yueh [States]: Wu Yueh ch'un-ch'iu
The Storehouse of All Things: Kuei tsang
Supplementary Material to "Biographies of Immortals" and to "Biographies
    of Holy Immortals": Hsien chuan shih yi
The T'ao-wu Demon of Shu: Shu t'ao-wu

A Treatise on Extraordinary and Strange Things: Tu yi chih
The Treatise on Research into Nature: Po wu chih
The Vale of a Myriad Flowers Embroidered on Brocade: Chin hsiu wan hua ku
The Water Margin: Shui hu chuan
The Yellow Emperor Questions the Dark Lady on the Art of War: Huang Ti wen Hsuan nü chan fa

Bibliography

The following is a select bibliography that lists the works cited or referred to in the text. It is arranged in three parts: the first lists classical Chinese works, showing, where available, reliable translations into Western languages; the second lists modern Chinese, Japanese, and Western works on the classical texts and on general aspects of Sinology related to mythology; the third consists of works on world mythology and comparative mythology. Some abbreviations have been used: *ch.: chüan,* volume(s); rpr.: reproduced; rpt.: reprint.

Classical Chinese Texts

Chan kuo ts'e (Intrigues of the Warring States [403–221 B.C.]). Anon. (third century B.C.). Commentary by Kao Yu (fl. A.D. 205–212); Huang P'ei-lieh (1803). 33 *ch.* SPPY. Trans. James I. Crump.

Chiang Tzu wan chi lun (The Myriad Sayings of Master Chiang). Attributed to Chiang Chi (fl. ca. A.D. 250). 1 *ch.* Fragments collated by Ma Kuo-han (1794–1857); edited by Yen K'o-chün (1762–1843). SYTS.

Chien chu T'ao Yuan-ming chi (Collected Works of T'ao Yuan-ming, with a Commentary). Collated and edited by Li Kung-huan (Sung-Yuan). 10 *ch.* SPTK. Trans. James R. Hightower; A. R. Davis.

Chin hsiu wan hua ku (The Vale of a Myriad Flowers Embroidered on Brocade). Anon. (first published A.D. 1188). 120 *ch.* Facsimile of Ming ed.; postface dated A.D. 1536. Taipei: HHSC, 1969.

Chin shu (A History of the Chin [Dynasty]). By Fang Hsuan-ling (A.D. 578–648). 130 *ch.* Rpr. from Palace ed. of 1739. SPPY.

Ch'in ts'ao (Compositions for the Lute). Compiled by Ts'ai Yung (A.D. 133–192). 2 *ch.* TSCC.

Ching Ch'u sui shih chi (A Record of the Seasonal Customs of Ching Ch'u). By Tsung Lin (ca. A.D. 498–ca. 566). 1 *ch.* Fragments preserved in various works: reconstituted text. HWTS.

Ching hua yuan (The Fate of the Flowers in the Mirror). By Li Ju-chen (1763–

ca. 1830). Edited by Chang Yu-hao. 100 *ch.* Peking: Tso-chia, 1953. Trans. Lin Tai-yi.

Chou shu (A History of the Chou). Also known as *Yi Chou shu* or *Chi-chung Chou shu.* Commentary by K'ung Ch'ao (third century A.D.). 10 *ch.* HWTS.

Chou yi. See Yi ching.

Ch'u hsueh chi (Sources for Beginning Scholarly Studies). Compiled by Hsu Chien (A.D. 659–729) et al. 30 *ch.* Facsimile of Ming ed. SPCY.

Ch'u Tz'u (Songs of Ch'u). Compiled, with a commentary, by Wang Yi (A.D. 89–158). Supplementary commentary by Hung Hsing-tsu (A.D. 1070–1135). 17 *ch.* Photolithic rpr. of Ming rpr. of Sung ed. SPTK. Trans. David Hawkes.

Ch'u Tz'u pu chu (The *Ch'u Tz'u,* An Amended Edition with a Commentary). By Hung Hsing-tsu (A.D. 1070–1135). TSCC.

Chu shu chi nien (The Bamboo Annals). Anon. (? late Chou). Fragments collated and edited by Chu Yu-tseng (1838), Wang Kuo-wei (1877–1927), *Chu shu chi nien chi-chiao.* 1 *ch.* Hai-ning: Wang Ching-an hsien-sheng yi-shu, 1917.

Ch'üan Shang-ku San-tai Ch'in Han San-kuo Liu-ch'ao wen (A Compilation of Prose Texts from Antiquity, the Three Eras, Ch'in, Han, Three Kingdoms, and Six Dynasties). Compiled by Yen K'o-chün (1762–1843). 741 *ch.* Originally published 1815. Kuang-chou: Kuang-ya, 1887–93.

Chuang Tzu (Master Chuang). Attributed to Chuang Chou (ca. 369–ca. 286 B.C.). Commentary by Kuo Hsiang (d. A.D. 312); glosses by Lu Yuan-lang (d. A.D. 626). 33 *ch.* SPPY. Trans. Burton Watson; Angus C. Graham.

Chuang Tzu chi shih (Collected Explanations of *Chuang Tzu*). By Kuo Ch'ing-fan (1844–96). 10 *ch.* Preface dated 1894. SHCSK.

Ch'un-ch'iu (Spring and Autumn [Annals]). Text is included with *Tso chuan.*

Ch'un-ch'iu fan lu (Heavy Dew of the Spring and Autumn Annals). Attributed to Tung Chung-shu (?179–?104 B.C.). 17 *ch.* Facsimile of 1910 ed. Taipei: Ho-lo t'u-shu, 1974.

Ch'ün fang p'u (A Botanical Treatise). Compiled by Wang Hsiang-chin (1561–1653). 30 *ch.* Commentary by Yi Ch'in-heng, CFPCS. Chung-kuo nung-shu ts'ung k'an ts'ung ho chih pu. Peking: Nung-yeh, 1985.

Erh ya (The *Erh ya* [Dictionary]). Anon. (late Chou–early Han). 3 *ch.* Commentary by Kuo P'u (A.D. 276–324). Photolithic rpr. of Sung ed. SPTK.

Erh ya yi (Material Appended to the *Erh ya* [Dictionary]). By Lo Yuan (1136–84). Edited by Hung Yen-tsu. 32 *ch.* TSCC.

Feng su t'ung-yi (Explanations of Social Customs). Compiled by Ying Shao (ca. A.D. 140–ca. 206). *Feng su t'ung-yi fu yi wen.* Peking: CFCE, 1943.

Han Fei Tzu (Master Han Fei). By Han Fei (d. 233 B.C.) et al. Commentary by Ku Kuang-ch'i (1816). 20 *ch.* Rpr. from 1818 ed. of Wu Tzu from print of ca. A.D. 1165. SPPY. Trans. W. K. Liao.

Han shih wai chuan (Han [Ying]'s Outer Chapters on The [Classic of] Poetry). Compiled by Han Ying (fl. 157 B.C.). Edited by Chou T'ing-tsai. 10 *ch.* TSCC. Trans. James R. Hightower.

Han shu (History of the [Former] Han). By Pan Ku (A.D. 32–92). Commentary by Yen Shih-ku (A.D. 581–645). 100 *ch*. Rpr. from Palace ed. of 1739. SPPY. Partial trans. by Homer H. Dubs; Burton Watson.

Han shu yin yi (Pronunciation and Meaning in the *History of the [Former] Han*). By Hsiao Kai (late sixth century A.D.). Fragments preserved in various texts, collated and edited 1799 by Tsang Yung (1767–1811). 3 *ch*. Pai-ching t'ang ts'ung-shu.

Han T'ang ti-li shu ch'ao (A Collation of Fragmentary Texts on the Geography of the Han to the T'ang). Compiled by Wang Mo (fl. 1778). *Han T'ang ti-li shu ch'ao fu Lu-shan ching-she chi-pen liu-shih-liu chung*. Peking: CH, 1961.

Han Wu ku shih (The Old Fable of [Emperor] Wu of the Han). Attributed to Pan Ku (A.D. 32–92), but probably anon. (Six Dynasties). Ku-chin yi shih.

Han Wu-ti nei chuan (The Inner Chapters of Emperor Wu of the Han). Attributed to Pan Ku (A.D. 32–92), but probably anon. (? sixth century A.D.). 1 *ch*. Edited by Ch'ien Hsi-tso (d. 1844). TSCC. Trans. Kristofer Schipper.

Hsi yu chi (A Record of the Journey to the West). By Wu Ch'eng-en (ca. A.D. 1506–82). 2 *ch*. Peking: Tso-chia, 1955. Trans Anthony C. Yu.

Hsien chuan shih yi (Supplementary Material to *Biographies of Immortals* and to *Biographies of Holy Immortals*). [Attributed to Liu Hsiang (79–8 B.C.) and to Ko Hung (A.D. 254–334), respectively.] Compiled by Tu Kuang-t'ing (A.D. 850–933). 5 *ch*. Edited by Yen Yi-p'ing. Tao-chiao yen-chiu tzu-liao.

Hsien-yuan pen chi (Basic Annals of Hsien-yuan [sometimes identified as the Yellow Emperor]). By Wang Ch'üan (T'ang). In *Yun chi ch'i ch'ien*. SPTK.

Hsin shu (New Documents). Attributed to Chia Yi (201–169 B.C.) and also to Liu Hsiang (79–8 B.C.). 10 *ch*. Photolithic rpr. of 1514 ed. SPTK.

Hsu shih shih (A Continuation of *The Origin of Things* [by Liu Ts'un, T'ang]). Compiled by Feng Chien (ca. tenth century A.D.). Fragments reconstituted into a text. 5 *ch*. Ming ed., *Shuo-fu*.

Hsun Tzu (Master Hsun). By Hsun Ch'ing (ca. 298–ca. 238 B.C.). Commentary by Yang Ching (A.D. 818); edited by Hsieh Yung (1786). 20 *ch*. SPPY. Complete trans. Homer H. Dubs. Partial trans. Burton Watson; John Knoblock.

Hua-yang kuo-chih (Gazette of Hua-yang). By Ch'ang Chü (fl. ca. A.D. 347–350). 12 *ch*. Photolithic rpr. of Ming MS of Ch'ien Shu-pao. SPTK.

Huai-nan Tzu (Master Huai-nan). Compiled ca. 139 B.C. by Liu An, king of Huai-nan (ca. 170–122 B.C.) et al. Commentary by Hsu Shen (ca. A.D. 100); Kao Yu (fl. A.D. 205–215). 21 *ch*. Rpr. of Chuang K'uei-chi ed. of 1788. SPPY. Partial trans. Evan Morgan; Charles Le Blanc.

Huang lan (Imperial Survey). Compiled by divers hands, ? Liu Shao (fl. A.D. 215–245) and Wang Hsiang (? A.D. 222), or ? Wang Hsiang and Mu Hsi (A.D. 186–245). 1 *ch*. Fragments collated and edited 1802 by Sun P'ing-yi. TSCC.

Huang Ti wen Hsuan nü chan fa (The Yellow Emperor Questions the Dark Lady on the Art of War). Anon. (? Six Dynasties). Fragments preserved in various texts.

Jung-mo hsien-t'an (Gossip from the Barracks). By Wei Hsun (T'ang). Chiu hsiao-shuo.

Ku shih k'ao (An Examination into Ancient History). Compiled by Ch'iao Chou (A.D. 201–270). 25 *p'ien*. Text reconstructed by Chang Tsung-yuan (1752–1800). Wu-hsien: P'ing-chin kuan ts'ung-shu, 1885.

Ku-shih shih-chiu shou (The Nineteen Old Poems). Anon. (Han). In *Wen hsuan*, *ch.* 29. (1936) Hong Kong: Shang-wu, 1965. Trans. Jean-Pierre Diény; Anne Birrell.

Kuan Tzu (Master Kuan). Attributed to Kuan Chung (d. 645 B.C.). Commentary by Fang Hsuan-ling (A.D. 578–648). 24 *ch.* Photolithic rpr. of Sung ed. SPTK. Trans. W. Allyn Rickett.

Kuei tsang (The Storehouse of All Things). Anon. (? Chou-Han). Fragments preserved in various works, edited by Hsueh Chen. 1 *ch.* Han Wei yi-shu-ch'ao.

Kuei tsang ch'i shih (Explanations of Divination in *The Storehouse of All Things*). Anon. (? second century A.D.). Fragments scattered in various texts.

K'uo ti chih (A General Treatise on Geography). Compilation attributed to Li T'ai (fl. A.D. 638–642); or Hsiao Te-yen (seventh century A.D.) et al. Fragments collated 1797 by Sun Hsing-yen (1753–1818). 8 *ch.* Tai-nan-ko ts'ung-shu.

K'uo ti t'u (A General Atlas). Anon. (? Han). Fragments cited in various works reconstructed by Wang Mo (fl. 1778). Han T'ang ti-li shu-ch'ao.

Kuo yü (Discourses of the States). Attributed to Tso Ch'iu-ming (? fifth century B.C.). Commentary by Wei Chao (A.D. 204–273). 21 *ch.* Photolithic rpr. of Ming rpr. of Sung ed. SPTK.

Li chi (Record of Ritual). Anon. (late Chou and Han). Commentary by Cheng Hsuan (A.D. 127–200); K'ung Ying-ta (A.D. 574–648); glosses by Lu Yuan-lang (d. A.D. 626). 20 *ch.* Rpr. of ed. of Yueh K'o (1173–1240), *Li chi chu-su*. SPPY. Trans. James Legge; Séraphin Couvreur.

Li T'ang (Prefect Li T'ang). By Li Kung-tso (? A.D. 770–850). A short story written in A.D. 765. In TPKC, *ch.* 467.

Lieh hsien chuan (Biographies of [71] Immortals). Attributed to Liu Hsiang (79–8 B.C.), but probably anon. (Six Dynasties). 2 *ch.* Facsimile from *Ku-chin yi shih* ed., TSCC. Trans. Max Kaltenmark.

Lieh nü chuan (Biographies of Women). Attributed to Liu Hsiang (79–8 B.C.), but probably anon. (Six Dynasties). 7 *ch.* Rpr. from ed. of Wang K'ang-nien (1839, 1874) from ed. of Liang Tuan (1793–1825), *Lieh nü chuan chiao-chu*. SPPY.

Lieh Tzu (Master Lieh). Attributed to Lieh Yü-k'ou (? late Chou), but probably a forgery by Chang Chan (fl. A.D. 370). 8 *ch.* Rpr. from *Liu tzu ch'üan shu* ed., 1533. SPPY. Trans. Benedykt Grynpas; Angus C. Graham.

Liu t'ao (The Six Sword-Bags). Attributed to Lü Wang (early Chou), but probably anon. (late Ch'in-early Han). Collated and amended by Yuan Feng-chien (Sung). 6 *ch.* Photolithic rpr. of Sung MS. SPTK.

Lo shen fu (Prose poem on the Goddess of Lo River). By Ts'ao Chih (A.D. 192–232). In *Wen hsuan*, *ch.* 19. SPTK. Trans. K. P. K. Whitaker; Burton Watson.

Lü-shih ch'un-ch'iu (Annals of Master Lü). Compiled by Lü Pu-wei (d. 235 B.C.). 28 *ch.* Commentary by Kao Yu (fl. A.D. 205–212); edited by Chu Meng-lung. Photolithic rpr. of Ming ed. SPTK. Trans. Richard Wilhelm.

Lun heng (Disquisitions). By Wang Ch'ung (A.D. 27–100). 30 *ch.* Photolithic rpr. of Ming ed. SPTK. Trans. Alfred Forke.

Lun yü (Analects). By K'ung Fu Tzu [Confucius] (551–479 B.C.) and disciples.

20 *ch.* Commentary by Ho Yen (d. A.D. 249); Chu Hsi (1130–1200). *Chu-tzu chi-ch'eng.* Trans. Arthur Waley; D. C. Lau.

Meng-ch'i pi-t'an chiao cheng (Collected Editions of Essays Written from Dreaming Pond). By Shen Kua (ca. A.D. 1031–95). 26 *ch.* Edited by Hu Tao-ching. Facsimile of CH of 1962. Shanghai: Shanghai ku-chi, 1987.

Meng Tzu (Master Meng [Mencius]). By Meng K'e (ca. 372–ca. 289 B.C.). Commentary by Chao Ch'i (d. A.D. 201). 14 *ch.* Photolithic rpr. of Sung ed. SPTK. Trans. D. C. Lau; W. A. C. H. Dobson.

Mo Tzu (Master Mo). By Mo Ti (ca. 479–ca. 381 B.C.) and disciples. 15 *ch.* extant. Photolithic rpr. of 1553 ed. SPTK. Complete trans. Mei Yi-pao; Alfred Forke; Angus C. Graham. Partial trans. Burton Watson.

Mu T'ien-tzu chuan (The Chronicle of Emperor Mu [trad. 1001–947 B.C.]). Anon. (trad. ? ca. 318 B.C., or A.D. 281; probably fourth century A.D.). Commentary by Kuo P'u (A.D. 276–324); edited by Hung Yi-hsuan (1800). 6 *ch.* Rpr. from P'ing-chin-kuan ts'ung-shu (1806). SPPY. Trans. Rémi Mathieu.

Pai hu t'ung-yi (The Debates in White Tiger [Hall]). Compilation attributed to Pan Ku (A.D. 32–92). 4 *ch.* Edited by Lu Wen-ch'ao (1717–96) and Chuang Shu-tsu (1751–1816). Facsimile of Pao-ching-t'ang ts'ung-shu. TSCC. Trans. Tjan Tjoe Som.

Pao-p'u Tzu (Master Embracing-Simplicity). Attributed to Ko Hung (A.D. 254–334). 70 *ch.* Photolithic rpr. of 1565 ed. SPTK. Partial trans. James R. Ware; Jay Sailey.

Pei-t'ang shu-ch'ao (A Collation from the North Hall). Compiled by Yü Shih-nan (A.D. 558–638). Edited 1888, with commentary, by K'ung Kuang-t'ao. 160 *ch.* KC, 1893.

Po wu chih (The Treatise on Research into Nature). Attributed to Chang Hua (A.D. 232–300), but probably anon. (Six Dynasties). 10 *ch.* Commentary by Chou Jih-yung et al. Rpr. from the *Shih-li-chü Huang-shih ts'ung-shu* ed. of 1804. SPPY. Trans. Roger Greatrex.

San chiao sou-shen ta ch'üan (A Compendium of Information on the Gods of the Three Religions [Confucianism, Taoism, Buddhism]). Anon. (Yuan). Edited ca. A.D. 1592. Yeh Te-hui ed. (1909), *San chiao yuan-liu sheng-ti fo-shih sou-shen ta ch'üan.* 7 vols. Taipei: Lien-ching, 1980.

San Wu li chi (Historical Records of the Three Sovereign Divinities and the Five Gods). By Hsu Cheng (third century A.D.). Fragments collated from various works. 1 *ch.* Yü-han shan-fang chi-yi-shu.

Shan hai ching (The Classic of Mountains and Seas). Anon. (late Chou–Han, third century B.C.–first century A.D.). 18 *ch.* Commentary by Kuo P'u (A.D. 276–324). Hao Yi-hsing (1757–1825) ed., *Shan hai ching chien chu.* SPPY. Trans. Rémi Mathieu; Anne Birrell.

Shan hai ching hsin chiao-cheng (The Classic of Mountains and Seas: A New Amended Edition). Pi Yuan (1730–97) ed. Rpr. of 1781 ed. Shanghai: Hui-wen t'ang, 1917.

Shang shu (Ancient History). Anon. (parts date between late Chou and third century A.D., with forged sections). Also known as *Shu ching* (The Classic of History). 20 *ch.* Commentary by K'ung An-kuo (second century B.C.);

subcommentary by K'ung Ying-ta (A.D. 574–648). Rpr. from A.D. 1815 ed. of Yüan Yuan, *Shang shu chu shu*. SPPY. Trans. Bernhard Karlgren.

Shang shu ta chuan (Major Tradition of the *Ancient History*). Attributed to Fu Sheng (d. early second century B.C.). 5 *ch*. Commentary by Cheng Hsuan (A.D 127–200). Photolithic rpr. of ed. of Ch'en Shou-ch'i (1771–1834). SPTK.

Shen hsien chuan (Biographies of [84] Holy Immortals). Attributed to Ko Hung (A.D. 254–334). 10 *ch*. HWTS.

Shen-nung pen-ts'ao ching (The Classical Pharmacopoeia of the Farmer God). Attributed to Wu P'u (third century A.D.). 1 *ch*. Edited by Huang Shih. Peking: Chung-yi ku-chi, 1982.

Shen yi ching (The Classic of Spirits and Strange Beings). Attributed to Tung-fang Shuo (ca. 161–ca. 87 B.C.). 1 *ch*. Commentary by Chang Hua (A.D. 232–300). HWTS.

Shih chi (Historical Records). By Ssu-ma Ch'ien (ca. 145–ca. 86 B.C.). 130 *ch*. Commentary by P'ei Yin (fifth century A.D.); Ssu-ma Chen (A.D. 730); Chang Shou-chieh (fl. A.D. 725–737). Rpr. from Palace ed. of 1739. SPPY. Partial trans. Edouard Chavannes; Burton Watson.

Shih ching (The Classic of Poetry). Anon. (compiled ca. 600 B.C.). Commentary by the scholar Mao (second century B.C.); Cheng Hsuan (A.D. 132–200), *Mao-shih chu-shu*. SPPY. Trans. Bernhard Karlgren; Arthur Waley.

Shih pen (The Origin of Hereditary Families). Anon. (? Han). Commentary by Sung Chung (late second–third century A.D.). Fragments collated by Sun P'ing-yi (1802 ed.), edited by Chang Chu. TSCC.

Shih pen pa chung (The Origin of Hereditary Families, in eight editions). Anon. Commentary by Sung Chung (late second–third century A.D.). Fragments collated and edited by Ch'in Chia-mo (Ch'ing). 10 *ch*. Shanghai: Shang-wu, 1957.

Shih Tzu (Master Shih). By Shih Chiao (fourth century B.C.). Text reconstituted by Sun Hsing-yen (1753–1818); Chang Tsung-yuan et al. from fragments. 2 *ch*. Rpr. from ed. of Chu Chi-jung, 1884 from the 1806 ed. of Sun Hsing-yen, P'ing-chin-kuan ts'ung-shu. SPPY.

Shih yi chi (Researches into Lost Records). Attributed to Wang Chia (Wang Tzu-nien, fl. A.D. 335–386). Text reconstructed by Hsiao Ch'i (sixth century A.D.). 1 *ch*. HWTS.

Shu ching (The Classic of History). See *Shang shu*.

Shu t'ao-wu (The T'ao-wu Demon of Shu). By Chang T'ang-ying (A.D. 1029–71). 2 *ch*. HH.

Shu wang pen chi (Basic Annals of the Kings of Shu). Attributed to Yang Hsiung (53 B.C.–A.D. 18). Fragments preserved in various works, including *Han T'ang ti-li shu-ch'ao*.

Shu yi chi (A Record of Accounts of Marvels). Attributed to Jen Fang (A.D. 460–508). 2 *ch*. HWTS.

Shui ching chu (Commentary on the Classic of Rivers). Compiled by Li Tao-yuan (d. A.D. 521). 40 *ch*. Photolithic rpr. of Wu-ying chan chen pan of 1774. SPTK.

Shuo-fu (A Garland of Minor Literary Works). Compiled by T'ao Tsung-yi (fl.

A.D. 1360–96) in 1396. 100 *ch.* Rpr. from six Ming eds., edited by Chang Tsung-hsiang in 1922. Shanghai: Shang-wu, 1927.

Shuo-wen chieh-tzu (An Explication of Written Characters). By Hsu Shen (ca. A.D. 100). Edited by Hsu Hsuan (A.D. 986) et al. 30 *ch.* Photolithic rpr. of N. Sung ed. SPTK.

Shuo yuan (A Garden of Anecdotes). Attributed to Liu Hsiang (79–8 B.C.). 20 *ch.* Photolithic rpr. of Ming ed. SPTK.

Sou shen chi (A Record of Researches into Spirits). Compilation attributed to Kan Pao (fl. ca. A.D. 317). 20 *ch.* TSCC. Trans. Rémi Mathieu.

Ssu hsuan fu (Prose poem on Rapture for Mystery). By Chang Heng (A.D. 78–139). In *Wen hsuan, ch.* 15. SPTK.

Sui shih chi (Seasonal Customs and Festivals). Compiled by Ch'en Yuan-ching (fl. A.D. 1225–64). Fragments scattered in various works. TSCC.

Ta Tai Li chi (The Elder Tai's Record of Ritual). Compiled by Tai Te (fl. 72 B.C.) and Tai Sheng (ca. first century B.C.). Of 85 *ch., ch.* 39–81 extant. SPTK. Annotated ed., with trans. by Kao Ming, *Ta Tai Li chi chin-chu chin-yi.* Taipei: Taiwan shang-wu, 1975. Trans. Benedykt Grynpas; Richard Wilhelm.

T'ai-p'ing huan-yü chi (Atlas of the Whole World in the T'ai-p'ing Era [A.D. 976–984]). Compiled by Yueh Shih (A.D. 930–1007). 200 *ch.* Nanching: Chinling shu-chü, 1882.

T'ai-p'ing kuang chi (A General Record of the Writings of the T'ai-p'ing Era [A.D. 976–984]). Compiled by Li Fang (A.D. 925–996) et al., completed A.D. 978. 500 *ch.* Peking: JMWH, 1959.

T'ai-p'ing yü-lan (An Imperial Survey of Writings of the T'ai-p'ing Era [A.D. 976–984]). Compiled by Li Fang (A.D. 925–996) et al.; presented to the throne A.D. 983. 1,000 *ch.* SPTK.

Tao Te ching (The Classic of the Way and the Power). Attributed to Lao Tzu (ca. third century B.C.). Commentary by Kuo P'u (A.D. 276–324). Peking: CH, 1984. Trans. D. C. Lau.

Ti wang shih chi (The Genealogical Records of Emperors and Kings). Compiled by Huang-fu Mi (A.D. 215–282). 1 *ch.* Fragments preserved by divers hands in the Yuan and Ming eras, in *Ti wang shih chi chi chiao.* TSCC.

T'ien-ch'iu Tzu (Master T'ien-ch'iu). Anon. (late Chou). 1 *ch.* Edited by Mao Kuo-han (1794–1857), Yü-han shan-fang chi-yi-shu. Changsha: Lang-huan-kuan, 1883.

T'ien-chung chi (Records from T'ien-chung). Compiled by Ch'en Yao-wen; preface dated A.D. 1569. 60 *ch.* SKCS.

Tso chuan (Chronicle of Tso). Attributed to Tso Ch'iu-ming (? fifth century B.C., with later passages, generally fourth century B.C.). 30 *ch.* Commentary by Tu Yü (A.D. 222–284). Rpr. from ed. of Yueh K'o (1173–1240), *Ch'un-ch'iu ching-chuan chi-chieh.* SPPY. Complete trans. Séraphin Couvreur. Partial trans. Burton Watson.

Tu Shan hai ching (On Reading *The Classic of Mountains and Seas*). By T'ao Yuanming (A.D. 365–427). *Chien chu T'ao Yuan-ming chi.* 10 *ch.* SPTK. Trans. A. R. Davis; James R. Hightower.

Tu yi chih (A Treatise on Extraordinary and Strange Things). Compiled by Li Jung (fl. ca. A.D. 846–874). TSCC.

Tun chia k'ai shan t'u (A Chart of the Magic Art of Being Invisible). Anon. (? Latter Han). Fragments collated in *Shuo-fu*.

Wen hsuan (Anthology of Literature). Compiled by Hsiao T'ung (A.D. 501–531) et al. 60 *ch*. Commentary by Li Shan (?–A.D. 689). KHCP, ts'ung-shu chien pien. Partial trans. Erwin von Zach; Burton Watson; David R. Knechtges.

Wen hsuan (as above). Commentary by Li Shan and five others, *Liu-ch'en chu Wen hsuan*. Photolithic rpr. of Sung ed. SPTK.

Wen hsuan k'ao-yi (Critical Research on the *Wen hsuan*). Compiled by Ku Kuang-ch'i and P'eng Chao-sun; edited 1809 by Hu K'o-chia (1757–1816). 10 *ch*. Facsimile of 1809 Canton ed. Taipei: Cheng-chung, 1971.

Wu tu fu (Prose poem on the Capital City of Wu [State]. By Tso Ssu (ca. A.D. 250–ca. 305). In *Wen hsuan, ch. 5*. SPTK. Trans. David R. Knechtges.

Wu Yueh ch'un-ch'iu (Spring and Autumn Annals of Wu and Yueh [States]). Compiled from ancient material by Chao Yeh (fl. ca. A.D. 40). Commentary by Hsu T'ien-yu (1306). 10 *ch*. Rpr. from *Ku-chin yi shih*. SPPY.

Wu yun li-nien chi (A Chronicle of the Five Cycles of Time). Attributed to Hsu Cheng (third century A.D.). Fragments preserved in various compilations, such as *Yi shih*.

Yi ching (Classic of Change). Anon. (early-middle Chou, with Han additions). Also known as *Chou yi* (Chou Change). 9 *ch*. Commentary by Wang Pi (fl. A.D. 226–249) et al. Rpr. from 1815 ed. of Yüan Yuan, *Chou yi chu-su*. SPPY. Trans. Richard Wilhelm.

Yi shih (Hypotheses on History). Compiled by Ma Su (1621–73); preface dated 1670. 160 *ch*. PCTP. Taipei: Kuang-wen, 1969.

Yi-wen lei chü (An Encyclopedia of Belles-Lettres). Compiled by Ou-yang Hsun (A.D. 557–641), Ling-hu Te-fen (A.D. 583–666) et al. 100 *ch*. Edited by Wang Shao-ying. Facsimile of Sung-Ming ed. (1959). Peking: CH, 1965.

Yi wu chih (A Treatise on Strange Creatures and Plants). Compiled by Yang Fu-hsiao (fl. A.D. 90). Fragments collated by Tsang Chao (Ming). TSCC.

Yu-yang tsa-tsu (A Miscellany from Yu-yang [a mountain in Hunan]). By Tuan Ch'eng-shih (d. A.D. 863). 20 *ch*. SPTK.

Yueh chueh shu (A History of the Glory and Fall of Yueh [State]). Compiled by divers hands in several periods, from Yuan K'ang (fl. A.D. 40) and later. 15 *ch*. Rpr. from Ming ed. SPPY.

Yun chi ch'i ch'ien (Seven Tomes from the Cloudy Shelf). By Wang Ch'üan (T'ang), or by Chang Chün-fang (fl. A.D. 1004–20). 122 *ch*. Photolithic rpr. of the *Tao tsang* text. SPTK.

Yung-ch'eng chi hsien lü (A Record of Immortals, Compiled in Yung-ch'eng [West China]). Compiled by Tu Kuang-t'ing (A.D. 850–933). In TPKC, *ch*. 56. Peking: JMWH, 1959.

Chinese, Japanese, and Western Research Works

Allan, Sarah. "Drought, Human Sacrifice and the Mandate of Heaven in a Lost Text from the *Shang shu*." *BSOAS* 47.3 (1984): 523–39.

Allan, Sarah. *The Heir and the Sage: Dynastic Legend in Early China.* San Francisco: Chinese Materials Center, 1981.

Allan, Sarah. *The Shape of the Turtle: Myth, Art, and Cosmos in Early China.* SUNY Series in Chinese Philosophy and Culture. Albany: State University of New York Press, 1991.

Allen, Joseph R. "The Myth Studies of Wen I-to: A Question of Methodology." *Tamkang Review* 13.2 (1982): 137–60.

Barnard, Noel. *Studies on the Ch'u Silk Manuscript.* 2 vols. Monographs on Far Eastern History, vols. 4, 5. Canberra: Australian National University, Dept. of Far Eastern History, 1973.

Birrell, Anne. *Chinese Love Poetry: New Songs from a Jade Terrace: A Medieval Anthology,* 1982, 1986. Rev. ed. Penguin Classics. London: Penguin Books, 1995.

Birrell, Anne. *The Classic of Mountains and Seas.* Penguin Classics. London: Penguin Books, 1999.

Birrell, Anne. *Popular Songs and Ballads of Han China.* 1988. Rev. ed. Honolulu: University of Hawaii Press, 1993.

Bodde, Derk. *Festivals in Classical China: New Year and Other Annual Observances during the Han Dynasty, 206 B.C.–A.D. 220.* Princeton, N.J.: Princeton University Press, 1975.

Bodde, Derk. "Myths of Ancient China." In *Mythologies of the Ancient World,* edited by Samuel Noah Kramer, 369–408. Garden City, N.Y.: Anchor Books, 1961.

Boltz, William G. "Kung Kung and the Flood: Reverse Euhemerism in the *Yao tien.*" *T'oung Pao* 67.3–5 (1981): 141–53.

Chang, Kwang-chih. *The Archaeology of Ancient China.* 1963. 4th ed., rev. New Haven, Conn.: Yale University Press, 1986.

Chang, Kwang-chih. *Art, Myth, and Ritual: The Path to Political Authority in Ancient China.* Cambridge, Mass.: Harvard University Press, 1983.

Chang, Kwang-chih. "Chung-kuo ch'uang-shih shen-hua chih fen-hsi yü ku shih yen-chiu" (Chinese Creation Myths: A Study in Method). *Bulletin of the Institute of Ethnology, Academia Sinica* 8 (1959): 47–79.

Chang, Kwang-chih. *Early Chinese Civilization: Anthropological Perspectives.* Harvard-Yenching Institute Monograph Series, vol. 23. Cambridge, Mass.: Harvard University Press, 1976.

Chavannes, Edouard, trans. *Les Mémoires historiques de Se-ma Ts'ien [Shih chi].* 6 vols. 1895–1905. Rpt. Paris: Adrien-Maisonneuve, 1967–69.

Chavannes, Edouard. *Le T'ai chan: Essai de monographie d'un culte chinois.* Annales du Musée Guimet, Bibliothèque d'Etudes, vol. 21. Paris: Leroux, 1910.

Cheng, Te-k'un. "Ch'ih Yu: The God of War in Han Art." *Oriental Art,* n.s., 4.2 (1958):45–54.

Cheng, Te-k'un. "*Shan hai ching* chi ch'i shen-hua" (The Classic of Mountains and Seas and Its Myths). *Shih-hsueh nien-pao* 1.4 (1932): 127–51.

Chiang Liang-fu. *Ch'u Tz'u hsueh lun-wen chi* (A Collection of Essays on *Songs of Ch'u* Studies). Shanghai: Shanghai ku-chi, 1984.

Chou, Tso-jen. *Hsi-la ti shen yü ying-hsiung.* 1950. Shanghai: Wen-hua sheng-huo, 1953. [Claims to be a translation of *Gods, Heroes and Men of Ancient Greece* by W. H. D. Rouse, but no such title by William Henry Denham Rouse exists; perhaps the reference is to *Atlas of Classical Portraits; Greek,* London, 1898.]

Chow, Tse-tsung. "The Childbirth Myth and Ancient Chinese Medicine: A Study of Aspects of the *Wu* Tradition." In *Ancient China: Studies in Early Civilization*, edited by David T. Roy and Tsuen-hsuin Tsien, 43–89. Hong Kong: Chinese University Press, 1978.

Conrady, August, trans. *Das älteste Dokument zur chinesischen Kunstgeschichte, T'ien-wen: Die "Himmelsfragen" des K'ih Yüan.* 1931. Revised by Eduard Erkes as "Zu Ch'ü Yüan's *T'ien-wen:* Ergänzungen und Berichtigungen zu Conrady-Erkes." *Monumenta Serica* 6 (1941): 273–339.

Couvreur, Séraphin, trans. *Li Ki, ou mémoires sur les bienséances et les cérémonies* [*Li chi*]. 2 vols. Ho Kien Fou: Mission Catholique, 1913.

Couvreur, Séraphin, trans. *Tch'ouen Ts'iou et Tso Tchouan; Texte chinois avec traduction française* [*Ch'un-ch'iu/Tso chuan*]. 3 vols. Ho Kien Fou: Mission Catholique, 1914.

Crump, James I., trans. *Chan-kuo Ts'e.* Oxford: Oxford University Press, 1970.

Davis, A. R., trans. *T'ao Yuan-ming (A.D. 365–427), His Works and Their Meaning.* 2 vols. Cambridge Studies in Chinese History, Literature and Institutions. Cambridge: Cambridge University Press, 1983.

Dennys, N. B. *The Folk-Lore of China and Its Affinities with That of the Aryan and Semitic Races.* London: Trübner, 1876.

Diény, Jean-Pierre. *Aux origines de la poésie classique en Chine: Etude sur la poésie lyrique à l'époque des Han.* Monographies du T'oung Pao, vol. 6. Leiden: Brill, 1968.

Diény, Jean-Pierre. *Les Dix-Neuf Poèmes Anciens.* Bulletin de la Maison Franco-Japonaise, n.s. 7.4. Paris: Presses Universitaires de France, 1963.

Diény, Jean-Pierre. "Mythologie et sinologie." Review of Rémi Mathieu, *Anthologie des mythes. Etudes Chinoises* 9.1 (1990): 129–50.

Dobson, W. A. C. H., trans. *Mencius: A New Translation Arranged and Annotated for the General Reader [Meng Tzu].* UNESCO Chinese Translations Series. London: Oxford University Press, 1963.

Dubs, Homer H., trans. *The History of the Former Han Dynasty [Han shu].* 3 vols. Baltimore: Waverly Press, 1938–55.

Dubs, Homer H., trans. *The Works of Hsüntze [Hsun Tzu].* London: Probsthain, 1928.

Eberhard, Wolfram. *The Local Cultures of South and East China.* Rev. ed. of vol. 2 of *Lokalkulturen in alten China,* 2 vols., trans. Alide Eberhard. Leiden: Brill, 1968.

Eberhard, Wolfram. Review of Bernhard Karlgren, "Legends and Cults in Ancient China." *Artibus Asiae* 9 (1946): 355–64.

Erkes, Eduard. "Chinesisch-amerikanische Mythen Parallelen." *T'oung Pao,* n.s. 24 (1926): 32–54.

Feng Yun-p'eng and Feng Yun-yuan, *Shih suo* (Research on Stone Carving). Part 2 of *Chin shih suo* (Research on Bronze and Stone Carvings). 12 vols. 1821. Rpt. Shanghai: Shangwu, 1934.

Finsterbusch, Käte. *Verzeichnis und Motivindex der Han-Darstellungen.* 2 vols. Wiesbaden: Otto Harrassowitz, 1966–71.

Forke, Alfred, trans. *Lun heng: Philosophical Essays of Wang Ch'ung.* 2 vols. 1907–11. Rpr. New York: Paragon, 1962.

Forke, Alfred, trans. *Mê Ti, des Sozialethikers und seiner Schüler philosophische Werke [Mo Tzu].* Berlin: Kommissionsverlag, 1922.

Fracasso, Riccardo. "Holy Mothers of Ancient China." *T'oung Pao* 74.1–3 (1988): 1–46.

Fried, Morton H. "Tribe to State or State to Tribe in Ancient China?" In *The Origins of Chinese Civilization*, 467–93. See Keightley 1983.

Fu-tan University, Department of Chinese Classical Literature, Research Section. *T'ien wen, T'ien tui chu* (A Discussion of the "Questions of Heaven" and "Answers about Heaven," by Liu Tsung-yuan, A.D. 773–819). Shanghai: Jen-min, 1973.

Fung Yu-lan. *A History of Chinese Philosophy*. 2 vols. 1934. Translated from the Chinese by Derk Bodde. Princeton, N.J.: Princeton University Press, 1953.

Giles, Lionel. *A Gallery of Chinese Immortals: Selected Biographies Translated from Chinese Sources*. Wisdom of the East. London: John Murray, 1948.

Gipoulon, C. *Qiu Jin [Ch'iu Chin], Pierres de l'oiseau: Jing-wei [Ching Wei] — Femme et Révolutionaire en Chine au dix-neuvième siècle*. Paris: Des Femmes, 1976.

Girardot, Norman J. *Myth and Meaning in Early Taoism: The Theme of Chaos (hun-tun)*. Berkeley and Los Angeles: University of California Press, 1983.

Girardot, Norman J. "The Problem of Creation Mythology in the Study of Chinese Religion." *History of Religions* 15.4 (1976): 289–318.

Graham, Angus C., trans. *The Book of Lieh Tzu*. UNESCO Chinese Translations Series. London: John Murray, 1960.

Graham, Angus C., trans. *Chuang-tzŭ: The Seven Inner Chapters and Other Writings from the Book Chuang-tzŭ*. London: Allen & Unwin, 1981.

Graham, Angus C. *Chuang-tzŭ: Textual Notes to a Partial Translation*. London: School of Oriental and African Studies, University of London, 1982.

Graham, Angus C., trans. and ed. *Later Mohist Logic, Ethics and Science*. London: School of Oriental and African Studies of the University of London, and Chinese University of Hong Kong Press, 1978.

Granet, Marcel. *Danses et légendes de la Chine ancienne*. 2 vols. Annales du Musée Guimet, Bibliothèque d'Etudes, vol. 64. 1926. Rpt. (2 vols. in 1). Paris: Presses Universitaires de France, 1959.

Granet, Marcel. *Festivals and Songs of Ancient China*. (First published 1919, in French.) Translated by Eve Edwards. London: George Routledge, 1932.

Greatrex, Roger. *The Bowu Zhi: An Annotated Translation [Po wu chih]*. Stockholm Skrifter utgivna Föreningen för Orientaliska studier, vol. 20. Stockholm: Orientaliska Studier, 1987.

Grynpas, Benedykt. *Les Ecrits de Tai l'ancien et le Petit Calendrier des Hia: Textes confucéens taoïsants*. Paris: Maisonneuve, 1972.

Grynpas, Benedykt, trans. *Lie tseu: Le Vrai Classique du vide parfait [Lieh Tzu]*. UNESCO Chinese Translations Series. Paris: Gallimard, 1976.

Hashimoto, Jun. "Momo no densetsu ni tsuite" (On the Peach Legend). *Shinagaku* 1 (1922): 857–68.

Hawkes, David, trans. *The Songs of the South: An Anthology of Ancient Chinese Poems by Qu Yuan and Other Poets*. 1959. Rev. ed. Penguin Classics. Harmondsworth: Penguin Books, 1985.

Hentze, Carl. *Mythes et symboles lunaires*. Anvers: Editions de Sikkel, 1932.

Hightower, James Robert. "Ch'ü Yüan Studies." In *Silver Jubilee Volume of the*

Zinbun-Kagaku-Kenkyu-syo, edited by Kaizuka Shigeki, 192–223 (Kyoto University, 25.1, 1954). Kyoto: Tōhōgakuhō, 1954.

Hightower, James Robert, trans. *Han Shih Wai Chuan; Han Ying's Illustrations of the Didactic Application of the "Classic of Songs."* Harvard-Yenching Institute Monograph Series, vol. 11. Cambridge, Mass.: Harvard University Press, 1952.

Hightower, James Robert, trans. *The Poetry of T'ao Ch'ien.* Oxford Library of East Asian Literatures. Oxford: Clarendon Press, 1970.

Hino, Iwao. *Shokubutsu kaii densetsu shinkō* (A New Appraisal of Legendary Plants). Tokyo: Yūmei shobō, 1978.

Ho Hsin. *Chu shen ti ch'i-yuan: Chung-kuo yuan-ku shen-hua yü li-shih* (The Origin of the Gods: The Primeval Myths and History of China). Peking: Hsin-hua, 1986.

Hoshikawa, Kiyotaka. *Soji no kenkyū, fu Kutsu ji yakuchi* (Studies on the Verses of Ch'u, with Translations and Annotations of Verses by Ch'ü Yuan). Tenri, Nara: Yotokusha, 1961.

Hosoya, Sōko. "Kan Shō Baku Ja setsuwa no tenkai" (The Evolution of the Legend of Kan Chiang and Mo Yeh). *Bunka* (Tōhoku University) 33.3 (1970): 48–71.

Hsiao Ping. *Ch'u Tz'u yü shen-hua* (Myth and the *Ch'u Tz'u*). Nanking: Kiangsu ku-chi, 1986.

Hsu, Cho-yun, and Katheryn M. Linduff. *Western Chou Civilization.* Early Chinese Civilization Series. New Haven, Conn.: Yale University Press, 1988.

Hsuan, Chu. *Chung-kuo shen-hua yen-chiu* (Studies on Chinese Myths). 2 vols. Folklore and Folkliterature 48–49. 1928. Rpt. (2 vols. in 1). Taipei: Orient Cultural Service, 1971.

Huang, Hui. *Lun heng chiao-shih* (Collated Exegeses of *Lun heng*). 2 vols. Changsha: Commercial Press, 1938.

Izushi, Yoshihiko. *Chūgoku shinwa densetsu no kenkyū* (Research on Chinese Myth and Legend). 1943. Rpt. Tokyo: Chūō Kōronsha, 1975.

Jan, Yün-hua. "The Silk Manuscripts on Taoism." *T'oung Pao* 63 (1978): 65–84.

Kaizuka, Shigeki. *Kamigami no tanjō* (The Gods and Longevity) Chinese History, 1. Tokyo: Chikuma, 1963.

Kaltenmark, Max, trans. *Le Lie-sien tchouan: Biographies légendaires des immortels taoïstes de l'antiquité [Lieh hsien chuan].* Peking: Chinese Research, 1953.

Kaltenmark, Max. "La Naissance du monde en Chine." In *La Naissance du monde,* edited by Marcel Leibovici, et al., 453–68, vol. 1 of *Sources Orientales.* Paris: Editions du Seuil, 1959.

Kao, Karl S. Y., ed., *Classical Chi.ese Tales of the Supernatural and Fantastic: Selections from the Third to the Tenth Century.* Chinese Literature in Translation. Bloomington: Indiana University Press, 1985.

Kao, Ming. *Ta Tai Li chi chin-chu chin-yi* (A New Annotated Translation of the Text of the *Elder Tai's Record of Ritual*). Taipei: Taiwan Commercial Press, 1975.

Karlgren, Bernhard. "Legends and Cults in Ancient China." *Bulletin of the Museum of Far Eastern Antiquities* 18 (1946): 199–365.

Karlgren, Bernhard. *Some Fecundity Symbols in Ancient China.* Stockholm: Bulletin of the Museum of Far Eastern Antiquities, 1930.

Karlgren, Bernhard, trans. "The Book of Documents" [*Shu ching*]. *Bulletin of the Museum of Far Eastern Antiquities* 22 (1950): 1–81.

Karlgren, Bernhard, trans. *The Book of Odes* [*Shih ching*]. Stockholm: Museum of Far Eastern Antiquities, 1974.

Keightley, David N. "The Late Shang State: When, Where, and What?" in *The Origins of Chinese Civilization. See* Keightley 1983.

Keightley, David N., ed. *The Origins of Chinese Civilization.* Studies on China, vol. 1. Berkeley and Los Angeles: University of California Press, 1983.

Knechtges, David R. "A New Study of Han *Yüeh-fu.*" Review of Anne Birrell, *Popular Songs and Ballads of Han China. Journal of the American Oriental Society* 110.2 (1990): 310–16.

Knechtges, David R., trans. *Wen xuan, or, Selections of Refined Literature.* Vols. 1, 2. Princeton Library of Asian Translations. Princeton, N.J.: Princeton University Press, 1982–87.

Knoblock, John. *Xunzi: A Translation and Study of the Complete Works [Hsun Tzu].* Vol. 1. Stanford, Calif.: Stanford University Press, 1988.

Kominami, Ichirō. *Chūgoku no shinwa to monogatari* (Chinese Myths and Tales). Tokyo: Iwanami, 1984.

Kominami, Ichirō. *Seiōbo to shichi seki denshō* (Legends of the Queen Mother of the West and the Seventh Night). Tokyo: Heibonsha, 1991.

Ku, Chieh-kang, ed. *Ku shih pien* (Critiques of Ancient [Chinese] History; author of preface and several articles). 7 vols. 1926–41. Rpt. Shanghai: Shanghai ku-chi, 1982.

Lai Whalen. "Looking for Mr. Ho Po: Unmasking the River God of Ancient China." *History of Religions* 29.4 (1990): 335–50.

Lanciotti, Lionello. "Sword Casting and Related Legends in China." Parts 1, 2. *East and West* 6.2 (1955): 106–14; 6.4 (1955): 316–22.

Lau, D. C., trans. *Confucius: The Analects [Lun yü].* Penguin Classics. Harmondsworth: Penguin Books, 1979.

Lau, D. C., trans. *Lao Tzu Tao Te Ching.* Penguin Classics. Harmondsworth: Penguin Books, 1963.

Lau, D. C., trans. *Mencius, Translated with an Introduction [Meng Tzu].* Penguin Classics. Harmondsworth: Penguin Books, 1970.

LeBlanc, Charles. *Huai Nan Tzu: Philosophical Synthesis in Early Han Thought.* Hong Kong: Hong Kong University Press, 1985.

Legge, James, trans. *The Li Ki [Li chi].* The Sacred Books of China: The Texts of Confucianism, vols. 3, 4. 1885. Rpt. Delhi: Motilal Banarsidass, 1966–68.

Lewis, Mark E. *Sanctioned Violence in Early China.* SUNY Series in Chinese Philosophy and Culture. Albany: State University of New York Press, 1990.

Li Chien-kuo. *T'ang-ch'ien chih-kuai hsiao-shuo shih* (A History of Pre-T'ang Fables and Fiction). T'ienchin: Nank'ai ta-hsueh, 1984.

Li, Hui-lin. "The Domestication of Plants in China: Ecogeographical Considerations." In *The Origins of Chinese Civilization,* 21–63. *See* Keightley 1983.

Liao, W. K., trans. *The Complete Works of Han Fei Tzu.* 2 vols. London: Probsthain, 1939–59.

Lin, Hui-hsiang. *Shen-hua lun* (Mythology: A Discussion). n.d. [1930s]; 1968. Rpt. Foochow: Fu-chien jen-min, 1981.

Lin, Keng. *T'ien wen lun chien* (A Discussion of the "Questions of Heaven"). Peking: Jen-min, 1983.

Lin, Tai-yi, trans. *Flowers in the Mirror* [*Ching hua yuan*, by Li Ju-chen, 1763–ca. 1830]. Berkeley and Los Angeles: University of California Press, 1965.

Liu, Ch'eng-huai. *Chung-kuo shang-ku shen-hua* (The Myths of Ancient China). Shanghai: Shanghai wen-chi, 1988.

Liu, Ming-shu. "Han Wu-liang tz'u-hua-hsiang chung Huang Ti Ch'ih Yu ku chan t'u k'ao" (A Study of the Picture of the Ancient Battle between the Yellow Emperor and Ch'ih Yu in the Han Shrine to Wu Liang). *Chung-kuo wen-hua yen-chiu-hui k'an* 2 (1942): 341–65.

Loewe, Michael. *Crisis and Conflict in Han China, 104 BC to AD 9*. London: George Allen & Unwin, 1974.

Loewe, Michael. "The *Juedi* Games: A Re-enactment of the Battle between Chiyou and Xianyuan?" [Ch'ih Yu and Hsien-yuan, alias the Yellow Emperor]. In *Thought and Law in Qin and Han China*, edited by Wilt L. Idema and E. Zürcher, 140–57. Leiden: Brill, 1990.

Loewe, Michael. *Ways to Paradise: The Chinese Quest for Immortality*. London: George Allen & Unwin, 1979.

Loewe, Michael, and Anthony F. P. Hulsewé. *China in Central Asia, The Early Stage: 125 B.C.–A.D. 23; An Annotated Translation of Chapters 61 and 96 of The History of the Former Han Dynasty* [*Han shu*]. Sinica Leidensia, vol. 14. Leiden: Brill, 1979.

Lu Hsün. *A Brief History of Chinese Fiction*. (First published 1925, in Chinese.) Translated by Yang Hsien-yi and Gladys Yang. Peking: Foreign Languages Press, 1964.

Major, John S. "Myth, Cosmology, and the Origins of Chinese Science." *Journal of Chinese Philosophy* 5 (1978): 1–20.

Maspero, Henri. "L'Astronomie chinoise avant les Han." *T'oung Pao* 26 (1929): 267–356.

Maspero, Henri. "Légendes mythologiques dans le *Chou king*" [*Shu ching*]. *Journal Asiatique* 204 (1924): 1–100.

Mathieu, Rémi. *Anthologie des mythes et légendes de la Chine ancienne: Textes choisis, présentés, traduits et indexés*. Connaissance de l'Orient, vol. 68. Paris: Gallimard, 1989.

Mathieu, Rémi. "Critique d'une critique critique." Reply to Diény, "Mythologie et sinologie." *Etudes Chinoises* 9.2 (1990): 151–60.

Mathieu, Rémi. *Etude sur la mythologie et l'ethnologie de la Chine ancienne* [*Shan hai ching*]. 2 vols. Mémoires de l'Institut des Hautes Etudes Chinoises, vol. 22. Paris: Institut des Hautes Etudes Chinoises, 1983.

Mathieu, Rémi. *Le Mu tian-zi zhuan: Traduction annotée — Etude critique*. Mémoires de l'Institut des Hautes Etudes Chinoises, vol. 9. Paris: Institut des Hautes Etudes Chinoises, 1978.

Mathieu, Rémi, et al. *À la recherche des esprits (Récits tirés du SOU SHEN JI [Sou shen chi] par Gan Bao [Kan Pao])*. *Traduit du chinois, présenté et annoté sous la direc-*

tión de Rémi Mathieu. Connaisance de l'Orient. UNESCO Chinese Series. Paris: Gallimard, 1992.

Mei, Yi-pao, trans. *The Ethical and Political Works of Motse [Mo Tzu].* Probsthain's Oriental Series, vol. 19. London: Probsthain, 1929.

Meskill, John, ed. *The Pattern of Chinese History: Cycles, Development, or Stagnation?* Problems in Asian Civilizations. Boston: D. C. Heath, 1965.

Mitarai, Masaru. *Kodai Chūgoku no kamigami kodai densetsu no kenkyū* (The Deities of Early China: Research on Early Legends). Oriental Studies Library, vol. 26. Tokyo: Sōbunsha, 1984.

Morgan, Evan, trans. *Tao, The Great Luminant [Huai-nan Tzu].* Shanghai: Walsh & Kelly, 1934.

Mori, Mikisaburō. *Chūgoku kodai shinwa* (The Myths of Ancient China). 1944. Rpt. Tokyo: Shimuzu Kōbundō Shobō, 1969.

Mori, Yasutarō. *Kō-tei densetsu; Kodai Chūgoku shinwa no kenkyū* (The Yellow Emperor Legends: A Study of Ancient Chinese Mythology). Kyoto: Kyoto Joshi Daigaku Jinbun Gakkai, 1970.

Münke, Wolfgang. *Die klassische chinesische Mythologie.* Stuttgart: Ernst Klett, 1976.

Needham, Joseph. "The Cosmology of Early China." In *Ancient Cosmologies,* edited by Carmen Blacker and Michael Loewe, 87–109. London: George Allen & Unwin, 1975.

Plaks, Andrew H. *The Four Masterworks of the Ming Novel, Ssu ta ch'i shu.* Princeton, N.J.: Princeton University Press, 1987.

Rickett, W. Allyn. *Guanzi: Political, Economic, and Philosophical Essays from Early China. A Study and Translation [Kuan Tzu].* Vol. 1. Princeton, N.J.: Princeton University Press, 1985.

Rickett, W. Allyn. *Kuan-tzu: A Repository of Early Chinese Thought: A Translation and Study of Twelve Chapters.* Hong Kong: Hong Kong University Press, 1965.

Rudolph, Richard C. "Bull Grappling in Early Chinese Reliefs." *Archaeology* 13.4 (1960): 241–45.

Sailey, Jay. *The Master Who Embraces Simplicity: A Study of the Philosopher Ko Hung, A.D. 283–343 [Pao-p'u Tzu].* San Francisco: Chinese Materials Center, 1978.

Schafer, Edward H. *The Divine Woman: Dragon Ladies and Rain Maidens in T'ang Literature.* Berkeley and Los Angeles: University of California Press, 1973.

Schafer, Edward H. "Ritual Exposure in Ancient China." *Harvard Journal of Asiatic Studies* 14 (1951): 130–84.

Schiffeler, John William, trans. *The Legendary Creatures of the Shan Hai Ching.* Taipei: Hwa Kang, 1978.

Schipper, Kristofer, trans. *L'Empereur Wou des Han dans la légende Taoïste Han Wou-ti nei-tchouan.* [Han Wu-ti nei chuan]. Publications de l'Ecole Française d'Extrême-Orient, vol. 58. Paris: Ecole Française d'Extrême-Orient, 1965.

Schlegel, Gustave. *Uranographie chinoise, ou preuves directes que l'astronomie primitive est originaire de la Chine, et qu'elle a été empruntée par les anciens peuples occidentaux à la sphère chinoise.* 2 vols. Leiden: Brill, 1875.

Schneider, Laurence Allen. *Ku Chieh-kang and China's New History: Nationalism and the Quest for Alternative Traditions.* Berkeley and Los Angeles: University of California Press, 1971.

Shen Yen-ping (Mao Tun). "Chung-kuo shen-hua ti yen-chiu" (Research on Chinese Myth). *Hsiao-shuo yueh-pao* 16.1 (1925): 1–26.

Shen Yen-ping (Mao Tun). *Shen-hua tsa lun* (Essays on Mythology). 1929. Shanghai: Shih-chieh, 1971.

Shih Yen. *Chung-kuo tiao-su shih t'u lu* (A Record of Historical Chinese Carvings and Brick Illustrations). *Chung-kuo mei-shu shih t'u lu ts'ung-shu.* 1 vol. Shanghai: Shanghai Jen-min mei-shu, 1983.

Shirakawa, Shizuka. *Chūgoku no shinwa* (Chinese Mythology). Tokyo: Chūō-kōronsha, 1975. Translated by Wang Hsiao-lien into Chinese as *Chung-kuo shen-hua.* Taipei: Ch'ang-an, 1983.

Sofukawa, Hiroshi. "Konronzan to shōsenzu: (Kun-lun Mountain and Pictures of Ascent to Immortality). *Tōhōgakuhō* 51 (1979): 83–186.

Soymié, Michel. "La Lune dans les religions chinoises." In *La Lune: Mythes et rites,* edited by Marcel Leibovici, et al., 289–319, vol. 5 of *Sources Orientales.* Paris: Editions du Seuil, 1962.

Su Hsueh-lin. *T'ien-wen cheng-chien* (A Review of Research on the "Questions of Heaven"). Taipei: Kuang-tung, 1974.

Sun Tso-yün. "Ch'ih Yu k'ao" (A Study of Ch'ih Yu). *Chung-Ho yueh-k'an* 2.4 (1941): 27–50; 2.5 (1941): 36–57.

Thompson, Paul M. *The Shen Tzu Fragments* [*Shen Tao*]. London Oriental Series, vol. 29. Oxford: Oxford University Press, 1979.

Tjan, Tjoe Som, trans. *Po Hu T'ung, the Comprehensive Discussions in the White Tiger Hall* [*Pai hu t'ung-yi*]. 2 vols. Leiden: Brill, 1949–52.

Tu, Erh-wei. *Shan hai ching shen-hua hsi-t'ung* (The Mythlological System of *The Classic of Mountains and Seas*). 1960. Rpt. Taipei: Taiwan hsueh-sheng, 1977.

Uehara, Jundō. "Shen Shu Yü Lü ni tsuite" (On Holy Shu and Yü Lü). *Tōhō Shūkyō* 1 (1951): 75–81.

von Zach, Erwin, trans. *Die chinesische Anthologie* [*Wen hsuan*]. 2 vols. Cambridge, Mass.: Harvard University Press, 1958.

Waley, Arthur, trans. *The Analects of Confucius* [*Lun yü*]. London: George Allen & Unwin, 1938.

Waley, Arthur, trans. *The Book of Songs* [*Shih ching*]. 1937; New York: Grove Press, 1960.

Walls, Jan, and Yvonne Walls. *Classical Chinese Myths.* Hong Kong: Joint Publishing Co., 1986.

Wang, C. H. "Chou Tso-jen's Hellenism." *Renditions* 7 (1977): 5–28.

Wang, Hsiao-lien. *Chung-kuo ti shen-hua yü ch'uan-shuo* (Chinese Myths and Legends). Taipei: Lien-ching, 1977.

Ware, James R., trans. and ed. *Alchemy, Medicine and Religion in the China of* A.D. *320: The Nei P'ien of Ko Hung* [*Pao-p'u Tzu*]. 1966. New York: Dover, 1981.

Watson, Burton, trans. *Chinese Rhyme-Prose: Poems in the Fu Form from the Han and Six Dynasties Periods.* UNESCO Chinese Translation Series. New York: Columbia University Press, 1971.

Watson, Burton, trans. *The Complete Works of Chuang Tzu.* New York: Columbia University Press, 1968.

Watson, Burton, trans. *Courtier and Commoner in Ancient China: Selections from the History of the Former Han by Pan Ku* [*Han shu*]. New York: Columbia University Press, 1974.

Watson, Burton, trans. *Hsün Tzu: Basic Writings.* UNESCO Chinese Translations Series. New York: Columbia University Press, 1963.

Watson, Burton, trans. *Mo Tzu: Basic Writings.* UNESCO Chinese Translations Series. New York: Columbia University Press, 1963.

Watson, Burton, trans. *Records of the Grand Historian of China, Translated from the Shih chi of Ssu-ma Ch'ien.* 2 vols. New York: Columbia University Press, 1961.

Watson, Burton, trans. *The Tso chuan: Selections from China's Oldest Narrative History.* Translations from the Oriental Classics. New York: Columbia University Press, 1989.

Wen, Yi-to. *Wen Yi-to ch'üan chi* (The Complete Works of Wen Yi-to). 4 vols. Edited by Chu Tzu-ch'ing. Shanghai: K'ai-ming, 1948.

Wen-wu Publishers, eds. *Hsi Han po hua* (The Western Han Silk Painting). Portfolio with Chinese text and 12 color reproductions of the funerary Ch'u silk painting in the tomb of the wife of the Marquis of Tai, Ma-wang-tui, Ch'ang-sha. Hunan Province, ca. 190 B.C. Peking: Wen-wu, 1972.

Werner, Edward Theodore Chalmers. *A Dictionary of Chinese Mythology.* Shanghai: Kelly & Walsh, 1932.

Werner, Edward Theodore Chalmers. *Myths and Legends of China.* London: Harrap, 1922.

Whitaker, K. P. K., "Tsaur Jyr's Luohshern Fuh" [Ts'ao Chih, *Lo shen fu*]. *Asia Major* n.s. 4.1 (1954): 36–56.

Wilhelm, Richard, trans. *Frühling und Herbst des Lü Bu We* [*Lü-shih ch'un-ch'iu*, Lü Pu-wei]. 1928. Rpt. Dusseldorf: Eugen Diederichs,1971.

Wilhelm, Richard, trans. *The I Ching, or, Book of Changes.* Translated from the German by Cary F. Baynes. Bollingen Series, vol. 19. 1951. 3d ed. London: Routledge & Kegan Paul, 1968.

Wilhelm, Richard, trans. *Li Gi: Das Buch der Sitte des Älteren und Jüngeren Dai; Aufzeichnungen über Kultur und Religion des Alten China* [*Ta Tai Li chi*]. Jena: Eugen Diederichs, 1930.

Wu, Hung. *The Wu Liang Shrine.* Stanford, Calif.: Stanford University Press, 1989.

Yamada, Hideo. *Hokudō shoshō insho sakuin* (Index to the *Pei-t'ang shu-ch'ao*). Nagoya: Saika, 1973).

Yang K'uan. "Chung-kuo Shang-ku shih t'ao-lun" (A Discussion of Ancient Chinese History). *Ku shih pien*, 7.1 (1941): 65–318.

Yen Ping. *Chung-kuo shen-hua tsa-chih* (Studies in Chinese Mythology). Folklore and Folkliterature, 91. Facsimile of 1973 ed. Taipei: Orient Cultural Service, 1973.

Yu, Anthony C. *The Journey to the West* [*Hsi yu chi*]. 4 vols. Chicago: Chicago University Press, 1977–83.

Yu, Kuo-en. *T'ien wen tsuan-yi* (Collected Interpretations of the "Questions of Heaven"). Peking: Chung-hua, 1982.

Yuan, K'o, comp. *Chung-kuo ku-tai shen-hua* (The Mythology of Ancient China). 1951. Rev. ed. Shanghai: Shang-wu, 1957.

Yuan, K'o, comp. *Chung-kuo shen-hua ch'uan-shuo tz'u-tien* (A Dictionary of Chinese Myths and Legends). Shanghai: Shanghai tz'u-shu, 1985.

Yuan, K'o, ed. (1980.1). *Shan hai ching chiao-chu* (Collated Notes to *The Classic of Mountains and Seas*). Shanghai: Ku-chi, 1980.

Yuan, K'o. (1980.2). *Shen-hua hsuan-yi pai-t'i* (One Hundred Myths: An Anthology with an Annotated Translation). Shanghai: Ku-chi, 1980.

Yuan, K'o. *Shen-hua lun wen chi* (Essays on Chinese Myth). Shanghai: Ku-chi, 1982.

Yuan, K'o, and Chou Ming, comps. *Chung-kuo shen-hua tzu-liao ts'ui-pien* (A Source Book of Chinese Myth Texts). Ch'eng-tu: Ssu-ch'üan sheng she-hui hsueh-yuan, 1985.

Research Works on Comparative Mythology

Bascom, William. "The Forms of Folklore: Prose Narratives." In *Sacred Narrative*, 6–29. *See* Dundes 1984.

Bettelheim, Bruno. *Symbolic Wounds: Puberty Rites and the Envious Male.* Glencoe, Ill.: Free Press, 1954.

Blacker, Carmen, and Michael Loewe, eds. *Ancient Cosmologies.* London: George Allen & Unwin, 1975.

Boas, Franz. *Race, Language and Culture.* 1940. New York: Free Press, 1966.

Bonnefoy, Yves, ed. *Mythologies.* 2 vols. Translated from the French by Wendy Doniger. Chicago: University of Chicago Press, 1991.

Campbell, Joseph. *The Hero with a Thousand Faces.* Bollingen Series, vol. 17. 1949. 2d ed. Princeton, N.J.: Princeton University Press, 1968.

Campbell, Joseph. *The Masks of God: Oriental Mythology.* London: Secker & Warburg, 1962.

de Vries, Jan. "Theories Concerning 'Nature Myths.'" In *Sacred Narrative*, 31–40. *See* Dundes 1984.

Dorson, Richard M. "The Eclipse of Solar Mythology." *Journal of American Folklore* 68 (1955): 393–416.

Doty, William G. *Mythography: The Study of Myths and Rituals.* University: University of Alabama Press, 1986.

Dumézil, Georges. *Mitra-Varuna: Essai sur deux représentations indo-européenes de la souveraineté.* Bibliothèque de l'Ecole des Hautes Etudes, Section Religieuse, vol. 46. Paris: Presses Universitaires de France, 1940.

Dundes, Alan. "Earth-Diver: Creation of the Mythopoeic Male." In *Sacred Narrative*, 270–94. *See* Dundes 1984.

Dundes, Alan, ed. *The Flood Myth.* Berkeley and Los Angeles: University of California Press, 1988.

Dundes, Alan, ed. *Sacred Narrative: Readings in the Theory of Myth.* Berkeley and Los Angeles: University of California Press, 1984.

Durkheim, Emile. *The Elementary Forms of the Religious Life.* Translated from the French by Joseph Ward Swain. 1915. Rpt. New York: Collier Books, 1961.

Eliade, Mircea. "Cosmogonic Myth and 'Sacred History.'" In *Sacred Narrative*, 137–51. *See* Dundes 1984.

Eliade, Mircea. *The Myth of the Eternal Return, or, Cosmos and History.* Translated from the French by Willard R. Trask. Bollingen Series, vol. 46. 1954. Princeton, N.J.: Princeton University Press, 1971.

Erdész, Sándor. "The World Conception of Lajos Ámi, Storyteller." In *Sacred Narrative*, 316–35. *See* Dundes 1984.

Frazer, James George (Sir). *Creation and Evolution in Primitive Cosmogonies, and Other Pieces*. London: Macmillan, 1935.

Frazer, James George (Sir). "The Fall of Man." In *Sacred Narrative*, 74–97. *See* Dundes 1984.

Frazer, James George (Sir). *The Golden Bough: A Study in Magic and Religion*. 13 vols. 1890. 3d ed. 1911–15. Abridged ed. New York: Macmillan, 1922.

Freud, Sigmund. *The Interpretation of Dreams* (*Die Traumdeutung*). 1900. Rpt. New York: Avon, 1965.

Goldenweiser, Michael A. A. "Totemism: An Analytical Study." *Journal of American Folklore* 23 (1910): 179–293. Rev. version in Alexander Goldenweiser, *History, Psychology and Culture*. London: Kegan Paul, 1933.

Gould, Eric. *Mythical Intention in Modern Literature*. Princeton, N.J.: Princeton University Press, 1981.

Hammond, N. G. L., and H. H. Scullard, eds. *The Oxford Classical Dictionary*. 1948. 2d ed. Oxford: Clarendon, 1970.

Harrison, Jane Ellen. *Themis: A Study of the Social Origins of Greek Religion* (with essays by Gilbert Murray and F. M. Cornford). 1912. 2d ed. London: Merlin Press, 1963.

Hynes, William J. and William G. Doty, eds. *Mythical Trickster Figures: Contours, Contexts, and Criticism*. Tuscaloosa: University of Alabama Press, 1993.

Jung, Carl G. *The Collected Works of C. G. Jung*. 20 vols. Edited by Sir Herbert Read, Michael Fordham, and Gerhard Adler. Translated by R. F. C. Hull. Bollingen Series, vol. 20. London: Routledge & Kegan Paul, 1953–79.

Kirk, G. S. *Myth: Its Meaning and Functions in Ancient and Other Cultures*. Sather Classical Lectures, 40. Cambridge: Cambridge University Press, 1970.

Kramer, Samuel Noah, ed. *Mythologies of the Ancient World*. Garden City, N.Y.: Anchor Books, 1961.

Lang, Andrew. *Modern Mythology*. London: Longmans, Green, 1897.

Lang, Andrew. *Myth, Ritual and Religion*. 2 vols. 1887. New ed. London: Longmans, Green, 1899.

Leach, Edmund, ed. *The Structural Study of Myth and Totemism*. 1967. London: Tavistock, 1968.

Lévi-Strauss, Claude. *The Raw and the Cooked*. Translated from the French by John Weightman and Doreen Weightman. New York: Harper & Row, 1970.

Lévi-Strauss, Claude. "The Story of Asdiwal." Translated from the French by Nicholas Mann. In *Structural Study*, 1–47. *See* Leach 1968.

Lincoln, Bruce. *Myth, Cosmos, and Society: Indo-European Themes of Creation and Destruction*. Cambridge, Mass.: Harvard University Press, 1986.

Lincoln, Bruce. *Priests, Warriors, and Cattle: A Study in the Ecology of Religions*. Hermeneutics: Studies in the History of Religions, 10. Berkeley and Los Angeles: University of California Press, 1981.

Littleton, C. Scott. *The New Comparative Mythology: An Anthropological Assessment of the Theories of Georges Dumézil*. Berkeley and Los Angeles: University of California Press, 1973.

Lloyd, G. E. R. "Greek Cosmologies." In *Ancient Cosmologies*, 198–224. *See* Blacker and Loewe 1975.

Lowie, Robert H. *The Crow Indians*. New York: Holt, Rinehart, & Winston, 1935.

Lucretius (ca. 94–55 B.C.). *De rerum natura*. Edited and translated by W. and I. D. Rouse. London: Heinemann, 1924.

Malinowski, Bronislaw. *Magic, Science, and Religion, and Other Essays*. 1948. Rpt. Garden City, N.Y.: Doubleday Anchor Books, 1954.

Mendelson, E. M. "The 'Uninvited Guest': Ancilla to Lévi-Strauss on Totemism and Primitive Thought." In *Structural Study*, 119–139. *See* Leach 1968.

Morris, Ivan. *The Nobility of Failure: Tragic Heroes in the History of Japan*. New York: Holt, Rinehart, & Winston, 1975.

Müller, Friedrich Max. *Chips from a German Workshop*. Vol. 2. 1869. Rpt. New York: Scribner, Armstrong, 1891.

Numazawa, K. "The Cultural-Historical Background of Myths on the Separation of Sky and Earth." In *Sacred Narrative*, 183–92. *See* Dundes 1984.

Ovid (43 B.C.–A.D. 17). *Metamorphoses*. Translated and edited by Frank Justus Miller. London: Heinemann, 1929.

Plumley, J. M. "The Cosmology of Ancient Egypt." In *Ancient Cosmologies*, 17–41. *See* Blacker and Loewe 1975.

Preminger, Alex, ed. *Princeton Encyclopedia of Poetry and Poetics*. Princeton, N.J.: Princeton University Press, 1965.

Puhvel, Jaan. *Comparative Mythology*. Baltimore: Johns Hopkins University Press, 1987.

Raglan, F. R. R. S. (Lord). *The Hero: A Study in Tradition, Myth, and Drama*. 1936. New York: Oxford University Press, 1937.

Rank, Otto. *The Myth of the Birth of the Hero, and Other Writings by Otto Rank*. (First published 1909, in German.) Edited by Philip Freund. Translated by F. Robbins and S. E. Jolliffe. New York: Random House, 1959.

Rooth, Anna Birgitta. "The Creation Myths of the North American Indians." In *Sacred Narrative*, 167–81. *See* Dundes 1984.

Rose, Herbert Jennings. "Sacred Animals," "Artemis," "Sacred Birds," and "Euhemerus." In *The Oxford Classical Dictionary*, 65, 126–27, 169, 414–15. *See* Hammond and Scullard 1970.

Schelling, Friedrich Wilhelm Joseph von. *Philosophie der Mythologie*. In *Sämmtliche Werke*, 3–131. Stuttgart: J. G. Cotta, 1857.

Showalter, Elaine (subject). (1991.1). "Sexual Déjà Vu at the Fin de Siècle" (interview by Joe Joseph). *Times*, 27 March 1991.

Showalter, Elaine (1991.2). *Sexual Anarchy: Gender and Culture at the Fin de Siècle*. London: Bloomsbury, 1991.

Smith, Ron. *Mythologies of the World: A Guide to Sources*. Urbana, Ill.: National Council of Teachers of English, 1981.

Snorri Sturluson (A.D. 1178–1241). *Edda*. Edited by Anne Holtsmark and Jon Helgason. 2d ed. Copenhagen: Munksgard, 1976.

Strenski, Ivan. *Four Theories of Myth in Twentieth-Century History*. London: Macmillan, 1987.

Thompson, Stith. *Motif-Index of Folk-Literature, A Classification of Narrative Elements in Folktales, Ballads, Myths, Fables, Mediaeval Romances, Exempla, Fabliaux,*

Jest-Books, and Local Legends. 6 vols. 1932–36. 2d ed., rev. Copenhagen: Rosen-
    kilde & Bagger, 1955–58.
Tylor, Edward Burnett. *Primitive Culture.* 2 vols. 1871. New York: Harper, 1958.
Wheeler-Voegelin, Erminie. "Earth Diver." In *Standard Dictionary of Folk-lore,
    Mythology, and Legend,* edited by Maria Leach, 1:334. New York: Funk and
    Wagnalls, 1949.
Wojkowitz, René de Nebesky. *Oracles and Demons of Tibet: The Cult and Iconog-
    raphy of Tibetan Protective Deities.* New York: Gordon Press, 1977.

Index of
Chinese Names
and Terms

Note: ch', k', p', t' are aspirated, as in English; *ch, k, p, t,* are unaspirated and are pronounced as *j, g, b, d; j* is pronounced *rr; ü* and *u* are pronounced *u* and *ou.*

Beast of White Marsh: divine being; knows human language and language of birds and beasts; knows natures of all creatures and location and former appearance of metamorphosed beings; linked to Yellow Emperor myth. *Motifs:* animal features of deity, cosmic knowledge, 231, 235–36. *See also* Yellow Emperor

Black-haired people: name given to the people in antiquity; refers to black hair or black headband, 72

Black Jade insignia: Taoist regalia; jade thought to be purest substance on earth; black, or dark, signified north, negative, mysterious, and was a mystical, emblematic color in Taoism, 159. *See also* Taoism

Block, the (T'ao Wu): one of the god Chuan Hsu's worthless sons; two traditions: (1) mythical monster; (2) historicized as one of a group of evil men. *Motifs:* destructive monster, rebel, unloved son, 95–99. *See also* Chuan Hsu

Cha Yü (or Ya Yü): killed by two gods; corpse kept incorrupt in western mountain paradise by shamans; depicted with serpent's body and human head. *Motifs:* animal feature of deity, immortality, murder, paradise, 90, 183, 184, 214. *See also* Shaman

Cha-yü beast: one of six world plague monsters killed by Yi the Archer; had dragon's head and tiger's claws. *Motifs:* monster, solar, 77–79. *See also* Yi the Archer

Ch'ang-hsi. *See* Mother of the twelve moons

Ch'ang O: moon goddess; also known temporarily as Heng O, due to taboo of imperial Han name; married to Yi the Archer; stole elixir of immortality received from the Queen Mother of the West; assumed to the moon; metamorphosed into toad. *Motifs:* immortality, lunar, metamorphosis, regeneration, trickster-figure, 11, 144–45, 160, 176, 189, 190, 195, 231. *See also* Queen Mother of the West; Yi the Archer

Ch'en star: star god; quarreled with brother; both punished by metamorphosis into stars in separate parts of the sky; astronomical emblem of Shang; identified with Antares. *Motifs:* fraternal enmity; punishment; stellar dynastic emblem, 100–101. *See also* Shen star

King Wen *(continued)*
was his posthumous title. *Motifs:*
conquest, exemplar of the good
king, foundation, military hero,
moral crusade, 110–11, 116, 220, 254,
259–60, 261. *See also* Chou (people
and dynasty); Great Lord Chiang;
King Wu; Shang

King Wu: semihistorical figure;
founder king of the Chou dynasty;
son of King Wen; named Fa; defeated last Shang ruler, King Chou
(different graph); established the
Chou dynasty, trad. 1123 B.C.; aided
by his brother, the duke of Chou.
Motifs: binary opposites, conquest,
deposed king, exemplar of the adviser, exemplar of the good king,
foundation, military hero, moral
crusade, 110, 116, 254, 261. *See also*
Duke of Chou; King Chou of the
Shang; King Wen

King Yen of Hsu: semilegendary, semi-
mythical figure; two traditions of his
reign: (1) in the era of King Mu of
the Chou (tenth century B.C.), (2) in
the reign of King Wen of Ch'u
(689–677 B.C.); Hsu is one of the
Nine Provinces in mythogeography;
miraculous birth from an egg; successful and good king; unwilling to
lead his people into war; took them
into exile; created a new kingdom;
depicted with strange features and
without bones. *Motifs:* dog, egg,
exemplar of a good king, exodus,
foundation, miraculous birth,
strange features, 113, 125–26. *See also*
Nine Provinces

K'ua-fu: a god; grandson of Hou-t'u,
Earth Deity; challenged the sun to a
race against light and time; died of
thirst; in variant myth killed by
Responding Dragon, a drought
deity; after his death his wooden
staff turned into a grove of trees.
Motifs: contest, death, drought, execution, failed hero, hubris, metamor-

phosis, sun, 133, 181, 215–16. *See also*
Hou-t'u; Responding Dragon

K'uei: storm god; one-legged mountain god; killed by the Yellow Emperor; skin used as a cosmic drum;
historicizing tradition makes him
master of music under the sage-
kings Yao and Shun. *Motifs:* deformity, murder, music, storm, 130, 134.
See also Yellow Emperor

Kun: demigod; tried to save the world
from the flood; stole god's magic soil
to dam the water; executed by the
fire god; corpse did not decompose
for three years; his son born from his
belly; metamorphosed into a yellow
bear (var. turtle, dragon), and disappeared. *Motifs:* execution, failed hero,
flood, incorrupt corpse, magic soil,
male birth, metamorphosis, savior,
11, 41, 79–82, 84, 121, 122, 146, 190,
202, 214, 222. *See also* K'ai; Self-
renewing soil; Yü

K'un: gigantic fish; metamorphosed
into a massive bird called P'eng.
Motifs: giant creature, metamorphosis, size, 191

K'un-lun: western mountain range;
mountain paradise; presided over by
the Queen Mother of the West; place
where shamans carried out immortality rite; later the dwelling of humans who have become immortals.
Motifs: axis mundi, female deity,
immortality, mountain paradise,
sacred beasts and birds, 10, 90, 183–
84, 230. *See also* Cha Yü; Grain Tree;
Queen Mother of the West; Shaman;
Shih-jou

K'ung Chia: mythological figure; trad.
13th king of the Hsia; favored by
god; granted two divine dragons;
betrayed god's trust; historical tradition charges him with the downfall
of the Hsia. *Motifs:* betrayal, dragon,
mythical dynasty, 60. *See also* Hsia

Kung Kung: a mighty god; in a war
with the god Chuan Hsu damaged
the cosmos by knocking down one

of the supporting pillars between earth and sky; separate myth says his irrigation works caused the damage, and that the people rejected his leadership and Heaven turned against him; another tradition makes him ruler of the Nine Provinces, with Hou-t'u as his son; several versions of his death: (1) exiled by Shun; (2) exiled by Yü; (3) executed by Chuan Hsu; historicizing tradition places him in the era of Yao as minister for public works. *Motifs:* cosmology, flood, marplot, punishment, war of the gods, 7, 27, 69, 89, 97, 146, 217. *See also* Chuan Hsu; Shun; Yü

League: translation of the Chinese term, *li*, one-third of a mile

Leaning Mulberry (Fu-sang): a worldtree in the east; where soiled suns were washed and hung to dry after the day's journey across the sky; sun carried to the top of the tree at dawn. *Motifs: axis mundi,* plant, solar goddess, sun, 10, 38, 231, 234. *See also* Hsi-Ho; Mother of the ten suns; Mulberry *in the* Index of Concepts

Li Chu, probably the same mythical figure as Li Lou, gifted with supernatural eyesight. *Motif:* supernatural eye

Li Ping: historical figure (third century B.C.) to whom legends attached; Ch'in official; governor of conquered Shu; foiled local river god; stopped local custom of female sacrifice. *Motifs:* battle between human and god, female sacrifice, hero, metamorphosis, river god, savior, 87–88, 213

Lo: one of the ancient capital cities of King Wu of the Chou; by Lo River, modern Loyang, Honan

Lo-pin: river goddess; wife of the Lord of the [Yellow] River; abducted by Yi the Archer after he killed her husband. *Motifs:* abduction of female, murder, river goddess, 101–2, 140–41.

See also Lord of the River; Yi the Archer

Lo River: tributary of the Yellow River, Honan; site of ancient city of Lo; focus of numerous myths and legends; its goddess Fu-fei. *Motifs:* goddess, sacred river. *See also* Fu-fei

Lord of the Granary (Lin Chün): named Wu-hsiang; founding hero of the Pa people, modern Szechwan; established mythological city of Yi-ch'eng; became chief by archery and boating contests; battled with the Goddess of Salt River when she seduced him. *Motifs:* foundation, hero, murder, sexual contest, sitiology, weapon, 12, 179, 204–5, 213, 253, 254, 265–66. *See also* Goddess of Salt River

Lord of the River (Ho-po): god of the river (*ho*), usually denoting the Yellow River; consort of Lo-pin; shot dead by Yi the Archer, who abducted his wife; in one version he was killed because he had been murdering humans; aided the Chou in their campaign against the Shang. *Motifs:* divine aid, murder, punishment, river god, 88, 101–2, 140–41, 263. *See also* Chou (people and dynasty); Lo-pin; Shang; Yi the Archer

Many-Splendored Bird: a divine bird of evil omen; had double pupils; Yao's era; image used in the Han era to ward off evil spritis. *Motifs:* divine bird, evil, supernatural eye, 237

Master Yen: legendary inventor of automaton; linked to the era of King Mu of the Chou. *See also* King Mu, 63–64

Miao: a people mentioned in mythological and historical texts; sometimes known as San Miao, and other variants; southern region; known as a rebellious tribe; two traditions: (1) disrupted the cosmic power between gods and humans; (2) tyrannized the

Shao Hao *(continued)*
  Sang, Exhausted Mulberry, after the place where his parents courted; also named Ch'ing Yang with the title of Metal Sky; Ch'iung Sang was a sacred place where a world-tree grew; metal associated with the west; Shao Hao usually identified with the east; in one tradition, raised as a child by the god Chuan Hsu; founded Niao (Bird) kingdom. *Motifs:* bird emblem, divine birth, elemental correspondence, foundation, metal, plant, 92, 135, 207–8, 267. *See also* Chuan Hsu; Mulberry
Shen star: star god; astronomical emblem of the mythical Hsia; quarreled with his brother; punished by metamorphosis into a star; separated in the sky from his brother, also a star god; equivalent to stars in Orion; named Shih Ch'en. *Motifs:* dynastic emblem, quarreling brothers, star god, 100–101. *See also* Ch'en star
Shih-jou: mythological creature guarding K'un-lun paradise; shaped like an ox's liver and regenerated when eaten. *Motifs:* guardian of paradise, sitiology, strange creature, 76–77
Shou-yang Mountain: in modern Shansi
Shu: ancient state in southwest, modern Szechwan; divine descent from the god of sericulture; divine kingship. *Motifs:* culture bearer, divine descent, divine kingship, hero, sericulture, 61–62, 87–88, 197–98, 227, 253, 264. *See also* Ch'in; Li Ping; Ts'an Ts'ung; Tu Yü
Shu Chün: identified in one tradition as Shang Chün; buried in same place as Shun; descended from the god Ti Chün. *Motifs:* burial, divine descent, 66, 77. *See also* Shun; Ti Chün; Ts'ang-wu
Shun: demigod; known as Yu Yü or Yü, also name of his period of rule; also named Ch'ung Hua; divine descent from Chuan Hsu; most tradi-

tions depict him as the archetype of filial piety; numerous myths of his trials as the hero who foils the plots of his father and half-brother; some traditions say he banished his father and killed his half-brother; chosen by the demigod Yao as his successor; given two daughters by Yao; similarly passed over his own sons in favor of Yü; depicted with double pupils; traditional burial place in Ts'ang-wu, or Ming-t'iao, with his grave tended by his half-brother; second sage-king of the Golden Age. *Motifs:* divine descent, evil father, filial piety, fraternal quarrel, Golden Age, succession, supernatural eye, trials of the hero, 18, 55, 74–77, 81, 104, 115, 167–69, 193, 213, 237. *See also* Chuan Hsu; Hsiang; Hsiang queens; Yao; Yü
Silkworm Horse: divine horse; supernatural power of human intelligence; given vow of marriage by a girl; killed; avenged broken vow by metamorphosing himself and her into a huge silkworm. *Motifs:* broken vow, death, divine horse, etiology of mulberry, love, metamorphosis, 199. *See also* Mulberry
Sky River: celestial replica of the Yellow River; its mythical source; equivalent to the Milky Way; linked to stellar myth of lovers; legendary voyage in space by a man in the Han. *Motifs:* separation of lovers, space travel, star gods, 166, 206–7. *See also* Draught Ox; Weaver Maid
Snake: in myth endowed with supernatural powers; often forms lower half of deity's body; worn in the ears or on the head of gods, and trodden underfoot as sign of the gods' knowledge of and power over the cosmos. *Motifs:* cosmic knowledge and power, divine creature, emblem of deity, 185
Son of Heaven: divine ruler; title of

Taoism *(continued)*
parable, fable, reversals of historical truth, fictionalized interviews, rhapsodic passages, anecdotes, pseudological discourse, and inanities; incorporated and distorted mythological material; first seven chapters considered authentic. Next datable text, but considered to be much older than the third century B.C., is *Lao Tzu,* written in short, poetic pieces in a peremptory and prescriptive style; primitivist concepts, and cult of the simple or inane; anticivilization and opposed to intellectualism. After the Han period, Taoism developed into a new system of thought incorporating Confucian elements called Neo-Taoism; also developed into a religious system. Taoist texts of the late Chou and early Han are valuable sources of myth, especially cosmogonic mythic vestiges

Ten suns: born of the goddess, Hsi-Ho; each rinsed by her after the day's journey in the sky; once they all rose together and threatened the world with extinction; shot down by Yi the Archer; the number ten is associated with the ancient calendar; the traditional week is ten days. *Motifs: See* Mother of the ten suns, 77–78, 123–25. *See also* Hsi-Ho; Mulberry; Yi the Archer

Three and Five: numbers denoting the Three Eras of the Hsia, Shang, and Chou, or the three sage-kings, Yao, Shun, and Yü, and the pantheon of five gods, usually T'ai Hao, the Flame Emperor, the Yellow Emperor, Shao Hao, and Chuan Hsu (different names given in some texts)

Three Sovereigns: Heaven, earth, and humankind in their divine emanations; may also refer to Fu Hsi, the Farmer God, and Nü Kua (different names given in various texts)

Ti. *See* God/goddess

Ti Chün: a god; consort of the sun goddess Hsi-Ho; consort of the moon goddess, Ch'ang-hsi; favored by a bird of paradise; gave Yi the Archer the bow and arrows to shoot down the ten suns when they all rose at once; ordered Yi to go down to earth and save humankind; major deity of *The Classic of Mountains and Seas. Motifs:* culture bearer, foundation, moon, sun, weapon, 65–66, 77–78, 123–25. *See also* Ch'ang-hsi; Hsi-Ho; Yi the Archer

Ti K'u: a god; also named Kao Hsin; consort of Chiang Yuan, ancestress of the Chou people; also consort of Chien Ti, ancestress of the Shang; Ti K'u's two sons metamorphosed into star gods because of their quarrels; culture bearer, music. *Motifs:* divine ancestry, divine bird, foundation, grain god, metamorphosis, music, star god, 53–54, 101, 114, 116. *See also* Ch'en star; Chiang Yuan; Chien Ti; Hou Chi; Hsieh; Shen star

T'ien (lit. Sky): *See* God/goddess

Torch Dragon: animalian god of light in the northwest. *Motifs:* dragon, light, mythogeography, supernatural eye, 68, 232

True Person, or True Man: Taoist term for one who attains transcendental perfection by following regimen and ritual; one who becomes an immortal among the gods, 71. *See also* Taoism

Ts'an Ts'ung (lit. Silkworm Cluster): god of sericulture; first ancestor of the kings of Shu; inaugurated markets; developed sericulture; known as the Green God, or God in the Green Clothes. *Motifs:* divine ancestry, divine kingship, etiology of the market, etiology of the silkworm, foundation, 61–62, 197, 253, 264. *See also* Mulberry; Shu

Ts'ang-wu: mythogeographical place where Shun died and was buried; name of a mountain, also known as

Index of
Concepts